The First Woman Judge

The First Woman Judge

THE LIFE AND LEGACY OF FLORENCE ALLEN

Tracy Thomas

UNIVERSITY OF CALIFORNIA PRESS

University of California Press
Oakland, California

Library of Congress Cataloging-in-Publication Data

Names: Thomas, Tracy A. author
Title: The first woman judge: the life and legacy of Florence Allen / Tracy Thomas.
Description: Oakland, California: University of California Press, [2026] | Includes bibliographical references and index.
Identifiers: LCCN 2026009893 (print) | LCCN 2026009894 (ebook) | ISBN 9780520399600 cloth | ISBN 9780520399624 ebook
Subjects: LCSH: Allen, Florence Ellinwood, 1884–1966 | Women judges—United States | LCGFT: Biographies
Classification: LCC KF373.A4 T46 2026 (print) | LCC KF373.A4 (ebook)
LC record available at https://lccn.loc.gov/2026009893
LC ebook record available at https://lccn.loc.gov/2026009894

GPSR Authorized Representative: Easy Access System Europe, Mustamäe tee 50, 10621 Tallinn, Estonia, gpsr.requests@easproject.com

35 34 33 32 31 30 29 28 27 26
10 9 8 7 6 5 4 3 2 1

publication supported by a grant from
The Community Foundation for Greater New Haven
as part of the *Urban Haven Project*

For those women in my own history:
Linda, Kaye, Hazel, Helen, and especially Caroline

Contents

Introduction

Florence Allen was the first woman judge many times over. She was the first in the nation appointed to a federal appellate court and the first repeatedly shortlisted for the U.S. Supreme Court. Before that, she was the first woman in the country elected to a common pleas court and the first voted onto a state supreme court. In the early half of the twentieth century, she was considered "the most famous woman judge in the world," widely recognized as the "first."[1] There had been women before her serving in quasi-judicial roles, but Allen was the first judge elected to a regular, general jurisdiction court, thus earning the accolade of "first."[2]

Allen became the first woman judge in the country when she was elected to the Cuyahoga County Common Pleas Court in Cleveland in 1920. She then became the first woman elected to the highest supreme court in *any* state, chosen for the Ohio Supreme Court in 1922 and reelected in 1928. Allen ran as an independent, describing herself as a liberal conservative, conveying her progressive values and moderate inclinations—but she was decidedly a new Democrat.[3] Allen was also the first woman appointed to a federal appellate court, nominated by President Franklin Roosevelt in 1934 to the U.S. Court of Appeals for the Sixth Circuit, where she served for twenty-five years and became the first woman to serve as chief judge of a circuit court. When announcing the historic appointment of Allen to the federal court, Roosevelt's attorney general, Homer Cummings, emphasized that Allen "was not appointed because she was a woman."[4] "All we did," he said, "was see that she was not rejected because she was a woman." Allen's gender was ignored rather than embraced, discounting the seismic change the first woman made to the courts.

Allen came close to extending this historic impact by being the first woman Justice on the U.S. Supreme Court. She was the first woman shortlisted for the U.S. Supreme Court—considered for the highest appointment twelve times by three presidents from both parties trying to capture the women's vote.[5] The nomination looked like it would surely happen in 1938, as Allen was invited to dinner at the White House and championed by Eleanor Roosevelt. But a conflict over a case pending before Allen that put the constitutionality of FDR's New Deal agenda on trial made any appointment look like a bribe.[6] The spot would go instead to the unassuming Stanley Reed. Allen's name rose again in subsequent nominations that would go to William Douglas and Frank Murphy, making it to advanced stages of administration and media shortlists. But a devastating media exposé erroneously claimed that Allen was disqualified because Douglas supporters torpedoed her nomination by giving Attorney General Murphy "a list of her cases in which she has been reversed by the upper courts," saying it proved that "Judge Allen's record perhaps is worse than any other prominent federal judge's."[7] It was said to have "ended the possibility of a woman on the Supreme Court," implying that Allen and women generally were not competent to be on the Court. Allen was outraged because the allegation was "absolutely false," as she had been reversed only once on the federal court and once on the state court.[8] She sent this response to the attorney general, but Murphy disclaimed any knowledge of the list.[9] It was too late, however, as the damage to Allen's reputation was done. "The malice behind the article was evident," she said. "They meant to kill me off forever."[10] Murphy himself got the nomination.

Women activists persisted in demanding a woman on the Supreme Court.[11] Finally, in 1949, President Harry Truman stated he was willing to appoint a woman. Convinced by India Edwards, director of the Democratic National Committee Women's Division, the president agreed that a woman Justice was a good idea, especially one of "Sister Allen's reputation and capability."[12] However, he had to first consult his close friend and advisor, and poker buddy, Chief Justice Fred Vinson. Truman needed "to find out how he and the other Justices would feel about having a woman in their august group." Vinson reported back that the Justices said no. No, they would "not willingly have a woman as a Justice" because it would impede their conference deliberations and ability "to meet informally with robes off," "shoes off, feet up, and shirt sleeves rolled up, in a casual discussion that could not be done in the presence of a woman."[13] Edwards was incensed and called out the blatant sexism of the Court—for the lack of collegiality and contentiousness among the "Brethren" on the Court was public knowledge.[14] The Justices called each other names, bullied like "school boys," and even came to blows.[15] A frustrated Edwards said facetiously, "I am certain that the old line" about there being no adequate bathrooms for a female Justice was also one of their claimed rationales.[16]

Truman proposed a compromise to appease the men: Appoint Allen for just one year.[17] The nomination would gain him political points with women, but it would limit any disruption a woman could make on the Court. For women, it would at least break the last judicial glass ceiling of gender, even if it marginalized a woman Justice into a second-class citizenship. No appointment, however, ever materialized. Truman instead appointed two other political cronies and poker buddies, Attorney General Tom Clark and Senator Sherman Minton.[18] As Edwards said years later, "I tell you we would have had a woman on the Supreme Court if it hadn't been that Fred Vinson vetoed it."[19]

Florence Allen was a frequent contender for the U.S. Supreme Court and a successful judicial pioneer because she was a highly qualified candidate. She was well educated at prestigious schools including Case Western Reserve University, the University of Chicago Law School, and New York University School of Law, graduating at the top of her class. She had prosecutorial experience, serving in the Cuyahoga County Prosecutor's Office as one of the first women prosecutors in the country handling trials and grand juries. Allen had good trial experience, rare for a woman lawyer at that time, handling civil matters in multiple courts as well as criminal defense and legal aid cases. She earned her stellar legal reputation handling constitutional cases of women's suffrage in Ohio. The women's suffrage movement and the fight for the Nineteenth Amendment to the U.S.

Constitution gave Allen her political experience and national connections. She worked as a leader in the national movement in New York City and in Ohio, where she shepherded litigation and grassroots activism. Allen was a progressive, believing in the role of government to regulate and protect economic and social welfare. She was a "New Woman" of the emerging feminist movement, apprenticing with social feminists of the reform movement and training with legal equality feminists.

On the bench, Allen accrued four decades of judicial experience with two years on the trial court, eleven years on the state supreme court, and twenty-five years on the federal appellate court. Allen proved herself to be a constitutional progressive, a strong New Dealer, supportive of federal legislation and government's response to the devastating Great Depression. She was also politically well connected—earning the support of First Lady Eleanor Roosevelt, Democratic political bosses in Washington and Cleveland, and most national women's organizations from temperance to business, buoyed by family connections including her mother's reform activism and her father's term as a first congressional representative from Utah. She gained further political support from the Democratic Party, running twice for Congress—once for the Senate in 1926 and once for the House in 1932—though both bids were unsuccessful. Centered in the bellwether state of Ohio that foretold the turn of the political tides, Allen was well located and well qualified to be the first woman judge.

RESENTMENT AND RESISTANCE

As the first woman judge, Allen was also among the first to suffer the backlash and resistance of the majority who believed that women had no place on the court. After shattering the judicial glass ceiling, Judge Allen encountered sexist slights, shunning, sidelining, hostile environments, disrespect, and outright discrimination. She was paid less than her male colleagues. She was not assigned complex or important cases, and her fellow common pleas jurists wanted to segregate her on a special domestic relations division. Colleagues excluded her from lunches at male-only clubs, joked about her age and hair, and refused to extend common professional courtesies. The press teased about her frumpy clothes, sturdy shoes, and plain face. Lawyers disrespected her by calling her "Miss" instead of "Judge" as she insisted, a problem faced by other early women judges such as the first Black woman federal judge, Constance Baker Motley.[20]

Allen's fellow attorneys and judges in Cleveland belittled and sabotaged her behind her back. An FBI report prepared for her federal nomination detailed the comments and views of "a large majority of prominent members of the Cleveland bar and U.S. District Judges West and Jones [who] strongly oppose appointment."[21] "Many members," the report summarized, "admit a natural prejudice against women in the judiciary, particularly Federal, as being naturally unqualified." These men said Allen was unqualified to handle masculine, scientific issues before the court like patent, tax, and admiralty cases. They called her "untrained" because "she had no knowledge of Federal practice." They said she was unethical, citing her campaigning for Congress while retaining her judicial seat. They criticized her for not recusing from cases involving banks because she had significant debt after the stock market crash from a failed investment in the Alcazar Hotel. Other FBI reports mentioned allegations that Allen was a communist, citing her peace activism, international work, and dissent in a case defending communist political beliefs as free speech. The Cleveland bench and bar criticized Allen as "politically ambitious with aspirations to the U.S. Supreme Court." These men said her appointment would be "lamentable, laughable, disastrous," as a woman's presence would make the Sixth Circuit "ridiculous" and demean the "high traditions of that bench." In response, Attorney General Cummings sent a representative to Cleveland to interview the common pleas judges about Allen. Cummings concluded that Allen was "preeminently qualified" and supported her appointment to the Sixth Circuit. Allen later said that she wondered whether Roosevelt appointed her only for "shock effect."[22]

The local media generally championed Allen, proud of her notoriety as the first woman judge, but as she rose higher, the national media was unimpressed. When she was nominated to the federal bench, *News-Week* called her appointment underwhelming and presented an unflattering picture of the fifty-year-old Allen.[23] The national magazine portrayed her as a mediocre judge who didn't know her own mind. "Bobbed-haired, stout, pleasant, she is distinguished for soundness and good sense rather than brilliance," it wrote. "Her judicial opinions are a composite of liberalism and conservatism. She does not believe in capital punishment, but she once sentenced a man to the electric chair. Though an ardent dry, she advocated a referendum on Prohibition. She admired Herbert Hoover but says she has also admired Franklin Roosevelt since he assumed office." It emphasized that she was "an unmarried woman earning her own living." Using gendered language of women's domesticity, the magazine said that Judge Allen's "recipe for success" was to "take one generous dose of persistency; add one large measure of industry. . . . Mix thoroughly and season with a goodly portion of sense of humor and several ounces of tact." It added snarkily, "So far her recipe has not proved potent enough to carry her to the National Capitol, to which she has longed to go."

After her appointment, a Cincinnati newspaper editorial made fun of the male opposition to a woman on the bench—an article Allen saved for posterity.[24] "A skirt, gentlemen? . . . A skirt on the federal bench? . . . Is it constitutional? . . . There is no precedent for this, gentlemen!" Indeed, it argued, tongue in cheek: "From the first the Federal Court always had worn trousers. By practice and tradition trousers had become the official regalia of a Federal Court. Upon study, trousered legs, like pillars of the Constitution, the Federal Court always had stood; and in all the years since Chief Justice John Jay no skirt had appeared to challenge the supremacy of trousers."

A WOMAN-CENTERED WORLD

Allen was beloved as a heroine and role model to women who appreciated her revolutionary appointment. She was larger than life to women activists, lawyers, reformers, friends, family, and the general public. To her friends, she was "Cap," a nickname for Captain, because she directed the ship among her friends. "Known for her keen sense of humor," Allen led the social group of friends, entertaining by her expert piano playing, initiating animated discussions, and horsing around with games and charades. She was very close to her three sisters and became the matriarch of her extended family, financially supporting siblings, nieces and nephews, elderly parents, and partners who lived with her. She loved the outdoors, growing up in the mountains of Salt Lake City, Utah. She was an avid hiker, climbing mountains, snowshoeing in winter, leading hiking groups along beaches and farmlands in Northeast Ohio, walking each day to work, and exercising her cocker spaniels. She also had a creative side, writing poetry, working as a newspaper music critic, and adoring the theater.[25]

Allen was considered tall for a woman, and commanded an even larger presence. At five feet six inches, she was taller than the average woman at that time and the same height as the average man. She was a tomboy, athletic in build and activity, described by some as a "mannish woman" or a "man woman."[26] The *Washington Post* described her as "Junoesque in stature, dressed simply in black with a rather severe hat on her big head, friendly in her manner, with a low delightful chuckle."[27] In her early years, she often dressed in masculine ways, in pants, knickers, long neckties and bowties, and men's hats, later replaced by a standard uniform of a somber black dress and, in her senior years, floral dresses and pearls. She wore spectacles and swirled her long auburn hair on top of her head in an old-fashioned double coil, until she cropped her hair as short as a man's.

Allen placed herself in a woman-centered world, drawing her energy and strength from sisters, partners, friends, suffragists, lesbians, and politically active female leaders. She took pride in being called a "spinster." Despite its derogatory connotation, she embraced the label and its idea of an autonomous, self-supporting woman who was not reliant on a man. She deliberately rejected marriage for herself and embraced alternative partnerships.[28] Like the majority of professional women in the 1920s who opted out of marriage, the assumption was that a woman could not be both wife and professional.[29] Allen's diaries note pivotal moments at which she contemplated marriage and same-sex relationships, always choosing autonomy. She was influenced by reading *Marriage as a Trade*, feminist and lesbian English playwright Cicely Hamilton's diatribe against the oppressive economic institution of marriage and advocacy of singlehood.[30] In her diary, Allen recounted one memorable weekend in the country, visiting with friends Edna Brush Perkins and Charlotte Jordan who were in a committed same-sex relationship, where after dinner there was "much talk of suffrage and lesbianism." A year earlier she and Edna had similarly discussed "women's friendships."[31]

Allen was part of the modern sexual revolution that questioned women's domestic status and explored other social constructs. Two years spent in Berlin, Germany, after college exposed her to the emerging gay rights movement at the time when Anna Rüling made her famous speech defending lesbian relationships as part of the larger discussion of the male "sexologists" who claimed to have newly discovered women's heterosexual sexuality.[32] Allen noted to herself that she disagreed with this hyper-focus on the physical rather than companionate aspects of marriage.[33] While in Berlin, she debated love and marriage with her sister Helen, rejecting the idea of any evolutionary need to produce children and "propagate" the human race.[34] As a law student in New York City, Allen interacted with the vibrant feminist Heterodoxy Club in bohemian Greenwich Village, whose membership of "unorthodox" professional women intellectually discussed and lived out feminism and practiced cohabitation, bisexuality, lesbianism, and divorce.[35] Important mentors to Allen like lawyer Frances Kellor, reformer Jane Addams, political organizer Molly Dewson, and New Deal administrator Harriet Elliott all modeled affirming ways to live in intimate personal relationships with women.[36]

Beginning in her late thirties, Allen lived in long-term domestic partnerships with women—first her campaign manager Susan Rebhan, and then school principal Mary Pierce. These so-called Boston marriages were socially tolerated at the time because women were assumed to be asexual and emotionally devoted to their female friends.[37] This allowed women to hide their sexuality in plain sight and enjoy "a certain freedom to carry on relationships with other women outside of the public eye, often without scrutiny or judgment."[38] Few documents survive revealing the intimate details of these relationships, as Florence, Mary, and Mary's family destroyed many personal documents and ripped pages out of diaries when donating papers to national archives. From the remaining evidence, historians have concluded that Florence was a lesbian, though family descendants disagree, characterizing her partnerships simply as friendships.[39] But Florence arranged her partnerships as a single domestic unit, serving as the breadwinner to her partner's caretaking role, sharing her finances and home, bequeathing all to her partner, and sharing daily life in a cohabitating relationship.

Florence first lived with Susan Rebhan for fourteen years. Susan had been a school principal and then leader with the Young Women's Christian Association in Youngstown, Ohio, and out West. She became the force behind Florence's successful campaigns as her savvy manager and private secretary. Susan later went to law school at Ohio State University while she lived with Florence and her family in Columbus, famously earning a top score of 95.5 percent on the bar exam. She then practiced law in Cleveland and served a term on the Cleveland City Council. Family and friends treated them like a couple in correspondence.[40] Newspapers commented on Susan and Florence's close relationship, noting that the "two can be found together," as "very good friends" who have "been pals for years," emphasizing Susan as a "close personal friend" who traveled widely with Florence to Alaska, Europe, and the West.[41] Susan was described as tall and shorthaired, with a love of nature and playing baseball with the boys, full of "grit and determination" and able to handle "business deals as good as any man."[42] Florence, however, in her autobiography, mentions Susan only twice, and only as her campaign manager.[43]

Florence Allen, Susan Rebhan, Mary Pierce, and Bertha (Bert) Miller, Florence's law school roommate, spent summers in Estes Park, Colorado, in the Rocky Mountains, returning to Florence's treasured West, where she bought a cabin.[44] The friends relaxed by hiking, fishing, and cooking over the campfire. For a time, Florence, Mary, and Susan lived together back in Cleveland, where "the three of them shared life's joys and sorrows in a comfortable family setting without the benefit of men. Their commitments to each other were deep and enduring."[45] They would caravan together out from Cleveland in "Gypsy," Florence's Ford Model T car, with multiple dogs, tents, and trailers. Photos taken of "the girls" at Estes Park show the women's fun times, silly antics, and close connection.

After Susan's untimely death from the flu in 1935, Florence lived in partnership with Mary for thirty-one years, until Florence's death in 1966.[46] Mary was a school principal at the progressive Park School in Cleveland Heights and later a homemaker. Florence called Mary her "cousin," but there was no family relationship. In their domestic partnership, Florence was the sole breadwinner while Mary was the domestic housekeeper and Florence's personal assistant. The two sent joint holiday cards depicting them together with their dogs on the lawn of the country cottage, "Briar Patch," which they called their "feminist retreat" for friends in Lake County east of Cleveland. Later in life, they together raised a young ward who came to live with them. Family and friends wrote to them as a couple and they responded as partners.[47] At Florence's death, President Lyndon Johnson sent a telegram to Mary with his condolences, as one might send to a bereaved spouse.[48] Mary inherited all of Florence's property, but when she moved closer to extended family in Massachusetts as a senior, her relative cleared out the farmhouse and destroyed the remaining effects.

WOMEN'S TRANSFORMATIVE IMPACT

This book tells the story of the first woman judge—but it is more than just one woman's story. It is also the story of how women infiltrated the courts as judges, lawyers, jurors, and lawmakers and transformed the legal system to a more representative institution attuned to social justice. It reveals what women did with their newly gained authority as citizens after passage of the Nineteenth Amendment, demanding political accountability and participation as agents in the institution of law. The biographical lens of Allen's life illuminates the systemic changes women's integration made to the law and the courts, as she stands at the forefront of the first generation of women lawyers who broke through the gender barrier in the courts. Allen was part of women's reform of the law on multiple fronts where women shifted the legal status quo, for in addition to her impact on the local, state, and federal courts, she pioneered women's entry as a law student, suffrage activist, women's rights lawyer, prosecutor, international peace advocate, and Supreme Court contender. This book uncovers the voluminous archives of Allen's life—two thousand documents she donated to libraries, eight hundred case opinions, and hundreds of newspaper articles—to craft the narrative of the first woman judge.

Allen lived through times of radical social change, from the Progressive Era of modernity and bohemian experimentation, through the years of despair with two world wars and a Great Depression, to periods of stark conservativism including the Cold War and Red and Lavender Scares. She was elected the first woman judge in November 1920 during a window of time that was ripe for innovation and modern evolution. The Nineteenth Amendment had just passed after a seventy-two-year battle, finally removing gender barriers to the right to vote. Women had been contesting their exclusion from political citizenship, emphasizing the need for active roles in the law beyond the vote, including participation in lawmaking as lawyers, judges, jurors, and legislators.[49] With the passage of a federal constitutional amendment enfranchising women, the time was now right for women to be empowered to bring on this transformation.

This decade of the Roaring Twenties following World War I offered a hopeful time for renewal after the devastation of global war. As Allen then described it: "We live in a remarkable time, swift moving, fascinating, diverting, tending to pull us away from our mooring and to turn our minds out of the old current of thought and action."[50] It was an era of innovation with airplanes, automobiles, and radio. It was a more socially tolerant time of flappers, the Harlem Renaissance of Black writers and musicians, and bohemian exploration of lived experience including the binary boundaries of sexual identity.[51] It was also the high point of Progressivism, a political movement offering a third party and a liberal philosophy of populism, bringing an acute social consciousness about the consequences of urban life and a monumental shift in how America viewed government, business, and society.[52] It rejected the corruption and excess of the Gilded Age, during which an insidious corporate wealth presented a false shine of gold obscuring vast inequalities and harm to the welfare of regular people.

Women were at the center of this social transformation. "Certainly never before, . . . did a group of self-proclaimed innovators tie their ambitions so tightly to women, and not just a token handful but whole troops of women, waving the flag of sexual equality."[53] Women entered public life in greater numbers during the Progressive Era, many agreeing with the progressive platform of social welfare and seeking to inject moralism and an ethic of care into a corrupt system. Feminism emerged as a recognized identity and ideology of gender consciousness on the political left centering women's lived experience and demanding equitable social and legal treatment of women.[54] Feminism was associated with the "New Woman," women committed to "economic independence, sexual freedom, and psychological exemption from the repressive obligations" of wife and mother, a "jettisoning of family duties for a heightened female individualism" embracing "female assertiveness and independence."[55]

At the same time, the first Red Scare exposed a nationalistic fear of communism in the wake of the Russian Revolution, resulting in witch hunts targeting socialist organizations including labor and feminists. In response, civil libertarians created the American Civil Liberties Union (ACLU), committed to defending free speech and political activism. 1920 also brought "Red Summers" when hot tempers and blood ran in violent racial conflict in riots in twenty-five towns, including Cleveland, Tulsa, St. Louis, and Chicago.[56] The nascent National Association for the Advancement of Colored People (NAACP) expanded its work and presence in response as the Ku Klux Klan gained renewed prominence. Meanwhile, Prohibition had passed in 1918 as a constitutional ban on the sale and transport of alcohol, spawning organized crime and legal concerns over flaunting the rule of law.[57]

This book begins as the Nineteenth Amendment is on the horizon and women are contesting their anemic citizenship and demanding an equal role in the system of law. It opens as Florence Allen seeks a meaningful life with a fulfilling profession that contributes to society. Chapter 1 follows her through law school as one of the first women to attend coed schools, rejecting gender-segregated programs even as many schools remained firmly and formally closed to women. Allen became one of the first 1 percent of women lawyers, distinguishing herself as a trial lawyer, handling criminal, civil, and legal aid cases. She was appointed county prosecutor by a progressive local party with a shadow woman boss, becoming one of the first women prosecutors in the country. During this time, Allen fought in the revitalized women's suffrage movement in its penultimate decade. Chapter 2 traces Allen's pivotal work in state and national suffrage organizations from the grassroots of street-corner advocacy to constitutional litigation in the halls of justice. In the suffrage movement, she trained with feminists from across the theoretical spectrum, exposed to new ideas of social welfare, equal rights, and women's agency. Days after passage of the constitutional amendment for women's suffrage in 1920, Allen ran for judicial office in the trial court of common pleas.

Chapter 3 traces Allen's ascent and women's rising electoral power as Allen runs as a nonpartisan, launched into office by the power of women and a few male allies. On the bench, Allen initially judged through a social feminist lens, instituting procedures to integrate women jurors and mandate a fair and speedy process for criminal defendants, bringing professional ethical management to a dishonest system. She adopted a tough judicial persona taking on Mafia murderers, corrupt judges, and lying attorneys, zealously enforcing perjury laws and imposing the death penalty—surprising the public as the first woman judge to render such a punitive sentence.

After two years, Allen ran for a seat on the Ohio Supreme Court, desiring a position where she could have more impact on the progressive development of the law. Chapter 4 explores how Allen, as the lone Democrat on the court, developed a constitutional jurisprudence endorsing the new state progressive constitution upholding rights for workers, voters, and municipalities, even as she remained tough on crime during the era of Prohibition and flagrant disregard for the law. However, Allen was quickly frustrated by male colleagues, an adversarial chief justice, and routine cases of little significance that sidelined her efforts to make larger social contributions. Chapter 5 shows how Allen turned to other venues of policymaking nationally and internationally. Inspired to action by the devastation of World War I, she dedicated her life to peace, leading the public and former suffrage colleagues in the legalistic movement to outlaw war. Allen ran twice for Congress, presenting as a party Democrat rather than a woman's candidate with feminized agendas for maternal welfare legislation or an Equal Rights Amendment.

While these legislative campaigns failed, they strengthened Allen's political connections, and President Roosevelt appointed her to the U.S. Court of Appeals for the Sixth Circuit. However, as a first woman judge, Allen experienced discrimination on the basis of sex, ranging from microaggressions to formal inequalities. Chapter 6 reveals how the first woman judge dealt with these problems often faced by women in male spaces by using deflection, super-performance, and, where necessary, public challenge. She assimilated to the masculine norms of the profession, pleased when complimented for her "manly mind" or told that she could "think like a man," determined to prove women's legal competence and pave a more welcoming way for other women judges after her.[58] But as a feminist journalist deduced, Allen's "men colleagues soon found out . . . that she had a mind of her own."[59]

Chapter 7 details how, as a federal jurist, Allen continued to develop public law for an expanded role for government. Her most important cases—*Tennessee Electric Power Company v. Tennessee Valley Authority* and *Wickard v. Filburn*—endorsed broad views of governmental powers for economic and social justice.[60] In a sole case of women's rights, *Walker v. Chapman*, her ruling upheld protective labor legislation of a gendered minimum wage.[61] These landmark cases were mixed in with other cases of patents, criminals, and communists. In the wake of *Brown v. Board of Education*, Allen emerged as an aggressive enforcer of civil rights remedies for race discrimination in schools and housing, taking seriously the new command of *Brown* to enforce civil rights with "all deliberate speed."[62] This legacy stands in stark contrast to a decision early in her judicial career on the state supreme court in *Weaver v. Ohio State University*, where she joined a unanimous per curiam opinion refusing to enjoin racial discrimination in women's college housing.[63] Yet Allen's generally liberal record was significant enough to earn her consideration for the U.S. Supreme Court twelve times. Chapter 8 discusses the winding vicissitudes of politics in the Court appointment process and shows how sexism and cronyism blocked her nomination in favor of less remarkable men.

Allen's story is also the parallel story of women's transformation of the legal system more broadly. In many speeches over the decades, Allen spoke often of the significance and magnitude of women's entry into law. The Nineteenth Amendment was critical to opening these doors to full legal agency as political citizenship as voters, jurors, elected officials, and judges facilitated women's equal participation in the adjudication of law. Suffrage, Allen often noted, symbolically identified for all women their right to power and encouraged their participation in the system of law. Women forced their entry into the profession of law with the help of some male allies, slowly deconstructing the masculinized fraternity resistant to their entry and presumptions of emotionality and incompetence. Requiring the law to end its own discrimination, Allen said, was instrumental in exemplifying the need to end gender discrimination everywhere.

She encouraged women to work to "restore the principle of equality before the law," though male judges balked at women "seeking a special privilege for their sex" or advancing only the causes of their own "emancipated sex."[64] Women also brought new perspectives gained from their own social experience and appreciation of the experience of other women. Allen said they brought to law a "superior sense of integrity," and a "conception that law is the expression of the moral feeling of the community," evidenced by a heightened ethical process and an expanded view of social justice.[65] Women reformers experimented with reforms of legal process like alternative problem-solving approaches to law, integrating social work in women's and juvenile courts and leading the advent of dispute resolution processes. They demanded legislative attention to policies addressing mothers, marriage, children, and formal equality. At the end of the day, women knew they needed to be equally represented as agents in all lawmaking capacities to ensure equal justice and stop an application of justice that ignored or subordinated them and their interests.

Viewing Allen in context, the picture of the first woman judge that emerges is more Elena Kagan than Ruth Bader Ginsburg—neutral arbiter rather than gender champion. Despite a lifetime dedicated to women's causes, Allen, recognized as a "crusader for the rights of women in professional and public life," did not take that crusade to the bench.[66] Only a few women's rights cases came before Allen, but even then, she took a backseat, deferring to male colleagues or reading the gender out of the issue presented. Allen did not adopt a feminine approach to judging based on mercy or problem solving, but instead embraced the mantra "to do justly," emphasizing judgment strictly enforcing legal commands. She embodied the emerging legal thought of legal process, rejecting the classic formalism of the law as a merely logical deduction, insisting upon a balanced, principled approach that appreciated consequences without devolving into results-oriented legal realism.[67] Allen's gender justice operated not through case law but through the system as a whole, shepherding incremental change to incorporate women as equal agents of justice and integrating women's prioritized issues of public law and social justice.

Florence Allen's model of professionalism and gender exceptionalism forged the path allowing women to enter and transform the courts of justice. Allen was acutely aware of the honor and burden of being a pioneer.

One of her favorite speech anecdotes repeated the short story "Three Dreams in a Desert" by Olive Schreiner, a South African feminist and novelist.[68] In it, a woman is deterred from journeying across a deep dark river and steep hills to reach the land of freedom. She is lying motionless, buried in the hot desert sand, weakened by the subjugation of the ages. The lone woman is encouraged by the masculine voice of reason to rise up, though knowing ultimately "she must help herself." She is finally persuaded by the promise of the feet of the thousands of women who would follow behind her on the path she made easier. Florence Allen knew she was this first woman.

1 Integrating the Legal Profession

Florence Allen dedicated her life to integrating the legal profession, for her own actualization and as a trailblazer for other women. She came from a family tradition of public service and had been taught the importance of vocation. Early on she traveled the path of her mother, looking for fulfillment and meaning in women's social reform and in conventional feminine pursuits of music and writing. She soon, however, found that this was not a satisfying avenue, and so she gravitated to her father's work in politics and law. To Allen, the legal profession was attractive because it offered women economic privilege and opportunities for public office. It was a "respected and learned profession" that provided "more interesting and rewarding" work than had been historically available to women. Allen liked that a legal career presented an extra challenge "because the profession was dominated by men."[1] She also believed that women lawyers like herself offered transformational value in social reform of the legal system by morally enhancing the administration of justice and moving the law away from a mere system of private regulation to a social system of "positive standards of rights."[2]

When Florence Allen chose her path of law in the early twentieth century, law was the profession most "engendered and closed to women," relative to teaching, science, and even medicine.[3] Only 1 percent of lawyers were women, and thus Allen faced an uphill battle.[4] Formal rules and statutes provided that only men could be lawyers, excluding women from bar exams, bar licensure, law schools, and bar associations. The long-prevailing cultural assumption was that women were intellectually inferior to men, naturally inclined emotionally only for family nurturing and thus lacking any aptitude or need for a professional life. Law practice was said to put a woman in contact with "baser natures" and "insult," making her unfit for a domestic life.[5] The law profession developed as a fraternity, a social brotherhood riding the circuit of early courts where lawyers and judges would arrive at county seats, hold court before rustic crowds eager for drama, and stay together in inns of court drinking and fraternizing as friends.[6] Law was considered masculine in professional ideology—formal, logical, hierarchical, abstract, and competitive.[7] Lawyers were valorized for being "fearless" and "manly," depicted as the hero fighting in the arena for their clients. Women were said not to meet this ideal because they lacked the physical strength, intellectual capacity, and mental tenacity to handle aggressive competition and abstract, nonemotional reasoning. As crusading attorney Clarence Darrow told a group of Chicago women lawyers, "You can't be shining lights at the bar because you are too kind. You can never be corporation lawyers because you are not cold-blooded." At best, he said, women might work as unpaid pro bono counsel in divorce or criminal defense matters.[8]

Women fought these gendered assumptions, demanding acceptance into the legal profession. Chicago legal editor Myra Bradwell challenged the denial of her admission to the bar, but the U.S. Supreme Court held that women did not have the privilege of profession under the Fourteenth Amendment Privileges or Immunities Clause. A concurrence more broadly opined that women were unfit for law because of the "natural and proper timidity and delicacy which belongs to the female sex."[9] D.C. lawyer Belva Lockwood brought suit at every juncture of her qualification for profession. She challenged the refusal of the National Law School to issue her diploma at graduation, sued when the bar did not accept her exam and made her take it twice, and lobbied for special legislation to admit women to federal court. When Virginia denied her right to practice there, the U.S. Supreme Court upheld the prohibition, contorting a state statute allowing a *person* to practice law to mean only men under an originalist interpretation of the history and tradition of the term.[10]

The turning point for women's admission came as some male allies changed or ignored these conventional rules. The first woman lawyer in the U.S., Arabella Mansfield, was admitted to the Iowa bar in 1869 because a male judge disregarded the express text of a statute limiting admission to white men, finding that interpretation would work an injustice.[11] In Ohio, early women lawyers came up through apprenticeship facilitated by male friends and family, including first-in-the-state sisters Nettie and Florence Cronise in 1873; the first in Cleveland, Mary Spargo Fraser, in 1885; and the first Black woman lawyer, Daisy Perkins, in 1919.[12]

Allen's search for legal profession was driven by deep feminist convictions in the fundamentality of women's economic autonomy.[13] The progressive feminism of the time as theorized by the "preeminent feminist intellectual" Charlotte Perkins Gilman centered feminist theory on economic independence. The idea was that women should all engage in market work—whether profession, trade, or domestic service—to gain monetary power and escape the subordination of the isolated home sphere.[14] This emerging feminism of the early 1900s meant "different things to different people," from equality of employment to protection for women's labor, but the fundamental tenet was economic freedom for all working women. Allen articulated her own "new kind of feminism" for the professional woman, blending radical and progressive ideals. She advocated "a sweet-natured feminism, not strident but nevertheless firm, steady, clear-headed and organized for the protection of the whole human group as well as for the protection of women as a sex."[15] This "dynamic as well as protective" feminism, she argued, offered a "particular social perspective" to the "new order of economic structure" and the use of profession for social good.

THE SEARCH FOR PROFESSION

Allen spent her educational years and early twenties searching for a meaningful life purpose and profession. In her autobiography, she recalled this time as one of "fast-developing psychological conflict" over contemplating a future path, colored by periods when she "felt blue" about her prospects.[16]

She was searching for something more than women expected at the time, more than marriage or a paycheck. Allen's parents, Corinne and Emir Allen, fundamentally influenced her to aspire to work in a vocation that was socially conscious and publicly engaged.

Both of Allen's parents were active in political, community, and social reform work, modeling for their children a life of service and contribution to others. Florence nostalgically recalled her childhood "as one of love and understanding from her parents," who had instilled "their sense of morality, justice, and civic responsibility that sustained her for a lifetime."[17] Just before she was born, the Allen family relocated to Utah from Northeast Ohio because of her father's failing health from tuberculosis.[18] Florence Ellinwood Allen was born in Utah on March 23, 1884, the third of six surviving children. Utah was then governed by the Mormon Church, but there was a national battle against its practice of polygamy, and railroads and silver mining interests vied for power in the state.[19] The Allens were non-Mormons who at first worked alongside their neighbors before later challenging their religious governance.

Florence's mother, Corinne Tuckerman Allen, built a vocation of reform and community activism. Corinne came from a family of reformers in Northeast Ohio. Her father, Jacob Tuckerman, ran the New Lyme Institute, a progressive coed college preparatory school. Her brother Louis Bryant Tuckerman was called "the Father of Cleveland liberalism," his name "a synonym for radicalism of the soundest kind."[20] Corinne had been one of the first students to attend Smith College, one of the women's colleges founded in the 1870s to provide women a college education like that of men, even as they perpetuated the idea of separate female spheres. She said that her father believed in intellectual training for women the same as men, and that women's rights leader Lucy Stone, his classmate at Oberlin College, had converted him to suffrage and feminism.[21] Corinne actively worked for public libraries and for women's suffrage, and helped found the National Congress of Mothers (later the National Parent Teacher Association).[22] Corinne's conservative politics of women's domestic authority evolved into a moralism that took on the issues of polygamy and sexual purity.[23]

Florence had a good relationship with her mother, but it was her father, Clarence "Emir" Allen, whom she emulated and sought out for advice. She often recounted that her father, a "giant" over six feet tall, loomed large in her life as a role model of lawyer, legislator, and teacher.[24] Emir Allen was one of the first U.S. congressional representatives from the new state of Utah in 1895.[25] He was a Republican running on pro-silver opposition to party presidential nominee William McKinley, an Ohioan who advocated the gold standard backing paper money.[26] Before that, Emir served in the Utah territorial legislature, a populist of the Liberal Party of non-Mormons known for his bills on worker's compensation, labor protections of eight-hour workdays for miners, and free public schools.[27] He was of Puritan stock and traced his lineage to Revolutionary war hero Ethan Allen. Emir had worked as a silver mine manager and as a professor of Greek and Latin at Western Reserve Academy in Hudson, Ohio.[28] His claim to fame was that he was the first college baseball pitcher in Ohio to throw a curveball, helping Western Reserve clobber Oberlin College and going on to play semiprofessional baseball for the Erie Keystones.[29]

Florence was educated in Utah and Ohio. She attended her grandfather's New Lyme School at age twelve when she moved to Ohio to live with her maternal grandparents while her father served in Congress in Washington, D.C. She completed high school at Salt Lake College back in Utah.[30] Florence had been an athletic child, climbing mountains, hiking streams, and volunteering for outdoor chores like chopping wood and mowing lawns rather than anything domestic in the house. In family photos, she is often seen in pants, menswear hats, and long neckties. She was described as a "precocious," "husky little girl."[31]

Florence returned to Ohio for college at age sixteen, attending Western Reserve College for Women (now Case Western Reserve University). Like many women, she studied languages and English, assumed to be appropriate female concentrations. Florence emerged as a leader among her peers, elected president of the freshman class, serving as editor of the literary magazine, and winning lead roles in theater productions, often male roles, earning her the nickname "Cousin Jo" after her resemblance to the character in Louisa May Alcott's classic book *Little Women*.[32] When she graduated Phi Beta Kappa, the college's president, Charles Thwing, wrote her a reference, stating, "In efficiency, as well as character and scholarship, Miss Allen represents the best."[33]

Following her college graduation in 1904, twenty-year-old Florence accompanied her mother and siblings to Berlin for two years. They went to Germany so that her sister Esther—a musician and later violin teacher, college dean, and professor—could study violin at the Stern Conservatory. Corinne used the trip for her suffrage and other activism.[34] While abroad, Florence studied music and piano, with dreams of being a concert pianist, and worked as a newspaper music critic.[35] She dabbled in poetry, writing "patriotic poems" from abroad that exploited "the duality of nature" in subjects about law, friendship, and the American West that were published as a book called *Patris,* meaning "homeland" in Greek. A review of the book commented on the "masculine qualities" of the work, finding "there is no sex in good writing."[36] Allen's poems, the reviewer wrote, "have, moreover, a masculine standard of ethics; an elemental manly code of justice. If you read the poem 'Law' you will see how complete is Miss Allen's intellectual divorce from sex; how surely she has grasped and expressed the man-idea of the subject."

When Florence returned to Cleveland, she searched for a meaningful and financially supportive career. She tried working as a freelance music critic for the *Plain Dealer* newspaper, and as a teacher at Laurel School for girls instructing on German, Greek, and history.[37] Her memoir notes the drudgery and boredom of teachers' meetings and the endless papers to grade.[38] She said her mind hungered for "words and ideas," and so she took graduate courses for a master's degree in political science at Western Reserve University. This graduate work studying constitutional law, comparative governments, and municipal law ignited her interest in law, encouraged by Professor Augustus Hatton, a progressive who helped form the innovative Cleveland city management. Allen said it then "came to her 'like a flash out of the blue'" and a "revelation on high" that she wanted to be a lawyer.[39] However, another professor, Dr. Curtis, gave a speech dismissing such aspirations, saying that a "woman is morally, aesthetically, physically, . . . intellectually inferior to man."

LAW SCHOOL

When Florence Allen applied to law school in 1909, many schools were still closed to women. This educational exclusion was increasingly detrimental to women as the apprenticeship system was replaced by formal education. Law schools served as barriers to entry and could also more systemically inculcate the profession's "orthodox masculine ideals" in a stricter normative way.[40] They developed the "scientific" Socratic method that replaced lectures with teacher-directed questioning, requiring a competitive, individualistic dialogue for discernment of legal principles. This "machismo view of the case method" was said to require manly courage and survival instincts.[41] A few women broke through these formal barriers and became the first to attend law school in the early 1870s: Lemma Barkeloo and Phoebe Couzins at St. Louis Law School (now Washington University School of Law), Ada Kepley at Union College of Law (now Northwestern University Pritzker School of Law), Sarah Killgore Wertman at the University of Michigan Law School, and the first Black woman law student, Charlotte Ray, at Howard University School of Law.[42] Most law schools, however, continued to prohibit women until 1920, when some began opening slowly, and then only for a token few students, while others continued to resist, like Harvard (until 1950) and Washington and Lee (until 1972).[43]

Women established their own separate institutions at the Washington College of Law (now American University Washington College of Law) in 1896 and Portia Law School (now New England Law Boston) in 1908.[44] But these schools were diminished by the practicing bar because they were part-time institutions, with night schools, minimal admission requirements, and low tuition. While part-time schools provided good opportunities for women, many with limited income and work or family obligations, as well as for poor, immigrant, and racial minorities, they were targeted by the legal educational elite as inferior.[45] These law schools "alarmed" the practicing bar, concerned about producing too many lawyers and protecting their own income and reputation. The establishment rejected these schools, as well as admission paths such as apprenticeship and diploma privilege, for a rigorous bar exam requiring intensive, and more expensive, academic study.[46] Yet an experiment into an elite, exclusively women's law school, Cambridge Law School for Women, instigated by college women at Radcliffe and located on the edge of Harvard using the Harvard methods of instruction, lasted only a few years.[47]

Allen's alma mater, Western Reserve University, did not admit women to law school when she sought to enroll. Later, when Allen became a lawyer, she would use her authority to pressure the university to admit women to the professional schools of law and medicine, which it did in 1918.[48] Allen's hometown did offer an evening law school, Cleveland Law School (then at Baldwin Wallace University, now at Cleveland State University), which had just graduated its first women in 1908. But the part-time school did not offer the prestige of other schools discounted by legal gatekeepers.[49]

Allen instead enrolled at the University of Chicago Law School in 1909. Her mentor, Professor Hatton, encouraged her to attend his alma mater, where he had recently completed his PhD and taught.[50] Chicago was one of the top schools attended by women graduate students in the social sciences at the turn of the twentieth century. It was an academic center of women researchers and social feminists and served as "the seed-ground for the theories undergirding radical feminism" on progressive issues of social welfare and sex-based differences.[51] The university offered distinguished faculty and rigorous science, challenging East Coast schools for national intellectual preeminence.[52] Chicago's law school accepted women from its first days, opening in 1902 with express principles of extending "opportunities from all departments of higher education to persons of both sexes on equal terms."[53] Its commitment to sex equality, though, was more a function of financial sustainability, to attract a sufficient number of paying students after its founding on John Rockefeller's money. Sophonisba Breckinridge became the first woman law graduate at Chicago in 1904, ranking at the top of her class and going on to a career in academia.[54]

Allen was one of only four women at the Chicago law school. She was sometimes the only woman in a classroom of one hundred men and said that as a "shy person," she "found it an embarrassing ordeal."[55] The rules of "ladies first" applied, as a woman's arrival at the door of a classroom prompted a dozen men to stand aside when she entered, a form of attention Allen said was "terrifying." For, as feminist theorists have explained, the first women law students "experienced exaggerated attention combined with near-total invisibility, seldom seen but always center stage."[56] Allen confirmed this experience, saying that the "first women who studied law . . . after incredible efforts to gain admission endured real persecution in their classes, ridicule from students and lack of sympathy from faculty."[57] By the end of the winter quarter, Allen was ranked second in the class and was recognized by her male colleagues for having "a masculine mind," ruled by reason rather than emotion.[58]

Yet Allen was unhappy in Chicago, where money was short and friends were few. Jobs as a housemaid and then as a library clerk cataloging French and German legal treatises were pure drudgery.[59] Allen noted in her diary that her Contracts professor, Roscoe Pound, the renowned legal scholar and later dean of Harvard Law School who taught at Chicago for one year and who was known for his "orotund pomposity," didn't like women students, and "whale[d] against one woman over contracts." She noted in her autobiography that she and her three women classmates "felt he discouraged us in our wish to practice law. He thought it was no field for a woman."[60] Allen encountered Pound a decade later at a business luncheon when she was a judge, but he seemed to have no recollection of her as one of his few women students.

Disillusioned in Chicago, in the summer of 1910, Allen transferred to New York University School of Law, where she found a more supportive environment. It was one of the largest law schools in the country admitting women, with eighty-two women enrolled.[61] NYU first opened its doors to women in 1890, four years after the state legislature passed a statute admitting women to the state bar. At the same time, it established a community non-credentialed certificate program called the Woman's Law Class to educate women generally in law and create a pipeline for future professional students.[62] Allen had preferred to attend the prestigious Columbia University Law School in New York but was denied admission. Columbia "vehemently resisted coeducation" and "often turned women away with a remarkable lack of civility"; its dean, Harlan Stone, later Supreme Court Chief Justice, threatened that women would be admitted only over his dead body.[63] Taking a dig at the school in her memoir, Allen wrote, "Unlike Columbia and many other law schools, New York University constantly encouraged women law students" and "I can never repay what I owe to New York University. There we were in the Law School on equal terms with men, and we said to ourselves, if we pass our examinations and are admitted to the bar, no one can prevent us from practicing. This was the spirit given us by New York University Law School." NYU, she said, "gave us a sense of the dignity and purpose of the law" and "gave us our profession—think what that means!"[64]

NYU offered lectures in the morning, afternoon, and evening so that students from different socioeconomic classes could study law. The morning session offered small classes and individual attention, attracting full-time students who could afford to go to school without working. The afternoon sessions were designed for students who had part-time jobs, and the evening school attracted students who worked full-time to support their legal education. NYU's night school, however, attracted the concern of Ivy League accreditors that denigrated the educational standards of such part-time programs. The dean of NYU refused to discontinue the night program, committed to working and minority students.[65] Allen first enrolled in the evening division, as she worked full-time the first semester, but then switched to the day division as she prioritized law school even though money was extremely tight.

At NYU, Allen took the usual menu of rigorous law courses. She reported struggling with some, such as Wills and Equity. Like the typical law student, she worried about being called on in class, later recalling one time when she was grilled over the *Slaughter-House Cases* on the civil rights amendments and another when she successfully recited on a difficult case of voidable minors' contracts.[66] Allen noted in her diary that she got "quite good at bluff" when called on.[67] She was upset by some of the readings about marital rape and embarrassed about being singled out to recite an old English case about the will of Julia Poulton, the Countess of Clarenza, complicated by her bigamy, adultery, cohabitation, and illegitimate sons.[68] Despite these worries, Allen succeeded, earning an L.L.B. and graduating second in her class—behind a man, it was noted, who had clerked for seven years in a law office.[69] Recognizing her achievement, NYU law school later established scholarships for women students designated as "Florence Allen Scholars," now extended to all students in the top 10 percent of the class at the end of their second year.[70]

Women law students at NYU also were required to attend "ladies' lectures" designed to compensate for their supposedly deficient life skills, for example to learn general business knowledge like reading a broker's statement. They must learn, they were told, to "work round the clock" and "be at the beck and call of business when it comes" rather than being detoured by some side personal issue. Women were also told they must compensate for the fact that the voice and physical appearance of the average woman lawyer "does not produce the impression of authority and aggressiveness" that are key characteristics of a lawyer (defined as male).[71] The school had legal sororities to support women's mentoring and networking needs. However, several of these excluded women of color and Jewish women, and for this reason, Allen rejected the invitation to join.[72]

In New York, both at school and in the city, Florence found a supportive environment personally and professionally. She lived in Greenwich Village near the law school with college friends Bertha Miller and her sister Marie. Her brothers Jack and Emir came to visit from Yale for weekends and holidays. She had an active social life and a lot of fun with her friends in New York City, going to the theater, ice skating, taking sleigh rides, getting their fortunes told, visiting museums, and day tripping to Staten Island. A few times, she also recorded in her diary that she smoked and got drunk. Florence was a dedicated foodie, enjoying dinners with friends and inventive food like scalloped oysters, lobster salad, mock turtle soup, and sardines with bologna. She had a huge sweet tooth and often overindulged in candy, making herself sick. Florence also obsessed over her weight, recording it every day for months on end as it fluctuated between 206 and 216 pounds, trying to walk for exercise, "the pedometer clicking all day." While a law student, Florence remained politically engaged, attending lectures on suffrage, peace, orphan asylums, and the Lowell mill women's strike.[73]

APPRENTICING WITH FEMINISTS

During law school, Allen continued her search for profession through volunteer and work experiences. Each of these experiences exposed her to different theories and practices of feminism, as she sought examples of professional paths for her way forward. She rejected her mother's maternalism of domesticity and nonmarket labor, incorporating the ideals of progressive social feminism to work for reform and welfare, and gravitating to formal ideals of equality in liberal feminism to eradicate gender barriers to professional work and political action.[74]

While in Chicago for law school, Allen encountered the social feminists of the progressive settlement house movement, who expanded her thinking to emphasize values of social and economic reform. The University of Chicago was the center of academic social feminism, where scholars like Sophonisba Breckinridge developed the theoretical underpinnings of social feminist theory and social activism. Chicago was also the center of the settlement house movement, with Jane Addams's Hull House, where Allen volunteered during her year in Chicago and was heavily influenced by Addams's ideas.[75] Settlement houses were located in low-economic urban areas, where middle-class women social reformers lived among the impoverished communities they served and offered childcare, kindergarten, education, and job and home training. These social feminists extended ideas of authority for women derived from domesticity to external venues of "enlarged housekeeping," where women had a collective duty to care for society and reform the laws to protect those vulnerable communities from the evils of industrialization.[76] Social feminists focused on social change, conceiving private organizations where volunteer aid work helped those in need, such as juvenile justice reform and legal aid organizations.[77] Allen internalized their tenets of social consciousness and care for the poor and vulnerable, which would dominate her political and legal thinking throughout her life.

Allen left Hull House after one year to move to New York City—"induced," she said, by a job offer from lawyer and activist Frances Kellor to work with her legal aid organization, the League for the Protection of Immigrants.[78] Allen said the offer came "as the result of a chance meeting of the two women in Chicago," but the opportunity was "above all others one she would have wished for," as Kellor's "genuine and fresh approach to the problems which interested me was so stimulating that I left Chicago to work for the League."[79] Allen worked with Kellor for about six months as a legal investigator on cases and services for new immigrants. Kellor's office was located across the docks from Ellis Island, where new immigrants arrived. Allen worked on the front lines assisting immigrants with legal issues, housing, and consumer fraud. She also worked briefly at the Henry Street Settlement House founded by nursing reformer Lillian Wald, dedicated to public health education for women and children.

Kellor and her life partner, trade unionist Mary Dreier, would become lifelong mentors to Allen.[80] Kellor offered an attractive role model for Allen, both personally and professionally, as Allen navigated her new role as a lawyer. Kellor was one of the first women graduates of Cornell Law School and conducted academic research at the University of Chicago on women's issues in criminology, harassment in domestic employment, and sports equality. She was high up in the leadership of the Progressive Party, drafting the immigration plank and advising Theodore Roosevelt on women's suffrage. Later, Kellor would be one of the founding officers of the American Arbitration Association, where she served for over thirty years, focused on an alternative noncompetitive method of conflict resolution.[81]

This was a politically charged time for Allen to be working with immigrants, as nativism and animus accelerated in response to a large increase in immigration and Congress responded by significantly curtailing immigration. This time was also the immediate aftermath of the Triangle Shirtwaist Factory fire in March 1911 that killed 146 workers, most of them young women who were Italian or Jewish immigrants.[82] The horrific stories of women trapped by locked exit doors and jumping from eight-story windows to their death on the concrete below exposed corrupt labor practices even as the business owners escaped criminal liability and profited from insurance payouts. Protests erupted in New York City, and law student Florence Allen joined in the demonstrations.[83] Protests and strikes by women over these types of dangerous working conditions a few years before led to wealthy feminist benefactor Alva Belmont bailing the women out of night court, telling the press: "There will be a different order of things when we have women judges on the bench."[84]

Allen did not last long in settlement house work, quitting after six months. She did not like the requirement that she live in the neighborhood of service. She was quickly disaffected by her living conditions, renting a room from an Irish landlady that had a significant infestation.[85] Her diary details how she sat up in a chair all night rather than "share the bed with its insect occupants."[86] More fundamentally, Allen rejected the ideology of social work grounded in the unpaid philanthropy of upper-middle-class women expected to volunteer their time. She valued the remuneration that signaled the legitimacy of profession. Allen needed to support herself financially, as she felt her parents had already paid enough for her graduate school and the family budget was strained by both brothers then attending Yale. She took on part-time work giving paid speeches on civics and music to local schools.

Allen then accepted a paid position with the College Equal Suffrage League as secretary to its leader, Maud Wood Park, that would support her for the rest of law school. She was paid $40 per month ($1,400 today). This position put Allen at the helm of the national suffrage movement and connected her with the leading feminists fighting for equal rights. These women exemplified equality feminist theory and the importance of public advocacy beyond private assistance. The suffrage movement would provide the jumping-off point for Allen's later career in politics and law.[87]

In New York City, Allen was further acclimated to feminism by her involvement with leading feminists active in the Heterodoxy Club, a vibrant luncheon debate club for "unorthodox women." Begun by fellow Clevelander Marie Howe in 1912, it flourished in bohemian Greenwich Village, where Allen lived. The "new women" intellectuals—feminists, writers, reformers, and professionals—"gathered over wine and food in frenzied discussions about arts, politics, and news" and became the center of intellectual feminism. These women rejected traditional roles of domesticity and marriage, and embraced a life of profession and alternative lifestyles of singlehood, lesbianism, divorce, cohabitation, and bisexuality. Photos show women "using little or no make-up or jewelry," wearing "ties, high stiff collars, mannish suits and hats and simple short hair styles." As Howe explained: "We're tired of being specialized to sex. We intend simply to be ourselves, not just our little female selves, but our whole, big human selves."[88] Allen attended meetings at Heterodoxy during law school, noting in her diary times when she attended "Mrs. Howe's club," highlighting one frustrating debate when a colleague "disputes my theory of justice." She met Heterodoxy members for lunch and dinner, including Mary Ware Dennett, a birth control advocate who was convicted of violating the Comstock obscenity law, lawyer and equality feminist Crystal Eastman, and Jeannette Rankin, a suffrage activist who would become the first woman in Congress. Heterodoxy kept feminism in the public eye by hosting a high-profile public forum on "What Is Feminism?"—which Allen missed due to a Torts exam.[89]

PRACTICING LAW

After graduating from NYU law school, Allen returned to Cleveland at age twenty-nine with "no job in sight."[90] As later reported in an article about

Allen in the *New York Times*, "The law seemed completely a man's game; no office wanted a woman solicitor, junior, or even clerk."[91] A Cleveland newspaper reported on Allen and the uncommon advent of a new woman lawyer in town, recommending the profession as a "boundless field for women who are anxious to help other women get a square deal in life" and noting that "more and more every year, young college women are cultivating the acquaintance of Blackstone and fitting themselves to win justice in 'a man's world.'"[92] Without a job, Allen took a gap year, spending time with family and friends, playing piano, and reading voraciously everything from classic women's literature to economic theory.[93] She remained politically engaged, attending meetings on progressivism and socialism, debating the "Comstock situation" of birth control, and reading left-leaning newspapers.[94]

After six months, Allen buckled down and devoted herself to studying in earnest for the bar exam. She studied at the local law library, getting old bar questions and reviewing the cumulative digests of codes and cases. She took the exam in June 1914, noting in her diary that it was generally easy, but there were "mean, technical, procedural questions in Crim Law." Two weeks later, she passed the bar with high marks.[95]

Allen said it was difficult to find work as a lawyer in Cleveland because "she was forced to fight against certain handicaps that went with being a woman, some of which were revealed to her, she said, in ludicrous ways."[96] Allen received one interview at a respected firm through connections of her father's college friend. The prominent lawyer, a "distinct product of the 'old school,' glanced out of the window where a light snow was falling and said: 'Miss Allen, it would be painful to me to have a woman in my office because I should not like to send her even to the courthouse on a day like this.'"[97] "After receiving this rebuff—and others," she decided to set up her own solo law office practice.

Allen hung up her shingle, put her name on the directory, borrowed furniture and money, and simply began work.[98] She made $25 her first month, later saying that "I had no clients. And I had no money. But I had great hopes."[99] Six months into practice, she affiliated informally with the Cleveland firm of Bartholomew, Leeper & McGill. She knew the lead partner, Robb O. "Barth" Bartholomew, because his wife was her college sorority sister. Barth gave her money and client referrals early on in her practice, and the named partners mentored her in practice.[100] Allen reported that she earned $780 ($24,000 today) in her first year of practice, but "fees for her work were small and slow in coming."[101] By 1918, she reported a salary of $2,200 ($45,000 today).[102]

Allen handled whatever cases that came in the door, struggling to be self-supporting. She described her work as general practice, including trial, probate, juvenile, consumer, and business matters.[103] She did the typical legal work of drafting papers, motions, and affidavits, filing notices and subpoenas, drafting wills and articles of incorporation, taking depositions, and attempting to settle cases. She litigated disputes, organized business partnerships and corporations, and handled collections.[104] However, she rejected low-paying social welfare work recommended by her suffrage friends at the juvenile detention home.[105] Allen did a significant amount of trial work in many courts, unusual for a woman lawyer then, including municipal, police, juvenile, and probate courts. In this work, she became familiar with many of the judges, which would later serve her well. Yet she said that visits to the police court were "especially unpleasant," and on at least one occasion she said the "vile, stinking place" made her physically ill.[106]

Early on, Allen began doing "divorce all day," and family law would be an area that sustained her practice.[107] Her first case involved an Italian woman seeking a divorce on grounds that her husband deserted her and their children; the woman's brother paid Allen $15.[108] Another involved helping a woman divorce her abusive husband, except that the client, Mrs. Nicolett, came back to Allen's office and said that "her husband will reform," then skipped further meetings with Allen. On another case, Allen noted how she lay awake at three in the morning "thinking of damn divorce case" that she was having a "terrible time trying to settle." She also handled cases of women seeking alimony of financial support after separation, guardianships and bastardy (child support) actions, and many juvenile cases.[109]

Early in her practice, Allen also volunteered for referrals from the Legal Aid Society of Cleveland. Her mentor, Barth, had just been selected as the contract attorney for the organization. She offered to do this work "for the sake of experience" and "began really to get some practice," while also fundraising for the organization.[110] She would later recommend the legal aid referral process as a good way for women lawyers to begin to build a practice and develop legal skills.[111] Her poverty clients, she said, had all sorts of "human interest cases," including landlord-tenant troubles, wage garnishment, juvenile delinquency, consumer and real estate fraud, and dental malpractice.[112]

Allen then branched out into criminal work. She consulted with her male mentors on how to get criminal defense business and court appointments. As a criminal lawyer, she handled a variety of cases, including one "white slave" sex-trafficking case. Another case involved a court appointment to represent a female defendant, Ms. Walters, who had been jailed. Allen thought the "policemen were in cahoots" and won the case on self-defense.[113] She then moved into more big-time criminal defense of Mafia defendants, representing one "Italian client" on a Corrupt Practices Act charge.[114] Another case in Akron put in her in the middle of a significant increase in criminal arrests as the city prosecutor, Cletus Roetzel, got tough on Mafia-related crime.[115]

Allen handled many matters for women clients who sought out a woman lawyer. In one successful appeal, she won a case for a woman claiming fraud by an executor of a will on grounds of tolling the statute of limitations.[116] The most important women's cases she handled were constitutional matters of women's suffrage litigated in the Ohio Supreme Court.[117] In addition, she served as general counsel to the Ohio women's suffrage organizations, drafting model suffrage legislation and petitioning against legislation, as she did, for example, in opposing a bill to make divorce harder in Ohio.[118] Allen handled a case challenging a birth control statute involving her suffrage friend Helen Mitchell.[119]

One of the most important cases for Allen was representing women streetcar "conductorets" in a labor dispute before the national arbitration board in *In re Employees v. Cleveland Railway Company*.[120] During World War I, the railway company hired two hundred women to replace streetcar conductors when the men left their jobs to fight in the war. As men began returning, they wanted their jobs back. The company initially refused but capitulated when the union threatened a strike, paralyzing Cleveland transportation and costing the company $2 million in revenues. A federal labor investigation found that the company was not required to retain the women.[121] The women conductors held "a spirited open meeting" at the streetcar barn, formed their own union, affiliated with suffragists, and hired Allen as their lawyer.[122] This was during the height of the Spanish flu pandemic, when Cleveland closed public spaces and tasked streetcar conductors, then mostly women, with arresting those who spat on the floor of the cars. Allen was very sick during this time, likely with the flu, though she continued her work on the case and at the courts.[123]

Allen filed a complaint on behalf of the women conductors with the National War Labor Board, an alternative dispute resolution forum providing mediation and arbitration services to keep labor from striking during the war.[124] She was the first woman attorney to appear before it.[125] The Board heard many cases of women's employment during the war, and its general precept was that all women hired in wartime were to receive equal pay for equal work. Initially, the Board summarily upheld the company's decision, allowing the replacement of the women by returning men, but recommended the company make "every effort" to assign the displaced women to other low-paying positions like selling tickets and cleaning cars.[126] Losing the first hearing and pressured by the company, the men's union, and the mayor to help end the strike, the women reluctantly agreed to "end their careers"—but they also voted to boycott the streetcars and appeal the decision.[127]

Allen petitioned for rehearing, which was granted on the basis of her arguments that the "women did not have their day in court." They were not given an opportunity to be heard at the first meeting, which was a closed meeting between investigators, the mayor, and the company improperly excluding the women.[128] The War Labor Board, in an opinion by joint chairs including former president (and later Chief Justice) William Howard Taft, reversed its prior decision, finding that an "injustice was done" by the previous order and determining that the company should restore the remaining women seeking employment to their positions.[129] The arbiters relied on an analogous War Labor Board decision for Detroit women conductors and were swayed by the factual reality that the railway had enough job vacancies to hire both men and the remaining women. The company, however, ignored the recommendation of the Board's nonbinding opinion, and so the women still lost their jobs.[130] The company hired women again as conductors when another labor exigency arose during World War II, disregarding Ohio law at the time that prohibited women from working as streetcar conductors and for long hours or night shifts.[131]

PROSECUTRESS

After five years in practice, Allen was appointed an assistant prosecutor for Cuyahoga County in Cleveland. The prosecutor position for Allen was a stable and financially rewarding job at a salary of $2,700 ($60,000 today). The *Plain Dealer* reported that the selection was "a surprise to everyone but her friends" who knew her legal reputation and political activism.[132] When she took office on April 1, the press asked Allen whether she thought it significant that her work began on April Fool's Day, intimating that the appointment was a joke.[133]

This was a game-changing appointment for Allen that would be pivotal to her success, as she entered mainstream politics and earned a key badge of professional reputation valuable for election or appointment to judicial office. Women's segregation from party politics as nonvoters had worked against them in patronage and political appointments, but Allen had become acquainted with Democratic Party leaders in Cuyahoga County and active in national Democratic politics as a national women's committee member for Ohio and campaigner for President Woodrow Wilson. While she was in the middle of the streetcar case, Cleveland political boss Burr Gongwer asked her to become an assistant prosecutor. Allen accepted immediately.[134] Gongwer was a progressive, innovative leader whose "farsightedness was best illustrated by the way he encouraged women to get actively into politics after women's suffrage became the national law." This support included promoting Bernice Pyke as women's political boss in the city and the first woman to serve in the mayor's cabinet, who in turn bolstered Allen's political career from behind the scenes.[135]

People celebrated Allen's appointment.[136] A historian described how "yellow roses, symbol of the woman suffrage movement, bedecked her office when she arrived, reporters interviewed her, photographers took pictures."[137] The newspapers trumpeted her appointment, reporting that she was the first woman in Ohio and in the entire country to hold the office of prosecutor. There had, however, been other women nominally serving as prosecutors before her. Clara Foltz was a deputy district attorney assigned to women and children's cases in Los Angeles, and Reah Whitehead was given the title of assistant prosecutor in Seattle though she worked as a secretary to a male attorney.[138]

The Cleveland prosecutor who supervised Allen, Samuel Doerfler, allayed concerns about her gender: "I consider that Miss Allen will do a man's job in our office. . . . I rate her as the equal of virtually any male attorney in Cleveland."[139] In a letter to the editor, Doerfler emphasized the revolutionary meaning of this appointment: "It is an indication of the increasing liberality of the public mind concerning women's position in the business and professional world." He continued, "It is not so long ago that an appointment of this kind would have been ridiculed and condemned, yet so rapidly have the views of the public changed, that today Miss Allen's appointment has been met with almost universal approval."[140]

Allen acknowledged the significance of her appointment: "Women lawyers have always had a hard row to hoe. That's why I am so happy for my appointment—not of myself, but of a woman—to public office."[141] She reassured the public that "I will do the same work the men do" and "try every case assigned to me no matter what it is."[142] While she noted that "criminal cases aren't quite so nice to handle perhaps as civil cases," she said "a woman who trains herself to fighting will not notice the difference. I expect to be interested tremendously in helping turn the wheels of justice."

No one knew what to call the woman prosecutor. Papers referred to her as "prosecutoress" or "prosecutress." Allen preferred the regular, gender-neutral term *prosecutor*. Professional terminology had become a point of contention for women lawyers. They rejected gendered titles like *Miss*, *Madam*, and *Lady* typically used for women in court. As scholars explained, "they saw these titles as symbols of male condescension and hostility toward women in the courtroom, even as subtle weapons in the hands of the judge and opposing counsel to call attention to women lawyers' femininity and to belittle them in court."[143] Allen encountered even more direct sexism from opposing counsel. In one case, a defense lawyer who "had an extremely raucous tongue" looked her "up and down with contempt" as she stepped into the courtroom with a police file and said loudly in front of the jury, "What does the prosecutor's office mean by sending a skirt in here?" Allen dismissed the slight, saying that the defense lost the case from that statement because the jury credited her authority with the prosecutor's office.[144]

Allen was surprised that she was "slung into cases without preparation" because the office was so backlogged.[145] She was only able to brush up on the fine points of criminal law at a new courthouse library and dive in. A decade later, she criticized this lack of training for prosecutors as a systemic failure of government and law schools.[146] She attacked the "neglect of the public branches of law," "where law students of small experience as prosecutors, learning the practice as well as they can by rule of thumb" battled "well-paid adroit and long-schooled" defense lawyers over "all-important criminal questions involving liberty, life, banditry, racketeering and the public safety." The failure, she said, was that the "great phases" of public law are "not at all adequately taught in law schools," as their "emphasis is upon private property rights."

Allen won her first criminal trial, supervised by a senior lawyer, of a domestic violence case convicting Albert Stahr of manslaughter for killing his wife, Mary. In opening argument, Allen emphasized the husband's conflicting testimony as to when he left and returned home to find his wife dead. The coroner testified that Mary "met death through kicking or trampling." The jury returned its verdict in less than one hour. She also won the first case she tried alone, a conviction for an $18 robbery.[147]

Allen tried criminal cases "just as the men prosecutors do." She reported that she had tried "about fifty in all" at a rate of three to six cases weekly, winning about three out of four. She handled a variety of cases, including burglary, robbery, manslaughter, forgery, embezzlement, bigamy, shootings, slander, breach of peace, concealed weapons, kidnapping, strike assaults, and "heaps of arraignments."[148] She noted that she handled one case against Arthur Smith for grand larceny that was "mixed up with sodomy."[149] She made mistakes—in one case, she forgot to put on the police as witnesses, but used them in rebuttal and won the case. In another manslaughter case that she lost, Allen said the "judge charged me out of court on it."[150] She had been given one rape case to handle, but was quickly pulled off that case by her supervisor.

Allen also noted that she had "presided in the grand jury, questioning the witnesses and drawing the indictments."[151] The grand jury was responsible for bringing criminal indictments or charges against alleged defendants on the basis of evidence presented by the prosecutor. She had been put in charge of the grand jury by her supervisor, Stephen Young, a Democrat who had been in the state legislature and would go on to serve in the U.S. Congress. He later took credit for persuading political leaders to appoint Allen as the first woman prosecutor.[152] Young strictly tasked her with preventing delays and demanded long hours. Allen excelled at this job, and during her quarterly appointment, the grand jury returned a record number of more than 1,100 indictments. She reported that at first, the grand jury, "composed mainly of elderly men, some of them retired police captains," "did *not* enjoy the idea of being supervised by a woman prosecutor." As the months went on, however, they "became good friends," and at the end of the session just before Christmas, they presented her with a gift of an expensive pair of white gloves, three sizes too small. The former police captain said, "We didn't think we would like a woman to have charge of the grand jury; we didn't think much of this idea of women lawyers but all I have to say to you is, may your shadow never grow less."[153]

Looking back, Allen reflected that the prosecutor's office had given her good legal experience. She said that it "was excellent trial training and full of constant and varied interest."[154] As a prosecutor, she became acquainted with the judges and practice of the common pleas court and developed the trial experience necessary for prestige and advancement as a lawyer and judge. Forty years later, an editor of the *Cleveland News* remembered the excitement over the "higher standards that she, one lone woman, had brought to that very average prosecutor's office."[155] Allen believed that the innovation of having a woman prosecutor did not "arouse great comment" because, while many may theoretically have a prejudice against women entering the legal profession in their mind, "when they are confronted with the actual situation" of a woman lawyer, "they're very willing to concede equal intellect and to give credit for hard work wherever it is put forth."[156]

WOMEN IN THE PROFESSION

Allen advised others that "the law is an excellent profession for women." She shared her experience officially in response to two surveys of all two hundred women lawyers in the country by the Bureau of Vocational Information.[157] The bureau's study of women in the vocation of law showed that women worked predominantly in civil solo practice, government positions, and transactional practice like probate and real estate, while men worked more in large corporate law firms and courtrooms. The study recommended that women face their fears and embrace trial work, though Allen sympathized that it was "hard at first for women to enter upon active trial work." She was realistic, noting that while law could be a highly paid profession, it would likely be "a long time to come" before women shared in this monetary reward, as "the more lucrative part of the law practice will be in the hands of men lawyers." She noted some disadvantages, like the "consequent association with characters not of the best type" that "tends to destroy your faith in human nature." She said women "must be willing to work hard" and must "learn to be very patient with people." For, Allen said, "it's the little fellows who are mean. A man hates to lose to a woman; it's especially hard because his clients rile into him much more than if he had been vanquished by a brother lawyer."[158]

Allen gave practical, frank advice to women in interviews and public speeches, saying women should "forget they are feminine."[159] She said that any girl contemplating the "workaday world outside the home" would "spare herself many heartaches" if she realized the brutal truth "that the world demands more of the business and professional women" than of men. Women were expected to outperform men, to "do something outstanding, do the work infinitely better than any man has ever done or fail!" She pointed out that "professional women are criticized more than professional men" and expected to work longer hours with "more spectacular achievements." And she admitted that "the woman in business will find prejudice. She will find that some people will not come to her in her professional capacity because she is a woman." Her advice to women was "to work hard, give conscientious service, and ask no special favors." She also advised: "Neither forget nor remember that you are a woman, paradoxical as that sounds. Ask no sex favors and don't be masculine in dress or manners," but avoid "unconscious femininity." As to housekeeping, Allen said, women "should not do double duty. A woman who works outside the home all day should no more go home at night to a round of domestic work than a man supporting a family should go home to wash clothes and dishes."

Allen epitomized the role of the woman lawyer as leader in the community. She used the gravitas of her position, particularly the prosecutorial role, to demonstrate women's authority as she continued to speak to women's clubs and public audiences on topics like suffrage, citizenship, good government, and current events.[160] Allen believed strongly in mentoring the next generation of women, and extending the metaphorical ladder down to help other women climb the profession's rungs of success. She was active in affinity groups of women's bar associations like the National Association of Women Lawyers and was a prime mover in the International Federation of Women Lawyers, using these roles to encourage other women in the profession and advocate for legal reform.[161] While women lawyers were still "hampered by lingering prejudice in state bar associations," they nevertheless had great potential to impact the legal system. Women, she said, transformed the administration of justice by their presence in the legal system and their social consciousness.[162] These lawyers served a representative function of allowing women litigants and public citizens to see they were entitled to be represented by "women pleading their rights" and women playing "their part equally with men" in the execution of justice. Women lawyers, Allen said, also made a substantive difference to justice by adding a female perspective that enlarged the scope of the profession to include "vital social problems" like economic justice, family life, and children's matters.

This public role for women in the law, however, was limited by their lack of the right to vote. The vote granted political citizenship and the corollary political rights to run for public office like judge and prosecutor and to serve on juries. Suffrage was thus critical to full realization of women's professional objectives and desired impact on the courts. Allen would take a leadership role in the movement for suffrage on the state and national stage, gaining an outsized reputation useful in further transformation of the law.

2 Demanding Suffrage and Citizenship

While Florence Allen was a pioneer in the legal profession, she came into prominence and "won her spurs" as a leader of the women's suffrage movement.[1] She earned her reputation as a smart, careful, reform-minded advocate through persistent activism and legal work for the women's vote. She was introduced to women's demand for the vote through her mother's efforts as a suffragist in Utah. At the national level, Allen worked for the college division of the national suffrage organization, campaigning for a federal constitutional amendment as well as independent rights in various states. In her home state of Ohio, she was an indefatigable grassroots activist, covering the state in two campaigns for women's constitutional suffrage. As a lawyer, she was the primary advocate formulating the ideas and shepherding test constitutional litigation for women's voting rights to the Ohio Supreme Court. Allen's accomplishments for constitutional change received commemoration in the nation's first social justice park, established in Columbus, Ohio, just blocks away from the supreme court where she served.[2]

Allen joined the sixty-year-old women's suffrage movement just as it began to regain momentum, rising to its pinnacle of eventual success in the Nineteenth Amendment ratified in August 1920. Allen was part of the energized leadership and organization that worked to increase the visibility, lobbying, and activism that would eventually produce a constitutional amendment. Before this, the suffrage slog had been long and slow, with little to show for it. Only seven states in the West had granted full enfranchisement to women; many had limited school suffrage, and a few had municipal voting for local elections.[3] Proposals for federal voting rights had been sidelined by the U.S. Supreme Court. In *Minor v. Happersett*, the Court recognized the self-evident but contested point that women were in fact "citizens" under the Constitution, but held that voting was a state right, not a federal privilege protected by the Fourteenth Amendment.[4] The case forced suffragists into the "slow glacial process" of state-level action, requiring decades of repeated, time-consuming, and costly campaigns in each of the many states that delayed and denied the voting promise of a federal amendment.

Women had been advocating for women's equal voting rights since the time of abolition, working alongside antislavery activists for universal suffrage for all, and then proposing their own Sixteenth Amendment for women's suffrage as part of the reconstructed Constitution. Voting was one of eighteen demands for equal rights embodied in the blueprint of women's rights in Elizabeth Cady Stanton's 1848 "Declaration of Sentiments" issued at Seneca Falls, New York, as part of a comprehensive plan to revolutionize women's civil and political status in all private and public spheres of society. Voting emerged as the primary demand for women's rights bolstered by consensus across the spectrum of conservative to radical women reformers. Voting was seen as the key determinative factor of citizenship, guaranteeing women public roles as electors, officials, and voters long denied. Traditionally, women's emaciated citizenship had been defined only by their secondary private domestic role and ascribed importance in raising children as moral citizens. Men's citizenship was public, defined by political and military action instrumental to the survival of democracy, and legally covered that of their wife.[5] The right to vote would fundamentally shift these anemic visions of women's citizenship both symbolically and functionally, providing a concrete mechanism of democratic participation and forced accountability for women.[6]

FAMILY SUFFRAGE REFORM

Allen's parents introduced her to women's suffrage activism early in life. Both her mother and father were active in the suffrage movement, a key issue in their adopted state of Utah. The Utah territory had granted women the right to vote in 1870, the second in the country, in part to demonstrate that Mormon women were not oppressed under polygamy.[7] However, Congress disenfranchised women in the federal anti-polygamy Edmunds-Tucker Act of 1887 as a penalty for the territory's continued polygamy and emerging threat of theocratic power. Utah had become a national pariah for its perceived immoral endorsement of plural marriage, attracting national outrage and federal intervention. When Utah leaders and the Mormon Church renounced polygamy in order to gain statehood, women's right to vote was restored. Corinne Allen took an eleven-year-old Florence to a meeting celebrating the victory where national leaders Susan B. Anthony and Anna Howard Shaw spoke.[8] Florence's father participated in the convention to write the first state constitution that included women's suffrage. He and Corinne were then invited to participate in the National American Woman Suffrage Association's (NAWSA) 1896 convention and were introduced by national leader Anthony.[9]

Florence sometimes helped her mother with her work from afar, sending her mother research and giving a few related speeches on the history of women's suffrage in Utah.[10] She also accompanied her to Berlin, where Corinne had been invited to give a talk at the meeting of the International Council of Women, a transatlantic group working for women's rights and suffrage.[11] Corinne, however, took the opportunity to speak against polygamy and excoriate Mormon women, seeking their expulsion from the suffrage group. Former colleagues were blindsided and appalled at the vitriol, as Corinne had worked alongside Mormon women for years on suffrage, women's clubs, and reform.[12] In the interim, Corinne had become an anti-polygamy zealot, living as she did in the midst of what had been polygamous Utah, believing that the practice had merely gone underground. She continued to rant against the indecency of polygamy and proselytize about monogamous morality and social purity long after polygamy had been formally abandoned.[13]

Corinne Allen's politics were grounded in notions of maternalism, a gender consciousness of moral authority rooted in women's biological and social role of motherhood, emphasizing women's moral difference from men.[14] Florence, however, rejected her mother's maternalism and its limitation of women's role to the family under the husband's headship. While she often shared a nostalgia that sentimentalized the home, she expressly rejected the role of mother as the sole moral and social force. "The mother, simply by remaining in the home," Florence wrote, "cannot protect her family," given the multitude of social "acute problems." She said "the mother's responsibility is not limited to cleaning the house and making excellent pie, and the father's responsibility is not limited to paying the grocery bills. There is an ethical and spiritual responsibility which rests upon every one in the home, and . . . the cooperation of both the mother and father . . . is essential." The more important role of parents, she said, was their political participation in the wider world and their informed voting in elections.[15]

SUFFRAGE ACTIVISM

Allen launched her own influential career in suffrage advocacy when she took a job during law school with the College Equal Suffrage League, an affiliate of NAWSA. She worked as executive secretary to Maud Wood Park, the leader and a founder of the League.[16] Allen had met Park years before when she came to Cleveland to establish a suffrage chapter at Western Reserve College. Park said, "I found an intelligent young woman and pounced upon her."[17] The suffrage organization was "dedicated to recruiting university students and alumni" to suffrage and adding intellectual prestige and professional organization to the movement.[18] As League assistant, Allen scheduled speakers, organized local chapters for college women, and engaged in grassroots outreach. Allen helped arrange visits for British suffragist leader Emmeline Pankhurst, the originator of militant actions of protests, marches, and even bombs.[19] She began to collect suffrage cartoons, later donated to the Library of Congress, that humorously portrayed anti-suffrage images of aggrieved husbands and women trying on suffrage like fashion.[20] Allen juggled the work with law school and occasionally noted that her work supervisors gave "her hell for calls being delayed."[21] Her association with the national suffrage organization led to close connections with national leaders. Philosophically, Allen embraced the classic political ideology of suffrage based on natural rights to equal citizenship. This liberal, equality feminism of formal individual right would become the dominant legal feminism of the twentieth century.[22]

Allen also learned activism from the suffragists, joining the front lines of the new demonstrations and parades raising the visibility of the voting demand. She marched in the third large-scale New York City suffrage parade, "Votes for Women," on May 4, 1912, organized by suffragist Harriot Stanton Blatch, building on British suffrage and labor tactics Blatch had seen while living in England. Blatch wanted this parade to "give evidence of a massive, disciplined suffrage army" and create a spectacle that "was to be an emotional and sensual evocation of women's power."[23] The parade was a success, drawing between ten thousand and seventeen thousand marchers. Allen recorded in her diary that she marched to Carnegie Hall with friends and supporters to hear Blatch and Anna Howard Shaw in the "biggest speech we ever heard." The next day it rained, stopping anti-suffragists from their opposition march, causing her to write in her diary, "The Lord is a suffragist!"[24]

In February 1913, Allen and her roommate Bertha Miller marched as day hikers in the "On-to-Washington" march, a grueling 250-mile suffrage hike from New York to Washington, D.C., in the dead of winter. Led by "General" Rosalie Jones, a radical suffrage organizer, two hundred women encountered cheers, jeers, intimidation, and violence along the march.[25] Once Jones's pilgrims reached Washington, they joined the famous mass suffrage parade on March 3, 1913, memorialized by the iconic lady on the white horse, Allen's law school classmate, Inez Milholland. Organized by Alice Paul, the dramatic parade utilized public and militant tactics Paul had also learned in Britain to call attention to President Wilson's opposition to suffrage on the eve of his second inauguration.[26] Milholland led the great parade down Pennsylvania Avenue, dressed in a regal white cape astride a white horse, like a Valkyrie representing the "New Woman." She was followed by nine bands, twenty-four floats, and five thousand marchers dressed in white, the color of moral right, with yellow sashes and roses for sisterhood and light, and purple connoting royalty and respect.[27] Allen was at the front of the Ohio contingent helping to carry the state banner.[28] Black women were segregated at the back, though Ida B. Wells-Barnett refused this arrangement by moving up to her state contingent halfway through the parade.[29] Crowds comprised mostly of men attending the inauguration attacked the marchers, and over one hundred women were sent to the hospital. The police did little to stop the "horrible howling mob" of men who "shoved, jostled, pushed, hooted, jeered" at the women marchers and broke into the march line to trip or slap the women—they arrested the women instead.[30]

ADVOCATING WOMEN'S SUFFRAGE IN OHIO

Allen put her theories of suffrage and feminism to work in Ohio, first as an activist and then as an advocate. Ohio was a leading battleground in the state strategy for women's suffrage. "Ohio stood well to the front," explained Harriet Taylor Upton, secretary of the national suffrage association then headquartered in Youngstown, Ohio, and leader of the Ohio Woman's Suffrage Association for eighteen years. "When the history and the philosophy of the movement is really written, Ohio will be credited with the second place, New York with the first."[31] The state had been one of the earliest states after the Declaration of Sentiments to organize with the Salem Women's Rights Convention in 1850. Another early meeting in the state, the Akron Woman's Rights Convention in 1851, was made famous by Sojourner Truth's "Ain't I a Woman?" speech, "a canonical text in accounts of nineteenth century feminism and of the role of Black women in the fight for woman suffrage," though historians later questioned the accuracy of this speech embellished by a journalist.[32] As Allen described it in her book *The Ohio Woman's Suffrage Movement: A Certain Unalienable Right*, written to "set the record straight" on Ohio, these meetings were "like a snowball gathering snowflakes to itself," and "one convention grew out of another."[33]

Women were advocating full equal suffrage, seeking to overturn a state law that defined electors as "male" and "white." Ohio women organized one of the first state associations for suffrage, and Cleveland and Cincinnati hosted several of the early national suffrage association conventions. Ohio came close to being the first state in the union to adopt women's suffrage, when the constitutional amendment vote in 1858 was tied. The Woman's Christian Temperance Union was also founded in Ohio, focused on prohibition of alcohol and quickly adopting suffrage as the tool of "home protection" to enact laws protecting women from alcohol-related domestic violence. Thus, "women across the nation looked to Ohio as a leader in the suffrage cause."[34]

In 1912, significant progressive reform of the Ohio Constitution provided another opportunity for women to demand equal suffrage. Empowered by a renewed national suffrage movement and the new Progressive Party's endorsement of suffrage, women were hopeful they would succeed this time. That summer, on break from law school, Allen came to Ohio to help Maud Wood Park campaign for an amendment to the Ohio Constitution granting women the right to vote by eliminating the words *white male* in voting requirements. The 1912 "Amendment 23" campaign incorporated new tactics like the state's first suffrage parade in Columbus. There, an audience of one hundred thousand watched three thousand suffrage advocates, including Black suffragists, led by a young woman "representing Joan of Arc" who, "clad in shiny tin armor, rode astride a huge truck horse" ahead of marchers and floats. Allen, "clad in cap and gown," marched and was one of the speakers. A reporter commented that "the eternal feminine showed in the parade," where there was a "stunning display of millinery and gowns," and a "score of dainty parasols" that protected the marchers from the burning rays of the August sun.[35]

Allen was a "chief orator" for suffrage, canvassing the state in mostly rural areas, giving ninety-two speeches in eighty-eight counties.[36] She traveled by trolley, buggy, and train, giving speeches from atop literal soap boxes, automobile back seats, and train platforms. She spoke at mills, hotels, churches, courthouses, street corners, and even a circus.[37] She had one of the first "moving pictures" made of her giving a suffrage speech in a "banner bedecked automobile."[38] She learned to deal with hecklers by refining her arguments, adopting the classic arguments of suffrage pioneer Stanton that women were unjustly taxed without representation, mirroring the key American demand for freedom. Allen's summer suffrage tour also established significant friendships among suffragist women of both parties who would be valuable to her as supporters when she later ran for judicial office. Allen's work in the summer of 1912 came to be memorialized in one of the most iconic photos of the women's suffrage movement. In a widely familiar picture, she stands out in front of the Cleveland suffrage headquarters, dressed in black menswear and waving the suffrage flag.

Despite the national attention, campaigning, and parades, the suffrage amendment in Ohio failed. Male voters rejected women's suffrage by a vote of 336,875 to 249,420 (57 percent). But it was the most votes ever cast in favor of suffrage in the country.[39] Elsewhere, it was a good election for women's suffrage, approved by voters in Arizona, Kansas, and Oregon, bringing the total nationally to ten states where women had full suffrage.

In 1914, Ohio women again organized to amend the state constitution for women's suffrage. This time they took advantage of a new constitutional amendment authorizing voter-initiated amendments with petitions of valid signatures.[40] Such voting changes were part of broader national progressive reforms to decentralize lawmaking to enhance responsiveness and accountability to the people. Allen, now working as a lawyer in Cleveland, traveled the state, circulating petitions to get the required number of signatures for a citizen initiative.[41] As World War I began in Europe, in Ohio the women symbolically kicked off the suffrage campaign with a pilgrimage to Salem, retracing the historical origins of suffrage, and then held tea parties, garden parties, bake sales, and bazaars to raise money and support.[42] Allen later recounted the women's efforts: "They canvassed the people, they followed political meetings, they held street meetings, they did *everything*. Suffragists were uniquely unselfconscious. They kept no records for posterity. They did not realize that they were making history. Perhaps they were too busy."[43]

Allen canvassed the Ohio counties again, giving speeches, marching in parades, and getting petition signatures. She spoke to women across the political spectrum, from radical socialists to fringe spiritualists and conservative Daughters of the American Revolution. In one highly publicized and acrimonious debate, Allen took on anti-suffragist Lucy Price at Grays Armory in Cleveland, attacking her opponent by calling her a "girl" who traded on her "sex-appeal," revealing she was paid a large salary to parrot the views of wealthy industrialists. They sparred over the effects of suffrage, whether it brought equality and social improvements, as Allen argued, or divorce as Price claimed.[44] Allen also spoke to lawyers, and, at a meeting of the Ohio State Bar Association, the newly admitted lawyer Allen was "given the floor after some protest" and challenged the bar association that its "duty" was to listen to the three hundred thousand women of the state and support women's suffrage.[45] "The only way you can stop the women in their fight for the ballot," she said dramatically, "is to exterminate them."

Allen bemoaned the difficulty of the initiative petition process: "I can't get men to sign." Several times she noted that she ended her crazy campaigning days with beers and cigarettes.[46] Finally she succeeded, and in July she went to the Ohio Statehouse in Columbus with 176 suffragists, two from each Ohio county, to present the successful petition at the capitol. The secretary of state refused to appear, even though he had met the liquor industry for their proposed amendment hours before.[47]

The women's suffrage amendment was defeated in November 1914 more soundly than two years before. Allen had been optimistic, predicting a win based on what she saw on the campaign trail.[48] But strong anti-suffrage sentiment came from the industrialists who opposed protective labor legislation and the liquor industry that feared women's temperance. The liquor interests hosted picnics for working men with free beer and plastered anti-suffrage posters on trolleys and in public spots. Opponents were well funded, spending $630,000 to defeat the amendment compared to the suffragists' $40,000.[49]

With so many defeats in Ohio and other states, the national suffrage organization leadership rethought its political strategy. In 1916, Carrie Chapman Catt, returning to the national leadership, announced her "Winning Plan" strategy embracing a two-track approach: renewing the priority of a federal amendment while also continuing to pursue selective state reforms. This dilution of effort, however, from fighting the suffrage battle on too many fronts, was challenged by the younger generation of suffragists who demanded a concentrated effort on the federal amendment.[50] Following Catt's plan, Allen turned back to helping with women's suffrage in other states, going to Boston and New York, until refocusing her main efforts on her home state of Ohio.[51]

LITIGATING THE CONSTITUTIONALITY OF WOMEN'S SUFFRAGE

Allen turned her legal acumen to help secure partial suffrage in Ohio as a way into full voting rights. In 1916, she led the efforts to gain municipal suffrage for women. A new amendment to the Ohio Constitution in 1912 gave home rule to municipalities, allowing cities to legislate their own affairs, thus creating an opportunity for women to vote in municipal or city council elections.[52] Women's municipal suffrage had first been adopted in Kansas in 1887.[53] However, the momentum of local suffrage was stymied by a decision of the Michigan Supreme Court in 1893 striking down the state's municipal suffrage law on grounds that the legislature had no authority to create a new class of voters.[54] Illinois turned this tide twenty years later, in 1913, when its Supreme Court upheld municipal suffrage law as constitutional.[55] Allen thought the Illinois case would be good precedent for a similar result in Ohio. By 1916, eight states had passed some form of municipal suffrage.[56]

Allen also thought that a twenty-year-old Ohio Supreme Court case upholding school board suffrage for women would support the legality of municipal suffrage. The Ohio legislature passed school board suffrage in 1894 by large majorities, after three previous unsuccessful attempts.[57] When Ida Earnhart, a state senator's wife, registered to vote under the new law, a case was brought against her and the Columbus Board of Elections to strike her name from the registration, claiming the statute was invalid. The Ohio Supreme Court, in *Mills v. Board of Elections*, summarily upheld women's school suffrage.[58] The court stated that the constitutional power of the legislature to pass laws for public schools overrode the constitutional definition of voters as "every white male citizen." Immediate attempts to repeal school suffrage were thwarted by defensive moves of Ohio women suffragists.[59]

Suffrage organizers selected the prosperous middle-class city of East Cleveland as their test case. They hired Allen to draft a new city charter for East Cleveland granting municipal suffrage to women and to handle the resulting test case in the courts.[60] Allen spent weeks in the office and library reading law books, constitutions and charters, and election laws. She filed briefs in which arguments "went back to the time of the old

English Kings to study the powers of municipalities."[61] There was a series of public meetings, in which the election committee members initially seemed opposed to municipal suffrage. The committee kept requiring Allen to submit additional briefs, and debated whether suffrage could technically be part of the charter or a separate law. At one contentious hearing, an attorney from the committee resigned in protest of the unfair process that had been established. He said, "It is a slap at the elections committee and a rotten deal to the women. I'm opposed to suffrage but I stand for justice and that the suffragists will not have at the hands of a committee of anti-suffragists."[62] Public hearings continued, and the East Cleveland municipal suffrage proposal was passed in June 1916 by the male voters.[63] Allen later noted that "the measure as it was inserted was not as we drew it, nor quite as we wished to have it; but we are very happy that it went in at all."[64] However, the Board of Elections refused to allow women to vote. Allen then filed a taxpayers' mandamus action in the Ohio Supreme Court to compel the Board of Elections to allow the women to vote.[65] She chose a highly visible plaintiff, businesswoman Sophia Taylor, president of Cleveland department store William Taylor & Son Company.

While the case was pending, Allen visited her family in Utah. She took the opportunity to campaign for President Wilson, a Democrat, in Montana—in direct contradiction to her Republican family and Alice Paul's suffragists picketing Wilson at the White House for his failure to support a federal suffrage amendment. The Democratic Party work, however, would earn her a powerful ally in Washington in Homer Cummings, who directed the Montana campaign, as he was later attorney general under Roosevelt and instrumental in shepherding Allen's federal judicial appointment. Women wanted to make suffrage the key issue of the 1916 presidential election, but the looming world war dominated the debate, and the incumbent Wilson won narrow reelection over Supreme Court Justice Charles Evans Hughes. At that time, the Democratic Party was still the conservative party of the South, though it would soon change into the liberal party of today—in large part due to the efforts of women like Allen.[66] Montana was a key state because women were voting there for the first time, and they would elect the first woman to Congress, Republican Jeannette Rankin.[67]

While in Montana, Allen received a wire notifying her that oral argument in the East Cleveland municipal suffrage case would be heard by the

Ohio Supreme Court in a few days. Allen recounted in her autobiography the mad dash to return to Ohio in time for the hearing.[68] Allen had been the lead attorney on the case since the drafting of the charter, and she wanted to be the one to argue before the court. She caught the train in Great Falls, Montana. She wired two friends from Chicago Law, Alice Greenacre and Greta Coleman, who met her at the connecting station in Chicago with a suitcase of law books, which Allen reviewed overnight on the train to Columbus in preparation for the argument.[69] Allen made it in time and successfully argued the case.

The Ohio Supreme Court upheld the constitutional validity of municipal suffrage by a vote of six to one in *Taylor v. French* (1917).[70] The court's opinion, written by Democrat James Johnson, relied on the *Mills* decision upholding women's school board suffrage, as Allen had predicted. She argued in her brief that the principle in *Mills* allowing a specific legislative power to preempt the general electoral definition of the male voter applied analogously to the specific municipal power of home rule.[71] The court found it unnecessary to reach Allen's second argument that the constitutional definition of elector applied only to specific political authorities named in the state constitution, which did not include municipalities, an argument that had been important to the decision in the analogous case in the Illinois Supreme Court.[72] Without this broader ruling, the *Harvard Law Review* noted, the *Taylor* opinion was "difficult to support either on principle or authority."[73] As the lone dissenter in *Taylor*, Justice Thomas Jones, a Republican, argued that the *Mills* precedent of school suffrage was based specifically on the constitutional power to provide for schools and schools only. He also found that the decision produced irrational results, enfranchising women in cities but not in rural townships and establishing "the fatuous position" allowing women to vote but not to serve as mayor, making them a "queen with a tarnished crown!"[74]

Despite the victory, the Ohio Supreme Court delayed announcing its decision until April 1917, blocking women's ability to vote in the 1916 election. The successful women, however, said Allen, were already "starting out to spread the poison among other Ohio cities," persistently demanding from state officials lists of other cities adopting the new home rule that could now have the potential of women's limited suffrage. Among eleven cities with new charters, Columbus and Lakewood subsequently adopted charters for women's municipal suffrage.[75] In Columbus, women used their newfound power to "cleanse" politics, and they organized through voluntary associations to dump the city boss who had been mayor for sixteen years and who had labeled them the "shrieking sisterhood."[76] Allen's charter and brief became a model for other states, as women reached out to her for assistance in crafting similar reforms.[77]

After the municipal suffrage success, Allen began to work on a presidential suffrage bill, an idea she had thought about for several years.[78] "Presidential suffrage" meant the right to vote for president, technically by voting for members of the Electoral College in each state as set forth in Article II, Section 1, of the U.S. Constitution. It would be a limited measure but would allow women in Ohio to weigh in on the national presidential election. A few years earlier, in 1913, Illinois had become the first state to pass presidential suffrage for women by legislative enactment, which was upheld as constitutional.[79] Politically, presidential suffrage seemed more expedient, given that in most states it was not subject to public referenda like a state constitutional amendment. It would prove to be an effective strategy on the road to the Nineteenth Amendment, as ultimately seventeen states would pass presidential suffrage for women.[80]

In Ohio, Allen drafted the proposed bill, which was then introduced to the state legislature by Representative James A. Reynolds of Cuyahoga County, a Democrat.[81] Allen "did much legal work in connection with" the Reynolds bill and handled the hearings before the Ohio General Assembly.[82] Her legal work again was a model for other states, and Allen also did on-the-ground campaigning "in more counties probably than any other woman in the state of Ohio."[83] During debates on the bill, advocates packed the women's balcony of the House chambers, spilling into the men's galley and the lobby. They became vocal only when one Republican legislator attacked the women's "pestiferous lobby" to cajole votes. Reynolds, the bill's sponsor, refused to call out his colleague, deferring to the gentlemen's rules of the chambers and further angering women. In early February 1917, presidential suffrage passed both houses of the Ohio legislature, seventy-two to fifty in the House and twenty to sixteen in the Senate.[84] Presidential suffrage was signed into law by the progressive Democratic governor, James M. Cox, who would run for president in 1920.

But success would not last. Anti-suffragist petitions immediately began to circulate, calling for a referendum on the new law.[85] Opponents used the new constitutional referendum power to veto the legislation.[86] The women appealed to Newton Baker, Wilson's secretary of war and former mayor and Democratic Party leader in Cleveland, to use his political capital to help fight the referendum, but he refused. It was a betrayal the Ohio suffragists did not excuse, even though Baker was immersed in the U.S. entry to World War I.[87]

Allen thus had a new battle to try and defeat the challenge. In the summer of 1917, she was checking the minutiae of the referendum petitions, finding many fraudulent signatures easily identified by a distinct green ink and similar handwriting as well as other irregularities. On behalf of the women's suffrage organizations, Allen filed lawsuits in four counties to challenge the petitions, and the courts issued injunctions invalidating 90 percent of the signatures.[88] However, the boards of elections in the many remaining counties with allegedly fraudulent signatures refused to take action. Allen appealed to the Ohio Supreme Court to invalidate and stop the referendum.[89]

The Ohio Supreme Court declined to hear the case.[90] The court dismissed the suffragists' petition on procedural grounds, finding that it was untimely because it was not decided forty days in advance of the election, seemingly announcing a new rule that such challenges to referenda had to be decided, not merely filed, by the deadline.[91] The referendum went forward and passed by a 144,000 majority, recalling the legislative grant and retracting presidential suffrage for women. The wording of the ballot asking whether to "sustain" the law was confusing to nonlawyers.[92] Opposition from the "antis" was strong, as businesses, churches, and liquor interests continued to block women's suffrage.[93] Animosity to the suffragists in Ohio was also fueled by rejection of the militant suffrage tactics happening on the national stage. Alice Paul's national pickets of the White House during a time of war, calling the president "Kaiser Wilson," were unpopular among the conventional public and mainstream suffragists.[94] Moderate suffragists like Allen were embarrassed by the aggressive actions, believing them unprofessional and counterproductive in antagonizing opponents. When one of these activists, Gail Laughlin, gave a speech in Cleveland, Allen attacked her as a "bitter feminist."[95]

These publicity efforts, however, would be the push suffrage needed to win the public to its side. Behind the scenes, long-standing suffragist lobbying efforts finally paid off, finding an ally in Wilson's daughter and navigating the "bewildering maze of Congressional procedure" to get the suffrage amendment out of its lockdown in the Judiciary Committee.[96] By then, the Progressive and Republican parties had officially endorsed women's suffrage. Wilson finally capitulated, saying he was now persuaded of women's qualification for full citizenship and "partnership of privilege and right" with men, given their patriotic efforts during the war.[97] The federal suffrage amendment quickly passed Congress in June 1919 by strong majority votes, and Ohio representatives wrote to Florence Allen to report the victory.[98]

Many states quickly ratified the Nineteenth Amendment within a week of its passage, Ohio being the fifth to do so.[99] But the ratification battle had not been that easy in Ohio, for women's suffrage was threatened by yet another new state amendment permitting ratification of federal constitutional amendments by popular referendum rather than legislature.[100] It had been designed by the liquor industry to fight off federal Prohibition but applied also to women's suffrage. The Ohio suffrage leaders sought legal opinions on the validity of the ratification amendment, receiving conflicting advice as to its constitutionality.[101] Allen counseled the leaders that for any court challenge to the Ratification Amendment, "time is of the utmost importance," as they learned the hard way in late timing that preempted their challenge to the presidential suffrage referendum. And she noted that most judges would be gone during the summer vacation and that they would "have to take pot luck in the chance of getting a Judge who can understand a legal proposition." While she thought that it was better if the drys (the Prohibition advocates) rather than the suffragists spearheaded the litigation, she emphasized that someone needed to do so.[102] The drys did take the litigation initiative, but lost their challenge when the Ohio Supreme Court upheld the state Ratification Amendment. The U.S. Supreme Court, however, reversed in June 1920, holding easily and definitively in *Hawke v. Smith* that state referenda on federal amendments were unconstitutional given the Constitution's mandates for the amendment process.[103]

On August 18, 1920, Tennessee became the last state to ratify the Nineteenth Amendment, barely passing it by two votes after a close national battle epitomized by the supporters wearing yellow roses and opponents red roses.[104] Allen gleefully announced at a women's club beach picnic that "it's all over but the shouting."[105] She also went to work registering women voters and speaking to them about the obligations of citizenship and "What to Do with the Vote."[106] However, challenges to women's suffrage continued, with cases brought in the U.S. Supreme Court contesting ratification, though they were easily and unanimously dismissed.[107] The Nineteenth Amendment in practice also did not enfranchise all women, because racially discriminatory laws continued to operate denying Black, Native, and Asian women the right to vote.[108] In the absence of federal enforcement legislation for the Nineteenth Amendment, as had been passed for other civil rights amendments, states were left to individually interpret the reach of the voting right, and many refused to extend that right to the related political rights of public office and jury service. Not surprisingly, the courts and political branches did not easily accept these new women citizens into the established structures of law.[109]

Through the suffrage movement, Allen became a national leader of women's rights and social justice. The suffrage movement gave Allen the experience, exposure, and gravitas needed for a political career. Reflecting on her work on the front lines, Allen observed: "To the young men and women of today with their free companionship and equality of privilege, the subject of woman suffrage is as obsolete as a prehistoric animal."[110] Equality was now assumed, as men and women "buy cokes together, go to school together, plan their homes together, spend and save their money together, keep their checking accounts together, care for their babies together, and—vote together." She noted, "It is hard for them to realize that in the nineteenth century this free partnership was the rare and not the usual thing," and that all had been changed by "universal suffrage with all of its ramifications." Indeed, the personal ramifications of suffrage for Allen were significant and transformational. With the Nineteenth Amendment, she not only won the right to vote, but secured the right to run for elective office. She did not wait to execute this right.

3 Judging the Trial Court

Days after ratification of the Nineteenth Amendment, Florence Allen initiated her campaign for judicial office. In August 1920, she declared her candidacy for judge of the Cuyahoga County Court of Common Pleas in Cleveland.[1] She thereby immediately implemented a long-standing goal of the women's suffrage movement—to place women in judicial office where laws were made and interpreted, and social norms created and enforced.[2] Women were needed in lawmaking to provide substantively better justice and to more fairly represent women in a legal system imbued with the "biases of man" and "created and executed by man" from the "masculine standpoint."[3] Allen explained that her purpose in pioneering as a woman judge was "to stimulate interest among women in the administration of justice and particularly in jury service," and to help women realize their equal "partnership with men in the making, application and enforcement of laws for the benefit of mankind."[4]

Women's first opportunity to infiltrate the bench came with the presidential election of 1920, just a few months after passage of the Nineteenth Amendment. The 1920 election pitted two Ohioans against each other: Senator Warren Harding, a Republican, versus Governor James Cox, a Democrat. Harding ran on a promise of "return to normalcy," a nostalgic renewal of traditional values after the disruption of World War I and the international rise of leftist ideologies like communism, socialism, and Marxism.[5] At the same time, he courted the new women voters, promising them everything under the sun, including their demands for equal pay for equal work, an eight-hour workday, expansion of administrative bureaus for women and children, an end to child labor, enforcement of Prohibition, prevention of lynching, protection of maternal and infant health, appointment of women to federal posts, and creation of a cabinet department of social welfare. Harding won by a landslide with 60 percent of the popular vote, and journalists claimed women voted for him because he was handsome. Later called "the worse president in history," defined by corruption and scandal, Harding rode into office on the "Red Wave" of Republican sweeps of national, state, and local offices.[6] This Republican victory affirming the traditional status quo seemed an unlikely time to facilitate the advent of the first woman judge. Yet Democrat Allen successfully emerged from this conservative haze.

The threshold question of women's right to public office, however, was not as self-evident as women thought. While women had long assumed that the grant of suffrage included the corollary political citizenship rights of public office and jury service, the courts did not all agree.[7] Some states, like Ohio, permitted women to run, finding that every political distinction based on women not being "electors" was now changed by amendment to the U.S. Constitution.[8] However, many other states retained their longstanding opposition to women's eligibility for public office, interpreting the Nineteenth Amendment thinly to apply only to voting.[9] These states used originalist arguments of women's historical inferior legal status as the "chattel of man" to disqualify them from public and judicial office.[10] As the *New York Times* surmised, it would take time to "to cut the old useless timber out" of laws explicitly excluding women.[11]

EARLY WOMEN IN THE COURTS

Before the Nineteenth Amendment, women had served in quasi-judicial administrative capacities.[12] Some of these "pseudo-judges" served in ministerial positions of factfinding, such as referees or special masters, providing recommendations to judges. Some were law clerks or stenographers to male judges or temporary substitutes. Others served in ceremonial positions, performing marriages like a justice of the peace, but as one woman explained, the fees for this position "are not large enough to tempt men to seek the office."[13] Esther Hobart Morris was the first, appointed justice of the peace for eight months in 1870 in a Wyoming frontier mining town after the territory was the first to enfranchise women. Morris was fifty-seven years old, stood six feet tall, and had no formal education or legal training. She performed marriages, heard small disputes, held her drunken husband in contempt of court, and sanctioned her predecessor who refused to turn over the court docket to a woman.[14] Catharine Waugh McCulloch, who worked in tandem with Allen on presidential suffrage and inspired her to run, was elected justice of the peace in Evanston, Illinois, in 1907 and then appointed master of chancery in Chicago.[15] In Seattle, Reah Whitehead was elected justice of the peace in 1914 but was criticized for being "too pretty for a woman judge."[16]

Women found new opportunities for judicial leadership and redesigning legal systems in the specialized courts of women and juveniles.[17] These separate courts of limited jurisdiction were innovations founded "at the height of progressivism" as structural reforms providing better ways to solve social problems.[18] These venues were considered more social work than legal, and law degrees were not always required for these administrative positions.[19] Women appointees "benefited from the cultural assumption that women judges could best understand the legal needs of children," families, and women, and the women arbiters brought a moral authority to these courts.[20] Mary Bartelme served on the Chicago Juvenile Court as an "assistant" to the male judge, put in charge of girls' cases, and only officially became a judge a decade later.[21] Women on these courts often adopted more caring models of justice. For example, Orfa Jean Shontz, referee in Los Angeles Juvenile Court in 1915, "created an all-female court, with a homelike atmosphere, to make women feel comfortable, and especially girls involved in sex cases to have the privacy she felt they were entitled to."[22]

Women also found early opportunities on the women's courts, police courts for prostitution. Georgia Bullock headed up the Los Angeles Women's Court in 1914, working for the first years without pay as a voluntary judicial clerk.[23] Jean Norris was appointed to the Women's Division of the New York City Magistrates' Court in 1919, later replaced by Anna Moscowitz Kross, who used the sociological approach to create a problem-solving court for domestic violence.[24] While public opinion began to accept the idea of women judges in some contexts, these courts were "clustered at the very bottom of the judicial hierarchy," "outside of the established court system, lacking the prestige, power, and permanence of the mainstream courts, which were dominated by men." As separate forums, they reinforced the idea that only certain secondary posts were available to women, and so ambitious women lawyers resisted these inferior social work appointments.[25]

Allen rejected an opportunity to pursue a position on the juvenile court. Reformer Jane Addams had encouraged Allen to consider a juvenile judgeship in August 1920. Allen had handled cases as a lawyer in juvenile court in Cleveland, and thus had experience with the specific matters of this court. However, her mentors at her law firm quickly talked her out of it.[26] These men appreciated that this court focused on children and social work would be of diminished reputational value as a limited jurisdiction court, and that suffrage promised greater opportunities on the horizon. This domestic path, however, would be advantageous to other women, like Jane Bolin, the first Black woman judge appointed to the New York City Domestic Relations Court in 1939, recommended by another woman judge on that court, Rosalie Whitney, before whom Bolin had practiced as a city attorney.[27]

Women, though, faced significant barriers to entry on the general courts. They were unsupported by political parties, lacked connections to government and business networks, and were excluded by bar associations. They also faced palpable sexist opposition to women directing men in the courtroom.[28] "Women will not be great jurists," a 1921 Carnegie Foundation report on legal education concluded, because they were not "domineering and cruel enough" to be combatants in the male-dominated courtroom.[29] "Embedded in the judicial office was a set of assumptions premised on the belief that dispensing justice was a manly duty" that equated "dispassionate decision making with responsible manhood" that could not be fulfilled by women.[30] Allen faced all of these barriers but managed to break through, buoyed by the campaigning efforts of women from her former suffrage networks.

AN INDEPENDENT WOMAN

Allen's choice to run for Cuyahoga County Common Pleas Court was a sound strategic decision, as she had a good reputation gained from her six years of trial experience and two years as prosecutor there. She received key endorsements from prominent male judges such as Frank Stevens and Republican Judge Willis Vickery, a former Cleveland common pleas judge elected to the court of appeals, serving as dean of Cleveland Law School.[31] U.S. Assistant Attorney General Frank Davis, an Ohio lawyer who knew Allen from the suffrage litigation, came out strong: "Miss Allen is a real lawyer. She has had large experience in the preparation and trial of cases in all of the Ohio courts, and in my judgement she has unusual ability."[32] The influential Cleveland *Plain Dealer* endorsed Allen early on in the campaign: "Her training and experience make her candidacy a notable event in local politics and voters should take advantage of the opportunity to support one whose qualifications raise her far above the ruck of common office seeking," like many men previously elected who were "qualified neither by experienced nor temperament."[33] "She will take to the bench," the paper added in a later article, "a sympathy with those in distress, an understanding of human problems and a breadth of view sufficient to make her a people's judge."[34] The *Cleveland News* agreed, noting that Allen was a "good lawyer" with "a fine sense of justice and active sympathies, controlled by a clear and trained mind."[35] It added, for those concerned about the suitability of women as jurists, that "she has vision, but she does not forget logic in her flights of imagination."

Allen and Ohio suffrage leaders had been thinking about her possible judicial candidacy for six months, hopeful that political citizenship for women was imminent.[36] In February, a delegation from the Ohio Federation of Business and Professional Women was formed for the specific purpose of supporting an Allen candidacy and reached out to Governor Cox and male judicial allies, seeking her appointment to a vacancy on the common pleas court.[37] The common response was that a woman could not serve in elective position because she was not an "elector" under state law, though given the pending ratification of federal suffrage, that disability would "probably be removed soon."[38] One state executive official encouraged the delegation, saying, "I have a very high regard of Miss Allen. She made a real impression on the members of the Supreme Court in her representation of a case not long ago," citing her constitutional suffrage case.[39] In addition, he said, "the attorneys in the state who know her are united in their estimate of her ability." The supporters continued to campaign for support, garnering more endorsements in the fall from judges, law firm partners, and women's club leaders that helped legitimize Allen's candidacy. A committee of forty to sponsor her campaign was organized, comprised of influential people, and she received public endorsements from the Cleveland Bar Association, labor and streetcar unions, the newly formed League of Women Voters, the business and professional women's organizations, the *Farm Journal*, and the four leading newspapers.[40]

Allen had missed the primaries, so she entered the race as an independent, nominated by petition.[41] She was not identified on the ballot as a Democrat and received no public or financial support from the Democratic Party. However, her diary reveals that Cleveland Democratic political boss Burr Gongwer was assisting her behind the scenes.[42] Gongwer's support was likely secured by Bernice Pyke, whom he deputized to run the women's arm of the local party, as she "became the most powerful woman in Democratic politics in Cleveland and Ohio."[43] Pyke knew Allen from suffrage circles, working together to gain municipal suffrage in the city of Lakewood where Pyke served on the school board. Any local party support was quiet because Allen had alienated party leadership by resigning her prominent position on the women's advisory group to the Democratic National Committee, where she served with Pyke, over her public opposition to a compulsory national draft in peacetime.[44] She was criticized for this party defiance, with a Cincinnati newspaper warning that "the ladies must learn, like the men, that resignation carries away all the political chips in front of the player."[45] An independent candidacy was therefore Allen's only option.

Allen justified the independent, nonpartisanship identification of judicial candidates as "traditional in Ohio."[46] But this was a relatively new tradition allowing judicial candidates to run either by party primary or by independent nonpartisan petition. The progressive amendment to the Ohio Constitution passed in 1912 and its predecessor, the state's Nonpartisan Judiciary Act of 1911, explicitly abolished the formal party convention process for nominating judges and established a separate, general ballot for judges omitting party affiliation—a practice that continued until 2021.[47] This process was intended to be more democratic and "curb attempts by politicians to corrupt the courts."[48] Allen said she had "always believed that judges should be non-partisan" and that in all her judicial campaigns she "chose to run by independent petition, although very few candidates for judge followed this course" because it required signatures on petition papers over a large number of the eighty-eight Ohio counties.

Despite this nonpartisan strategy, Allen was clearly a new Democrat. In January 1920, while women were awaiting state ratification of the Nineteenth Amendment, Allen discussed her political views with a newspaper writer in an article entitled "Why I Am a Democrat." She said that she was a Democrat because she believed a political party should exist to "render service to the people." Such service and humane progressive legislation, she argued, was achieved under Democratic President Wilson through laws on child welfare and women in industry, the first such laws in over forty years. For almost half a century, she chided, "one would have thought only men, and adult men, peopled America." Allen also cited Wilson's plan of international peace and the pending League of Nations as a strong reason for her political affiliation. In addition, she noted the progressive Democratic mayor of Cleveland, Tom Johnson, and his innovative city-manager form of governance as a reason for her party support. Of course, it was also the Democratic administration in Cleveland who appointed Allen prosecutor, and a Democratic state representative who introduced women's presidential suffrage in Ohio. Allen's progressive values mirrored those of her Republican parents on labor, education, and women's suffrage, but Allen now saw those progressive values as residing with the Democrats, rather than the Republicans. This same shift would occur nationally as the Republicans moved away from their role as reformers to the party representing businesses and conservativism. The majority of women, however, were still Republican at this time, in contrast to Allen's affiliation.[49]

Allen's independent candidacy also conformed to the political approach long adopted by women. They had worked outside the political parties, excluded as nonvoters, but also suspicious of the corruption, patronage, and gamesmanship of the parties. A high priority for progressive and moralist women as they first entered mainstream politics was the "purification of politics" and elimination of the fraudulent system of boss politics and political machines. Nonpartisanship was a core principle.[50] Allen agreed, believing initially that women could transform the political parties by "bringing something of a cleansing with them" rather than being forced into the corrupt process. Women, she said, "would not be whipped into line by machine domination to quite the same degree as men."[51] She said women did not have to accept politics as a "colossal if interesting game," and could instead bring a new approach to politics focused on issue rather than party that secured a "higher grade of judge" than the partisanship of political cronies.[52] However, a similar bipartisan, woman-centered approach had not worked for Republican Bertha Rembaugh the prior year in New York City, when she lost the race to be the first woman municipal court judge.[53]

Allen's nonpartisan stance was also a savvy political move, for it engaged the waiting and willing, newly enfranchised women voters of all parties. She had just ten weeks to seek nominating petitions and generate support for her candidacy. As an independent, she drew on the broad bipartisan support of the women's suffrage movement for a woman judicial candidate. Her nonpartisan affiliation was one of the key reasons people endorsed her, as the *Plain Dealer* confirmed: "Miss Allen as judge will owe no debt except to the people of Cuyahoga county. No party organization can ever dictate to her."[54]

Women from all parties activated their preexisting grassroots suffrage channels and promoted Allen's candidacy. She had many foot soldiers on the ground, circulating endless petitions and canvassing door to door, first for the nomination and then for the campaign. She spent relatively little in the campaign, a total of $1,043 ($16,000 today), including $318 of her own money.[55] She continued working at the prosecutor's office during the day, because she needed the money to support herself, and campaigned all evening in a grueling schedule. She spoke at the high schools, at all denominations of churches, at the Jewish Club, the Italian Club, the Junior League, and the Business Women's Club.[56] One of her key speeches addressed her "judicial belief" of what was required of a judge: knowledge of the law, integrity, backbone, and avoidance of political corruption.[57]

Her former boss, Maud Wood Park, now national president of the League of Women Voters, came to Cleveland and spoke for Allen's candidacy, as did Belle Sherwin, president of the Cleveland League—making exceptions to their rule against endorsement of candidates because Allen was nonpartisan. She was endorsed by many women's organizations, the Parent Teacher Association, and seventy-five lawyers who endorsed her on the front page of the paper. These organizations doubled down to get out the vote of the newly enfranchised women, conducting voter education classes, running registration drives, and writing articles on the candidates and voting process.[58]

This women-centered power and political network was thus the key to Allen's initial election success. Allen always credited women and women's political organization with catapulting her into office, and would continue to draw on this universal support in subsequent elections and nominations even as her appeal expanded to male political circles. Asked about her individual success, Allen demurred: "All of this sounds personal and yet it was not personal. I was the beneficiary of the entire woman movement. . . . It was the women—Democrats, Republicans, and independents—who made my campaign and elected me."[59] Her victory, she said, was "the vindication of the right of women to hold public office." Allen emphasized the loyalty of women in politics: "No one can be more conscious of the support and sympathy of women in political contests than I. . . . the women were always the driving force. . . . That I was elected was certainly due to the women." She elaborated: "Never tell me that women do not stand by women. All that I have had in my professional life I owe to the sympathy and support of women and of men who believe in women."[60]

Allen won the election in November 1920, leading the ticket in a field of ten judicial candidates for four positions. She was "elected by the largest popular vote ever cast for any judge in Cuyahoga County . . . and she outdistanced in number of votes the three other county judges elected, all of whom were men."[61] Yet Allen had been the sixth choice of the bar association, which did not affirmatively endorse her. Instead, it backed Judge George Addams of the Insolvency and Juvenile Court, and the three returning incumbents. In January 1921, Judge Allen took the bench in the relatively new Cuyahoga County Courthouse, a beautiful Beaux-Arts building that conveyed the pomp and majesty of the law.[62]

WHY FLORENCE WAS FIRST

Florence Allen emerged relatively easily as the first woman elected trial judge because she was the right candidate at the right time in the right place. She was the right candidate—a highly educated and qualified lawyer with six years of extensive trial work in both criminal and civil matters before the very court in which she sought office. Her prosecutorial experience had earned a reputation for toughness and respect with the judges and the public. Allen was politically well connected from her women's suffrage work nationally and in the state and her Democratic connections in Cleveland and nationally. Her family added Cleveland community connections on her mother's side and her father's connections in Congress. It was the right time, as the Nineteenth Amendment had just passed and women were voting nationally and in Ohio for the first time.[63] Moreover, Allen's suffrage affiliation gave her a ready grassroots network and political organization to deploy in her service. Allen was also in the right place, geographically located in a large urban city, generally more supportive of women, with a recent progressive history of idealistic reform.[64] Ohio was a bellwether state, signaling shifts in national political trends, with a long tradition of women's rights of suffrage, temperance, and college education.[65]

Allen also emerged as a first woman judge because of the use of multiple-candidate voting in her judicial election. These progressive voting reforms allowed a voter to select several from a group of candidates, sometimes in ranked choice, which often resulted in the election of more representative and diverse candidates like women and minorities. Cleveland and Ohio emerged as early leaders in the national movement for proportional representation reform. Ashtabula, just east of Cleveland—where Allen would ultimately reside—was the first city in the country to adopt proportional representation in 1915. Nationally, from 1913 to 1932, the Proportional Representation League "pursued a vigorous national campaign" for proportional voting, believing that it restored voting to ordinary people, as opposed to corruption funding single winner-take-all candidates.[66] Multiple-candidate voting also allowed voters to strategize by not voting all their possible choices, thus increasing the total number of votes for preferred candidates and decreasing the totals for other candidates.[67]

Allen candidly admitted that this strategy of withholding votes, colloquially called "plunker voting," explained her victory. She recounted a conversation she had after her election at a luncheon with Roscoe Pound, her infamous professor at Chicago and now dean of Harvard Law, who was giving a speech about his study of criminal justice administration in the Cleveland courts. She introduced herself by saying, "You will not remember me," and he said snarkily, "I remember you perfectly: you're Miss Allen." Another lawyer jumped in to mediate, saying this is Judge Allen, a presiding judge in the court of common pleas. Pound said, "Oh! You're the woman! Plunker votes, I fancy," thus discounting her elective victory. But Florence ignored the slight. "I had to laugh at this. Unquestionably so-called plunker votes had aided me to lead the ticket. Persons who voted for me and for no one else on the list of ten candidates had deprived other candidates of possible votes."[68]

Women activists led the movement for proportional voting and city manager governance in Cleveland.[69] The progressive women idealistically believed that women candidates would benefit from these proportional voting reforms because women were a "numerical majority but drastically underrepresented in political life." The national and local League of Women Voters and the Cleveland Women's City Club led advocacy efforts for voting reforms and "were joined in the fray by Democratic attorneys Florence Allen and Susan Rebhan of Cleveland" as Allen gave speeches in support of proportional representation and the city manager plan.[70] This new system achieved its objective, as it saw the election of the first women to the city council: Marie Wing, Allen's friend and executive secretary of the YWCA (Young Women's Christian Association); Helen Green, president of the temperance union in Cuyahoga County; and, a few years later, Allen's partner, Susan Rebhan. Wing and her longtime partner Dorothy Smith remained close friends and "very kindred spirits with Allen" and Rebhan. Wing would organize Rebhan's funeral at her death in 1935.[71]

In Allen's very first opinion written as a judge newly elected to the Ohio Supreme Court, she upheld the constitutionality of the proportional voting she had endorsed, which had helped elect her and her friends to office. Judge Allen wrote the opinion for the Ohio Supreme Court in *Reutener v. City of Cleveland* (1923), validating the constitutionality of the constitutional amendment allowing proportional representation on the principle of municipal home rule.[72] Allen said it was the "first decision in the United

States" to uphold "the radically different system of voting and counting," which was technically true, though Michigan and California courts had reached similar results.[73] In her opinion, she dismissed arguments that the voting system nullified votes, finding that it is "axiomatic" and "a matter of common knowledge" that minorities can determine outcomes, citing John Quincy Adams's presidential election and the common practice of gerrymandering voting districts. In a companion case, she also upheld proportional voting against federal constitutional challenge.[74] Cleveland's proportional voting, however, would be repealed ten years later as wins by Italian and Irish candidates in Cleveland drew public ire, and as Democratic reformers became the majority party and lost interest in systemic reforms. In 2026, Ohio passed a law prohibiting any city from adopting alternative voting systems, in direct contravention of Allen's finding of the constitutional right to home rule.[75]

MISS JUDGED

A woman judge was at first an oddity. Spectators packed her public courtroom "to see how a woman judge administers justice." Her bailiff reported that "it's not the usual court followers," but rather "citizens from every walk of life" that watch, as "men bring their wives" to see the novelty of a woman judge.[76] One male reporter wrote that "probably not one person in a thousand has ever met a woman judge" and "I admit that I looked forward to the meeting with curiosity tinged with considerable doubt. I had no prejudices against a woman acting as a judge; but I was afraid she might be somehow queer. I wondered how she would dress and how she would do her hair! She might be a fine woman and a most excellent judge, and yet might look ridiculous presiding over a court of law." He wrote, "You might tell yourself that inside of her head, not outside, was the important thing. But it will be a good long time before women judges become so common that we won't think about how they look." He highlighted Allen's appearance, noting her plain dark dress with a simple white lace collar, and hair with a "natural wave" that pleased the eye. "The most impressive thing about Judge Allen," the reporter concluded, "is this simplicity and unaffected naturalness. She is direct, without a trace of aggressiveness. She has dignity, without self-consciousness. She says what she thinks."[77] Some typecast Allen into existing gender roles, calling her "the eternal mother."[78] Others characterized her as masculine, finding that more reassuring of her judicial authority. A Lisbon, Ohio, newspaper wrote: "Judge Allen is physically as well as mentally a big woman, hearty and wholesome looking . . . her complexion fresh . . . with abundant light brown hair dressed in the style of fifteen years ago . . . a good face, a face to inspire confidence. She cares little for frills." It added: "The lady walks with a stride like a man and wears roomy, common sense shoes. Her voice has a masculine depth and lends itself easily to open air speaking."[79]

Lawyers did not know what to make of the first woman judge. Allen told a story from early in her judicial tenure when a young male attorney who had worked with her in the county prosecutor's office was in "the midst of an impassioned plea to the Jury" and turned to address a question to the bench, but stumbled over how to address a woman judge. He stuttered, "Miss Allen—," then hesitated and began again, "Please, Your Honor—Judge—Oh, well, Miss Allen—in this case—." "Everyone in the court room laughed," according to Allen. But she emphasized that it was not long before all the attorneys addressed her as Judge Allen, the same as they did other judges on the bench.[80]

Allen deliberately crafted her judicial persona in masculine form. She wanted to prove that women could think and judge like a man, because a man was the existing model of a good judge. She said she "took every case like a man."[81] That meant that she strove to exemplify masculine qualities of objectivity, formal reasoning, rationality, and linear logic and distanced herself from feminine traits of informality, emotion, and subjectivity.[82] Allen said the key to her success was old-fashioned hard work, as she knew that "her work must be as nearly letter-perfect as possible because people are ten times more critical of a woman in an unprecedented position than of a man in the same position."[83] In her first year on the court, she developed a work ethic of devoting long hours, being the first person to the office each day at 5 a.m. and working through the summer vacation. In her eighteen months on the court of common pleas, she disposed of a record number of 892 cases, including 579 civil and criminal trials, including seven murder trials.[84]

Allen had to take deliberate action to avoid being relegated to subordinate gender roles. Less than a week after she was elected, Allen adamantly refused a proposal by her male colleagues that she head up a new, specially created divorce division.[85] Just days after the votes were counted, she reported in her diary that she was "agitated about Dom. Relations Ct," but noted that Barth, her mentor and law partner, "advises me to go slow."[86] Publicly she was more diplomatic in saying, "This did not appeal to me," as "I did not care to spend my life hearing and deciding divorce controversies."[87] "Since I was unmarried," she jested, "I thought these eleven men, most of them married, were better qualified than I to carry their share of this burden." Allen not only declined, but went public to expose the perceived sexism of her new colleagues. She made a statement to the press, stressing that there was no particular reason why she should consent to this proposition, emphasizing instead her broad civil practice and prosecutorial experience—although she had in fact handled many divorces in practice. In her first week on the bench, she stated emphatically to another reporter, "I am not going to try any divorce cases this term," refusing to start on the path of women's work either formally or informally.[88] The *Cleveland News* joked that "we certainly never expected to live long enough to hear a spinster decline appointment as judge of a court of marital relations on grounds that she was ignorant of the subject."[89] But Allen, as the first woman judge, knew she needed to fight back against this type of detrimental typecasting to family matters that would limit not only her but all women judges who came after.

Judge Allen continued to hear more than her fair share of divorce cases, which made up 44 percent of her regular docket of the common pleas court. She handled 397 divorce cases, twice as many as any other judge, even though cases were supposed to be distributed randomly among all judges.[90] She reconciled the couple in 101 of these cases, saying that the divorce law itself was not problematic or "evil" as some claimed, but that cases needed to be pending longer to allow for reconciliation. Her commonsense advice for couples was not to enter into "hasty marriages," to provide for the wife to receive a regular allowance and be a "business partner" to the husband, and for the wife to be sympathetic and never nag her spouse.[91] Cuyahoga County created a separate Domestic Relations division in 1923, but cases were still heard by rotating common pleas judges until 1959.[92] The Cleveland judges had been considering a domestic division before Allen was elected, following the progressive innovation of other cities and as strongly endorsed by local women reformers. Women wanted this special attention because most of the divorce cases were brought by women (75 percent), and the majority were low-income women who had been married as minors and needed careful consideration by the courts.[93]

A MORE ETHICAL PROCESS

As Judge Allen started her new position in the depths of winter, she walked to the courthouse each morning.[94] On her first day in office, the newspaper reported the historic occasion: "Portia sat for the first time on the common pleas bench in Ohio." "Portia" referred to a Shakespearian character in *The Merchant of Venice*, a woman who pretended to be a male lawyer in the courtroom to cleverly resolve a legal conflict. "Judge Allen," it said, "took charge of the routine of court procedure like an old timer and decided the questions of evidence and law raised by the contending attorneys with speed and dispatch."[95] Allen had run her campaign on reform of the existing system. She developed a six-point platform promoting "law enforcement, justice for all, business methods applied to the courts, efficient work by public servants, respect for law, order, and the courts, and moral standards functioning in government."[96] Like social feminists and progressives, she sought to clean up the moral fraud and streamline efficient procedures. Drawing on her prosecutorial experience, she emphasized the rule of law and strict enforcement of the laws during a time when bootleggers defied Prohibition and flaunted respect for the law. Her "justice for all" promise sought to counter the bribes and payoffs that dominated the courts. "The court needs the woman's conscientiousness and her respect for law," Allen said, to imbue a moral backing to remedy the defects of the court administration.[97]

Judge Allen quickly confirmed her instinct, gained as a lawyer, that there was a need for reform on the common pleas court. As judge, she was concerned about the lack of speedy trials, which allowed the accused a chance to jump bail, risked witnesses dying or forgetting facts, and left prosecution witnesses stuck in jail, where they were kept for their protection and to guarantee their testimony.[98] She adopted a "no passing" policy, prohibiting criminal lawyers' practice of passing or delaying the case to wear out witnesses and the prosecutor, unless they had an affidavit of due diligence presented in court with the defendant. Allen also adopted a procedure in her courtroom that all cases with witnesses in jail were immediately set for trial. But other judges did not have to follow her procedures, and few did. This lack of consistency and administrative oversight was also a concern of Allen's, as cases rotated among the twelve common pleas judges with no overall management of the different staffs, "each a law unto himself," leading to extreme backlogs of six thousand cases.[99] The solution she proposed was a single administrative judge, a recommendation from the Cleveland women's clubs that had called out the court mismanagement, ultimately resulting in a state bill mandating the appointment of such an administrator. Allen later called on women to continue this great interest in the "delay of the law," explaining her strong views on the "radical need of reform" in the system of criminal procedure.[100]

Another contributing factor Judge Allen identified for the case backlog was the court's practice of shutting down over the summer months while the judges took long vacations. She proposed to her new colleagues that they hear cases over the summer. Not surprisingly, they did not like the idea and refused. So Allen instituted her reform unilaterally. She traded her civil term and vacation period with a judge assigned criminal cases, and she cleaned up practically all the criminal cases in which the defendant was in jail awaiting trial in the summer.[101] The idealistic Judge Allen was staying true to her campaign promises and proclaimed judicial values—but she wasn't making any friends along the way.

The corruption in the courts was another reform focus for Allen. The new judge, emulating progressive theory, demanded ethical behavior by all court officials and eschewed the common practice of partisan influence.[102] "It is because we let influences creep in," she said, "which twist the law to selfish interests that injustices come out of the law."[103] Some members of the Democratic Party felt that because she had been appointed prosecutor by them, she "should pay attention to an influential member of the organization when he desired some specific court action." Allen said that "whenever an intimation of this kind came to me I ignored it." Shortly after her election, she was told that an influential Democratic ward leader said, "This Florence Allen is the worse [*sic*] thing that ever happened. You go into her court and ask her for some usual favor and she pays no attention to it. She hardly knows who you are and if she did, it would not make any difference." Allen took that as a compliment: "I thought this was testimony that I was carrying out my platform—'Justice for all.'"[104]

Allen was not the only one who saw the need for reform. At the same time, the Cleveland Bar Association asked the Cleveland Foundation to fund a study of the criminal justice system in the city and the alleged corruption and systemic problems.[105] The 1921 Cleveland Criminal Justice Survey was the first thorough study of the criminal justice system of a major city and served as a model for surveys in other states and in President Herbert Hoover's administration. The Cleveland survey "epitomized the Progressive outlook, relying on objective professional experts," including Harvard law professors Felix Frankfurter and Roscoe Pound as chairs, to recommend nonpartisan civic reform. The survey provided a "frank diagnosis" detailing errors and making recommendations for the work of the police, prosecutors, criminal courts, and correctional system. For the courts, the report found inefficiency, a lack of training, and corruption among bailiffs, court personnel, and criminal defense lawyers. The report validated Judge Allen's concerns with the lack of administrative management, "fluctuating policies," and "loafing judges." The report favorably noted some of Allen's reforms as good solutions, including the "no passing" policy. Allen's initiatives in combination with the Cleveland survey quickly improved the fairness and operation of the court. By the end of her term in 1922, the Cuyahoga County Court of Common Pleas was called one of the best trial courts in the nation.[106]

PROVING HERSELF TOUGH AS A MAN

Judge Allen set out from the beginning on the bench to prove herself as tough as a man. She demonstrated that she was tough on the law, tough on crime, and strong enough to impose punitive sanctions such as the death penalty and life imprisonment.[107] Allen was aware of the double bind of women in law: criticized for being too emotional, squeamish, and afraid of criminal work, but also stereotyped for being strict, schoolmarmish, and unforgiving.[108] She leaned into the criminal work, drawing on her prosecutorial experience and demonstrating that women were equally suited to handling these provocative and dangerous cases. She claimed that as a woman she would be tougher on criminals than the "masculine courts," whose judges were weak when it came to women defendants because their "oversentimentality" was easily wooed to leniency by a pretty face.[109] Women in her court, she said, "should expect a fifty-fifty deal in court and nothing more." A woman judge adjudicating a case of a woman defendant before a woman prosecutor made national news when Allen presided over a criminal arraignment for Australia Crape, said to be "the first time in the history of the United States and probably of the world that such a thing has taken place."[110] Reporting on the woman judge's first month on the bench, a newspaper commented that, with Judge Allen, "justice is tempered with mercy" and that the "precision with which justice is administered has proven a surprise to veteran lawyers and prosecutors alike" who wished "we had more judges like her."[111]

When Allen joined the Cuyahoga County Common Pleas Court in 1921, it was a chaotic place of corruption and sensationalism. Political bribes for patronage or favors were the norm, and the era of Prohibition included corrupt police and Mafia involvement. Soap opera–like cases were featured in the newspapers, and spectators often filled the courtrooms for the entertainment spectacle. Allen heard both criminal and civil cases, though she seemed to prefer the criminal cases, given her prosecutorial background.[112] In her first weeks on the bench, she oversaw cases of murder, rape, a robbery (the defendant smiled at her a lot), and an embezzlement she found "very tiresome."[113] Several times her mentors, prosecutor Stephen Young and Judge Vickery, criticized her, telling her she ruled "wrongly."[114] She handled one dramatic case where Mrs. Miller, accused of murdering her husband either by mistaking him for a burglar or by premeditation, repeatedly faked swooning to avoid taking the stand and avoid cross-examination about "her past life."[115] In another case, the defendant was arrested on the doorstep of a Catholic Church immediately after his own wedding, accused of assault with the intent to rob and denied parole when Allen learned he had previously stolen from the foster mother who raised him.[116] One defendant even tried to trick the new woman judge and the female prosecutor, Eva Jaffa, by having the wrong defendant take the stand, with his lawyer's knowledge, in a play to trigger double jeopardy and free the robber, who had attacked an automobile and robbed two girls.[117]

The centerpiece of Allen's tough reputation was her most sensational case as a trial judge: the first-degree murder trial of Frank Motto, a member of the notorious Mayfield Road Mob, an Italian criminal gang affiliated with the "Black Hand" (a symbol of the Mafia). Motto was convicted of murder and Judge Allen sentenced him to the death penalty. Motto, a twenty-six-year-old "gang leader" who "terrorized people of Italian birth," was convicted of planning a payroll robbery and murdering two businessmen who were transporting the money. On New Year's Eve, Motto drove an automobile into a bridge railing, and when the businessmen got out of their car at the accident, six Mafia men opened fire, killing them. Motto allegedly needed the money to pay for his legal appeal of a prior conviction for several automobile thefts. Two of Motto's associates, Louis Komer (aka the "Toledo Kid") and teenager Sam Purpera, testified against him at trial.[118]

Allen began the double-murder trial by taking the jury to the scene of the shooting as requested by the prosecution. Motto was represented by Samuel Doerfler, Allen's former boss at the prosecutor's office. The sensationalized trial packed the courtroom and captured the public interest. Judge Allen and the jury were threatened several times during the trial. Armed spectators were found in her courtroom and one man was arrested and jailed for illegally carrying loaded weapons. In chambers, she received a "dirty smudgy" letter with "several black outlines of a hand" threatening that "the day Motto dies, you die." Judge Allen also eerily discovered a black hand painted on the cement wall of the storage basement of her apartment after her roommate heard someone prowling around outside. People she met in the community, including a young female waitress, warned her to be careful lest they "bump you off." Allen, reportedly, seemed remarkably calm to the court officers, who took these threats very seriously.

Allen found Motto guilty of murder and sentenced him to death. In other courtrooms, co-conspirator Purpera was also sentenced to death, while Komer, the only non-Italian defendant, was sentenced to life imprisonment. Motto's appeals were denied, and Judge Allen refused a last-minute stay, saying that only the governor could grant the request at that late hour. The newspaper reported that "there was no tremor in Judge

Allen's voice when she made this decision."[119] Frank Motto was executed by electric chair.[120]

Judge Allen thus became the first woman judge in the country to impose the death penalty. She said that she "did not enjoy this task" and that "it was an unpleasant duty to sentence a man to death, but I determined that as it was my duty under the law to pass that sentence, I should not be emotional about it."[121] She imposed the death penalty only once, but upheld the sentence several times when later sitting on the state supreme court, including in the case of Motto's accomplice. Throughout her career, Allen would be asked about the Motto case and whether ordering an execution was compatible with the nurturing role of women. Allen's sentence of death confused people, as women were assumed to be forgiving and merciful and opposed to killing. Her answer was simply that she had an obligation to enforce the law as it was written. The show of grit and strength earned her reputational points. One citizen, Benjamin Hubbell, an architect who played a major role in developing Cleveland, wrote to her: "When I voted for you it was as a compliment to the sex rather than with the hope that you had the necessary forcefulness to see that murders and other violators of the Law are properly convicted and sentenced." But in the Motto case, he wrote, Allen had proved her "courage" and "necessary qualifications" to hold judicial office.[122] Allen herself would repeatedly cite this experience as proof of her strength and ability to be a judge.

Judge Allen also demonstrated she was tough by showing she was not afraid to take on powerful foes of the establishment. In what she believed to be her most important case on the trial court, Allen sentenced Judge William McGannon to prison for perjury. The case dominated the *Plain Dealer*'s front page, and the *New York Tribune* called the conviction and sentencing "the most dramatic incident in the history of the Cuyahoga County courts."[123] McGannon, who had been the chief judge of the Cleveland Municipal Court, a "great bear" of a man considered a "dignified and respected pillar of the community," had been an excellent judge who brought reforms to the court.[124] But he had become involved with criminals and bootleggers during Prohibition in what was called "Dr. Jekyll and Mr. Hyde behavior." In the underlying case, McGannon was charged with the murder of Harold Kagy, who was shot and killed at midnight on a downtown street corner in Skid Row after exiting McGannon's car following an evening of drinking at a speakeasy. Two different juries acquitted McGannon, believing his fabricated story that he got out of the car earlier and walked to a streetcar stop. It then came to light that witnesses had been bribed and threatened and jurors tampered with.[125]

Judge Allen handled the subsequent perjury trial against McGannon. The star witness, Mary Neely, revealed that she had been paid to avoid testifying in the second trial that she saw McGannon at the "death corner" and witnessed him take the shot. In the perjury trial, Allen held in contempt several women jurors, witnesses, and a bailiff for subornation of perjury, coming down hard to set an example and halt the rampant bribery and corruption in the courts.[126] Judge Allen also ordered a psychiatric evaluation of the defendant, who was at a sanatorium after a nervous breakdown, which found he was fit to stand trial. Allen's charge to the jury emphasized the rule of law: "You are the ministers of justice and not of mercy." She said, "In a civilized state like this, it is absolutely essential to the preservation of social order that the law should be enforced." The jury was deadlocked after five ballots, but Allen refused to let them stop, and they reached a verdict after twenty-seven hours of deliberation. As the former chief judge awaited the verdict, he "tugged nervously at his tie and his fingers drummed an incessant tattoo on the table." When the guilty verdict was announced, "a look of stupefaction, almost terror, overspread" McGannon's face, which "gave way to one of almost malignant hatred" as "he stared stonily at the jury." He "seemed to fix his gaze on the two women" jurors, Bertha Reed and Ada Griffith, who had been firm in their conviction, "nodding his head at them as a sneer curled on his lips. . . . Haltingly, he arose and walked unsteadily to the bar, and in a low voice, tense with emotion, addressed Judge Allen and the jury."[127]

McGannon challenged the sentence, calling it the greatest miscarriage of justice. While he was speaking, a newspaper reported, "Judge Allen sat with her hands clasped on the desk before her, gazing out the window of her courtroom."[128] She then stood up behind her bench and leaned in closer to McGannon, who was menacingly close to the bench. She reprimanded him, emphasizing the particular wrongfulness of a judge, dedicated to truth and justice, lying in the courts of law: "Judge McGannon, a court never has been faced with a more disagreeable duty than that of sentencing a man before whom the court has practiced as a lawyer. However, our personal feelings cannot be permitted to prevent us from performing our duty. . . . Judges cannot think that they are above the law. . . . Judges know the law as well, or better, than private citizens. Judges ought to know the spirit of the law, which demands that all tell the truth in a court of justice, judges as well as private citizens."[129] Allen sentenced McGannon to an indeterminate term of one to ten years in prison. He was forced by the bar to resign and was prosecuted for contempt of court, as was Mary Neely, McGannon's junior counsel, and two reporters who had intimidated witnesses.[130] McGannon was released on parole after serving nineteen months because he was sick with diabetes, and he moved to Chicago, where he clerked for a law firm until he died four years later.[131] The McGannon trial exposed multiple levels of corruption in the court system and ignited calls for reform, precipitating the Cleveland Criminal Justice Survey that validated Allen's concerns about court corruption.

Judge Allen's strictness on ethical dictates for all in her court stretched at times into overzealousness. When a police officer improperly interrogated a suspect by promising he would be "let off easy," Allen granted the defendant's release and chastised the officer.[132] Twice, her strong sanctions were reversed by an appellate court. In one of her first cases on the court, also a "blackhander" gangster case, John Azzarello was convicted of first-degree murder and sentenced to life imprisonment. Allen was found to have committed prejudicial error by charging three defense witnesses with perjury in the presence of the jury. Azzarello was granted a new trial because of Allen's error.[133] But Judge Allen was not concerned, because she had intentionally waged a "campaign against perjury in criminal trials" and by being strict had effectively "stopped the practice."[134]

In a second case, Judge Allen held attorney Tim Long in contempt of court.[135] Long, a former prosecutor Allen had worked with, was defense counsel to George Crawford, an accountant who pled guilty to embezzling $15,000 ($500,000 today). Crawford had no prior record, and Allen initially sentenced him to parole, and his wife sold some jewelry to make partial restitution. The attorney then stated in court that there was no other money in hiding and that he had not received a fee. But it was later established that the defendant had deposited $5,000 in a bank account with a fictitious name and given control of it to the attorney as a fee. Allen summarily sentenced the attorney to five days in jail for his contempt of court and revoked the defendant's parole. The court of appeals reversed, finding that Allen had improperly imposed summary contempt instead of holding a full criminal trial with a prosecutor. Allen had spent several days working on a careful opinion to justify her ruling and concluded that summary contempt was appropriate because it had occurred in front of her in court. She had also consulted Stephen Young at the prosecutor's office, finding it would have been futile to refer it to that office, where Long had worked.[136]

A JURY OF HER PEERS

Judge Allen's final innovation of the court system was to shepherd in the new generation of women jurors. Women's jury service was a key agenda of the nascent League of Women Voters nationally and locally in Cleveland. It had been envisioned by women's rights activists from the advent of their Declaration of Sentiments, and Judge Allen was now empowered to implement the demand.[137] Jury service was an obligation of citizenship that gave women a role in meting out justice and governing the meaning and enforcement of law. Women had been historically excluded as jurors because of a claimed "defect of sex" of emotional frailty, inferior intellect, and need for protection from the public sphere of the courtroom and its theater of atrocities. They were only rarely called for a "jury of matrons" when there was a woman's issue like pregnancy or rape at issue. There was consensus among women's activists that jury service was important to establish this equality while also bringing women's perspective of care and mercy to legal justice.[138]

Allen was well aware of the magnitude of this political right, and of the national battle being waged by women demanding this right from resistant courts. She took what power she had in her own court to actualize women as jurors in a state that had accepted the full political meaning of the Nineteenth Amendment. Ohio interpreted straightforwardly the text of its laws authorizing "electors" to be jurors to now include women as constitutionally mandated. Later challenges to this application of the law in the Ohio Supreme Court when Allen sat on that court were rejected, though without opinion by the woman judge.[139] However, only a minority of states interpreted the new amendment to include the right to jury service, limiting the Nineteenth Amendment to voting only, thus reserving the democratic role of the jury for men. Under what women's advocates called "tortured reasoning," these courts interpreted gender-neutral terms defining jurors as "persons" to mean only men, rationalizing under originalist methodology that historically the common law disqualified women.[140] The U.S. Supreme Court would not hold that women were equally entitled to democratic participation through jury service until 1975.[141]

In Ohio, Judge Allen presided over some of the first juries in the country that included women. Her very first panel of jurors included two women, Nellie Chase and Mary Kalal, and a woman served as foreperson on the Motto death penalty case.[142] Allen matter-of-factly adopted procedures in her court to facilitate the process for women to serve as jurors, such as a separate woman bailiff to supervise the separate quarters for women when jurors were sequestered overnight, hiring a husband-wife team as her bailiffs. She ridiculed a procedure reportedly used in southern Ohio of putting curtains around women jurors' chairs to protect them from seeing any upsetting evidence. She quickly moved to a practice of impaneling juries of equal numbers of six women and six men, recruiting even numbers out of the jury waiting room to ensure a gender-balanced jury.[143] She also proactively reached out to include women as 30 percent of her grand juries.[144]

Judge Allen used her pulpit to convince people of the competence of women jurors and to encourage women to embrace this important public duty.[145] "The outstanding characteristic of the woman juror," she said, "has been her sense of responsibility, her conscientiousness, and her intelligence in following the evidence."[146] Women's eligibility, she argued, more than doubled the number of people available for service, educated the public and families about the jury's importance, and helped raise the ethical standards of jury service in comparison to the "old days" when "some juries threw dice and played cards to decide what the verdict would be."[147] She disabused the public of the common assumption that women were too emotional for this role, asserting that her own experience was that women could "keep their emotion in check and control their feelings in accordance with their view of the law and the evidence." She believed that "the participation of women in the courts alone, not only as attorneys, prosecutors, and judges, but as jury women, has immeasurably raised the tone of the administration of justice," especially in the criminal courts. She concluded that if no other results "come out of the enfranchisement of women but that of their participation in the work of the courts the extending of the vote to us would be amply justified."

Allen continued to promote jury reform for women's equality. She lobbied intensely behind the scenes in 1947 when a federal jury bill proposed guaranteeing women equal rights to serve on federal juries.[148] The year before, the Supreme Court had held in *Ballard v. United States* that federal juries in states that allowed women jurors must include women, but that still permitted states to exclude women.[149] The federal bill would have guaranteed women the right to serve on federal juries regardless of state law, a result achieved ten years later by the 1957 Civil Rights Act.[150]

Allen served for two years as a common pleas court judge until she was elected to the Ohio Supreme Court in 1922. Her work in those two years was significant and appreciated. On Judge Allen's last day on the Cuyahoga County Court of Common Pleas, she was called to her courtroom late in the day by a probation office claiming to have a last-minute case for deliberation.[151] Instead, Allen found the courtroom filled with well-wishers, including friends, court personnel, and her associate judges, while the women employees of the court filled the jury box. These supportive colleagues wanted to show their appreciation and thank her for her service. They presented Allen with a gift of a black leather suitcase with engraved ivory toilet articles to support her travel as she headed to Columbus to the Ohio Supreme Court. The newspaper reported that "Miss Allen was visibly affected. She inspected the case, looked away for a minute, and then smiled." "Nothing," she said, "since my election has touched me as greatly as this surprise gathering and gift of my fellow workers." The reporter concluded that there were "few women who enjoy a greater local popularity" than Florence Allen.[152]

4 Battling for Progressive Reform on the State Supreme Court

Allen's service on the common pleas court did not last long because, two years after her historic first election, Florence Allen ambitiously ran for the Ohio Supreme Court. She sought out this more visible role with a potential for wider impact to better effectuate her commitment to progressive policies and public service. Allen and her supporters had been eyeing opportunities on the supreme bench, which soon opened up when Judge James Johnson, a progressive Democrat, resigned from the court to run for governor.[1] She would serve on this high court for eleven years, winning reelection to a second term in 1928.

The Ohio Supreme Court was a different experience for Allen—a bench of consensus requiring majoritarian agreement among the judges, rather than the independent autonomy she was used to as a singular judge in her own common pleas courtroom. The high court was composed of seven judges, the same number it has today. Though colloquially referred to as "judge" or "justice," the members of the court were then officially called "judge" (except for the chief justice), until later changed to the honorific "justice."[2] Allen fought to establish a legacy of progressive jurisprudence on the Ohio Supreme Court, following her engrained progressive values and conforming to the progressive 1912 amendments to the state constitution. However, she was blocked by conservative colleagues and a controlling chief justice who sidelined her authority and influence. When Allen joined the court, she was the only Democrat.[3] She would remain the sole Democrat for most of her tenure, until a second Democrat was elected in her last year on that bench.[4] The court had a conservative reputation, criticized for its judges "having taken on age" and "emasculated every liberal tradition of the Constitution of 1912" by overturning "every liberal law that they had a chance at" through narrowing interpretations.[5] The "political climate of the twenties was conservative," backing away from progressive reforms of the prior decade.[6] The restructuring of the Ohio Constitution in 1912 was an "important dividing line in Ohio constitutional history," fundamentally revising the constitution by thirty-four amendments. Progressives passed widespread reforms like direct democracy of popular referendum and voter initiative, elimination of supermajority for constitutional amendment, and municipal home-rule power. Concerned about courts invalidating economic and social legislation and overcrowded dockets, the constitution limited appellate de novo review, narrowed supreme court jurisdiction of right, and required a near-majority to invalidate a law as unconstitutional if upheld by the appellate court. Other subjects of amendment included minimum wage, labor protections, natural resources, worker's compensation, civil service, and abolishing contracted prison labor.[7]

Ten years later, these issues were still legally new, and Judge Allen would be required to wade into the constitutional morass. Newspaper editors wrote that they were glad to see Allen on the supreme bench because she was "a liberal mind and realizes that we are in 1922 instead of in the eighteenth century, and more important, if any court ever needed of regeneration that very august tribunal . . . deserves an overhauling."[8] Allen would distinguish herself from her colleagues as a liberal moderate.

AIMING FOR THE HIGHER COURT

In the campaign for Ohio Supreme Court, Allen utilized the same game plan she had used for the common pleas election: running as an independent and relying on the organization of the women's suffrage network.

She continued her same platform emphasizing law enforcement, justice for all, business methods, efficiency by public servants, respect for the rule of law, and moral standards.[9] The cornerstone for Allen was justice for all, which meant nonpartisan judicial administration, for "if a democratic Judge favors democrats and a republican Judge favors republicans, obviously our liberties are at stake."[10] "Justice," she said, "should be administered without regard to the personality, condition or political connections of the parties before the Court. It ought not to make any difference whether the parties concerned are rich or poor, black or white." Allen ran on her common pleas record, emphasizing her "battle against perjury" and her record-setting disposition of cases in eighteen months that cleared the dockets and "surpassed the record of any Judge" on the common pleas court.[11] The Cleveland Criminal Justice Survey results were released at this time, ratifying Allen's superior and ethical court management.

Susan Rebhan, Allen's new partner and an organizer for the YWCA in Youngstown, became her campaign manager.[12] Rebhan supervised a team of women who covered the state through former suffrage county channels, bipartisan groups of women now rebranded as "Judge Florence Allen Clubs" to "boost the independent candidacy" of Allen.[13] Rebhan later wrote that it was "always women, women, marching on the voters like an army."[14] With this grassroots effort, Allen's campaign secured over forty thousand signatures needed for the nominating petitions as an independent candidate, and her petitions were submitted to the Board of Elections by an "august committee of men," including a former judge.[15] Allen said that most male candidates paid for signatures, paying circulators two cents per name, but the women working on her campaign were paid nothing, as her campaign operated on just several thousand dollars.[16]

Allen traveled the state, visiting most of the counties in her Model T automobile. She took the month of October off from the court, substituting for her summer vacation time. She was "booked for appearances like a vaudeville star," packing in meetings all day at clubs, homes, factories, theaters, and street corners.[17] During a time of heightened racial tension, she appeared before a "large race audience in Cleveland" of "race men and women of the city" with a "burning message" about equal justice in an event sponsored by the NAACP. It was noted that "Judge Allen was an active member of the National Association for the Advancement of Colored People, long before entering the field of politics."[18]

Once again, neither party supported her. Nor did the bar association. Women's organizations strongly backed her, including conservative temperance and patriot groups.[19] Her few male allies supported her again from behind the scenes, including her former law partner Robb Bartholomew, appellate judge Willis Vickery, and Cleveland Democratic political boss Burr Gongwer.[20] The Cleveland newspapers endorsed her because she was a woman, was running as a nonpartisan, and "had the courage of her convictions and put human rights ahead of selfish ends." The *Plain Dealer* strongly supported her, writing: "This much is certain, however, in Judge Allen's case: that her service on the lower bench fully entitles her to aspire to the higher office and that the state judicial campaign will be put on a higher plane of discussion by her presence in it."[21] Supporters disagreed, however, on whether they were getting a judge who was a solid "conservative" or "liberal without being radical."[22]

Allen's election success was due in large part to the sisterhood and their money, time, and significant individual and collective efforts. As a biographer noted, "she was the women's woman."[23] She again had bipartisan support among women. The Republican Party tried to prevent its women from working for Allen's campaign and uninvited Allen from Republican events.[24] They sent U.S. Assistant Attorney General Mabel Walker Willebrandt, the highest-ranking woman lawyer in the nation, who was in charge of Prohibition enforcement, to Ohio to "halt Republican women" by preaching "undeviating loyalty to the party"—an attack Allen took personally and would never forget.[25] Some Republican women complied and opposed Allen's candidacy.[26] However, many other Republican women, including those in Cleveland and from the temperance movement, ignored this command and some resigned from the party.[27] Her friend Rose Moriarty was reprimanded by the party, while Toledo lawyer Vadae Meekison said she stacked anti-Allen literature in her basement rather than distribute it.[28] Filed expense reports showed that "Allen's campaign was by far the most expensive one among the judicial candidates," spending $5,714 ($110,000 today) while other candidates spent between $1,000 and $1,500, her money "coming mostly from small contributions from individual women."[29] A Cleveland newspaper noted the positive change in political campaigning that women candidates like Allen brought with their social and personable informal receptions, as opposed to the circus-like drinking halls of the male partisans.[30]

Allen both embraced and deflected the woman card. In her official campaign announcement to the press, she said, "I believe there are women's interests that should be represented, and there is a place for a woman on the supreme bench."[31] Her campaign appealed directly to newly enfranchised women voters on women's issues. The campaign sent letters to women voters throughout the state saying that a vote for Judge Allen was "of especial importance at this time" because proposed laws affecting property rights and the general status of women were currently being discussed in public bodies of the state. "These laws will no doubt come up to the supreme court for adjudication," where the court will decide whether the laws affecting women are valid, "and will virtually legislate for women," so women are "entitled to representation."[32] Social feminist Lillian Wald wrote to remind Allen that she hoped her time living in the settlement house would help her, as judge, appreciate realities for women and the poor.[33] Allen carefully proclaimed, though, that "she was running as an independent candidate, however, and not as a woman."[34] Supporters also walked this fine line between ignoring and highlighting her gender. Circuit judge and law professor Frederick Henry said this: "Irrespective of her sex, Judge Allen is thoroughly qualified to sit on the supreme bench. Her knowledge of law, her personal poise and her varied experience—judicial, professional and otherwise—render her peculiarly fit to be the first representative of the women lawyers of Ohio to occupy a seat on the bench of the court of last resort in this state."[35]

Allen was successful in the election as the only nonpartisan, coming in second of five candidates for two spots on the high court. Robert Day was the clear front-runner, known as a respected lawyer and common pleas judge; he was from a distinguished family of judges, as his father, Luther Day, was a former chief justice of the Ohio Supreme Court and his half-brother, William Day, a U.S. Supreme Court Justice.[36] The real battle was for the second position, and it was "a surprising upset" when Allen beat popular Republican incumbent and World War I general Benson Hough. Her victory was challenged, however, when attorney Edward Dempsey, former mayor of Cincinnati, "protested the issuance of a certificate of election to Allen" on grounds held by courts in other states that the Nineteenth Amendment right to vote did not include the right to hold office, but no one else joined in his widely publicized challenge.[37] The same election also saw the victory of Allen's friend Mary Grossman to the Cleveland Municipal Court, and Allen had assisted in the campaign.[38] Allen credited the "political courage" of the voters "who believed in women enough" to elect her and trust her to write decisions of constitutional magnitude.[39]

Judge Allen was sworn in at a joint ceremony for all fifty Ohio judges of common pleas and appellate courts. She was selected to give the address. Allen refused to delay taking the bench by a few weeks to allow the upcoming Democratic administration in Cleveland to appoint her common pleas replacement, already embracing the cloak of impartiality.[40] The aftermath of the election was "a veritable love fest," with "tumultuous applause" and standing ovations following her at appearances, and congratulatory letters and telegrams pouring in. She was welcomed by everyone but her new male colleagues, four of whom publicly snubbed her by skipping a reception in her honor.[41] The press equated her again with Shakespeare's woman lawyer Portia, but the label referenced a female character who only play-acted at the male role of lawyer and abandoned law for matrimony.[42] Allen instead preferred a comparison to Deborah, the biblical symbol of wisdom and the prophetess of ancient Israel who sat under a palm tree while all nations came to her for judgment.[43] Lower-court male judges were a little worried at this forthcoming judgment. One trial judge wrote, "I hope you will not treat us common pleas judges too poorly," and appellate Judge Vickery wrote, "I have reversed you when I thought you were wrong, and I suppose you will be able to return the compliment and reverse me when I am wrong."[44] During the 1922 campaign, manager Susan Rebhan had promised: "We are going to make her the first woman on the supreme court of the United States, about five years from now." Allen only smiled and said that it would be a long time before any woman was appointed to that court.[45]

Allen moved to Columbus in January 1923 to begin her term on the highest state court. She bought a large house in Clintonville north of downtown and the courthouse. She continued her practice of walking to work early each day. Her Victorian house was something special, featured in an article in *Better Homes and Gardens*, which also narrated Allen's family life.[46] Her parents, now in their seventies, came to live with her. Allen became the matriarchal head of the family, providing a home and financial support on her judge's salary of $8,500 ($150,000 today) to her parents, partner Susan attending Ohio State University law school, disabled brother Jack and his wife and daughter, and later widowed sister Esther Gaw, who moved for a new job as dean of women at Ohio State, and her son.[47] When unmarried women were criticized for working during the Depression for what was assumed to be mere pin money, thus taking men's jobs, Allen spoke out at a speech in Chicago, emphasizing that "it was the salary of the 'old maid'" like herself that kept homes going during financially difficult times. Her unscripted defense of spinsters went viral in the national media, though she tried to explain that "in some many ways, the so-called old maid is the man of the family, and in many cases, of more than one family."[48] It was a heavy role she took on even as she balanced the increased notoriety and workload of the high state court.

STARTING OFF WITH A BANG

At the start of her term, the papers trumpeted history being made as Allen "donned the black robes of judicial office" on a supreme court and became "the first woman in the world to sit as a judge in such a court."[49] Judge Allen began determined to make her mark on the court, taking on big cases and writing important decisions. The Ohio Supreme Court was a relatively busy court, typically producing 175 opinions per year, with 40 percent of those designated "per curiam," meaning written collectively and anonymously "by the court" rather than identified by individual judge.[50] During her eleven years on the state supreme court, Allen wrote 227 majority opinions, about twenty per year. She wrote fewer secondary opinions—three concurrences and twenty dissents, placing her third in numbers of dissents. In her first year, she penned sixteen majority opinions and four dissents on significant issues of constitutional interpretation, voting, municipal home rule, public schools, and labor.[51] These first opinions became some of her most respected decisions and helped cement her legacy of progressive constitutionalism.

Florence Allen was the middle child in a close-knit family committed to public service. Her father, Emir, was a state and federal legislator in Utah, while her mother, Corinne, led national and state organizations for suffrage and maternal rights. Her eldest sister, Esther, was a prominent violinist and later a professor and college administrator as dean of women at The Ohio State University. The Allen family (ca. 1898), left to right, front row: Clarence "Emir," Esther, Corinne Tuckerman; middle row: Clarence "Emir" Jr., John "Jack"; back row: Elizabeth, Florence, Helen. *The Western Reserve Historical Society, Cleveland, Ohio.*

After Allen graduated from New York University Law School in 1913, she said there was "no job in sight," because law firms refused to hire a woman. Undeterred, she put out her own shingle, starting a solo law practice with referrals from Legal Aid for low-income clients. A college sorority sister's husband, Robb O. Bartholomew, loaned her furniture and referred clients, later affiliating Allen with his firm. She made $24,000 in her first year of law practice. Allen Law Office, Cleveland, Ohio, 1914. T*he Western Reserve Historical Society, Cleveland, Ohio.*

Allen joined the activism of the final decade of the women's suffrage movement, working in the national office and campaigning on the ground in Ohio. In the dead of winter in February 1913, she and her law school roommate, Bertha Miller (right), were new recruits of the militant "General" Rosalie Jones, who led suffrage pilgrims on a protest hike from New York City to Washington, D.C. Caught here by press photographers outside of Burlington, New Jersey, the two and their group encountered harassment and violence along their route. *The Western Reserve Historical Society, Cleveland, Ohio.*

In this iconic photo that has come to represent the entirety of the women's movement for voting rights, Florence Allen, dressed in menswear, waves the flag in front of the Woman Suffrage Headquarters on Upper Euclid Avenue in Cleveland. During the summer of 1912, while on break from law school, Allen campaigned with national suffragists for an amendment to the Ohio Constitution granting women's suffrage. She traveled the state by train, trolley, and automobile through all eighty-eight counties, speaking from street corners, soapboxes, churches, and even a circus. *Library of Congress.*

Allen led a renewed campaign for women's suffrage in Ohio in 1914, using a new state constitutional amendment that allowed citizen initiatives by petition to place proposed amendments to the Ohio Constitution on the ballot. Now a lawyer, Allen traversed the state giving speeches, marching in parades, and trying to get signatures and votes. She had a difficult time, however, getting men to sign. The suffrage amendment was defeated more soundly than two years before, led by opposition from industrialists and the liquor industry. Left to right: Florence Allen, Elizabeth Hauser, and Greta Coleman counting suffrage petitions. *Library of Congress.*

Florence Allen was sworn in as judge of the Cuyahoga County Court of Common Pleas in Cleveland, Ohio, in January 1921. She made history as the first woman in the nation elected judge of a general jurisdiction trial court. In this first election after ratification of the Nineteenth Amendment granting women a constitutional right to vote, she ran as an independent, fueled by the bipartisan support of suffrage women and networks. Allen came in first, gaining more votes than the nine men running for the judicial office. *The Western Reserve Historical Society, Cleveland, Ohio.*

Allen dedicated her two years on the common pleas court to reforming court practices for ethics and fairness. During a sensationalized time of Prohibition and crime, Judge Allen came down hard on perjury, bribes, backlogs, and obstruction by lawyers. She criticized her judicial colleagues for shutting down the court for the summer months while witnesses and defendants languished in jail. And she publicly rejected the attempt of the male judges to create a new domestic relations court for her alone, criticizing their suggestion that women belonged only on a family court. Judges of the Cuyahoga County Court of Common Pleas, Second Annual Summer Picnic, June 30, 1921. *The Western Reserve Historical Society, Cleveland, Ohio.*

Allen was elected to the Ohio Supreme Court in 1922, the first woman in the country to serve on the highest bench in any state. She was the only Democrat on a conservative court that resisted implementation of the progressive amendments to the Ohio Constitution passed in 1912. She immediately went to work writing liberal decisions to uphold the reforms for voter initiative, labor rights, schools, and municipal home rule. Yet it was her dissents that would be recognized as the most powerful opinions, as they upheld free speech and political rights. Judge Florence E. Allen, Ohio Supreme Court, ca. 1923. *The Western Reserve Historical Society, Cleveland, Ohio.*

For most of Judge Allen's eleven years on the Ohio Supreme Court, her male colleagues blocked and dismissed her. They unfairly criticized her work, refused to assign her opinions of significance, and made fun of her boyish haircut. It was only in her final years on the court, after the election of a few friendly colleagues, that she began to find professional acceptance. Ohio Supreme Court, 1932. *Bowling Green State University Library, Center for Archival Collections.*

Allen believed that her activism for peace was her most important legacy. Motivated by the profound loss of both of her brothers in World War I, she became a public advocate against war, converting the suffrage organizations to the issue of peace. She led public protests like the Cleveland Peace Parade of 3,600 women and a few men on May 18, 1924, orchestrated by the new Women's Council for the Prevention of War, which she chaired. Her most significant contribution came as a lawyer advocating the "outlawry" of war through the use of international law to prohibit aggressive military action unless for self-defense. *The Western Reserve Historical Society, Cleveland, Ohio.*

Allen remained an internationalist her whole life, committed to the priority of international law for peace. She presented an influential speech, "Peace Through Justice," at the second International Bar Association Conference at the Hague in August 1948, one of only a few women featured. In the speech, she emphasized the need for the United Nations and the World Court to enforce new international norms against instigating war. *The Western Reserve Historical Society, Cleveland, Ohio.*

Allen ran for Congress twice as a Democrat, in the Senate primary in 1926 and as the party candidate for the House in 1932. Allen's platform was peace, Prohibition, good government, and human rights for every citizen. She enjoyed the freedom on the congressional campaign trail to speak her mind on policy matters. However, Allen lost both races. In between, she returned to the bench, running successfully for reelection to the Ohio Supreme Court. She is pictured here campaigning at Geauga Lake Park, Ohio, at a family day of forty thousand people sponsored by organized labor. *Cleveland Plain Dealer*, Sept. 4, 1928.

Top Allen's male colleagues on the Ohio Supreme Court did not welcome her to the bench. They publicly shunned her, refusing to attend a reception in honor of her historic first election. The men played golf without her, relegating her to ladies' luncheons with their wives. Yet years later, one colleague, Judge Thomas Jones, ironically inscribed this placard of the jurists to Allen as "my dear friend . . . in remembrance of our pleasant association as members" of the state's highest court. Ohio Supreme Court Judges, 1927. *The Western Reserve Historical Society, Cleveland, Ohio.*

Left Chief Justice Carrington Marshall (right) actively obstructed Allen's legacy on the Ohio Supreme Court. After her first year on the bench writing significant opinions of constitutional import, he tightly controlled the case assignment process to deny her jurisprudential impact while keeping many important cases for himself. Marshall created his own rules, including constructing a platform to raise his seat higher than those of his colleagues on the bench. Ohio Supreme Court Judges Robert Day, Florence Allen, and Chief Justice Carrington Marshall on the statehouse roof at the governor's inauguration. *Cleveland Plain Dealer*, Jan. 21, 1923.

Right None of the judges on the U.S. Court of Appeals for the Sixth Circuit favored Allen's appointment to the court. One refused to speak to her in deliberations, one took to his bed for days, others criticized minutiae and word counts in her opinions, and they declined to assign her difficult patent cases. When court was in session, the men all ate lunch together at the male-only University Club, excluding Allen from their debates and collegiality. Sixth Circuit Judges Charles Moorman, Charles Simons, and Xenophon Hicks and District Judge Fred Raymond, Detroit, Michigan, Dec. 8, 1937. © *Detroit Free Press via Imagn Images.*

President Franklin Roosevelt appointed Allen as the first woman federal appellate judge, nominating her to the U.S. Court of Appeals for the Sixth Circuit in March 1934 on her fiftieth birthday. Attorney General Homer Cummings emphasized that Allen was "not appointed because she was a woman." Instead, the administration merely ensured that she was not discounted because of her sex. Judge Florence Allen, U.S. Court of Appeals for the Sixth Circuit, 1938. *Library of Congress.*

Left Judge Allen's most famous case was *Tennessee Electric Power Company v. Tennessee Valley Authority*. Her decision validated the constitutionality of Roosevelt's New Deal economic legislation, allowing the government to sell electricity in competition with private companies. Opening day of the *TVA* trial was a national media event featuring, front and center, the only woman federal judge. The government lawyers were initially concerned about having a woman judge, but they quickly came to appreciate Allen, who took command in the courtroom and tolerated no posturing or gamesmanship to delay or obfuscate the case. Judges John Gore, Florence Allen, and John Martin at the *TVA* trial. "Federal Judges in T.V.A. Cause Celebre," *International News Photo*, Nov. 18, 1937.

Right Judge Allen remained the lone woman on the federal appellate bench for decades. After she retired, having served for twenty-five years, the federal appeals court remained entirely male for almost a decade, until Shirley Hufstedler was nominated to the Ninth Circuit by President Johnson. Another woman would not be appointed to the Sixth Circuit until 1979, when President Carter nominated conservative Michigan judge Cornelia Kennedy. Judge Florence Allen at the Sixth Circuit Judicial Conference, 1941. *Library and Archives of the U.S. Court of Appeals for the Sixth Circuit*.

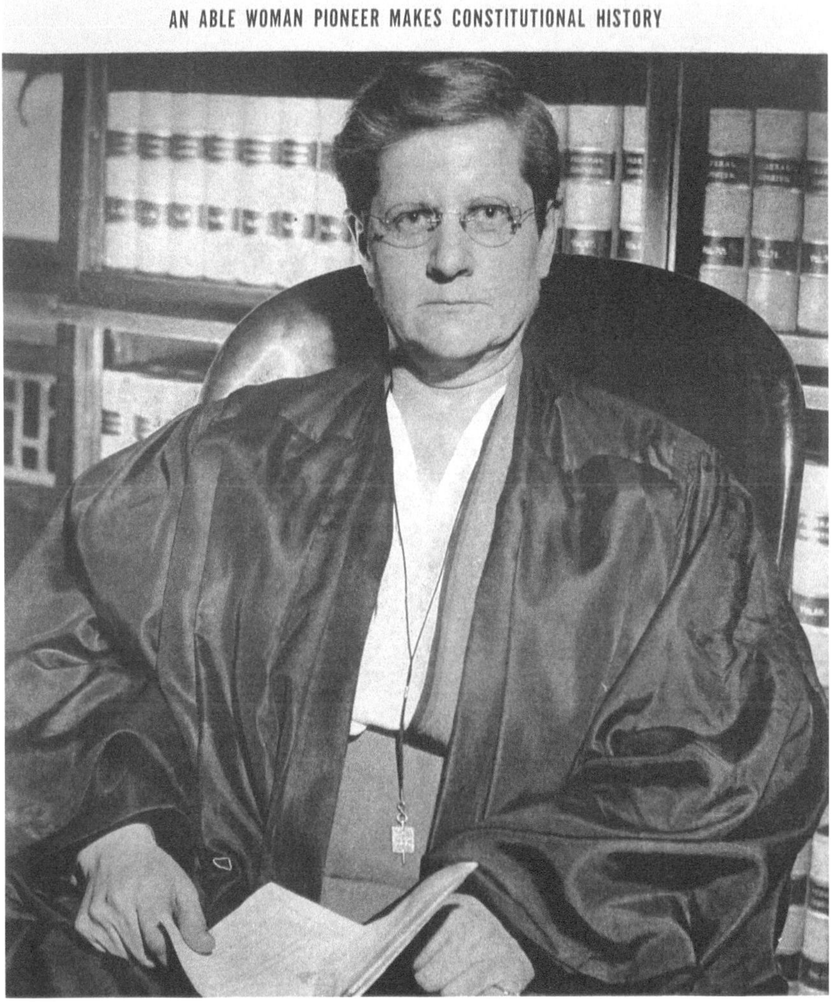

Allen came close to an appointment to the U.S. Supreme Court in January 1938. However, the pending *TVA* decision before her made the nomination look too much like a political bribe. The position went instead to Solicitor General Stanley Reed. But the press escalated its endorsements of Allen to be the first woman Justice. A week after the Reed announcement, *Life* magazine published this full-page portrait of Allen. The accompanying text read: "Because of the profound respect which Judge Allen has won by her ability and erudition, wiseacres would not be surprised if the precedent-breaking President were to choose her for this supreme distinction." "An Able Woman Pioneer Makes Constitutional History," *Life*, Jan. 24, 1938, 21.

Allen retired in 1959, at the age of seventy-five, after forty years of service. Her formal portrait commissioned for the federal courthouse was supported by a community of women: tax judge Marion Harron, D.C. federal district judge Burnita Shelton Matthews, the National Association of Women Lawyers, and Allen's personal community of partners, sisters, and nieces. In presenting the portrait, Chief Judge Thomas McAllister said that "the heart and mind of Florence Allen will flame for generations as a beacon for thousands of young women who will take their rightful place in government, in the practice of law, and in judicial service." *The Western Reserve Historical Society, Cleveland, Ohio.*

In her senior years, Allen dedicated her time to legal diplomacy for the rights of women internationally. She worked closely with the International Federation of Women Lawyers (Federación Internacional de Abogadas), founded in the aftermath of World War II when women were not welcome in the international bar associations. Allen traveled around the world on missions for the Federación, including a trip to Israel in 1950 to review the new country's religious regime of women's marital rights. Florence Allen with the International Federation of Women Lawyers, Athens, Greece, en route to Israel, 1950. *The Western Reserve Historical Society, Cleveland, Ohio.*

Florence Allen and Mary Pierce sent joint holiday greetings to their friends from what they called their "feminist retreat" in the farm country of Northeast Ohio. They depicted their lives enjoyed in the country relaxing, hiking, and playing with their many dogs. Friends visited them there often, treated to Florence's piano playing, clever games, and Mary's home cooking. Briar Patch Cottage, Waite Hill, Ohio, 1948. *The Western Reserve Historical Society, Cleveland, Ohio.*

Allen began her term as a challenger, dissenting in her first official decision. Her dissents would be called "the outstanding events of her judicial career" on the state bench, where she "dared to disagree with her colleagues" and "stand alone."[52] In this first case about caps on damages for wrongful death, she voted against her new colleagues' restrictive interpretation of the state constitution denying recovery of mental distress damages for the death of a ten-year-old child.[53] The text of a 1912 amendment to the Ohio Constitution expressly provided that "the amount of damages" for wrongful death "shall not be limited by law."[54] The majority interpreted the constitution narrowly to apply only to economic damages, relying on common law precedent and a historical state statutory prohibition excluding non-pecuniary emotional damages, even though the amendment intentionally changed those laws.

Allen's first written majority opinion, in the *Reutener* voting case, upheld Cleveland's "radically different system" of proportional representation, also interpreting a new provision of the state constitution establishing municipal power of home rule.[55] The decision drew scrutiny and criticism for its novelty of being the first written by a woman. Reports found her writing surprisingly satisfactory, with a "readable style," "sureness of tone," and abundance of citation without overload, while avoiding "involutions and convolutions"—though they couldn't resist mentioning pedantically her split infinitives and misuse of *shall.* Allen brushed it off, saying that "the writing of supreme court decisions by women, it would seem, lost all its ominous and unusual aspects before it began."[56] Allen issued a second voting decision that same year, dissenting in the *Noctor* case awarding a city council election to a Republican candidate where there was an error on the ballot, listing the Democratic candidate's name as both Democrat and independent. She penned a long and impassioned dissent protecting the historical, fundamental right of the voter to choose their candidate and not letting that constitutional right be infringed by a technical error.[57]

Judge Allen's progressive values shone through in these first-year cases supporting constitutional rights and community values. She wrote multiple decisions on public schools and labor—issues important to social feminists and advanced by her reform-minded father in the state legislature in Utah. Public schools, she wrote, are "a matter of grave public concern" of the "utmost importance" to the coming race, as required by "the moral sense of the community."[58] Her decision in *Miller v. Korns* upholding the constitutionality of legislation distributing funds for public schools was pivotal seventy-five years later in the Ohio Supreme Court's landmark decision in *DeRolph v. State* finding a right to an efficient and effective public education system and ordering legislative taxation reform.[59] She also upheld teachers' right to a retirement pension, legislation that had been invalidated prior to the major amendments to the Ohio Constitution passed in 1912.[60]

Allen's decisions generally endorsed labor unions. In a key early case, Allen authored a long, detailed opinion for a unanimous court in *La France Electric Construction & Supply Co. v. International Brotherhood of Electrical Workers* upholding a broad right of employees to strike and picket under the labor laws, subject to restrictions on violence or illegal interference with the employer's business.[61] In another important labor case, *Ohio Automatic Sprinkler v. Fender*, Allen interpreted workers' compensation laws to allow separate damages under tort law, thereby allowing employee Hannah Fender to recover for the amputation of her thumb from inadequately protected machinery.[62] In so ruling, Allen overturned two prior decisions that conservatively refused to interpret the legislation for workers, a result sought by state progressive reforms. The *Fender* decision split the court four to three along political lines, which Allen said was "probably as tense a conflict as I had to deal with during my eleven years in the Supreme Court of Ohio."[63]

SIDELINED ON THE STATE COURT

Allen's initial proactive progressive impact, however, did not last. After her impressive start in the first year, Allen was assigned less important cases. She was blocked by the coercive control of Chief Justice Carrington Marshall, who arbitrarily used his discretion to assign cases and keep the most significant ones for himself. Marshall tightly controlled opinion writing, penning two and sometimes three times as many opinions as his colleagues. In some years he wrote forty opinions while others wrote around six, with Allen usually authoring the second greatest number of opinions at around twenty, vying for influence and development of the law. Marshall seemed threatened by Allen's capabilities, viewing himself as the intellectual heavyweight on the court. The conservative judge also feared that Allen's liberal views were creeping into the state's jurisprudence. Marshall was chief for all but one year of Allen's tenure, which she vehemently believed prevented her from making a bigger impact on the court.

Allen's assigned opinions became restricted to routine, bread-and-butter cases of individual contract, tort, and property with little precedential value beyond the parties to the dispute. Personal injury, negligence, wills, and liens dominated her daily work. There were automobile accidents, wandering horses, dog bites, and a spectator hit by a baseball at a Cincinnati Reds game.[64] And there were an inordinate number of industry challenges to government regulation of motor transport as cars, buses, streetcars, trucks, and railroads battled for control of the roadways.[65] Allen later tried to put a positive spin on these "run-of-the-mine civil cases," saying they went beyond the basic "Whose cow was it?" because they entered "new and unexplored domains of the law" arising from industrialization of the automobile, rubber, and steel manufacturers concentrated in Ohio and the state's new efforts at economic regulation.[66] Yet they raised few novel or complex issues of law and merely sought final adjudication of an interpersonal monetary dispute.

Allen did use the routine cases as opportunities to insist strictly on fair process. Her rulings mandated that all legal and state actors follow the rules of fair play in the legal process and harshly punished any cheating of the system.[67] She voted against unfair practices involving the government, such as a city official defrauding constituents, public utilities padding values with fictitious items, and a public telephone company overcharging its subsidiary. From these decisions, it was reported that Judge Allen "condones no hair-splitting when it comes to questions of social import."[68] Allen followed these same strict rules of ethics for herself—for example, when disqualifying herself from a case brought by the Cuyahoga County Court of Common Pleas judges regarding salaries for years she was on the court.[69] She intended this due process concern to reform the work of the court, serving on the Judicial Council convened to improve and streamline the administration and procedures of the court.[70]

Allen's dissatisfaction on the court worsened the longer she was on the bench. She began to disengage by abstaining from votes, recording neither agreement nor dissent with the opinion. She gave up on persuading her colleagues on the merits and distanced herself from controversial issues.

Significantly, Allen did not seize the opportunity to add her voice to the few cases of women's equality that came before her on the Ohio Supreme Court. Two cases challenged women's eligibility to serve as jurors, an issue of vital importance to Allen at the trial court and in the suffrage movement, yet she issued no opinion or concurrence in the court's decision easily affirming women's political rights.[71] She may have deferred to her male colleagues as a politically more valuable act that would not be discounted as merely a woman voting for women. Allen remained silent as well in a case of gendered distinctions in criminal sentencing that garnered national attention. In that case, *In re Brady*, Virginia Brady brought a federal Fourteenth Amendment equal protection challenge to the juvenile court's sentence for her misdemeanor of contributing to the delinquency of a minor because of the state statute that sentenced women, but not men, to indeterminate rather than fixed sentences, causing women to remain in jail indefinitely up to the statutory maximum.[72] Four male justices upheld the gender-differentiated law on grounds that an indeterminate sentence was reasonable to facilitate the specialized reform for women prisoners who needed "radically different" moral rehabilitation to restore their purity rather than the "masculine type" of punishment for men.[73] The court upheld the sentencing law under rational basis scrutiny because the maximum term for the delinquency crime was the same for both men and women. Allen recorded no vote in the case, signaling her opposition, yet she did not dissent or pen an opinion in this significant gender discrimination case.[74] She may have been conflicted because, three years earlier in a similar case, *In re Fenwick*, she had voted to uphold the gendered sentencing law, where the court's rationale praised the progressive and social feminist reform of separate women's prisons for safety and reformation.[75] However, the court's decision in *Brady* may have been a step too far for her vote, as it explicitly endorsed women's natural differences. Courts did not overrule this line of cases of women's discriminatory indeterminate sentences until 1968, though Allen could have weighed in much earlier.[76]

The women's case Judge Allen did become known for, she said with humor as well as distress, was the case of a wife suing her husband's paramour for alienation of affection. The salacious case of *Snedaker v. King* enjoining the paramour's romantic actions gained national attention as a woman's catfight refereed by a woman judge. It titillated the public with its details of the adulterous affair.[77] The opinion, Allen explained, "was extensively quoted by professors in law schools throughout the country," for the "combination of the interesting case and of a woman judge delivering herself of outspoken views as to how to handle a triangle," which was "too much for the law professors to resist."[78] Grace King had sued Jessie Snedaker for five years of "wickedly, secretly, stealthily, and maliciously" causing King's husband, Homer, to dislike her. The dissent by Chief Justice Marshall called Snedaker a "vampire." The trial court had issued a broad injunction perpetually enjoining the paramour and her agents from going anywhere near Homer King, communicating with him, or interfering with his love for his wife in any way. The Ohio Supreme Court divided, with four justices reversing the injunction and two dissenting. The majority in its brief per curiam opinion considered the case a simple one of equity jurisdiction, finding the order to be an "extreme," "drastic" injunction that went too far in restraining personal relations and would be difficult to enforce. Judge Allen wrote a concurrence, noting the practical difficulties of enforcement of such an expansive injunction given the geography of the small Appalachian town where the parties lived and the need for testimony of the lovers in any contempt hearing. She emphasized she was not condoning the paramour's behavior, appreciating that the decision on the merits alone imposed a shaming sanction. Yet ten years later, Jessie Snedaker married Homer King.

CONSTITUTIONAL RIGHTS AND POWER

Despite these barriers from court administration, Judge Allen fought to carve out a record of constitutional jurisprudence. She succeeded in building a legacy of progressive opinions that expanded the governmental power of the state and municipalities. Her strong belief in public law and the governance of elected officials for social and economic welfare would guide her decisions on the state court, and later would extend to her views of expansive federal power under the New Deal. She also crafted opinions endorsing individuals' constitutional civil rights.

In the area of institutional powers, Judge Allen consistently upheld the sovereignty of municipal power of home rule, believing strongly in this expansive state constitutional power and having studied the issue theoretically and politically. She upheld municipal power to regulate utilities, take property through eminent domain, and regulate speed in a school zone.[79] She refused to vote in favor of usurpation of this local legislative power by the probate courts for park districts, though the U.S. Supreme Court disagreed and upheld the transfer to judicial power.[80] Allen's most long-lasting decision on municipal power was *Pritz v. Messer*, a well-known decision that enlarged city zoning authority.[81] Courts had limited cities' zoning power to only nuisances like slaughterhouses and gunpowder industries. Allen expanded that power to regulate geographic zones in the city generally, including for commercial reasons, based on the state's police power to regulate for public welfare, initiating a new trend in zoning law. Her holding in *Pritz* was mirrored one year later by the U.S. Supreme Court ruling in *Village of Euclid v. Ambler Realty Company*, which similarly upheld the constitutionality of broad zoning under an Ohio building law, rejecting a challenge by attorney Newton Baker.[82]

Judge Allen's state decisions on constitutional rights in the civil context included multiple issues of voting rights and a significant case on free speech. Her voting opinions demonstrate a pattern of strong views endorsing voting rights in all varieties of contexts. This is not surprising, as Allen, a former suffrage advocate and lawyer, knew the importance of the voting right and the powers that worked to disenfranchise public electors. In addition to her first-year opinions in *Reutener* upholding proportional voting and *Noctor* regarding a ballot error, she wrote five other key opinions on voting, several of them dissents. She wrote opinions upholding the legality of voting machines, a politically charged issue, and strictly requiring publication notice of the date of elections, which together reinforced the election right entrusted to the individual citizen.[83] In a case limiting the subjects for voter initiative, *Smith v. City of Fremont*, Allen penned a long dissent criticizing the court for impermissibly infringing on the sacred state rights of citizen action, a centerpiece of the progressive constitutional reform.[84] This *Fremont* dissent received among the most "favorable comments from Ohio lawyers" of all her decisions. She signed on in another closely divided case to a jointly authored dissent that would have permitted the Progressive Political Action Committee chaired by her Cleveland friend, Marie Wing, to be authorized for election by petition exception rather than statute.[85] And Allen was the sole dissent in support of Democratic candidates who had been disqualified by the Board of Elections for having voted in some Republican primaries, emphatic that the court should protect the "freedom of candidacy."[86] All these decisions show Allen's strong commitment to fair elections and harsh criticisms of "how far the courts have gone in ceasing to protect purity of elections."[87]

STILL TOUGH ON CRIME

Judge Allen also had the opportunity to continue her record of decisions that were tough on crime, harkening back to her prosecutor days and trials against Mafia defendants and corrupt judges. Yet she displayed a balanced approach to justice in criminal cases, insisting on fair process for criminal defendants while judging them strictly and moralistically for criminality. She wrote decisions endorsing the "fundamental right" of defendants to fully defend themselves in Prohibition hearings.[88] She upheld the right to consult with attorneys in prison.[89] And she upheld an indigent criminal defendant's right to plead an insanity defense and obtain a psychiatric "alienist" evaluation, and thereby overturn a sentence to death by electric chair, even in the heinous case of a defendant who had murdered a woman by throwing gasoline and lighting her on fire.[90] Judge Allen had no patience for tactical game playing and rejected a criminal defense attorney's demand for a bill of particulars, finding no such state requirement, excoriating the lawyer for his "fishing expedition" and trying to "multiply the technicalities by which a defendant may postpone the day of trial."[91]

Judge Allen saw cases of notorious criminals charged with Mafia and bootlegging activities, as she had during her short time on the common pleas court. And she continued to be fearless and tough on these criminals. In *Porello v. State*, she supported the government's warrantless search of a defendant's car revealing a gun, rejecting his defense of the constitutional right to bear arms.[92] That right under the state constitution, she said, was for defense and security, and she found "little soundness" in its extension to a car parked outside a restaurant at three in the morning. Allen admitted to a reporter during the case that she carried a gun in her car.[93] However, she explained in *Porello*, the right included a duty to not exercise it to the "annoyance and terror and danger of its citizens." The defendant, Rosario Porello, was one of seven brothers of a Mafia family engaged in hostilities against rival Mafia families in Cleveland over control of bootlegging and gambling. Having served fourteen months on the weapons charge affirmed by Allen, he was gunned down while playing cards in a cigar shop the following year.[94]

In another scandalous case, *In re Remus*, Allen dissented when the court, in a rare split of four to three, granted habeas corpus to release George Remus from an insane asylum, finding him restored to reason.[95] Remus, who had murdered his wife in cold blood, claimed "transitory insanity." Known as the "king of the bootleggers" and the "master mind of one of the most famous whisky rings in the United States" during Prohibition, Remus had made a fortune from illegal and legal "medicinal" liquor as a one-time pharmacist. A modern bourbon brand now bears his name and likeness. In Gatsby-esque grandeur, Remus threw elaborate parties, including one New Year's Eve party where "every guest found a $1,000 bill under the dinner plate, the men all got stick pins and gold watches as gifts, and the women each received brand-new Pontiac automobiles." Even in jail, he threw a lavish party for the employees and prisoners.[96]

Newly appointed federal Prohibition prosecutor Mabel Walker Willebrandt wanted to bring Remus down, flaunting as he did his criminality and the acquiescence of federal authorities.[97] She assigned her best federal investigator, Franklin Dodge, to the case, and Remus was soon arrested by federal agents for violation of the Prohibition Volstead Act and served two years in a federal penitentiary. While he was in prison, his wife, Imogene Holmes, began an affair with Agent Dodge, and they took control of her husband's fortune by selling off all his properties and possessions, which Remus had transferred to her to protect his assets. She then filed for divorce, tried to get him deported back to Germany, and hired a hit man. Remus publicly contested his wife's divorce suit, reminding everyone that he "picked her up out of the gutter" from her former days as a maid in his office. He began to stalk his wife, following her one day in a taxi as she left her hotel, resulting in a chaotic car chase through morning rush hour that ended at a park, where he ran after her on foot to a gazebo where he shot her point blank, while his nineteen-year-old stepdaughter watched in horror from the car.[98]

Remus, an attorney, represented himself at trial. He was acquitted on grounds of temporary insanity and sentenced to an asylum. Six weeks later, he petitioned for release, claiming he was "returned to reason." After a second rehearing, his petition was granted, freeing him from prison and absolving him of any further incarceration.[99] A split majority of the Ohio Supreme Court upheld the release, deferring to the question of fact regarding sanity even if it was an "unpopular decision." Judge Allen was incensed, writing in dissent that there was "not a syllabus of proof" in the record that Remus had been restored to sanity in a few short months, clearly through his "legal chicanery." She did not change the outcome, but she earned favorable media endorsements in her next campaign for the court that fall.[100]

SEEKING REELECTION

Despite these glimmers of interesting and impactful decisions, Judge Allen was uninspired by the routine work of the court. From the start, she was disillusioned with the work of the supreme court, in stark contrast to the energy she had devoted to her role on the trial court. She instead diverted her reform energies to public service engagement. She increased her public speaking on women's rights and peace and traveled extensively for public service and bar association presentations, including big trips to London and Europe with her father and Susan Rebhan. Allen was searching for opportunities to effectuate her commitment to making a difference in the world around her by influencing policy.[101] In 1926, while still on the Ohio Supreme Court, she ran for U.S. Congress. Her resounding defeat in the Senate Democratic primary cast doubt on whether she was still electable and a shadow over her ethics, as she was criticized for piercing the veil of judicial impartiality by campaigning as a Democrat.

In 1928, Allen ran for a second term on the Ohio Supreme Court. Her reelection was not a given in light of the intervening congressional defeat. Allen, however, won easily by a wide margin of 350,000 votes. The ballot again allowed multiple-choice voting for two of a group of six candidates.[102] Allen ran as a nonpartisan and won in the midst of another national Republican sweep of the 1928 elections that included the presidency and the Ohio governor's office.

In the court reelection campaign, Allen emphasized her bona fides as a sitting judge and her proven judicial abilities and experience.[103] She cited as most relevant her opinions on labor and worker's compensation, pandering to the powerful unions that had supported her.[104] Labor continued to back Allen, inviting her as a speaker at a family day for "friends of unionism" attended by forty thousand people at Geauga Lake Park, also featuring a speech by American Federation of Labor president William Green that was broadcast on the radio to millions.[105] As in past judicial elections, she ran as an independent. "Her politics," the *Cleveland Press* commented, "have been of the right sort. She is dependent upon a support based on confidence in her work, and attachment to her straightforward personality, rather than upon demagoguery and improper pledges, personal or public." Judge Allen's great following, it explained, is "built upon . . . the belief that no one can 'own' her."[106]

Allen now distanced herself from the women's movement. Her campaign literature featured quotes from newspaper editorials calling her "a woman who asks no odds because of her sex" and advocating her election "not because Florence Allen is a woman, but because she is an able judge and a great citizen."[107] Her campaign message was clear: "The Judge therefore makes no request for votes on the ground she is a woman. Although, that is having a strong appeal to the thousands of women voters in Ohio, through pride at having one of their number elevated to so high a position, she seeks a re-election on the far greater platform of efficiency in office and a faithful, conscientious discharge of duty, where justice was tempered with mercy only when a strict interpretation of law is not possible."[108] The papers followed this lead, saying that while many women were loyal to Judge Allen, "she is certainly no longer, if she ever was, a 'woman's candidate' in a narrow sense. She has a greater following among the best men of the state."[109] Allen featured these "best men" in her campaign—highlighting, for example, an influential endorsement from former U.S. Supreme Court Justice John Clarke, an Ohioan and a college classmate of her father's, that emphasized her merits: "Judge Allen is one of the most carefully educated judges that has ever been a member of our supreme court, she is studious, industrious, painstaking and patient in the performance of her judicial duties, and competent lawyers everywhere agree that her opinions are equal to any coming from that court in recent years. She is the first woman to hold so high a judicial office in our country, and she has proved herself so equal to its every requirement that she richly deserves re-election."[110]

The media supported Judge Allen as a success on the Ohio Supreme Court. One paper commented, in an article titled "Why Women Call Her Great," that "it is evident she holds her high position not because she has adopted the masculine viewpoint, but because her judicial mind commands the respect of men."[111] Yet rather than citing her judicial acumen, the article described the maternal appearance of her outdated hair, worn "in exactly the same fashion she followed in her teens," and how her dress matched her eyes and hung "comfortably on her rotund figure." Others saw a successful judge through gendered eyes while also respecting her accomplishments. Allen's true achievement on "behalf of women's rights" was not her mere election or presence on that court, "but her demonstration that women can keep pace with the professional achievements of men and still get along with them." The writer explained that "on the state supreme bench she has been a complete liberal; generally disagreeing with the conservative faction and yet never despairing of trying to win them, in court conferences, to the viewpoint that all laws must have been aimed at protecting the greatest number of people; and because she is known all over America for the militancy of her belief in the need for better protection of women who must work, and underprivileged children."[112]

CONTROVERSIAL OPINIONS

Late in Judge Allen's second term, in her last years on the court, she issued three controversial opinions. These decisions would continue to haunt her as they were used against her in appointment for the federal appellate court and consideration for the U.S. Supreme Court.[113] Moreover, they alienated political support from progressive groups like labor and Black organizations that had been her staunch supporters, for the trio of decisions seemed to betray her core principles.

The first decision was controversial for its radicalness. In *State v. Kassay*, Judge Allen dissented in favor of the communist defendant on grounds of First Amendment political free speech.[114] Her decision would be flagged in an FBI report as evidence of her potential extremist views and allegiance with an "ultra-radical communist element."[115] In the case, Paul Kassay was employed at an Akron airship hanger as a metal worker constructing a dirigible and was alleged to have threatened to loosen the rivets to sabotage the *USS Akron*, though he had no opportunity to act. In a split decision of five to two, a majority of the Ohio Supreme Court, in an opinion by Chief Justice Marshall, upheld the constitutionality of the state criminal syndication statute on grounds that the First Amendment applied only to the federal government and that Ohio's more limited free speech right allowed punishments for threats to safety. Allen wrote an important dissent "to add some further observations upon a case of so much moment to the liberties of the entire people, not only in Ohio, but throughout the United States." Her smart opinion explained that the law was "clearly unconstitutional" under both the federal and state constitutions, which distinguished protected speech from punishable violent action that creates a clear and present danger.[116] Allen criticized her Ohio colleagues who claimed that "the statute does not seek to punish academic and harmless discussion of the advantages of political and industrial reform. Perhaps it does not seek to, but it does." She wrote that "under the sweeping provisions of this act, even peaceful agitation against a law may well be considered a felony." Quoting a dissent by Justice Oliver Wendell Holmes, she concluded that "freedom of the press and of individual opinion, however markedly the views expressed differ from our own, are vital to our social progress." Allen's opinion foreshadowed the ultimate conclusion of the U.S. Supreme Court in the landmark case of *Brandenburg v. Ohio*, where it finally struck down the Ohio sedition law as unconstitutional when challenged by a Ku Klux Klan member.[117]

In the next controversial case, however, the problem was that Allen seemed to abandon her commitment to labor in contravention of her consistently liberal views. She joined a unanimous per curiam decision in *United District Heating v. State Office Building Commission* rejecting the government's argument that it could rescind a building contract bid when it learned the heating company was an open shop and did not employ exclusively union labor.[118] Unions were livid about the court's decision failing to enforce labor unions through closed shops. In a "hotly-contested" rehearing, Chief Justice Marshall took the opportunity to pen a dissent to politicize the issue and gain some points from labor, as he was running in a contentious reelection.[119] His dissent attacked the majority opinion, likely written by Allen, as it closely resembled her opinion in *La France* and its dicta about nondiscrimination against all workers and the right of businesses to avoid labor trouble. Labor felt betrayed, and thereafter the largest unions led by the president of the American Federation of Labor began to work actively against Allen's further election and appointment.[120]

The final controversial decision from her last year on the state court would remain a permanent stain on Allen's legacy and reputation. In *Doris Weaver v. Ohio State University*, she joined another unanimous per curiam decision that left college housing segregation in place and seemed to endorse social separation on the basis of race.[121] The opinion was labeled anonymous by the court, but Allen's diaries state that she "read the case" at conference, which she typically noted for cases she authored, and that she had "cleaned up all proof," further suggesting her authorship of the written decision.[122] Weaver challenged racial segregation in Ohio State's senior residential housing for an experiential home economics program, claiming a right to "equal residence opportunities." In this "Home Management House," twelve women students lived together to practice cooking and domestic management in a homelike environment. The university asserted that "it was not within their power to compel the people of one nationality or race to room with or live in such intimate relations as prayed for by the plaintiff with people of other races or nationalities, against their desires."[123]

The university had previously denied another Black student, Wilhelmina Styles, residency in the program in the first year of the experiential program on the grounds of "color and tradition." Styles completed the program through an inferior educational substitute of residing in a private home off campus with a Black family.[124] Doris Weaver could pass for white, which is why she was first mistakenly allowed to enroll in the residency program, until administrators learned she was Black and dropped her from the course. Chester Gillespie, a Black man newly elected as an Ohio legislator from Cleveland and a leading civil rights attorney, took up the cause demanding immediate integration and threatening the university with a loss of funds if it did not provide equal opportunity for Black students.[125] Weaver was then given the option to live in an apartment in the basement of the management house with the resident advisor, accessible by a separate entrance and having separate living and eating quarters, which she declined. Weaver completed her degree through a different class and continued at the university to earn a master's degree in chemistry, allowing her to teach home economics at the historically Black Wilberforce University, where Wilhelmina Styles also taught. But Weaver lost time and precious money in the delay of her occupation.[126]

The NAACP selected *Weaver* as a test case for its legal and political strategy to take on social discrimination in colleges, two decades before *Brown v. Board of Education*.[127] The Ohio Supreme Court issued a unanimous decision in which all judges, liberal and conservative, anonymously joined in agreement. The decision evaluated the operative Board of Trustees's regulations under the most deferential scrutiny, asking whether the housing rules were "reasonable, and not arbitrary."[128] It denied Weaver's claims of race discrimination on hyper-technical grounds, obtusely accepting the government's misleading depiction of the facts fumbled in admission at oral argument by plaintiff's counsel stating she had been offered a "compartment in the house" but turned it down. The court ignored the fact that this was a segregated offer, isolating Weaver from the collective living and group work of the program.[129] The court held that the student was not being denied equal opportunity but only "the social privilege of residing with white girl students and partaking in their family or communal life; of rooming, dining and sharing their common bath room and toilet facilities." Such "same social intercourse," it held, the "purely social relations of our citizens[,] cannot be enforced by law; nor were they intended to be regulated by our own laws or by the state and Federal Constitutions." It then quoted the "learned judge" from the U.S. Supreme Court's 1896 separate-but-equal case, *Plessy v. Ferguson*.[130] "The argument also assumes that social prejudices may be overcome by legislation, and that equal rights cannot be secured to the negro except by an enforced commingling of the two races. We cannot accept this proposition. If the two races are to meet upon terms of social equality it must be the result of natural affinities, a mutual appreciation of each other's merit and a voluntary consent of individuals." Law was "powerless to eradicate racial instincts or to abolish distinctions based upon physical differences, and the attempt to do so can only result in accentuating the difficulties of the present situation." The *Weaver* court added: "Were the case reversed, and had a white girl student, under the same circumstances, sought to compel social relations with a group of girls of another color we would feel compelled to deny her relief."[131] Allen parroted this exact phrasing when later called upon to defend her role in the case, relying like the court on an overly literal reading of the facts.[132] Her sister, Esther Gaw, was then dean of women students at Ohio State but did not publicly play a role in the case either as a defendant or as an advocate for the student.

The NAACP was outraged by the *Weaver* opinion. After the decision was announced, the organization called a mass meeting at which Weaver spoke, blaming the university faculty and administration for the discrimination rather than the students.[133] The NAACP argued that the *Weaver* decision was "contrary to the policy and the law of Ohio for the past fifty years" and decried the court's citation to the outdated racist decision of *Plessy*. It also excoriated the high court for improperly relying on an outdated 1870 Ohio case that was "rendered prior to the repeal of the 'black laws' of Ohio and was thus overruled by statute."[134]

The *Weaver* case became a lightning rod in Allen's consideration for the federal appellate court the following year. The NAACP now actively opposed her nomination. The organization also politically weaponized the case in a campaign to liberals, both Black and white, to "wreck the Democratic party in Ohio," appropriating Doris Weaver as a pawn.[135] Losing this support and that of labor, and "aware of the diminished organizational strength of her women supporters, Allen feared that she would not survive a third statewide election."[136] She was also questioning the value of continuing on the Ohio Supreme Court, where she was limited in her ability to influence the progressive development of the law or impact national policy. Allen began to lay the groundwork for an alternative path, whether that was through federal judicial appointment or legislative office in the U.S. Congress.

5 Legislating for Peace and Welfare

Constrained on the state supreme court, Allen sought other venues for progressive impact. She had a deep commitment to making the world a better place, both at home and abroad. As a leader of the women's suffrage movement, she knew that one key objective of enfranchisement had been to gain power in the legislative arena to transform the law by incorporating women lawmakers and including women's concerns of social welfare.[1] She wanted to contribute to what she identified as the issues of magnitude of her day: peace, war, Prohibition, and the Great Depression. These national problems of the time, Allen said, were to be solved by legislative, not judicial, action—which is why she thought she could "serve the people best in a legislative office."[2] After a few years on the Ohio Supreme Court, Allen pressed Democratic Party leaders to support her legislative candidacy. She ran for U.S. Congress twice: in the Democratic primary for Senate in 1926, and as a Democrat in the general election for the House of Representatives in 1932. She lost both times. The party did not assist Allen, first opposing her congressional candidacy and then sacrificing her in a losing district. Yet the partisan exposure gave Allen what she needed: an opportunity to speak on the national stage, on big issues, and secure party patronage and gravitas that would prove beneficial to a federal judicial appointment.[3]

The decade following women's enfranchisement initially saw a burst of political support for women's issues. Congress at first feared the influence of a unified bloc of twenty-six million new women voters who threatened to radically change politics by voting on moralistic grounds, uncontrolled by business and social allegiances of patronage.[4] The national legislature rushed to cater to women's prioritized interests.[5] Congress endorsed maternal welfare initiatives proposed by the Women's Joint Congressional Caucus, a conglomeration of twenty leading women's organizations representing two million women, led by Allen's former boss, suffragist Maud Wood Park. The Women's Caucus was called by some "the most powerful and highly organized lobby in Washington," and politicians clamored for its favor.[6] The caucus's initiatives for mother and child welfare had been percolating among women's groups and conformed to gender social norms of women in the family and thus were ripe for action. Congress quickly passed the Sheppard-Towner Maternity and Infancy Protection Act, the Cable Act reinstating married women's citizenship, the Child Labor Amendment, and authorization for women's prison reform, and later repealed the Economy Act of 1932 terminating married dual earners in the civil service.[7]

But just as quickly, Congress abandoned women's legislation. It was soon apparent that women would neither vote in large numbers nor vote uniformly for issues. Politicians realized they did not need women to maintain power and continued doing business in the old ways. Women were accused of squandering their vote, confirming the long-standing assumption that women were disinterested and unsuited for political action. Social barriers, like husbands' opposition and polling locations in raucous saloons and beer tents, also made some women reticent to vote. Women needed time to learn new political skills now that they were insiders in the "male sport" of politics—a system they had criticized and that did not welcome them.[8] Their developed power as outsiders to the partisan system, working externally through lobbying and administrative bureaus, was no longer effective. The women's movement, formally unified around suffrage, also splintered into numerous special interest organizations battling each other with different and often competing goals. Post-suffrage women's organizations advocated pacifism in the peace movement, voter education with the League of Women Voters, protective labor legislation with the social feminists, anti-lynching with Black leaders, and an Equal Rights Amendment (ERA) drafted by Alice Paul's National Woman's Party. Women's political influence was thus further diluted, as they divided and then were subsumed by the mainline parties.[9]

Experts proclaimed the Nineteenth Amendment a "failure." It was dubbed a great "nonevent" because women's vote made no difference to politics, and they had less political influence than they previously had. Allen defended women and the importance of women voters against the criticism of suffrage's failure. "Whether or not the ballot is exercised at all," she wrote, or "whether it is exercised foolishly, there is a potential power in the franchise which makes its holder more influential than the one who does not have the vote."[10] "The office-holder," she noted, now "views every woman as a possible voter, and does not dismiss her with the casual indifference which formerly so often was the rule." Citing research documenting women's substantive impact at the local level, Allen showed that women were making a significant difference, particularly in cities, but had "failed only in publicity!"[11]

Women demanded not only consideration of their concerns, but also a seat at the legislative table through elected office. Allen was part of this inaugural group of women who sought a national stage in Congress. At the time Allen contemplated running for office, fewer than ten women had served in the U.S. Congress.[12] The first woman representative, Jeannette Rankin, had been elected to the House in 1916, before national suffrage and soon after her home state of Montana adopted women's suffrage.[13] Rankin was a single woman, a progressive social feminist and suffragist who had worked with Allen on the ground in Ohio, and became renowned for her votes against U.S. entry to both world wars.[14] On the opposite front, another early representative, Alice Robertson of Oklahoma, was an anti-suffragist, a sixty-six-year-old Republican spinster who opposed all bills for women's rights or benefit.[15] The few other women in Congress were often substitutes for husbands or fathers who died in office, like the first woman senator, Hattie Caraway, a Democrat from Arkansas reelected in 1932. In 1924, the National Woman's Party mounted an extensive "Women for Congress" campaign designed to elect women to the House of Representatives as the first step toward the creation of a "woman's bloc," yet had little success.[16] One decade after passage of the

Nineteenth Amendment, less than 2 percent of legislators in both state and national chambers were women.[17] Politics remained a "male monopoly," and many women who entered political leadership had no gender consciousness, "no use for feminism," and "never bother with so-called women's measures or movements."[18]

Surprisingly, despite her long-standing identification with the women's movement, Allen as a legislative candidate distanced herself from designated women's issues. She did not use the national platform of her campaign to advance maternalists' proposals for mothers and children, even when a staffer drafted such recommended endorsements for her. She did not support her social feminist colleagues' advocacy of protective labor legislation of minimum wages and maximum hours for women. Nor did Allen publicly endorse the nascent movement for the ERA, introduced in Congress in 1923 as a blanket guarantee of gender equality.[19] Privately, however, Allen supported most all of these policies to help women. She highlighted the language of the ERA, when it was first proposed, by inscribing it on the inside cover of her diary for 1921. She was active in several women's organizations of lawyers and business professionals who actively worked for passage of the ERA. And she agreed with social feminists on the need for prison reform and protective legislation for working women, as evidenced in some of her judicial decisions. Yet Allen was politically astute, aware of the divisiveness of these issues among the newly enfranchised women, and the political ramifications of publicly aligning with one side over the other. She thus remained silent, taking the unexpected path of avoiding all women's issues.

Instead, Allen's campaign rhetoric featured a gender-neutral approach: "No longer need the achievements of women be viewed from a feminine angle alone. Now that the vote is won, the work of men and women is *blended*, as it should be, into a human whole."[20] Allen adopted instead the tenets of the Democratic Party's standard platform—against public corruption, opposing tariffs, supporting veterans' benefits, and proposing economic reform for the looming Depression.[21] For her party loyalty, Allen gained the strong endorsement of labor, which had not yet abandoned its allegiance to her. "Labor is not supporting Judge Florence Allen for the Senate because she is a woman," the large railroad union said. "Labor is supporting Judge Allen because she is comparably the best and biggest 'man' available for the job. In brains, character and experience, she towers head and shoulders above the field."[22]

Allen deviated from the Democratic Party, however, in supporting Prohibition enforcement and advocating peace. Global peace in the aftermath of the devastation of World War I was Allen's priority and her motivation for entering the congressional race. She would find, however, that the public was no longer interested in the issue of preventing war, given the preceding eight years of peace and isolationism. Instead, Prohibition and its repeal dominated their agenda. Allen's stubborn adherence to the moralism of Prohibition—in contradiction to her own Democratic Party—would prove to be her downfall.

OUTLAWRY OF WAR

With her fierce commitment to working for peace in the aftermath of the war, Allen initially tried to influence policy for peace through grassroots activism of protest, lobbying, and public speaking. Her peace activism began with a march in Cleveland in May 1915 in response to the German sinking of the passenger ship *Lusitania* that killed over one thousand people and triggered the eventual U.S. entry to the war after three years of isolation.[23] The next month, she wrote an op-ed in the *Plain Dealer*, amplifying the work of women and the "feminine mind" at the inaugural International Congress of Women at the Hague, where delegates had discussed world peace and a world court.[24]

Peace was a policy issue that continued to link Allen with women-specific initiatives. The issue of peace was becoming "as close to suffrage in unifying women's concern as any single issue," as many of Allen's former suffrage colleagues shifted to peace activism in light of global warfare.[25] Jane Addams led international organizations committed to pacifism, opposing war and advocating "peaceweaving" of social welfare work to ameliorate conditions that lead to war, which would earn her the Nobel Peace Prize. The Women's Peace Union wanted to enshrine disarmament and peace in a constitutional amendment making war illegal and prohibiting the use of funds for that purpose. Women were thought to be particularly suited for peace activism because their ethic of care allowed them to empathize with the human cost of war to women and children across borders.[26] With intensifying evangelism, Allen called on women to join the "world sisterhood" to eradicate war, using the "growing universal love of women for one another" to redirect the passion and energy of the "permanent sisterhood."[27]

Allen's commitment to peace intensified when she suffered the devastating loss of both of her brothers, who had enlisted when the U.S. entered World War I in 1917. Jack was then twenty-three and a student at Yale, and Emir was twenty-seven, having just graduated from Yale Law School and passed the California bar exam.[28] Emir was killed in action in July 1918 at the second battle of the Marne, hit by an exploding shell during repeated missions to rescue his men, heroism for which he posthumously received the Distinguished Service Cross. In December 1918, Jack was injured in action. He was a balloon observer and had been shot down and parachuted out four times; the last time, he hung in a tree for fifteen hours before rescue, which mentally incapacitated him. Jack returned home in 1919, but with serious post-traumatic stress disorder and possible nerve injury from the gas used in the war. He married and had one daughter, Corinne (Keenie), with whom Florence would grow quite close, and Keenie would name her own daughter after Florence. Jack was unable to hold down a job, lived with Florence, and often disappeared for long periods. He died in 1924 from blood poisoning after a minor injury.[29]

Impacted by this traumatic loss and harm to her brothers, Florence Allen resigned her position on the women's advisory committee to the Democratic National Committee, in protest over her opposition to the military draft.[30] In a letter to committee chair and family friend Homer Cummings, she stated that she was resigning because she was "unalterably opposed to compulsory military service in peacetime."[31] This defiance in support of her principles, however, threatened her developing political ties with the Democratic Party. It challenged the draft instituted by Wilson's secretary of war, Newton Baker. The papers made much of Allen's defection and the "persistent efforts on the part of the Democratic national committee" to "lasso" "the lady from Ohio" back into the fold.[32] Allen responded: "My decision is final. I agree with you that being a Democrat is more than skin-deep. There is something in me deeper than party affiliation, however, and that is the determination to fight the causes of war wherever I find them." Compulsory service, she said, "is so subversive of the whole structure of our democracy that I cannot understand how a Democrat can propose it." She added, "I do not consider that I have left the party. I have resigned a position in the party but I expect to work with the Democrats if, on the whole, they maintain Democratic principles."[33] Years later, in her autobiography, Allen commented on her resignation: "Perhaps I should have stayed in the office and fought compulsory service on the inside."[34] However, when the issue of military registration came before her thirty years later as a federal judge, Allen upheld the law in peacetime, finding sufficient necessity for it during the Cold War and rejecting the claim that religious beliefs absolved violations.[35]

In 1920, Allen began speaking publicly on peace and gravitated to the emerging legalistic movement for outlawry of war. "Outlawry" was the idea of using international law to prohibit aggressive, proactive war, permitting military action only for self-defense. It was a stark departure from existing international law that allowed a country to use aggressive military action as a legitimate diplomatic strategy. Outlawry, as a theory based on law, treaties, and codes, was a good fit for Allen's legal mind and training. The founder of the outlawry movement in 1921 was Salmon Levinson, a Chicago lawyer who had worked a little with Hull House. Florence Allen joined his American Committee for Outlawry of War early on and began to zealously advocate for this position.[36] Compared to the views of the women pacifists, outlawry was a moderate position; but compared to mainstream public opinion and emerging conservative "patriotism," it was a radical idea associated with socialism and communism.[37]

Allen's outlawry platform had three steps: Declare war a crime, codify that prohibition in international law, and establish a court with international jurisdiction to enforce it. She spent most of her speaking time on the "indispensable first step" of making war a crime.[38] She was passionate when speaking against war, using fiery language very different from her usual staid presentations. She said, for example, "We must crystalize the people's conviction into law and in law make deliberate aggressive mass-killing what it is in morals—international murder," and "It is not enough for us to regard war as the incalculable folly and tragedy of all time. We must go further and acknowledge that deliberate, premediated, aggressive war is the highest moral wrong which exists in civilization."[39] Responding to critics, she explained that outlawry of war, like homicide law generally, allowed narrow exceptions for self-defense. However, she admitted to peace audiences that "there never was a war which was started in self defense" and that "once we rid the world of aggressive wars, there will be no wars of self defense."

Outlawry was distinct from the movement for the League of Nations, which other women's peace groups supported. Allen opposed the League plan because she thought it was too weak and ineffective at preventing war, although she supported its limited measures in principle. The League of Nations was President Wilson's idea, established in the Treaty of Versailles ending World War I, for an international forum to provide security to member states by resolving international disputes by assembly, council, and world court through peacekeeping, arbitration, and sanctions. The United States, however, never ratified its own plan, as President Harding and Republicans opposed the League out of growing public isolationism and fear of entangling the nation in European wars at great financial cost. Allen's opposition relied on the work of her mentor, Frances Kellor, whose book *Security Against War* exposed the limits of the League of Nations and its World Court, which was a mere arbitration tribunal declaring a winner in conflicts without binding force of precedent to "lay down law."[40] Allen studied the issue carefully, observing the operation of the League of Nations during a trip to Europe.[41]

Publicly, Allen was careful to avoid a direct statement against the League, saying that due to judicial ethics, she could not "take any part in that controversy." U.S. Supreme Court Justice John Clarke, who was Allen's father's friend from Ohio, had resigned from the Court to advocate for the League of Nations, establishing a precedent that judicial ethics prohibited advocacy of this political position. Even though Allen, unlike Clarke, would not have had cases on this issue come before her on the state court, her public peace advocacy still drew censure, as she was criticized for abandoning her elected duties. One newspaper wrote, "It seems to be an unusual week when our own Judge Allen isn't away off somewhere, rallying her audiences to do something to outlaw war, bring all nations to brotherhood, or otherwise speed the advent of the new day, instead of helping the esteemed bar associations of Ohio to realize their dream of reform in Ohio judicial procedure."[42]

Allen would become one of the most recognized speakers on the topic of outlawry nationally. She would speak on the radio, reaching audiences across the country, have her message featured in the popular *Good Housekeeping* magazine, and have her words read into the Congressional Record.[43] Allen initiated her peace evangelism among friends, working to convince the newly formed League of Women Voters locally and nationally to adopt outlawry as its platform. The 1921 Cleveland Peace Plan endorsed Allen's outlawry idea and spun off a distinct peace organization. This separate group, the Women's Council for the Prevention of War and Promotion of Peace, named Allen its honorary chair. In that role, she led the Cleveland Peace Parade on May 18, 1924, followed by Marie Wing on a horse and 3,600 women (and a few men) from 250 women's organizations marching in thunderstorms and heavy rains.[44]

Allen also persuaded the national League of Women Voters to adopt outlawry as its platform beginning at its 1923 national convention in Iowa where she shared the podium and the spotlight with Herbert Hoover, then secretary of commerce, who supported an international court but opposed the League of Nations. The *New York Times* reported that Hoover was "put on the defensive before he started to speak" by the preceding speech by Allen demanding outlawry and calling the proposed court ineffectual; in response, he began his talk with an admonition to the two thousand women in attendance that they should "not be overcome 'by mere advocacy'" but should pursue "realizable ideals" through "practical government." The League of Women Voters then spun off its own peace organization, the Committee for the Causes and Cure of War, ultimately endorsing legalistic outlawry in response to Allen's speeches, rejecting suffrage leader Carrie Chapman Catt's broader vision of pacifism.[45]

Allen and the outlawry advocates believed that their theory of peace was validated when it emerged as the driving principle of the Kellogg-Briand Pact, signed in Paris in 1928. The peace agreement "made the war system illegal" by characterizing aggressive war as a crime and reversing the historical assumption of war as a legitimate strategy for resolving inter-country disputes.[46] At the time, the Pact was considered at best merely symbolic and innocuous, and at worst naive, childish, vacuous, and a waste of time. But today, the idea of "outlawing war only seems ridiculous to us because ours is a world in which it has already been outlawed."[47]

Scholars have shown how pivotal the Kellogg-Briand Pact was in shifting the international norms against aggressive war to those of the modern global order. They conclude that the Pact "was among the most transformative events of human history, one that has, ultimately, made our world far more peaceful." For example, its key principles provided the legal foundation for the prosecutions of Nazis at the Nuremberg trials.[48] Allen trumpeted women's role in creating the treaty. Kellogg-Briand, she said, "owes its very existence to the political support of women." When the U.S. balked at the idea, the women "covered the country with 14,000 meetings," successfully raising the visibility of the issue and demanding that their politicians enact the Pact.[49]

Allen continued throughout her life to be an internationalist, dedicated to using public advocacy and international law to secure peace.[50] In one notable example, she presented at the second conference of the International Bar Association Meeting at the Hague in 1948—the lone woman in a sea of men. Her influential speech "Peace Through Justice" emphasized the need for the World Court and the United Nations to enforce the new norms of outlawry principles, and lawyers' key role in that judicial process. "It is not an emotional exaggeration to say," she warned, "that atomic time is running out."[51] Always a vocal supporter of the United Nations as the only world organization dedicated to peace, Allen also offered constructive criticism in a book she authored, *The Treaty as an Instrument of Legislation*. She challenged the use of treaties for controlling U.S. law rather than operating as mere contracts and attacked the encroachment of specialized international agencies supplanting domestic American legislation. A reviewer noted that Allen was "a profound scholar of political science and international law," but the book was quickly out of print.[52]

Allen always believed that her most important legacy was her activism for peace and challenge to the "moral bankruptcy" of governments that caused war.[53] She preserved voluminous amounts of papers related to her outlawry activism, seeing historical value in preserving this record. NYU Law School recognized Allen's contribution to international law by establishing a professorship in her name awarded to an expert in international law, long held by Professor Gráinne de Búrca, a woman recognized as a leading scholar on European Union law.

A CONGRESSIONAL STAGE FOR JUDGE ALLEN

Since peace and the outlawing of war was Allen's primary objective, she chose to run for the U.S. Senate, which has a constitutional role in approving treaties and declaring war. She wanted to be able to speak out on political issues, but felt constrained in her judicial role by ethics of neutrality and nonpartisanship. Legislative office would give her a venue in which to speak her own views.

Allen first contemplated running for national office in 1922, early in her political career, but was convinced by state party leaders including Newton Baker to defer to the incumbent, Atlee Pomerene, and run for judge instead. Pomerene lost the election. The first woman candidate did, however, run for U.S. Senate that year when Allen's suffrage colleague, Virginia Green, one of the first women elected to the Cleveland School Board, ran as an independent, though she was soundly defeated.[54] Allen refused to abandon her ambition for a voice on the national stage. In 1925, Allen discussed running again with influential Democratic supporters and her father.[55] This time Baker initially encouraged her candidacy. Pomerene had decided not to run again, given his prior defeat and because his long career in politics was culminating in national notoriety as the prosecutor in the Teapot Dome bribery case, raising his hopes for a presidential run.

The women's rights community was thrilled that Pomerene was out because, as Allen explained, he "had won the hostility of the women leaders in Ohio by his bitter, discourteous and sarcastic opposition to their efforts to secure woman suffrage" and by withholding his one vote in the Senate to block the federal suffrage amendment.[56] And Allen had been one of his loudest public accusers.[57] With Pomerene out, she announced her intention to run in the primary and the Democratic Party endorsed her. Cleveland women's political organizer Bernice Pyke was a pivotal supporter behind the scenes along with her boss, Burr Gongwer.[58] Yet during the state convention in June, Democrats pressured Pomerene to reconsider and he agreed to run. Party politicos advised Allen to withdraw, to allow Pomerene to run uncontested in the primary, but she stayed in the race.[59] This set up a contentious internal battle for the Democratic primary.

Allen continued on, again without official party support and with a campaign run by women. Baker warned Allen that she couldn't win, but gave her a half-hearted endorsement praising her qualifications while canceling his planned address on her behalf.[60] He thought that her sacrifice of "burning the judicial bridge" might help with some voters, but that others like her "women friends" might prefer to keep her on the bench and thus vote against her for the Senate.[61] He had also advised her to resign from the bench before announcing her candidacy, based on lawyers' expressed misgivings that a conflict of interest presented an ethical problem and constitutional violation for judges engaging in politics.[62] The American Bar Association had just passed its first Canons of Judicial Ethics, stating that a judge "shall not engage in political or campaign activity inconsistent with independence, integrity or impartiality."[63] Allen consulted on the matter with Chief Justice Marshall and did not resign. She believed she could balance the obligations and trust of each position, and she depended on the income to support her extended family.[64]

Once again, Allen and Rebhan activated their grassroots women's network, including "flying squadrons" of Florence Allen Clubs that crossed the state and women law students at Ohio State, where Rebhan studied. However, this time, in a partisan race, they couldn't count on bipartisan women's support from Republicans. The National Woman's Party, in its national campaign initiative, backed Allen's race.[65] Allen worked almost around the clock, arriving at court early in the morning for her regular judicial duties, often staying up until four in the morning to read briefs for court, and then speaking for peace talks and campaign speeches during lunch, in the evenings, and on vacation days from the court.

As the challenger, Allen positioned herself as a critic of the status quo, running for the Senate because she was "interested in good government and a square deal for everybody." Her stated plank was outlawing war, supporting farmers and veterans, and enforcing Prohibition.[66] However, Allen presented much of her Senate campaign in moralistic, philosophical terms of "constitutionalism" rather than concrete proposals. She advocated a return to the "old standards" and "theory of government" expressed by the U.S. Constitution that "government had a moral responsibility to the people." "The government," she said, "should be used to maintain the human rights of every group, class, and citizen" to "establish justice, promote the general welfare, and insure domestic tranquility." Citing the Declaration of Independence, Allen used the sesquicentennial of that founding document to remind voters of the "no kings" core of American constitutional democracy. She pleaded with voters not to condone the pervasive corruption of public officials who had "reverted to sovereignty," failing to meet the basic standards of ethics and care "we demand in private life."[67]

Allen used her gender as an affirmative attribute in this race, trying to tap into her prior bipartisan support.[68] In a speech entitled "Why Should a Woman Be Elected to the Senate?," she answered that question by saying that women needed representation by their own sex because "women constitute one-half of the adult population of the country," and other women best "adequately expressed and protected" those women's concerns.[69] Representation of "women as a whole" by "capable, upright, and trained" women in Congress also helped women generally "become conscious" of their own political citizenship and "ownership in government."[70] Allen added that women provided a different voice, a "distinct contribution" and "viewpoint" that was "neither inferior to nor superior to that of man, but different, and therefore needing to be expressed." Supporters agreed, stating that with Judge Allen, "American women have at least one perfectly good chance to send to the Senate . . . a high-power woman of unquestioned ability and great dignity, and one who truly reflects the woman point of view."[71]

Allen concentrated much of her campaign on peace—the issue that brought her to seek legislative office. She advocated outlawry of war, denouncing the "so-called Christian nation" that "legalized murder," thus coming across as a radical. She used maternalist arguments to appeal to women voters, commenting that all women feel the question of war "with peculiar keenness" as mothers who have "borne the sons who have had to die in war," the young men sent to war by "old men" in Washington. Raising the specter of her brothers, she said that "if I had a son I couldn't look him in the face unless I had spoken and done everything in my power to stop war." This maternal approach earned her some male support, including that of one man who was impressed by the "large-endowed woman" who was so driven by her "spiritual force" to abandon motherhood to mother the world.[72] Most of Allen's audiences, however, were not interested in discussing war given the decade of peace. The topic was no longer a burning issue in a time of isolationism and anti-internationalism, and the academic issues of the League of Nations and outlawry that animated Allen bored her audiences. She seemed old-fashioned, a "figure of the past."[73]

Moreover, such radicalism of peace painted Allen as an antipatriotic "Red" during a time of reactionary politics and anticommunist witch hunts.[74] Antifeminist women's organizations extended the Red baiting into the decade after the first Red Scare, advocating an extreme nationalism of militarism and patriarchal power and stridently opposing women's peace and progressive reforms as antipatriotic. They accused feminist organizations and leaders of being agents or dupes of communism, all interconnected in a spider-like web.[75] The Daughters of the American Revolution (DAR) led the attack against Allen, even though she was one of them. A privileged club of upper-crust women claiming heritage traced to the Revolutionary founders, DAR had supported women's social legislation but, under new leadership, became a fringe reactionary group.[76] It blacklisted Allen because of her "un-American" pacifism, contacts with pacifists, and advocacy of outlawry. But Allen had been a member of DAR, deriving membership from her father's Puritan stock and revolutionary relative, Ethan Allen, and her mother was a charter member tracing her family back to the *Mayflower*.[77] Allen often spoke at their meetings, and DAR had endorsed her in prior elections. She was not too worried by the blacklisting, as she was in good company with others on the list including Justice Felix Frankfurter, Jane Addams, Roscoe Pound, the NAACP, and the Federal Council of Churches. In her next campaign, seeking reelection to the Ohio Supreme Court in 1928, Allen courted DAR with extra appearances and speeches at their meetings, and they easily forgave one of their own and leant her their support as they had earlier in her career.[78]

On the day of the election, a newspaper writer reported that "despite perfect weather," a light vote was expected for the primary because there were "no issues of importance at stake."[79] He said that the electorate had "shown nothing but apathy during the campaign," even with the candidacy of the "colorful bachelor woman." Allen reportedly spent $8,000 on her campaign, while the ex-senator Atlee Pomerene said he spent no more than $100 and had not been campaigning, "content to abide by the verdict of the people."

Allen lost the Democratic Senate primary by twenty thousand votes. She later called her run "a grave political mistake," though party leaders thought she had done well, as she lost only by a relatively small margin. Pomerene lost in the general election to the returning incumbent,

Republican Frank Willis. Nationally, it was another Republican landslide, reelecting President Calvin Coolidge. Feminist academic Sophonisba Breckinridge wrote that "Judge Allen's defeat was more than the failure of an individual candidate. It was a reverse in a cause which, to many women, they embodied"—seeking women in legislative office.[80] The legislative branch as the bastion of male power and privilege was proving to be one of the most difficult for women to infiltrate.[81]

CONGRESSIONAL AMBITION FOR THE HOUSE

Following her Senate loss, Allen returned to the bench, successfully reelected to the Ohio Supreme Court by a large margin.[82] However, she grew increasingly frustrated with the antagonistic situation in the court, with animosities escalating among her fellow judges over the assignment of opinions and ethical accusations. Allen still desired a larger national platform from which to impact important policies, unencumbered by the restraints of judicial office. She accepted an invitation from the Democratic Party to run for a House seat in 1932, convinced by Cleveland organizer Bernice Pyke.[83] It was a puzzling decision, as the House was not the forum that considered Allen's priorities of international war and treaties, which had motivated her prior run for the Senate. The House run also seemed to be a bad strategic move, unlikely to succeed because the district in which she ran, including the east side of Cleveland and its suburbs, was heavily Republican and the seat was held by a popular Republican incumbent, Chester Bolton. But Allen had won a large plurality of the votes in this district in her judicial reelection campaign, and the party thought she had a good chance of success to flip this district.

This time, Allen's campaign had the support of the new Women's Division of the Democratic National Committee and its leader, Molly Dewson. Dewson, called the first "female political boss," integrated women within the revitalized Democratic Party, winning places for women in politics and government on an unprecedented scale.[84] She was an effective political leader because she "learned to play the game by the men's rules while remaining connected to bases of female support in women's voluntary reform organizations and among prominent women in public life." The division sent several prominent national women politicians to speak on Allen's behalf, including Frances Perkins, soon to become the first woman cabinet member as Roosevelt's secretary of labor. It also scheduled Allen for four national radio talks, in which she would help the Democrats nationally by speaking on the topic of international trade and tariffs.

Allen was again criticized by the Cleveland Bar Association and the press for campaigning while in judicial office.[85] They said she should resign. Detractors alleged Allen was neglecting her judicial duties, improperly taking a judicial salary while out campaigning, and abandoning the "ideal fruit of a non-partisan judicial plan" that she had successfully envisioned. Allen responded with an official statement that there was no constitutional or ethical doubt that she had the right to campaign while in office, as judges routinely ran for higher office or reelection while on the bench. She emphasized that the work of the Ohio court would be "greatly hampered" by a resignation of a judge, in addition to the recent illness of one judge and the death of another, that would "throw the court into increasing confusion."[86] However, the intimation of ethical violations would rear its ugly head when Allen later sought federal court nomination.

Allen continued to work during the campaign because, as before, she needed the money. Finances were a heightened concern because, in addition to the usual money issues of supporting an extended household, Allen had incurred a colossal debt from a failed investment in the Alcazar Hotel. Susan Rebhan and Florence's former law partner Robb O. "Barth" Bartholomew purchased the Alcazar out of receivership in June 1929 for $854,200 ($15 million today)—just months before the Black Friday stock market crash.[87] The glamorous Alcazar, built in 1922 in the suburb of Cleveland Heights, was a 195-room apartment-style hotel, with Spanish architecture and an inner courtyard patio, that housed wealthy locals and celebrities and hosted dinners and weddings.[88] Susan may have pursued the investment for reasons related to campaign financing and recouping the costs of Florence's Senate and second judicial elections. It may have been made through inside connections and with some conflict of interest, as Barth was president of the Ohio State Mortgage Company. Florence then signed the notes as an accommodation maker or guarantor, which she later said was a "serious mistake" due to a "matter of friendship."[89] The fiasco led to a fissure and break in Susan and Florence's personal relationship. All hopes of financial return collapsed with the stock market crash in October 1929. The hotel went out of business and the bank foreclosed, leaving the investors liable. Both Susan and Barth died, leaving Florence singularly and fully responsible for repayment. She may have transferred other property to Mary Pierce to try to protect her assets from creditors, a possible fraudulent conveyance.[90] Allen's diaries are replete with worries over the Alcazar as she consults lawyers, her sisters, and friends about the problem.[91] The debt was eventually satisfied after the hotel was sold at foreclosure and Allen slowly paid off the balance over ten years.[92]

In her campaign for the House, Allen emphasized her ten years of judicial experience interpreting legislative statutes: "As to my training, there could be no better training for careful, conscientious legislative work than examining statutes for their defects," she said, with this judicial review giving her insight on how to better craft fair legislation.[93] This time, Allen downplayed the woman card, saying, "I have never believed, and I do not now believe that a woman should be elected to Congress just because she is a woman." "But," she added, "if a woman has governmental training and if she is competent and upright, I believe that she has some very definite contributions to make to our governmental life." She was willing to "sacrifice the higher salary and distinction of the Supreme Court in order to put the government training which the people have given her to the best use for the nation." Detractors targeted this judicial experience to defeat her, couching their opposition as a desire to keep Allen on the bench.[94]

As in the prior congressional campaign, Allen positioned herself as the candidate of change. Now, in the middle of the Great Depression, Allen argued, the "only hope for improving present conditions . . . is a drastic change in the government policy" of the past twelve years of Republican administration. Allen explained her candidacy as offering to "furnish leadership in a great national crisis."[95] She ran as an FDR Democrat, saying the Democratic platform "offers the greatest hope of real economic reconstruction."[96] Her platform followed the Democratic Party plank: for new economic legislation, against tariffs, and for getting people back to work. She was for the farmer and child nutrition, and for "equal rights to all and special privileges" to none of the corrupt business interests. Like the Democrats, she favored restriction of government expenses given the severe budgetary deficits, attacking the bloating of the Department of Commerce and the "mushroom growth of bureaucracy" for partisan gain. This opposition to administrative agencies, however, antagonized women's organizations that had long championed the Women's Bureau and Children's Bureau created by President Wilson as executive agencies in the Department of Labor. Allen dismissed these administrative agencies and "autocratic bureaucracy" as antidemocratic responses to the failures of the legislative process that violated separation of powers. Notes for her campaign, however, suggest she would have supported appropriations to the Children's Bureau advanced by the Democrats.[97] Despite this party loyalty, Allen couldn't let go of her convictions regarding peace and Prohibition; she kept talking about the politically obsolete issues of international goodwill, peace, and the gangster and the bootlegger.[98]

Allen lost the general election for the House of Representatives by nineteen thousand votes. Her opponent, the incumbent Bolton, was one of the few Republicans elected in a year that saw Democrats sweep the White House and Congress as Roosevelt was elected by a large margin. Even running as an FDR surrogate in a blue sweep wasn't enough to push Allen into office—because she was a woman who continued to hold tight to her old-fashioned views on Prohibition.

A REFERENDUM ON PROHIBITION

The sticking point in Allen's congressional campaigns was her stubborn and moralistic endorsement of Prohibition, which made her seem out of touch with voters. Despite all the issues candidate Allen wanted to discuss, her congressional candidacies were labeled by the national press as a "referendum on Prohibition."[99] It was the beginning of the end of Prohibition, as coalitions began to build for repeal. Allen's first Democratic primary was one of the earliest nationally to engage with the emerging opposition to Prohibition. Allen stuck with her strong support for enforcement of it, believing in the rule of law and in the feminist origins of temperance and Prohibition.[100] However, it was the Republican Party and President Hoover who politically supported the continued enforcement of Prohibition. Allen's endorsement of Prohibition thus made her a Democrat advocating the Republican policy.[101] It was that obstinate backing of Prohibition that cost Allen congressional office.

When directly asked about her position on Prohibition by voters or the press, Allen hedged, trying to evade the issue. She would reply, "I've repeatedly stated my position," and say that the "wet and dry question" was constantly being used as a "smoke screen" to distract from more pressing issues of foreign relations and the impending economic depression.[102] Her evasion jeopardized expected endorsements from temperance women as her lectures on the importance of the rule of law to prevent nullification of the Constitution failed to assure drys of her support.[103] Allen's reticence to endorse repeal doesn't seem to have been one of personal conviction, given that she was not a zealous teetotaler and imbibed an occasional drink of wine or beer.[104]

Allen's convictions seem to have been based in part on her experience on the state supreme court, where she strictly enforced the federal and state Volstead Acts prohibiting the sale of alcohol. In many cases, Allen had little sympathy for the defendants and ruled for the prosecution, rejecting ludicrous defenses offered by defendants.[105] So great was her commitment to Prohibition enforcement that she, along with the rest of the court, denied a challenge to the financing of municipal liquor courts by the payment of fines directly to the judge—a case reversed by the U.S. Supreme Court in *Tumey v. Ohio* as violating due process by allowing the judge to profit from a ruling.[106]

Allen's continued support of Prohibition was also due to her feminist understanding of Prohibition as a constitutional achievement of a broad mass movement of women, including the temperance and social feminists she had worked with in the suffrage movement.[107] Prohibition had prevailed with the strong national consensus in 1918 for an Eighteenth Amendment to the Constitution, won largely through the efforts of women's temperance groups.[108] Such groups as the Woman's Temperance Christian Union and the Anti-Saloon League had a deep history in Ohio. It was a feminist initiative, grounded in women's protective and moral challenge to domestic violence to regain "power over their lives within the home" through curbing the drinking that accelerated violence.[109] Prohibition was "concerned as much with overcoming the abuses of male power as with legally enshrining a Christian morality of temperance."[110]

Allen was keenly aware of these driving principles, and remembered all too well that strong opposition to women's suffrage had come from the liquor industry, and thus had trouble aligning herself with a political rival.

Prohibition enforcement was also female, as the "thankless task" of national enforcement under the Volstead Act had been placed in the hands of two women: first, briefly, Assistant Attorney General Annette Abbott Adams, the first woman appointed to that position; then, and primarily, her successor, Assistant Attorney General Mabel Walker Willebrandt.[111] Describing Prohibition as an "infant on the Justice Department's doorstep," Adams said that "as a woman I could not refuse to offer it shelter and neither did I want the men to think it was too big for me to undertake, so from the day of its christening, I mothered it." Willebrandt, who inherited the task of Prohibition prosecution from Addams, was not a temperance zealot, but rather a good trial lawyer and volunteer public defender from Los Angeles. As assistant attorney general, Willebrandt managed an office of more than one hundred staff and handled more than forty thousand cases per year. During her eight years in office, she submitted 278 cases for certiorari to the U.S. Supreme Court, and was fourth among members of the bar who had argued cases before the Court, a significant accomplishment when only a few women had admission to that bar. Yet Willebrandt encountered a hostile bench, especially newly appointed Justice James McReynolds, who objected publicly to the notion of women becoming attorneys and had a reputation for leaving the bench when female attorneys rose to argue their cases.[112] The Court upheld the full scope of the Prohibition law, yet defendants flaunted enforcement, and those in administration dismissed the little women trying to corral the boys. Yet Willebrandt and Adams also received accolades for the "man sized job" they had done "with as much ability as a man" in prosecuting dangerous criminal bootleggers and Mafia members, only reinforcing to Allen that Prohibition was an important avenue of women's success that should not be abandoned.

In 1932, Allen was still clinging to Prohibition. Yet virtually the entire country had moved on, seeing the writing on the wall that Prohibition was doomed for extinction. Even women converted to the repeal cause, fostered by the Women's Organization for National Prohibition Reform, created in 1929 by Republican National Committee leader Pauline Sabin.[113] The nonpartisan group flipped the narrative of home protection, previously used to argue for Prohibition to protect women from domestic violence, to a protection of women and the family from criminality and immorality fueled by liquor violations. The *Cleveland Press* and the *Plain Dealer* refused to endorse Allen in 1932, even though they had strongly supported her in the past. The *Plain Dealer* wrote, "We admire her liberal political attitude toward most public questions. Her position on prohibition, however, we think unsound and in a partisan sense illogical; she does not stand squarely on the national platform of her own party."[114] Democratic presidential candidate Franklin Roosevelt officially endorsed repeal of Prohibition at the June 1932 convention, as did his wife, social feminist Eleanor Roosevelt. All of Europe had already repealed the prohibition of alcohol, Finland being the last country to do so in 1931. Even the Republican Party abandoned oversight, pledging in its platform to return the enforcement power to the states. A coalition of big business, labor, intellectuals, and women, including former progressive supporters, had turned the tide, now opposing the law for its restrictions on personal liberty, link to organized crime, and taxation potential for the depressed national budget.[115]

As Prohibition became supremely unpopular and enforcement continued under the female direction of Mabel Willebrandt, it was easy for women to be the fall guy. Women's leadership made it easier to dismiss Prohibition as a giant failure—a naive moralistic experiment tried by unseasoned actors. At the end of 1933, one year after Allen's congressional campaign, Prohibition was eradicated by passage of the Twenty-First Amendment. Thus, the "only constitutional amendment to be repealed was an amendment engineered by a social movement led by women."[116]

Women saw Allen's loss as a harbinger of defeat for women lawmakers more existentially, demonstrating just how hard it was for women to break into the legislative arena. "It is clear," said an editorial, "that the barriers in the way of women being elected to any political office are almost insurmountable. The dominant political parties do not nominate women for political office if there is a real chance for winning. Political offices are the assets of the political machine. In general, they are too valuable to be given to women."[117]

Allen, however, was not too disappointed in the result. She noted to the national campaign chair that she had made a better showing in that

Republican district than any Democrat ever had in a presidential year. And she added that she was glad she had helped Roosevelt get elected through her campaigns and national radio speeches. This was perhaps the purpose of the campaign after all—national exposure from her own party—for Allen had "piled up some political chips" by sacrificing her current position to campaign for the national party in seeking a reversal of the past decade of Republican rule. Two weeks after the election, Allen went to New York to consult with her mentor Frances Kellor and Frances's partner, Mary Drier, close friends of now First Lady Eleanor Roosevelt, and there was "much talk of appointments." Allen had won after all, getting the attention of the national party that she needed for a federal judicial appointment.[118]

6 Challenging the Brethren

Gaining closer partisan identification through her runs for congressional office as a Democrat, Allen was now well placed for a political appointment to the federal court. In 1934, on her fiftieth birthday, President Roosevelt appointed Allen to the U.S. Court of Appeals for the Sixth Circuit. She became one of four judges then serving on the Sixth Circuit, one from each state in the circuit: Ohio, Michigan, Tennessee, and Kentucky. The court would expand to six judges during Allen's tenure, later growing to its current composition of sixteen. Allen would serve for twenty-five years on the federal bench, in the last year becoming the first woman jurist to serve as chief judge. The *Cincinnati Enquirer* repeated what had been said before, that Allen held such high judicial positions "not because she has adopted the masculine point of view, but because her judicial mind commands the respect of men."[1]

Women rejoiced at her appointment and packed the courtroom on the day of her inauguration. Judge Allen's office was filled with flowers sent by her supporters.[2] Dinners and banquets organized by women were held in her honor, celebrating this historic accomplishment of the first woman on the federal appellate court, the second highest appointment in the land.[3] The press documented the significance of this transformation "in the casting aside of the American tradition of keeping the various higher courts in masculine hands." One newspaper wrote, "Whether one approves or disapproves of such a drastic change in the status of womankind as a jurist," one must acknowledge "with felicitation the ability, education, and the assiduity of Judge Florence E. Allen."[4]

However, it was clear that most men did not welcome a woman to the courts. The Senate confirmed Allen's appointment favorably, but some on the reviewing Senate Judiciary Committee protested her nomination, and the chair from her home state of Utah "forwarded her name to the floor 'without enthusiasm.'"[5] The *Cincinnati Post* snidely greeted the new judge as a "temporary resident," hoping she would have a pleasant stay, reminding readers that the paper had endorsed a highly qualified male judge for the appointment rather than a mere "agreeable woman of fine capacity and genuine breadth of view."[6] Another paper ran an unflattering candid photo of Allen giving a maniacal laugh.[7]

On her first day on the federal bench, Allen portrayed confidence and graciously revealed none of the awkward undercurrent. She told the papers she "was perfectly at home" as she "sat down beside my colleagues and went to work and that's about all there was to it." She shared with reporters that she was "thrilled by the courtesy and consideration extended to her by her fellow judges and attaches of the court."[8] However, at best, Allen's male colleagues distanced themselves from her, aggravated with the breach of their male bastion. At worst, they ridiculed her, boycotted her appointment, and segregated her from important decision making, diminishing her potential impact on the court. Allen was familiar with these types of sexist slights from the judges. On the common pleas bench, reported the *New York Times*, "as the Woman Judge, she was not popular" because "this woman with her quiet manner" was a "new thing around the court house."[9] On the Ohio Supreme Court, her colleagues presented her with a surprise birthday cake only once in twelve years—on the day of her federal court nomination. Allen joked that they were celebrating her departure.[10]

Technical admission to the judiciary was not the same as belonging. Women were still outsiders, excluded from the collegial benefits of the male insiders. The social norms and prejudices of sex differences inadequately prepared men to work with women as equal colleagues.[11] Women like Florence Allen had to navigate this tightrope bias of walking a precarious, narrow line between the gendered societal expectations of women and the professional expectations for men and lawyers. Women judges were still seen as women first, society forcing them back into prescriptive stereotypes of caretaking nurturers. Allen encountered this when she was depicted as "Aunt Florence" by the press, a pleasant, "gracious homebody" who could "embroider a pillow case."[12] They clung to this gendered expectation even as Allen disabused them of her homemaking role, saying, "I don't cook or sew or shop, for the simple reason that I haven't the time or energy for these things, any more than the men judges have."[13] As one female reporter emphasized, Allen "is a judge, not a housekeeper, and the details of managing her home never cross her mind."[14] Allen's strategy for acceptance by the male establishment was assimilation—to act like men rather than appear too different or feminine in approach or persona. Men set the standard for what a good judge was: direct, assertive, formal, objective, dispassionate, and impersonal.

Despite trying to conform to existing masculine standards and do her job well, Allen attracted backlash and misogyny on the basis of her gender. Men were resistant to women joining the bench and did not accept it without pushback. Breaking barriers as the first woman judge meant being among the first to experience unleashed sexism and hostile work environments. Sexism operates in many forms, including explicit formal barriers like unequal pay, sidelining into separate and subordinate roles, implicit bias of discriminatory stereotypes and gendered incompetence, and microaggressions of seemingly small slights accumulating in death by a thousand cuts. Allen experienced all of these forms of sexism, littered throughout her years on the bench, on both the state and federal courts, which constrained her authority and contributions.[15]

SEXISM ON THE STATE COURT

The six male judges on the Ohio Supreme Court did not welcome their new female colleague. They were all significantly older than she; most were in their mid-fifties, some much older, while she was thirty-nine. Later, though, Allen noted tactfully that "there always is an adjustment when a new member enters a court," and that was simply magnified by her gender.

Days after Allen was first elected to the Ohio Supreme Court, she came to Columbus for a welcome reception with political dignitaries and fellow members of the court. The newspaper ran a prominent story, "Four Justices Fail to Greet Recruit," highlighting that most of the judges on the Ohio court shunned Allen by refusing to attend the reception: "Conspicuous by reason of their absence to-day were the four Justices who make up the majority of the Ohio Supreme Court."[16] Only Chief Justice Carrington Marshall and Judge R. M. Wanamaker "helped to welcome her," as "the other Supreme Court Justices refrained from attending." A few months later, at the inauguration of Governor Victor Donahey, a Democrat, Allen was pictured again with the chief, joined by the newly elected Judge Robert Day.[17] Both Day and Marshall did each, once, invite Allen to dinner, but Allen was more commonly invited to socialize with the judges' wives.[18] She noted one day on which the judges canceled the scheduled court conference and all the men played golf without her.[19]

Allen encountered an uncomfortable and hostile environment from the start of her term on the Ohio Supreme Court. On her first day hearing cases, Allen recounted how, when the judges retired to deliberation in the conference room, she was "was aware of a certain uneasiness among the men." She said to them, "While I don't smoke, myself . . . I shall be delighted if any of you will do so whenever he wishes," to which they responded by lighting up pipes and cigars.[20] Her diary notes that she asked a "pertinent" question on this first day, but only Judges Wanamaker and Day spoke to her.[21] The other associate judges, Edward Matthias, James Robinson, and Thomas Jones, the remaining part of the conservative "Big Four" that had dominated the court, refused to speak to her.[22] Allen reported that she clashed repeatedly with Chief Justice Marshall in these early days and immediately identified the "Marshall factions" on the court.[23] She appealed to her mentor and law partner Barth for advice on surviving the first week.[24] She initially tried to use persuasion to achieve consensus with her colleagues on the cases but quickly abandoned this effort. Her diary noted many incidences of strife: cases in which she "squabbled" with fellow judges, refused to agree with the vote, had to give in to the chief and "newcomer" Reynolds Kinkade, had judges "chew up" her opinion, or started a "row" over a legal issue.[25] Her diary repeatedly comments that "cases blow up" at conference and could not be resolved amicably.[26]

Allen had hoped for allegiance from the progressive Judge Wanamaker, who had run in alternate elections both as an independent and as a Republican. Early in her tenure, she had attended a Lincoln's Inn of Court lecture by Wanamaker and was inspired by his talk on identifying guiding principles for a judge's decision-making.[27] Yet the *New York Times* criticized Wanamaker's methodology: "Precedents meant nothing to him, many of his opinions being based on principle without resorting to authority. He did not permit himself to 'become lost in the labyrinths of the law nor stand upon mere precedents, however gray.'"[28] But Wanamaker rarely left his bed. He had been struggling with severe depression and skipped court hearings, voting only as necessary in tied cases. In Allen's second year on the court, Wanamaker was hospitalized with a nervous breakdown and "leapt to his death from the fourth floor of Mount Carmel Hospital."[29]

Allen wrangled with her fellow judge, James Robinson, who she said was a "high-tempered man," though a good lawyer and judge. He was "particularly outraged" at her election and "distinctly opposed to women in professional life."[30] Robinson was the great-grandfather of President George W. Bush on his mother's side. He was "built along conservative lines," a "gentleman" who "presented a most lovable phase of manhood," as an "out-of-doors man" who enjoyed hunting, guns, horses, dogs, and "fraternizing most agreeably with his fellow members of the bar."[31] Robinson unfairly called Allen out in an opinion for raising a new issue in dissent (a common practice), snidely commenting that "I do not concede the power of a nonconcurring judge to interpret into a decision that which the majority decision has not included."[32] Yet Robinson ruled for women's equality in several important cases, affirming women's right to serve on juries and dissenting in a referendum case that helped women's suffrage.[33]

Even after she had served many years on the court, Allen's colleagues could not resist personal jibes. When Allen cut her outdated long hair into a very short style, one of her fellow judges told her she looked like a football player. After the first haircut was "unsatisfactory and unbecoming," she quickly got a second, more "modish," "boyish bob" that was cut "soft around the face, shingled in the back." Her haircut drew media attention, as papers commented that Allen had long avoided the trend of the "bobbed hair epidemic" but had surprised her colleagues by returning from summer vacation having "cast aside the long chestnut-colored tresses." But there was "no statutory law," they reported, "on the subject of how a woman should wear her hair." Bobbed hair had been an identified subversive act of the female flappers, casting off the long hair of religious and Victorian meaning to embrace freedom and convenience. Allen, however, agonized over cutting her hair, believing that her classic coiled hair made her more dignified.[34] Papers made fun of Allen's plain appearance, downplaying her femininity, reporting that she had no mirrors in her home or courtroom.[35]

Allen was also slighted in the official record of the court. In volumes of the *Ohio Court Reports*, judges were often listed by gendered marital status, as "Miss Allen" or "Mr. Jones," rather than by the neutral convention of "Honorable," appropriately used at other times to grant her the same respect accorded to the male judges. Gender also trumped seniority in the official Ohio case reporters. Volumes during Allen's early years on the court randomized the order of judges each year in listing decisions by judge, but in later years, Allen always appeared last in the list, which was not by seniority or alphabetical order.

Then Allen discovered she was being paid less than her male colleagues. In her fourth year on the court, she noted in her diary: "Got salary."[36] Several months later, she noted: "Discussed salary raise." A week later, the diary mentions "Chief salary equalizations." It appears she had confronted Chief Justice Marshall about the unequal salary and successfully negotiated an equalization in pay. Allen was supporting a large extended family, and so the common explanation and assumption that women did not need the same salary as men to support others did not hold true. This experience fueled Allen's later outspokenness about the valuable economic role of spinster women and criticism of governmental policy that assumed it was extraneous.[37]

These mistreatments and microaggressions escalated to outright animosity on the Ohio Court when Allen pushed back against the unfair administrative practices of Chief Justice Marshall. Marshall was elected to the court three years before Allen and remained until her final year, thus controlling the administration of the court during most of Allen's tenure on the state bench. He was only the second chief justice elected after the 1912 reforms to the Ohio Constitution had changed the customary practice of rotating the administrative work of the court among all the judges to a new, specially elected chief.[38] His ego expanded to fill this new role. Chief Justice Marshall erected a pedestal for his court chair, physically "elevating his position on the bench above his associates," which "irked the other justices" for years. Fifteen years Allen's senior, Marshall was a Republican who had a general law practice in the small town of Zanesville.[39] The Ohio Supreme Court under Marshall's leadership was criticized for its splits—both splits in decisions (in an era of common unanimity) and "bitter differences" of personal opinion on administrative matters. Marshall used the opinion assignment power to give all the important cases to himself. He tightly controlled the assignments, blocking other judges from being able to share in influencing the development of law. Marshall envisioned himself the intellectual leader of the court, typically writing twice as many opinions as he allowed his colleagues, an average of forty to their ten and Allen's twenty.[40] He later wrote the multivolume *History of the Courts and Lawyers of Ohio* to solidify his reputation as a great jurist.

Allen's public revolt started when she wrote an opinion in a recusal case that implicated the chief justice. Marshall was "very angry" at Allen, perceiving the opinion as a personal attack. In *Turner v. Marshall,* the party had appealed to the chief to recuse the trial judge and assign a new judge to the case, which Marshall denied.[41] The party demanded recusal of the trial judge due to a significant conflict with his business and personal connections from having worked with the defendant bank and its attorney's firm. Allen agreed, overruling Chief Justice Marshall. In a divided, four-to-two opinion for the court, Allen wrote a terse opinion attacking the chief's judgment in what she called an "embarrassing case" where recusal was obvious under the facts, as "any one, whether consciously or unconsciously, would have a natural inclination to prejudge." She added that it was of "vital importance" for judges to maintain the appearance of impartiality. Chief Justice Marshall was offended that Allen's opinion insulted his intelligence as well as his ethical inclinations.[42]

Allen further antagonized Marshall and other judges in a second case where she called out her colleagues over a blatant political switch in votes on rehearing. In the original case, *Bowman v. Board of Commissioners of Allen County*, Judge Allen wrote the opinion for the six-to-one majority invalidating as unconstitutional a state law allowing taxation of an entire municipality for sewer improvements for only a small commercial or residential area. The decision had catastrophic financial effect, invalidating $210 million in tax bonds, leaving innocent stockholders holding meaningless stock during the height of the Great Depression and tanking the State of Ohio's credit. Judge Jones was the sole dissenter, arguing "vehemently and long against the decision." With millions at stake and sinking credit, the Ohio attorney general intervened, successfully petitioning for rehearing. The financial interests, Allen said, "appeared in such strength" to convince four of the judges to switch their vote on monetary, not legal, grounds. Allen and Robinson stayed true to their original vote. Allen then wrote the dissent in the revised decision, converting her original majority opinion to a minority view. With her opening line she implied there was no justifiable basis for the switch: "The case upon rehearing is even stronger against the validity of the bonds than it was upon the original hearing."[43]

The conflict over *Bowman* escalated when Chief Justice Marshall made a power grab and assigned the case to himself as writer. Jones, the original dissenter, wanted to write the new opinion, "having stood from the first as the court finally decided," wanting the opportunity to take the lead in explaining a "case of great public importance, not only in Ohio, but elsewhere." Allen "voiced open opposition to Marshall," saying that Jones, not Marshall, "should have the honor of writing an opinion for which he stood alone in the first instance." This was a particularly courteous overture by Allen, given that she had some personal frustration with Jones, who had written the sole dissent in her East Cleveland voting case years earlier opposing women's municipal suffrage.[44] The chief's "persistence in assigning such cases to himself resulted in a fiery session of the court." Yet, after all the drama, Marshall still wrote the opinion.[45]

Several months later, however, it was reported in the news that the judges had rebelled against the chief and Allen had led the mutiny. The judges voted unanimously against Marshall to remove the assignment authority from the chief, replacing it with a plan to "draw lots to determine who shall write the opinion." By then, all the allegiances on the court had shifted against Marshall. The action was said to "be the culmination of many years of bitter dissension" between the chief and associate justices.[46] Indeed, this "discord that reigned among the justices" had been in play for years, which Allen had noted immediately from her first days on the court, discerning that there was "trouble over assignments."[47]

Allen's final act was to make public her fight with the chief and his allies on the court. After a decade on the court, Allen cared less about collegiality and more about the fair administration of justice. When she announced she was running for Congress in 1932, she was pressed as to why she would resign from the bench—why someone "occupying the highest public office ever given to one of her sex, would consent to be a candidate for an office of far less public importance." She responded, quite frankly, that "she was 'tired' of having her utterances on matters of public import 'stifled' and 'sick' of the 'intolerable' situation in the court."[48] Modern studies have shown that women judges are less likely than their colleagues to receive opinion-writing assignments, ratifying Allen's concern with the gender bias limiting her work.[49] Allen noted in her diary that Marshall jibed back, giving speeches indirectly criticizing her pacifist views by arguing that "disarmament is fanatical."[50] Marshall also attacked her directly in the opinion in *United District Heating* about union closed shops, manufacturing a dissent not aligned with his views to draw negative political attention to Allen's antilabor ruling.[51]

This conflict ultimately cost Marshall his position on the court, as he lost reelection. As the *Cincinnati Times Star* explained in opposing his candidacy and endorsing his Democratic opponent, Cleveland Court of Common Pleas Judge Carl Weygandt, people cannot "count on a square deal in their courts of justice" if the judges do not have "a fine sense of fair play."[52] There was an unusual interest in the chief justice race, the paper said, as "the contest takes on dramatic interest because of the unusual character" of Marshall "and the storm of personal feeling which whirls about him." The article revealed: "For many years there has been a bitter feud among the Supreme Court. At the beginning, Judge Marshall had a number of them on his side. Gradually they have slipped away, until today all of the judges of the Supreme Court are hostile to him." "Some of them," it emphasized for effect, "are bitterly hostile." "Florence Allen, the capable and straight-thinking woman member of the bench," the paper revealed, "is now one of his outspoken critics." It concluded: "The sharp division of personal feeling in the Supreme Court has interfered with the efficiency of that court. The situation is preposterous."

Ironically, the chief justice's daughter, suffragist Constance Marshall, had previously written a glowing account of Allen's life and career, contradicting her father's indictment of the woman jurist.[53] Constance's portrayal seemed to appreciate the difficulties of a woman serving on a court of men—including her father: "Probably the most heinous crime of which a woman judge could be guilty, aside from making false decisions, would be to succumb to a case of 'nerves.'" While Judge Allen had no such nerves, the "business of being a woman judge involves a greater strain than people realize." For example, "all her work must be as nearly letter-perfect as possible because people are ten times more critical of a woman in an unprecedented position than of a man in the same position." She continued: "Besides the regular routine, considerable work is thrust upon Judge Allen simply because she is a woman," including an overwhelming number of invitations for speaking engagements and a volume of letters from people that "make her mail as heavy as that of a movie star." Yet Allen, she wrote, "is noted for the volume of work she accomplishes" and also cultivates "brain power," developing an impressive power of concentration and "sucking the essential meaning from even the driest of legal documents in a minimum of time," thus perfecting the "the masculine art of concentrating on essentials." In short, "she is doing a man's work."

GENDERED OPPOSITION FOR A FEDERAL APPOINTMENT

Allen was also bombarded with sexism from the legal establishment in the appointment process for the U.S. Court of Appeals for the Sixth Circuit. Her process was highly gendered: Women strongly endorsed and actively campaigned for her, while the old boys' network of politics, law, labor, and the press opposed her and discounted her competence.

Allen's successful appointment, like her earlier election success, was the direct result of women and their active lobbying and networks.[54] Supporters from women's law associations and women's political organizations proactively engaged in coordinated letter-writing campaigns to convince the president and his advisors to appoint Allen to the bench.

When Judge James Hickenlooper, a Republican appointed by President Coolidge to the Ohio seat on the Sixth Circuit, died in December 1933, lobbying efforts intensified. Former suffrage leader Carrie Chapman Catt immediately wrote Molly Dewson, the powerful political boss at the Democratic National Committee's Women's Division, conveying that Judge Allen was interested in the vacancy.[55] Dewson was credited by Eleanor Roosevelt for bringing a "new deal for women in politics" by securing key political leadership roles in the New Deal. Dewson's connection was critical to Allen's nomination.[56] Allen had two conferences with Dewson, and later wrote her that "I never can tell you how I feel about your coming to the front for me as you did . . . [as] you helped me over the biggest hurdle."[57]

Meanwhile, Allen's partner and campaign manager, Susan Rebhan, and her friend and colleague from the Ohio Supreme Court Judge Will Stephenson presented her name to Democratic Party representatives from Ohio, including Senator Robert Bulkley, who was to have the right of recommendation. Rebhan called for public support of Allen's appointment to bombard Attorney General Homer Cummings, Senator Bulkley, and President Roosevelt with letters. They reached out to Ohio's second senator, Republican Simon Fess, who said he would not oppose Allen's appointment because of recognition "of the enlargement of women's sphere," she was well qualified as a two-term high state court judge, and her "attitude is in line with the more liberal view of judicial interpretation, which seems to be commanding today."[58] Feminists and leaders of eighty-one national women's organizations wrote in support, as did over two hundred individual lawyers and proponents of her nomination.[59]

Allen herself wrote to President Roosevelt, nominally to congratulate him for appointing Frances Perkins as secretary of labor, the first woman to serve on a presidential cabinet, whom Allen had known from suffrage work. Allen said to the president that women everywhere "are proud of you for having had the courage to place a woman in this outstanding position."[60] She wrote a similar letter to Eleanor Roosevelt, whom she had gained as an inside supporter and intermediary through connections with her mentor Frances Kellor. The First Lady had praised Allen in magazine columns and subtly endorsed her for office, commenting that the judge's model of excellent work might eventually lead to the understanding that "sex should not enter into the question of fitness for office" and disqualify women.[61] After she was out of the White House, Eleanor gave a tribute to her "good friend" Judge Allen and endorsed her for the Supreme Court.[62] When Allen's anticipated nomination to the federal appellate bench seemed to be taking an unusually long time to materialize, Dewson pressed Eleanor, who wrote a memo to her husband asking about the judge's chances—for Rebhan had been told that the problem was that Allen was a woman.[63]

A few influential men also supported her, mostly family friends of the Allens. Attorney General Cummings was her father's friend, whom Allen had worked with on the Wilson campaign and the Democratic National Committee. Assistant Attorney General (and later D.C. Circuit Judge) Harold Stephens, a lifelong family friend from Utah, made the recommendation to Cummings.[64] Stephen Young, Allen's former boss at the prosecutor's office and now a congressional representative, actively endorsed her candidacy. New colleagues on the Ohio Supreme Court, Chief Justice Carl Weygandt and Judge Will Stephenson, strongly affirmed. Stephenson wrote: "There is no court too big for Judge Allen."[65] Former U.S. Supreme Court Justice John Clarke again wrote in support: "As the daughter of my college classmate I have had an especial interest in Judge Florence Allen. . . . I think her opinions equal if not superior to any others coming from the Ohio Supreme Court in recent years. You know of course of her thorough education and judicial methods."[66] Yet his infantilization of the fifty-year-old Allen in characterizing her as a "daughter" diminished rather than bolstered her credibility.

Beyond these few male allies, most of the men from the bench and bar abandoned Allen and whatever support or tolerance they may have previously given. Now they worked to actively oppose her nomination to the federal bench. Judges and lawyers who had worked with Allen now resented her for taking a revered male position. Notably, two district judges in Cleveland, West and Jones, who would serve under Allen if she were appointed, were among these emphatic critics.[67] These professional colleagues hurled personal accusations of intellectual incompetence and unethical behavior at Allen, alleging her lack of knowledge in complex subjects, stark ambition, financial conflicts, and partisanship. To these, they added generalized gendered attacks, claiming women's inclusion would make the distinguished court "ridiculous." In one stinging rejection, powerful Democratic supporter Newton Baker withdrew his prior support and mentorship, telling Allen only that he was not endorsing her "for reasons too complicated to bother her with."[68] While he had supported her in prior judicial and congressional elections, at least informally, this time his law firm, Baker & Hostetler, sent an attorney to Washington to actively oppose her appointment.[69]

Labor, once a leading proponent of Allen, now actively blocked her nomination. They were angered by her vote in the *United District Heating* case upholding open shops and the right to work of nonunion employees.[70] Allen blamed Chief Justice Marshall for antagonizing labor through his gratuitous politicized dissent in a desperate bid for reelection. Her mentor Kellor, though, had flagged this decision as likely to present a problem. However, a report prepared for the White House on labor's claims concluded that the balance of the judicial record showed, to the contrary, that Allen was "not unfriendly to labor," as other labor decisions she authored or concurred with "show her to be fair to labor and liberal."[71] Indeed, one legal expert telegrammed that "there has been no judge on the Ohio Supreme Court more liberal or more favorable to labor in the interpretation" of the worker's compensation law than Allen.[72]

The men leading the NAACP also launched a campaign against Allen. The Black civil rights organization had been a staunch promoter of Allen because she was one of its early members and had issued favorable decisions in a few race discrimination cases. They were "caught off guard" by her vote in *Weaver*, furious over the racist decision that shut down what could have been a "monumental" decision for civil rights.[73] Clayborne George and Chester Gillespie of the Cleveland NAACP branch wrote to the Senate Judiciary Committee opposing Allen's confirmation because of her "infamous" decision in *Weaver*. They stated: "We believe that by this opinion, an opinion reeking and pregnant with racial discrimination, Judge Allen and her associates disbarred themselves from any further judicial consideration."[74] The decision was "contrary to the law and policy of Ohio for the past 50 years," they wrote, while noting that "of course, this is a discrimination against a minority group, but we think the history of the world will show that one who discriminates against the fellow lowest down unfits himself to sit in judgment on the matters of the fellow highest up."

As the *Weaver* case became a national referendum on Allen's judicial eligibility, she stubbornly defended the decision. She appealed directly to the national office of the NAACP, reaching out in an attempt to explain the decision. She received a copy of the telegram to the Judiciary Committee and furiously scribbled in the margins—"*completely mispresented*. See opinion."[75] Writing to the NAACP's national secretary, Walter White, she proclaimed: "I never defend a decision and I do not now defend this one. . . . If I were sitting in the case again I should vote exactly the same."[76] She added: "As one, however, who believes in justice to all peoples, I wish to state to you that your telegram shows that you have been misinformed upon material facts in this case." Deflecting the implications of racial bias, Allen doubled down on legal technicalities and said the court was constrained by the facts and record in the case: "Whether Miss Weaver was admitted to the cottage for practical laboratory work in home management at first and then denied admission because of her race was not before us in the record of the case in any way, shape or manner" because of the factual concessions of her counsel and the pleadings. Thus, "no discrimination was made against her on the ground of her color and race." Allen added, "This judgment would have been rendered in the case of any white girl." Her concern about "the attitude of the Cleveland branch," she said somewhat disingenuously, "arises not from any effect which the case may have had or may in the future have with reference to myself," but she regretted "that honest and reputable people should believe that they have been done injustice by this court because of their color when exactly the same decision would have been rendered had the lawsuit been brought by a girl of any other race, under the facts admitted in open court by the lawyers for the Cleveland Branch of the NAACP." Years later, in her memoir, Allen added a self-serving anecdote to her defense, allegedly from college friend Mary Brown, "a very nice colored girl" and the first Black woman on the Cleveland Board of Education, saying she agreed with Allen that Weaver should have "stayed right there and graduated and made it easier for some colored girl to follow."[77]

In defense, Allen's judicial clerks also prepared a response memo arguing that the *Weaver* decision had been unanimous among both Democrat and Republican jurists and thus there was "no politics whatever in the decision."[78] The memo documented that the court and many of the same judges had unanimously struck down racial discrimination in two other per curiam cases: one invalidating segregation in Dayton schools, and the second affirming the prohibition against showing the inflammatory racist movie *Birth of a Nation*, on grounds that it was an "unfair presentation" and "tended to arouse race prejudice."[79] Allen had seen the movie, censored at the time in Ohio, in New York when it was first released.[80] Women attorney supporters reached out to appease prominent influential Black lawyers, like Jesse Heslip, president of the National Bar Association, arguing that Allen had "less prejudice in her make-up than any other person," had shown "eminent fairness to all creeds and races," and had a "colored woman housekeeper who is practically a member of the family."[81]

Allen's defense was effective enough. The White House's further investigation of these allegations disproved them sufficiently to the president's satisfaction. In a memorandum found in Eleanor Roosevelt's papers, an investigator describes the *Weaver* case, attaches the opinion and some pleadings, and adopts Allen's explanation that the student had in fact been offered housing on "the same terms as members of other races." A handwritten note on the papers says, "This is the case the colored people thought unfair."[82] The attorney general sent someone to Cleveland to follow up, and the report found sufficient testimony about Allen's qualifications.[83] Despite the aggressive attempts to keep a woman out of the federal court, Allen was appointed to the Sixth Circuit. It came with a big payday, an annual salary of $12,500 ($300,000 today).

MISOGYNY AND MICROAGGRESSIONS ON THE FEDERAL BENCH

On the federal bench, Allen's male colleagues were no different than the men on the state court. In fact, they were a little worse. An old clerk's tale holds that when Allen first arrived at the courthouse, there was a banner displayed reading "It's a girl," like one announcing a baby's arrival.[84] Her fellow federal jurists among the most respected branch of the judiciary were unwelcoming and exclusionary. Allen initially joined three conservative Republicans on the bench of four: Charles Moorman, Charles Simons, and Xenophon Hicks. All were about a decade older than Allen.[85]

Allen recounted in her autobiography that "none of the judges favored my appointment."[86] One "went to bed for two days," so distraught over the humiliation of having to work with a woman. Judge Hicks refused to write the customary note of congratulations welcoming her to the court. Allen viewed "the omission with some concern as it indicated that he was strongly opposed to a woman on the Court." Hicks avoided looking at her during their first working session, compounding the sexist slight. In her first session on the court, Allen said she "asked one or two pertinent questions, and in the conference after the cases I expressed myself in the normal way." "At the very last," she said, "he did look at me, and I thought, 'That's a victory.' We went on from there, I feeling my way, and asserting myself little except in the matter of voting."[87]

The animosity dimmed a bit when Allen proved her physical toughness and grit. Early in her tenure, she fell down a flight of stairs at the courthouse, landing on her face and breaking several teeth and battering her face. When Presiding Judge Moorman moved to postpone the case scheduled for the next day, which was a big Detroit bank case involving a number of lawyers already on trains headed for Cincinnati, Allen refused to postpone. Sensitive to the expense during the Depression, Allen continued the case despite how she looked, with her face wrapped in adhesive tape. Her fortitude in carrying on, even with a damaged and painful face, won over Judge Hicks a bit, and they were able to work together on the court. Allen later recollected that Hicks "became my real friend when I took this common sense decision. Some time later he remarked, regarding an opinion I had written, 'That's a damn fine opinion.' I felt I had joined the club."[88]

However, the men judges continued to interact as a separate group and exclude Allen. When sitting as a panel for weeks of argument in Cincinnati, the men took lunch at the University Club and other establishments that officially excluded women. Allen instead walked or swam during her lunch hour "to get rid of the stuffiness" and often made her own lunch on a hot plate. She went to the movies most nights and walked back to her hotel. These men's clubs, however, were important sites where conversations about work and informal collegiality on the bench were centered—shunning Allen.[89] When the second woman judge on the Sixth Circuit, Cornelia Kennedy, was appointed forty-five years later in 1979, she inherited the hot plate Allen had used to cook her lunch while her male colleagues lunched at the club. Kennedy enjoyed pointing out "the little marble-topped table in her chambers" where Allen kept her hot plate, and that table "occupied a place of some prominence in Judge Kennedy's chambers." Kennedy would become the first woman admitted to the University Club when it eventually changed its policy banning women.[90]

The official decorum of the court also emphasized gender. Potter Stewart, a junior colleague of Allen's on the Sixth Circuit until he was nominated to the Supreme Court, recalled: "Lawyers who wanted to be correct used to say, 'May it please the Court and Miss Allen,' which burned her up."[91] The court's drafting process also drew out criticism from Allen's male colleagues, Allen believed unfairly. In the exchange of drafts, she thought they were being overly critical on "trivialities and trumped-up criticisms" in commenting on opinions. Her diary was dotted with notations of "mean" letters, which she documented in detail.[92] Judge Simons, she said, "severely criticized" one opinion because it did not start out with language stating the action of the court as having "heard upon the record, briefs, and argument"—an irrelevant formalism that Allen knew Simons didn't really care about as he had approved opinions written by Judge Hicks without the language. Simons quibbled over rule statements and changed his mind on finalized decisions, forcing Allen to rewrite. Judge Moorman criticized Allen for citing Ohio cases in a negligence action, even though state law was relevant. In another case, Allen had to educate Moorman by providing him a copy of the statute he was interpreting. Both Simons and Moorman attacked Allen for making her opinions too long, though in another case Simons said Allen's opinion was too short.

In her first few months on the federal court, Judge Allen noticed that she was not being assigned any patent cases, considered technically and scientifically difficult. She thought it was "possibly because I was a woman."[93] Allen objected, saying that her background and experience in industrial cases qualified her to write patent opinions as capably as the men on the bench. The assigning judge, Moorman, initially balked at what he perceived to be Allen's improper request for a special case, until she explained she was asking not for a particular case, but only that she not be excluded from any class of cases. Her colleagues quickly agreed to her request to be assigned patent cases, as they didn't mind handing off these tedious cases with voluminous records of scientific technicalities that required extra hours and extra work.[94] Her "main motivation was to prove that a woman judge could handle a patent case as well as a man." Later, Allen prided herself on her patent knowledge, gaining the respect of the Cleveland Patent Bar, though patent lawyers were initially "aghast" that a woman had been appointed a federal judge.[95]

Years later, at her retirement, Judge Simons wrote to Allen about the judges' disagreement over the patent case assignments. He stated his "great regret" that "in the very early days of your incumbency we were impelled to disagree rather sharply in some matters, both of substance and procedure."[96] Allen replied, explaining why she had been concerned over the discretionary assignment system administered by Judge Moorman. She wrote that she had been a "little on edge," "because under the Chief Justice of the Supreme Court [of Ohio], I had seen deliberate manipulation of assignments so as to injure not only myself but some of the finest judges I had known up to that time."[97] Simons emphasized how much he now "valued greatly" her "contributions" to the court and her "industry" and "intelligence." He remarked that he was "deeply saddened by the impending breakup of our coordinated judicial group." Allen would remain the only woman on the Sixth Circuit during her twenty-five years on the federal bench.

FIGHTING FOR OTHER WOMEN JUDGES

While Allen often took the path of least resistance in responding to gendered affronts, she also knew when to stand up and fight. She challenged supervising judges who limited and devalued her work and paid her less. She took to the press to expose the dysfunction and internal politics of Chief Justice Marshall and objected to her common pleas colleagues typecasting her for an appointment in domestic relations. Allen also confronted systemic bias against women judges publicly and officially when one of her fellow women judges was targeted by the American Bar Association (ABA)—jeopardizing her own standing and political future.

Allen stood up for federal tax judge Marion Harron when she faced a contentious reappointment hearing in 1949 orchestrated by the American Bar Association. The ABA led the opposition to Harron's reappointment in one of the organization's first attempts to use its power as a professional association of lawyers to influence judicial appointments. Its newly formed ABA Standing Committee on Judicial Appointments created another barrier to women judicial candidates by defining judicial "quality" standards in credentials that excluded women. It identified criteria like Ivy League educations and work in corporate law firms that barred women, thereby disproportionately disqualifying women and reifying the gendered belief that women should not be judges.[98] The sexist attacks by the ABA were allegedly based on Harron's "temperamental" courtroom management. The opposition was also rooted in Harron's alleged "immorality," based on rumors of her five-year lesbian affair with journalist Lorena Hickok, previously connected romantically with First Lady Eleanor Roosevelt.[99]

Allen was a friend and mentor to Harron, twenty years Allen's junior, appointed by Roosevelt to the U.S. Tax Court in D.C. in 1936. Harron and Allen, as two women federal judges, had much in common, including sharing stories about similar disrespectful treatment by their male colleagues. They first met when they were both sitting for cases in Cincinnati. Harron wrote to Hickok of her dinner with Allen and Mary Pierce, whom she described as "the friend who lives with her." Harron noted, "The judge has about the same problem with her male colleagues that I have—which was interesting to learn."[100] During the rest of the dinner, they discussed Allen's four dogs, country house, and vegetable garden. Florence and Marion remained good friends, visiting at Allen's cottage, the Briar Patch, and in D.C. where Marion drove her around to see the city lights and the Lincoln Monument and where they broke their diets by having a "rapturous chocolate milk shake" at the Mayflower Hotel.[101]

Harron came up for reappointment during the frenzy of the "Lavender Scare." The Cold War–era Lavender Scare was a moral panic and political investigation of gay and lesbian people in the federal government that led to their mass dismissal from civil service and the military.[102] Following World War II, any prior benign ignorance gave way to moral panic and aversion to gay people as the medical community characterized homosexuality as a perversion of mental illness and the government defined them as "deviant."[103] The Lavender Scare paralleled the time of the second Red Scare of McCarthyism, both witch hunts targeting people on the basis of unfounded rumor, intense interrogations, and no due process.[104]

The persecution of gay federal employees escalated when a congressional subcommittee chaired by Senator Clyde Hoey, a seventy-three-year-old Southern Democrat, investigated "the employment of homosexuals in the Federal workforce."[105] The few important women in Washington cooperated in the investigation, with Senator Margaret Chase Smith (R-Maine) serving on Hoey's investigating committee and Frances Perkins testifying about methods of flushing out gay employees.[106] The Hoey Committee issued its report in December 1950, concluding that "all government intelligence agencies agree sex perverts in the Government constitute security risks" because gay men and lesbians were ripe for communist affiliation as they were immoral and more susceptible to blackmail.[107] In 1953, President Dwight Eisenhower signed Executive Order 10450 barring "homosexuals" from working in the federal government. Even the ACLU supported the government, refusing to defend gay people fired from their jobs.[108]

Marion Harron's reconfirmation hearing came up in the midst of animosity roused by the growing Lavender panic. One of the instigators, Senator Hoey, sat on her hearing committee. The hearing was described as a "nasty incident."[109] The ABA found Harron not qualified on the basis of a questionnaire it sent to mostly male lawyers who reported she was discourteous, bad mannered, had outbursts, had a temper, lectured counsel, acted "on emotion," and insulted and embarrassed counsel and clients. In gendered language, men reacted to a woman correcting them, explaining the law, and taking over their questioning. Lawyers said she did not follow accepted judicial procedure for evidence—asking questions directly of the witnesses, ordering the reporter to redact parts of the legal record, delaying opinions because no legal assistants would work for her—and had a poor record on appeal.[110] The ABA said that its opposition was not based on gender and that it had endorsed other women candidates such as Harron's predecessor on the tax court, Annabel Matthews.

Allen stuck her own neck out for her colleague, connecting her own reputation to an accused lesbian and taking on the powerful ABA even as it potentially threatened her own relationships and federal employment. She submitted an official letter to the reappointment proceedings, emphasizing that as an appellate judge, she knew Harron's work as decisions came to her Sixth Circuit court for review. "I am well acquainted with her work," she wrote. "She is able, intelligent, and highly industrious" and "has an excellent work record on what is, after all, a very hard-working court."[111] Allen then added a character endorsement: "I consider that Judge Harron has done an excellent piece of work, and that her integrity and standing are a credit to us all." Behind the scenes, Allen "made several trips to Washington to discuss the matter with her network of friends," engaged the Cleveland women lawyer's organization to write letters to the Senate Judiciary Committee in support of Harron, and wrote to Eleanor Roosevelt on Harron's behalf. Allen also pandered to FBI Director J. Edgar Hoover, exchanging sycophantic correspondence with him and his agents expressing her utmost respect and confidence in the agency, earning the agency designation "a good friend of the FBI."[112] However, when Harron later supported Allen in her candidacy for the U.S. Supreme Court by writing letters, Allen wrote pleading with her to remain "anonymous, for the protection of us both," saying she wanted to save them "both from possible embarrassment or worse."[113] She said her "sole concern was to protect You and Me. It is far too easy for someone unfriendly, to make trouble."

Harron was successfully reappointed and would serve another twenty years on the court. However, the American Bar Association would use the same playbook to stridently oppose the next woman proposed for federal court appointment, Frieda Hennock, nominated by President Harry Truman to the Southern District of New York in 1951. Hennock, a New York lawyer and commissioner on the Federal Communications Commission, was strongly opposed by the ABA and the New York bar associations. They rated her "totally unqualified," leading a sexist attack based on anonymous charges of ethical impropriety in suing her former business partner for defrauding her out of fees; salacious accusations of an "improper relationship" with a married state judge, Ferdinand Pecora; and a bizarre accusation about placing a public bet on a third term for FDR and then voting in the election. Hennock prepared a vigorous self-defense, calling the charges "hearsay of a nature which women are defenseless to combat." However, when political support stalled, she was forced to withdraw her candidacy.[114] The next woman nominated to that same district court, in 1966, Constance Baker Motley, faced the same resistance from the ABA, which hesitated to approve the nomination on grounds she lacked trial experience in New York, a "patently ludicrous suggestion given her extensive experience in courts nationwide" as a civil rights lawyer.[115] Political scientists have documented this institutional gender bias, showing that the "likelihood of women being devalued is particularly high when they occupy male-dominated roles or are evaluated by men."[116]

A STRATEGY OF ASSIMILATION

Judge Allen navigated this sexism and resistance to women judges by embracing the masculine values of the law and the judicial profession as she assimilated to the system. Assimilation meant blending in with the male judges by adopting their mannerisms and culture as she slowly calibrated the bench to an integrated system. Allen thus developed judicial traits of hard work, stoicism, formality, determination, and grit—valued masculine traits—that won men over. She steered clear of feminine attributes. "Don't be emotional," she counseled women, for it was assumed that women were "temperamental creatures, swayed by their emotions," and thus "unable by their very natures to render impartial justice."[117] She thus deflected jibes, letting them roll off her back to place the men at ease. Yet she did not shy away from public confrontations when necessary. Allen firmly believed that the best path to women's acceptance was familiarity, letting men get acclimated to a new but comfortable integrated norm by working with women daily as women "steadily and conscientiously" did their work. The strategy of assimilation, common for women both then and now, was one of finding acceptance on an individual basis of proof, thereby helping both the individual and the women who came after her.

Allen's strategy was generally successful, as she eventually won the respect of her male colleagues—even though "some of them no doubt had been shocked by the idea that a woman might sit with them as a judge."[118] When she resigned from the Sixth Circuit, Allen told President Eisenhower that "there could be no truer spirit of cooperation, mutual respect, and high principle than I have experienced in this court."[119] Tensions eased also with changes in personnel over the years, especially one welcome addition to the federal court, her good friend John Martin.

Allen did, however, grow tired of this masculine impersonation. In a speech given at a women lawyers' conference in Atlanta when she was seventy years old, she reflected introspectively on the duality of being both judge and woman. "The woman official," she said, "occupies a somewhat strange position which now and then presents a difficulty. She is doing what the world for centuries has considered a man's work. Many people think that we must be masculine in order to be doing such work, that we must have 'the masculine mind.' As I view it, our 'masculine mind' is just hard work, and women[,] a lot of them[,] have always worked hard." But, Allen concluded, the woman judge is also an outcast, "cut off from women because she is a judge" and "cut off from men, because she is a woman."[120]

Allen tried hard not to let the palpable gender bias of the courts get in the way of her work or success. She engaged the heavy workload of the federal court with efficiency and professional competency, for she had an important objective beyond pleasing her colleagues. Allen was intent on making a progressive impact in the cases, and focused on developing an intellectual record that might earn her a nomination to the U.S. Supreme Court.

7 Reshaping Federal Law for Economic and Social Justice

As Allen fought for her rightful place on the federal court, she extended her jurisprudential visions of public law and social justice to the national level. She expressed a broad commitment to human rights on the federal appellate bench, declaring that "the court is peculiarly the instrument of government which should and must protect these rights."[1] The twenty-five years she served on the U.S. Court of Appeals for the Sixth Circuit was the New Deal era of courts, when they were transitioning to upholding legislation for social and economic welfare in the shadow of the Great Depression.[2] Allen agreed with this theoretical development and showed a willingness to lead the way in laying the legal foundation for expansive governmental power.

Allen displayed an affinity for discerning the trends of the U.S. Supreme Court from dicta and dissent, carefully following the precedent and also its intimations for the future. The Supreme Courts governing her jurisprudence had a focus on economic legislation, initially overturning regulations under theories of substantive due process and the infamous *Lochner* case, then upholding New Deal legislation through legislative deference and judicial restraint.[3] During the Court's World War II era, it was confronted with questions of expansive executive power and infringements of civil liberties of racial and political minorities.[4] Later in Allen's tenure, the Court developed the civil rights laws of equal protection analysis and *Brown v. Board of Education* mandating remedies for racial desegregation of schools. Allen served through this transformational period from conservatism to liberality as courts reconfigured the understanding of federal judicial and legislative power for evolving concerns of public welfare.

Allen's jurisprudence collectively shows guiding principles of legal process and legal pragmatism. She had an appreciation for the practical realities and consequences of her decisions, and an understanding of the limiting importance of the facts as presented. She believed strongly in fair process for the adjudication of rights. She showed some motivation from the legal realists, deconstructing seemingly objective justifications to reveal bias or political motivation. She was a dedicated writer of judicial opinions, taking care with her clear and formal words. She authored 528 majority opinions in twenty-five years. She rarely concurred, writing only five concurring opinions and dissenting in eighteen cases, fewer than one per year. She was reversed by the Supreme Court five times on technical and evidentiary grounds that were not particularly significant.[5] In addition to appellate decisions from panels of three, she also issued decisions from three-judge district court tribunals convened at the trial level required under new federal law when an injunction invalidating a law as unconstitutional was requested.[6] She authored some of her most important decisions in this trial-court capacity, and seemed to be the most proactive when she ruled as the original arbiter of the merits.

Judge Allen explained her theory of opinion writing as straightforward: "Judicial opinions must be a statement of the law applicable, and nothing else."[7] Her law clerks helped research, but "Judge Allen always wrote her own opinions," usually by dictation.[8] She employed career law clerks, including Luke Lyman, Robert Toepfer, Richard Kuhn, Henry Brainard, and Mary Welles, while her legal secretary, Mrs. Ellis McClure, also performed research.[9] The federal appeals courts were first authorized to hire law clerks in 1930, and five of the first eight women serving as clerks worked for judges with connections to Allen: her family friend Judge Harold Stephens on the D.C. Circuit; law school classmate and friend Judge Jerome Frank on the Second Circuit; and Sixth Circuit colleagues Judge Thomas McAllister and Judge Elwood Hamilton. In the 1950s, all five federal judges in the Sixth Circuit's Eastern District of Michigan had female clerks, and they credited "our knowledge of the admirable judicial services of our good friend, Judge Florence E. Allen, . . . and our observation of women practicing before us" with that innovation. First woman federal district judge Burnita Shelton Matthews would hire only women clerks to balance out the refusal of other judges to do so.[10]

Judge Allen used a moderately formal style of writing, technical and thorough in detailing the facts and the controlling and analogous authority. Her opinions were commended for their "direct attack on the heart of the issues, their closely reasoned discussions, full documentation, and clear writing style."[11] Only rarely did Allen reveal personality or aggravation, reserved for a small paragraph at the end of her decisions. She proved herself through careful exposition following traditional rules of legal opinion writing rather than deviating into her own judicial voice or style. Her opinions were longer than most at the time.[12] Scholars have since demonstrated how women judges often "feel pressure to work harder than their white male peers to demonstrate their competence," by writing longer opinions, with more citations, that "go farther to explain and justify their rulings." These perfectionist tendencies of extra-high standards are strategies documented as used by women judges to continually prove their legitimacy on the bench.[13] At Allen's retirement, her Sixth Circuit colleague, Judge Thomas McAllister, recounted that she was viewed as "naturally hard working, and zealous in her determination to make a woman judge acceptable. As a result, she could be counted on to volunteer to take for opinion the cases with the most enormous records and complicated issues."[14]

Often, the most important legacy for a judge is the impact they have made in shaping and influencing the law through their decisions. As political scientists recognize, "to write a legal opinion is to exercise a fundamental form of legal power."[15] Allen's record, however, must be appreciated within the context of the constraints she faced. She was limited by arbitrary case assignments and contrarian colleagues from fully developing her jurisprudence. Modern studies have identified these constraints as a type of gender bias reducing women judges' influence on the law, as they are given less important and complex cases and fewer opinions to write, and draw unfair criticism based on presumptions of incompetence.[16] Yet Allen's most important decisions broke through these restraints, making important contributions to the interpretations of the scope of legislative and judicial power that made her a national figure.

WOMEN'S RIGHTS

The expectation of the first woman judge was that she would be a champion for women's rights on the bench—especially given Allen's work in the women's movement for suffrage and equal employment rights. Many today look for a woman judge like Justice Ruth Bader Ginsburg—a thought leader of gender equality jurisprudence who emphasizes cases challenging sex discrimination and gender stereotypes. Allen did not envision herself this way, embracing instead the cloak of impartiality and a record of liberal moderation on the full variety of issues.

Allen had only a handful of cases implicating women's rights brought before her in any court, thus limiting potential impact on gender law. In the early half of the twentieth century, women's rights litigation was not yet a coordinated program as it would become in the 1970s with Ginsburg's ACLU Women's Rights Project, the National Organization of Women's Legal Defense and Education Fund, the National Women's Law Center, and Cleveland's Women's Law Fund.[17] Instead, gender equity issues were scattered across a variety of legal contexts in isolated cases about labor, employment, property, and jury service that became more about legal doctrine than women.[18] For example, Allen heard an unfair labor practices case about women working on factory lines during World War II—Rosie the Riveters who were pressured by the company and the male union to work overtime without pay.[19] She treated the opinion as an exegesis of the labor law question of whether management interfered with a rival union, only vaguely referencing the gender issue of women working equally with men in the workplace and the union.

On the federal court, Judge Allen's sole case of women's rights was a case of protective labor laws in *Walker v. Chapman* (1936).[20] It was expected to be a big case, part of a national patchwork of labor legislation testing the constitutional rulings of the Supreme Court.[21] It also garnered national attention because of the predominant involvement of women—female employees Marquerite Walker and Kathryn Dakin, represented by a female attorney, Agnes Dickinson, before a female judge, challenging a women-specific Ohio law requiring a minimum wage.[22] Walker had lost her dry cleaning job because a man could be paid less, and thus claimed the law violated her equal liberty to freedom of contract. *Walker* was heard by a three-judge trial panel, and the final decision was designated per curiam, but Allen as the circuit judge would have been the presiding judge over the two district judges. She read the decision from the bench, as she usually did for her own opinions, and the writing reflects Allen's technical style and moderated reasoning.[23] Moreover, just after the case, she wrote to Roosevelt's ambassador to Mexico, "I thought, and of course still think, that the opinion is legally and ethically sound. It follows the distinction laid down by the Supreme Court itself, and I am proud to have had a part in rendering the decree."[24]

Walker seemed to present an easy case of striking down Ohio's wage law for women under a straight application of Supreme Court precedent. For as the *Walker* opinion itself noted, "the issue presented, in its broad aspect, is not new."[25] The Supreme Court had expressly invalidated such minimum wage legislation for women in the 1923 case *Adkins v. D.C. Children's Hospital*.[26] The split opinion in *Adkins* found that the Nineteenth Amendment embodied a structural change of all common laws that assumed women's inferiority, and thus mandated equality of treatment of women in all laws.[27] The Constitution, the Court said, now emancipated women from the old doctrine of "the ancient inequality of the sexes" and it was therefore "not unreasonable to say that these differences have now come almost, if not quite, to the vanishing point" in light of "the great—not to say revolutionary—changes which have taken place since that utterance, in the contractual, political and civil status of women, culminating in the Nineteenth Amendment."[28] The *Adkins* opinion was authored by conservative pro-business Justice George Sutherland, one of the so-called four horsemen of the judicial apocalypse striking down progressive economic legislation.[29]

Yet Sutherland wrote another opinion one year later, in *Radice v. New York*, upholding women-protective legislation. In that case, a unanimous Court upheld labor legislation for women that "protected" them by prohibiting them from working in large city restaurants at night.[30] The decision harkened back twenty years to pre–Nineteenth Amendment *Muller v.*

Oregon, which validated a maximum-hours law for women on grounds that woman was "properly placed in a class by herself" due to her frail physical nature, maternal biological function, and homemaking burdens—thus distinguishing women from men, who had a constitutional freedom to contract as identified in the infamous case of *Lochner v. New York*.[31]

Twelve years later, and while the *Walker* case was pending, the Supreme Court ratified *Adkins* by a close vote of five to four in *Morehead v. Tipaldo*.[32] *Tipaldo* struck down a New York law requiring a minimum fair wage for women. It was written by another conservative and one of the four horsemen, Justice Pierce Butler. Dissenting, Chief Justice Charles Evans Hughes textually distinguished the law in the controlling precedent of *Adkins*, finding the D.C. law there mandating a minimum wage for the cost of living to be materially different from the New York law in *Tipaldo* requiring a "fair wage" with adequate procedures for regulation.[33] He found nothing in the Constitution to prohibit legislatures from protecting "women from being exploited by overreaching employers." The other liberal Justices—Harlan Fiske Stone, Louis Brandeis, and Benjamin Cardozo—dissented on grounds of deferring to the legislature for economic legislation.[34]

Six months after the Court's pronouncement in *Tipaldo*, the ruling in *Walker* boldly adopted the dissenting view to uphold the Ohio minimum wage law.[35] It followed the moderate lead of Chief Justice Hughes and factually distinguished the statutory texts, finding the Ohio law to be clear in its requirement of a "fair wage" and devoid of the infirmities of the similar laws that had been struck down. Unbound by precedent, the *Walker* court summarily concluded without further analysis that the law was not unconstitutional.[36] Four months later, the Supreme Court followed this trend, rejecting *Adkins* and upholding women-specific laws in *West Coast Hotel v. Parrish*.[37] In the infamous political switch, which had been percolating earlier behind the scenes in other conferenced cases, conservative Justice Roberts changed his prior votes to now expressly uphold these same protective labor laws.[38] The decision by Chief Justice Hughes adopted the liberals' constitutional theory of deference for economic legislation, while the four conservative horsemen loudly dissented. The *Walker* decision thus positioned Allen as part of the New Deal judicial trend away from invalidation of economic regulation for workers.[39]

The decision in *Walker* also placed Allen squarely in the social feminist camp promoting protective labor legislation for women. Although it did not articulate rationales of women's physical sex differences as advocated by the social feminists, the decision expressly rejected the arguments of formal constitutional equality. It thus took an official stance in the post-suffrage feminist battle over the proposed Equal Rights Amendment demanded by equality feminists and feared by labor activists. Perhaps that is why Allen did not sign her name. She fell on both sides of the debate as Democrats and New Deal women heavily aligned with labor and protective legislation, while women lawyers' organizations advocated for the equality amendment. The ERA contest "splintered coalitions in the women's movement," alienating the equality feminists from reformers, labor, and progressives in a divisive "battle royal" that became the major concern of feminists for decades.[40] This political and philosophical clash played out behind the scenes in the Supreme Court's labor legislation cases leading up to *Walker*. Alice Paul and the equality feminists of the National Woman's Party assisted lawyers with the briefing in *Adkins* demanding equal treatment in employment, while social feminists led by Molly Dewson, then with the National Consumers League, argued for women's need for special labor protection due to physical weakness and unfair business practices using social science research presented in a "Brandeis Brief" in *Adkins* as they had successfully done in *Muller*.[41] Allen's anonymous decision in *Walker* allied her with the labor feminists, a public connection she had avoided when running for Congress. Her opinion, however, was consistent with her overall commitment to upholding progressive economic legislation that would be her defining jurisprudence.

THE TENNESSEE VALLEY AUTHORITY

Judge Allen rightly considered the case of *Tennessee Electric Power Company v. Tennessee Valley Authority* (1937) to be her most important opinion.[42] In the decision, Allen endorsed New Deal federal legislative authority to redress economic and social welfare enforced through administrative agencies.[43] The Supreme Court upheld her decision—demonstrating its full retreat from the *Lochner* era of invalidating economic legislation and fueling Roosevelt's reform agenda.[44] The *Tennessee Valley Authority* (*TVA*) case put Judge Allen on the national map and elevated her as a top contender for the U.S. Supreme Court. She took on the powerful national utility companies in a case worth $600 million, a brave effort reminiscent of her early trial court days, and she was immensely proud of the decision's effect. The *New York Times* heralded the case as "one of the most important and far reaching Constitutional cases in American history," testing "the extent to which the New Deal may carry forward the collectivist tendencies of its whole nation-wide power program as opposed to the individualism of existing private enterprise."[45] The *Chattanooga Times*, the local paper where the trial took place, appreciated that the case would "draw the eyes of the Nation's entire legal profession" to their town because of its "magnitude and the momentous nature of the issues."[46] Indeed, as *Life* magazine noted, the *TVA* case promised to be "one of the most far-reaching cases in U.S. constitutional history" and would determine "the fate of President Roosevelt's whole dream of reshaping American life."[47]

The controversy over the Tennessee Valley had been in the public spotlight for decades as the government tried to solve problems of navigation in this important water route obstructed by rapids. A project to build a dam at Muscle Shoals, Alabama, to provide electric power for a munitions plant was abandoned at the end of World War I, becoming a political controversy over the waste from the abandoned government project and the poverty and devastation of the river valley. Senator George Norris, a progressive Republican from Nebraska, proposed a plan for the government to complete the dams and generate electricity to produce and sell fertilizer or electric power. The idea of a government corporation competing with private business threatened the powerful and wealthy utility corporations, and raised accusations of socialism and unfair government competition as the companies claimed they would be destroyed by tax-subsidized competition. The feminists weighed in, as the National League of Women Voters carefully investigated the project and endorsed the Norris Plan for its help in addressing conservation and poverty and curbing corporate excess. Farm and labor organizations also favored the plan, which passed Congress twice but was vetoed by Republican presidents Coolidge and Hoover.[48] President Franklin Roosevelt renewed the idea and prioritized an expanded version of the plan as a "model of social and economic regeneration of a poverty area," and introduced legislation his first month in office. The Tennessee Valley Act, passed as part of FDR's New Deal, empowered a new agency, the Tennessee Valley Authority, to implement the act by building eleven dams to control the river, developing its navigation and agriculture, and producing and marketing electric power to municipalities in impoverished areas.[49]

The constitutionality of the Tennessee Valley Act was challenged by the private power companies, resulting in three cases sent to the Supreme Court. The first, *Ashwander v. Tennessee Valley Authority*, attacked the first proposed dam at Muscle Shoals, preliminarily blocking implementation until the Court later upheld the TVA as authorized by Congress's power to legislate for national defense.[50] It also held that the government corporation could legally sell its excess electric power and property like any other actor. In a second, related action, petitioners extended the challenge to all sites in Alabama in the case of *Alabama Power Company v. Ickes*.[51]

In a third mega-action, eighteen other private utility companies subsequently brought a separate suit to strike down the entirety of the TVA statute. They sued initially in Tennessee chancery court, but the government removed the case to federal court. Federal district judge John Gore granted a preliminary injunction in December 1936 prohibiting further TVA development, in flagrant opposition to the Supreme Court's contrary holding in *Ashwander*.[52] Judge Gore's unilateral action freezing the president's and Congress's action became the national example of the need for Roosevelt's court reform and three-judge district courts to prevent this type of judicial activism. They called for Gore's impeachment for defying the will of Congress, declaring melodramatically that his injunction was "doing more to promote communism than all the soap-box orators in America" for its disavowal of the government.[53]

A Sixth Circuit panel, including Judge Allen, dissolved Gore's preliminary injunction and sent the case back to the lower court for a full hearing.[54] An opinion written by Judge Charles Simons, a Republican appointed by Hoover, found that the *Ashwander* case called into question the validity of the injunction and thus an injunction was not in the public interest. Concurring, Allen elaborated that a preliminary injunction was never in the public interest in this type of case. Public law, she said, was different from private disputes as the public interest was generally always in favor of enforcement of all duly enacted laws. One congressional representative praised the Sixth Circuit decision, saying it was "a death blow to efforts of the power trust to paralyze the administration's power policies," while Secretary of the Interior Harold Ickes, charged with administering the TVA and the public works program, hoped the dissolution "foreshadowed an end of what he termed 'government by injunction.'"[55]

Judicial reform for the three-judge district court had just passed, transferring the *TVA* merits case to a three-judge panel, the first case in the nation litigated under this new procedure. The three judges on the panel were John Gore, the original district judge in the case from the Eastern District of Tennessee; John Martin, judge in the Western District of Tennessee; and Allen as presiding circuit judge. Allen, the most junior judge on the Sixth Circuit, got the appointment by default, as two of three other circuit judges were conflicted due to their close connections with the utilities industry and the third was out because of illness. Allen recounted that when the chief judge assigned her the case, he said, "They say you are not big enough for this case. You are big enough for any case."[56] Appointed in the spring, she spent the summer in Colorado reading and researching the relevant areas of law and Supreme Court decisions, laid up by a fractured ankle injured when she fell in a rocky river while fishing.[57]

That fall, Allen relocated to Chattanooga for the duration of the five-month trial.[58] She wrote to her friend Harriet Elliott that she "had the good sense" to "induce" Mary Pierce to come with her and a take a leave of absence from her job as a school principal.[59] She appreciated Mary's "good care" that "lightened considerably" her life and "made the difference between being sick and well, as the judges in this case have sat all day in a most controversial atmosphere, and then almost every night have studied briefs, and in addition to that, on almost every Saturday and Sunday have worked or had conferences." The two rented a cottage on Lookout Mountain, in an area called "Fairyland" where the judge could walk her dogs every day. Florence and Mary became well acquainted with Judge Martin and his wife, a topic of public interest when the local paper featured a spread and photo about dinner with the two couples at the Martins' home.[60] Thanksgiving that year was hosted by Florence and Mary, with Mary cooking an extensive dinner for them, the Martins, and law clerk

Luke Lyman and his wife, Helen. John Gore, described as a "confirmed bachelor who liked his whisky," kept to himself, staying at the hotel where he lived. Gore's death from heart failure at the age of sixty, one month after the *TVA* decision, was allegedly precipitated by the stress of the trial and his bad health.[61]

Opening day of the "momentous trial" on November 15, 1937, saw a packed courtroom. Allen took center stage on the bench in the majestic ceremonial courtroom. Behind the bench was a mural, newly commissioned by the New Deal administration, portraying the history of Chattanooga from its pioneers and Native American settlers to its Union role in the Civil War—and, featured in the center, the transmission tower of the TVA.[62] The audience was a who's who of political and corporate players. Democratic big whig Newton Baker, Allen's one-time political supporter and now nemesis, was chief counsel for the plaintiff utility companies. Baker, however, died during the course of the trial. He was replaced by a senior partner at his firm, Baker & Hostetler, Judge Arthur Denison, formerly of the Sixth Circuit. Wendell Willkie, later a Republican presidential candidate, appeared in the gallery as a potential witness in the case in his role as president of one of the largest utility companies and the industry's chief lobbyist and spokesperson. Willkie had long opposed the law and its implementation, but after the industry lost the case he would, outrageously, sell his private company to the TVA for a huge profit. James Fly, who headed the counsel team for the government, would later become head of the ACLU, known for his work opposing wiretapping. The government's team of "elite, brilliant lawyers" included Bessie Margolin, one of the few "prominent New Deal female lawyers," who was instrumental in drafting the briefs "against an avalanche of constitutional challenges."[63] "At the beginning of the trial," a member of the TVA legal staff told the press, "we were a little disturbed at having drawn a woman judge, but after the first day we were all very much impressed and quite satisfied. . . . She has some very decided facial mannerisms and at the same time a most disarming and engaging smile. She is inclined to lean over backward in her attempt to be absolutely fair."[64]

The TVA trial took seven weeks over the Thanksgiving and winter holidays in 1937, with 1,100 exhibits. Judge Allen ran a tight ship, utilizing a firm rule, "amusing to every one in attendance to the court," of operating every day from 9:30 a.m. to 4 p.m., with one hour for lunch, and continuing to a new witness even with only two minutes left in the day. She tried to wrangle the circus, prohibiting cameras in the courtroom after an unexpected photo of her and the other judges on the bench appeared in the papers. She also had to exert control over the obfuscation tactics of the industry lawyers, who were papering the court with voluminous pleadings and constant requests for evidence, documents, and depositions that wasted hours of the court's daily time. Judge Allen was not impressed with the delay tactics.[65] She later excoriated the industry in her opinion, chastising them for gaming the legal system with irrelevant, spurious, and unsubstantiated political opinions. When the industry appealed the decision, they claimed abuse of discretion in Allen and the district judges' handling of the trial evidence, a claim the Supreme Court easily dismissed in ratifying Allen's management.[66] Near the end of the trial, Allen's name swirled in the press over her possible nomination to the Supreme Court, drawing further attention and intrigue to the case. Chief Judge Charles Moorman grew impatient with Allen's absence from the appellate docket and demanded she make time during the Tennessee trial to hear a bank tax case.[67]

In her decision, Judge Allen granted a "clear-cut legal victory" to the TVA and President Roosevelt. The vote was unanimous, though it had been widely predicted that Judge Gore would vote with the companies, given his earlier order in the case and his Republican ties. Allen recorded Gore's surprise vote in her diary: "Read opinion and J Gore concurred!"[68] Judge Allen carefully read the fourteen-page decision from the bench in announcing the court's decision.[69] Allen said that "toward the close of the case I found myself unable to sleep, and often got up at night to work over the opinion." She offered the draft to her colleagues for rewrite and edit, and suggested that the opinion to be designated "per curiam" as authored by all three. The judges declined, perhaps appreciating the political value of having her name lead the opinion, given her imminent consideration for the Supreme Court and her judicial legacy. Allen noted in her diary that Judge Martin "says I must write opinion + not think @ being woman." Allen didn't want anything to detract from the legal credibility of the decision.[70]

Allen's *TVA* opinion was particularly well written, cutting through the morass of permutations and politicization of the legal arguments. She demonstrated a mastery of the complexities of the evidence, testimony, and science, expertly weaving together the facts, legal arguments, and conclusions while retaining the nuance. She synthesized points to avoid mere cutting and pasting of long-winded arguments, arriving succinctly at the heart of the matter. She took a vastly complex case and made it clear and understandable to lawyers, but also to the anticipated audience of the press, politicians, and public. Allen showed her expert understanding of the controlling precedent, carefully using the clues from *Ashwander*. She also effectively incorporated the Supreme Court's holding in *Alabama Power*, decided after completion of the TVA trial and just as she was finalizing her decision. The Court had dismissed the *Alabama Power* case on standing, holding that a private power company had no standing to challenge the TVA statute because it had no injury arising from a violation of law, given that there was no legal or equitable right granting the companies a monopoly or franchise with the right to exclude others from the market.[71] Allen also uniquely appreciated and noted the environmental context of the TVA, integrating progressive and feminist respect for conservation efforts and scientific development of hydropower for the future.

Allen rejected the industry's primary claim that the government authority was coercing and defrauding municipalities and companies into purchasing governmental power and abandoning private utilities. She dismissed the industry's assertions that the TVA statute was a "sham," a "pretense," created by Congress as a "cloak for the unlawful purpose" of creating a federal government monopoly of the power industry and corroborated the "sincerity" of the statute and its implementation. She found that the statute was authorized pursuant to Congress's constitutional authority to regulate for national defense, interstate commerce, and navigable waters. The generation and sale of electric power was authorized as incidental to those powers and necessary to liquidate the costs of the projects. Echoing the Supreme Court's recent decision in *Alabama Power*, she had strong cover and precedential support for her conclusion that this was a situation of *damnum absque injuria* (damage without legal injury), since the statute was valid and the companies had no protected franchise to legally immunize them from competition—even, she noted harshly, "if their business be curtailed or destroyed."[72]

The Supreme Court affirmed Judge Allen's decision one year later, with two archconservatives, Justices Pierce Butler and James McReynolds, dissenting.[73] Justice Roberts, of the infamous "switch in time that saved nine" staving off FDR's court-packing plan, wrote the majority opinion, the conservative having flipped again to uphold regulatory legislation. The Court rejected the companies' new arguments that the statute was a taking or interference with property. As in *Alabama Power*, it held that the power companies had no standing to sue because they had no injury due to any legal right of contract, franchise, or privilege allowing exclusivity in the market for power. The *New York Times* reported that the *TVA* decision unequivocally established the constitutional power for New Deal legislation and the Court's willingness to now approve that policy agenda.[74]

ENDORSING ECONOMIC JUSTICE

On the federal bench, Judge Allen remained committed to issues of governmental power as she had in *TVA* and in the state court. These issues repeatedly came to the forefront in cases about economic regulations and economic rights. Allen played a large role in interpreting the new economic legislation of the labor laws. These laws of the Fair Labor Standards Act, National Labor Relations Act, and National Industrial Recovery Act, among others, had Allen newly interpreting employees' rights to unionize, collectively bargain, and receive a minimum wage. She issued balanced decisions enforcing the commands of the new laws for workers, while taking into consideration the business rights of management.[75]

Two of Allen's most notable decisions in dissent endorsed expansive use of federal legislative power for economic regulation. In one, she wrote a dissent in an eminent domain case, disagreeing with the majority that struck down FDR's National Recovery Act. In *U.S. v. Certain Lands in Louisville*, the Sixth Circuit held that Congress had no power to enact the Recovery Act, thereby invalidating the use of eminent domain to condemn slums and develop the land by building low-cost housing.[76] Allen found that the slums caused by the pervasive homelessness of the Depression were a national problem that Congress had the power to resolve. The Roosevelt administration had planned to appeal these cases to the Supreme Court to test the scope of congressional power, but "abruptly sought dismissal" when the Court was striking down most all of the New Deal legislation.[77]

In another significant dissent, Judge Allen interpreted the Commerce Clause in a broad way—a decision that was unanimously adopted by the Supreme Court and provided the constitutional foundation for later expansive civil rights laws. In *Filburn v. Helke*, an Ohio farmer named Roscoe Filburn challenged a federal law that regulated the amount of wheat farmers could grow and penalized him for contributing to the problematic oversupply of wheat during the Depression. Filburn claimed that he used the wheat to feed his family and livestock and to save seeds for future planting, and thus that it was not in interstate commerce as required for federal regulation. Allen dissented from a three-judge district court decision enjoining the statute on "the equities." She did not decide like the majority on the basis of fairness to the farmer, even though she had supported farmers when running for Congress. Allen's dissent was based instead on constitutional power, finding the wheat regulation to be a valid exercise of the interstate commerce power based on Supreme Court precedent and congressional findings. She would have upheld the law because local market activity must be considered with "regard to the total effect" on the national system, which produced a direct effect on interstate commerce. As a legal scholar noted, "Judge Allen alone anticipated *Filburn*'s pivotal constitutional issues."[78]

After hearing reargument in the case, the Supreme Court unanimously upheld the law in the landmark case *Wickard v. Filburn*, accepting Allen's view of the broad scope of the Commerce Clause. Legal scholars note that "*Filburn* is regarded today as the high-water mark of the New Deal's constitutional revolution . . . and perhaps the most far-reaching example of Commerce Clause authority over intrastate activity."[79] Newspapers reported at the time that this was "the most liberal definition of the interstate commerce clause that has come down from the Supreme Court in years" and "ought to satisfy" the Court's New Deal critics.[80] However, the next year, Allen inexplicably departed from this broad interpretation in a case argued by government lawyer Bessie Margolin to vote with the conservative majority holding that a local beer distribution company was not in interstate commerce and thus not subject to the federal minimum wage. Judge Simons in the majority opinion took a potshot at her *Filburn* opinion, bemoaning the "abandonment of old distinctions between what is national and what is local" that put the court in the "twilight zone" and inappropriately supported "the persistence of administrative authority to seek the widest possible exercise of granted power."[81]

PATENTS, CRIMINALS, AND SPIES

Much of Judge Allen's federal docket, with its variety of civil and criminal cases, was similar to the routine cases she had heard on the state court. Cases included issues of negligence, insurance, contracts, bankruptcy, corporations, banking, and—to her despair—"innumerable tax cases."[82] Allen said that some of her more "interesting" cases included one about a quack medicine called "Glyoxylide," a case challenging the illegal seizure of a liquor still during Prohibition, and a case about a fraudulent housing loan, though none of these was particularly riveting.[83] None of these would place Allen on the public map; instead, it was the patent cases to which she devoted her energies and criminal cases that engaged the press.

Allen deliberately crafted an expertise in patent law, claiming the scientific field as an area of interest and aptitude for a woman. She was still seething about the many male opinions that had tried to block her federal nomination on grounds that patent and technology were subjects too complicated for a woman—views that seemed initially to be replicated by her federal colleagues and their reluctance to assign her patent cases. Allen intended to prove all of them wrong. About 12 percent of her total workload was patent cases, and she wrote sixty-five opinions on these issues of intellectual property for invention. U.S. Supreme Court Justice Potter Stewart, a colleague of Allen's for a short time on the Sixth Circuit, said he learned patent law from Allen.[84] She became a workhorse on these demanding cases that required heavy lifting with voluminous records, showing an ability to dive deep into the technology and mechanics at issue. One of her first written opinions on the Sixth Circuit was a dissent in a patent case, where she would have found the patent valid.[85] Three of her decisions were appealed to the Supreme Court, and two of them were reversed on fact-specific grounds.[86] Before the establishment of the Federal Circuit and its dedicated forum for patent appeals, patent cases were dispersed through the circuits by geography. Patent cases were prevalent in the circuit of Ohio, Michigan, Kentucky, and Tennessee, which included the automotive, steel, and machine tool industries.

Most of Allen's patent decisions were routine cases of technicality regarding infringement or validity of patents. She ruled in a balanced way, though more often in favor of alleged infringers. This followed the trend of Supreme Court precedent, which at the time was hostile to patents. Like a good appellate judge, Allen often affirmed the trial court decision below. Her patent decisions were generally unremarkable. One case, *Great Atlantic and Pacific Tea v. Supermarket Equipment Co.*, was appealed to the Supreme Court, which reversed Allen's finding of validity, and is now well known as important precedent in establishing the standard of obviousness for combination patents.[87] Other Allen patent decisions of minor interest include res judicata for licensing estoppel, lack of presumption for prior art not filed with the Patent and Trademark Office, and a ruling against two women inventors on a refrigerator patent.[88] Allen thought deeply about the patent topic, for example, writing a law review article offering her insightful views about consumer-oriented innovation.[89]

Despite crafting an expertise in patent law, Allen gained more attention in sensational criminal cases. One highly charged case of communist persecution during the height of the McCarthyite Red Scare era returned to Allen's long-held commitment to strict enforcement of the rules of fair play and her aversion to lying. Late in Allen's tenure, in *Brown v. United States*, the judge upheld a criminal contempt conviction and six-month imprisonment against Stefana Brown for refusing to answer questions on cross-examination after taking the stand in her own defense.[90] Brown faced cancellation of her naturalized citizenship for lying about her communist affiliation and refusing to name others. The prosecution relied on the Smith Act making it illegal to advocate or teach the overthrow of the government by force or belong to an organization with this objective. Allen upheld the conviction, holding that Brown had waived her right against self-incrimination by testifying on direct examination. "Having cast aside the cloak of immunity, the party may not resume it at will," she wrote. "To hold that a defendant, under claim of protection against self incrimination, may tell his full, self-serving story without any test of its truth by cross examination is to make a mockery of the judicial proceeding." Allen concluded the opinion by citing the eminent Judge Learned

Hand, with whom she occasionally corresponded, and his decision in the Second Circuit reaching the same result.[91]

The Supreme Court affirmed Allen's decision in *Brown*, but in a closely divided five-to-four opinion. Justice Felix Frankfurter wrote the majority opinion, deciding on grounds similar to those of Allen, while the dissenting civil libertarians attacked the erosion of the constitutional right against self-incrimination.[92] The Court upheld the contempt and underlying prosecution even though, in the previous year, it had limited the reach of the Smith Act in fueling communist targeting, holding that the First Amendment protected political speech unless it presented a clear and present danger.[93] Allen had ruled the same way in support of civil rights twenty-five years earlier in the Ohio case of *State v. Kassay*, where she dissented in favor of an accused communist on grounds of protected First Amendment political speech.[94] Yet she did not invoke this prior jurisprudence in *Brown*, perhaps because the *Kassay* case had been a black mark against her for Supreme Court appointment and used to support accusations that she was a Red.

Brown was Allen's second case of alleged treasonous insurgents conspiring in Detroit. She also ruled against an alleged Nazi spy during World War II in *Von Moltke v. Gillies*.[95] The case drew national headlines as Countess Marianna von Moltke, a German homemaker, was accused by double agent Grace Buchanan-Dineen of being a conduit to German leaders through her friend groups and a secret mailbox. The countess was arrested, dragged out of bed in the middle of the night, interrogated day and night by the FBI, and held incommunicado as an enemy agent denied due process and the right to counsel or visitors. Allen's ruling against von Moltke's claims of ineffective assistance of counsel—and upholding the conviction of espionage, which carried the death penalty—was based on the limited appointment of counsel for the purpose of entering a plea.[96] The Supreme Court disagreed—twice—with a plurality finding a violation of civil rights.[97] A tied vote, however, ultimately left Allen's order in place and von Moltke served a four-year sentence. These cases showed that the senior judge had grown conservative, moving away from her earlier record of demanding full and fair criminal process and empathy toward political minorities.

REMEDYING RACE DISCRIMINATION

Judge Allen's tenure on the federal court was also marked by the emergence of a civil rights law against discrimination on the basis of race. She wrote several important decisions on remedies for racial discrimination, enforcing the Supreme Court's edict in *Brown v. Board of Education* that racial segregation was unconstitutional. The Court decided *Brown* in 1954, finding that racial segregation of public schools violated the Fourteenth Amendment, and one year later, in *Brown v. Board II*, issued a remedial decision to enforce its constitutional command, ordering integration of the schools with "all deliberate speed."[98] Allen would strictly interpret this command to mean immediate action without excuse.

Allen's first application of *Brown*, however, was not in regard to schools. Just five months after *Brown II*, she extended the decision to the context of public housing, becoming the first federal judge to do so, when she authored one of the Sixth Circuit's most notable cases, *Detroit Housing Commission v. Lewis*.[99] The NAACP Legal Defense Fund brought this high-profile housing discrimination case, with Constance Baker Motley (later the first Black woman appointed a federal judge) as lead counsel and Thurgood Marshall (the future Supreme Court Justice) on the brief. In her decision, Allen held that racial segregation in Detroit's public housing was unconstitutional. Detroit had maintained separate all-white and all-Black housing and maintained separate eligibility lists resulting in vacancies in the white housing but wait lists for Black housing. Allen said *Brown* applied to invalidate this practice. But she also bolstered this holding of the new, and still contentious, decision in *Brown* with a series of Supreme Court cases since 1917 in which the Court had held racial segregation in housing to be unconstitutional, such as *Shelley v. Kramer*. Allen affirmed the district court ruling and ordered an immediate change with all deliberate speed, following the commands of *Brown II*'s remedial decision.

The next year, Judge Allen again interpreted *Brown II* strictly. In *Clemons v. Board of Education of Hillsboro*, she enforced racial integration against recalcitrant school authorities in a small Ohio town, demanding immediate remediation by the school district. Joyce Marie Clemons had challenged the school's establishment of gerrymandered elementary school zones that segregated all Black students into one school. Despite overcrowding at the two white schools, no white students were assigned to the Black school. The school claimed it was going to build a new elementary school to integrate children, but Allen saw this as a subterfuge to permit the continuance of segregation indefinitely. She emphasized that school segregation had been prohibited in Ohio since 1888, when the state supreme court upheld the repeal of a former statute allowing segregation. And she cited an opinion from her time on the Ohio Supreme Court in *Dayton v. Reese*, unanimously reaffirming that racial segregation in schools was prohibited.[100] Thus, while *Brown*'s dictate was new, school integration had long been required in the particular state of Ohio. Allen took the unusual step of writing that she wanted to remand with specific instructions to require integration immediately for all students, but could not obtain the vote of either of her two "brothers" on the panel and so was "compelled" to simply remand with remedial discretion to the district court. She called out the concurring opinion by Judge Potter Stewart (a future Supreme Court Justice) and the dissent by Judge Shackelford Miller, a Southern Democrat, both of whom wanted to defer to the school rather than mandate change.[101]

One year later, Judge Allen again commanded schools to immediately integrate, rejecting incremental proposals. In *Booker v. Tennessee Board of Education*, Ruth Booker challenged the gradual integration plan adopted by Memphis State College in response to *Brown*.[102] Tennessee had a long history of explicit statutes making it "unlawful" to allow "white and colored" students to attend any school or educational program together. After *Brown*, the college proposed to admit Black students at first only to graduate-level classes, and then, each year thereafter, to extend admission at one additional level of classes, descending in reverse rank. The district court accepted the incremental plan as a good-faith effort. Allen disagreed and reversed the district court. She said "this is a clear discrimination," requiring Black students to delay five years and be placed at the bottom of the admissions list because of race. Judge Miller again dissented.[103]

Judge Allen's aggressive oversight of recalcitrant school districts in racial integration reached a new level when she was confronted with a case of violence, hate, and mass resistance in *Bullock v. United States*.[104] Allen was now chief judge of the Sixth Circuit, the first woman in the country to serve in this role. In one of her last decisions, she adjudicated a case from Clinton, Tennessee, whose high school was the first southern school in the country integrated by judicial order. It would become an "explosive preview of what happened across all the South," with protests, mobs, and violent resistance to race integration.[105] The case had been filed by the NAACP in 1950, before *Brown* was decided. Joheather McSwain and her sisters, part of the "Clinton 12," twelve Black high school students seeking admission to the all-white school, sued the school district for its official policy of racial segregation and busing them to an all-Black school miles from their neighborhood school. A district court ordered the integration, resulting in eighteen students attending the school with eight hundred white students.[106] Protest and community opposition ignited as "every item in the apparatus of Southern civil-rights resistance . . . made an appearance in Clinton, from anti-Black slurs and heckling, to cross burnings, bombings, and Ku Klux Klan night riders."[107] The governor called out six hundred National Guard soldiers and tanks, further escalating the violence. Protesters formed a gauntlet where the Black students walked into the school, and attacked those who tried to protect or assist their access. President Eisenhower refused to act, saying the federal government cannot "step in with money every time something goes wrong with a school from a water faucet on up"—though he would soon do just that in sending federal troops to Little Rock, Arkansas, to protect and enforce school integration there.

John Kasper, the magnetic, villainous leader of the protests, was a twenty-six-year-old former bookstore owner from New Jersey who came to the South "on a mission to fight desegregation by any means." He led the violence in neighboring Nashville, then headed up the insurrection group that bombed and destroyed Clinton High School. He was repeatedly jailed for his criminal acts. Kasper's contempt violation of the injunction in the Clinton case came before Judge Allen. The U.S. attorney general prosecuted Kasper and several others who were found in criminal contempt for violating the injunction in the case prohibiting obstruction or interference with the desegregation of the school. Judge Allen showed no sympathy for the violent instigators and easily upheld the contempt charges against Kasper and the co-defendants.[108] She rejected their claims about freedom of speech, finding that the "right to speak is not absolute" and that speech cannot instigate unlawful conduct. This time, Judge Miller joined her. John Kasper retired from activism one year later, after serving a six-month sentence of hard labor in the workhouse.

However, in one of her final votes, Allen joined a decision in a third Tennessee case endorsing a delayed, gradual desegregation plan. In *Kelley v. Board of Education*, the challenge was to Nashville public schools' proposal to integrate one grade each year, starting with first grade, thus taking twelve years to remedy the unconstitutionality.[109] This overcautious plan still gave rise to a "reign of terror," "violence on the part of criminal elements opposed to desegregation," in large "unlawful crowds of disorderly persons" who "caused great trouble and turbulence" as they "wrecked" an elementary school "by bombing" and also bombed a synagogue, led again by Kasper.[110] The Board of Education then proposed a "parents' choice" plan supported by new oppositional state legislation allowing parents to voluntarily choose segregated schools, which was rejected by the district court as it approved the prior gradual plan. Thurgood Marshall was on the brief challenging the school's plan, and he cited Allen's *Booker* decision rejecting incrementalism in support. "This Court," he wrote, "has refused to accept generalized and unsubstantiated pleas for delay even when made in good faith, . . . and has held that a trial court has no discretion to continue the deprivation of basic human rights."[111] Allen, unexpectedly, did not rule for Marshall or follow her own precedent, instead deferring to her colleagues in *Kelley* and voting with them to uphold the slow, stairstep plan on the basis of sufficient evidence and the school's good faith. However, her initial inclinations in *Booker* as to the harm of incremental programs would prove right. The Nashville case would drag on for decades, as the Sixth Circuit subsequently acknowledged: "A whole generation of school children has gone through the complete school system of . . . Nashville . . . under circumstances now determined to have been violative of their constitutional rights. A second generation of school children is now attending school under similar circumstances—and the remedy is not in sight."[112] Allen's abdication in *Kelley* harkened back to her problematic holding in *Weaver* on the Ohio Supreme Court, both leaving in place official race segregation. Yet her other decisions on race stand in stark contrast, showing an evolving understanding of the harms of race discrimination and demonstrating the court's power to force its eradication.

Reflecting on her work on the federal court, Allen told close friends, "When you write a judicial opinion once in a while you think you have really struck a blow for right and justice." But, she qualified, it "usually" turns out to be just a "lawsuit," without a result of broader permanent reform.[113] Allen and her supporters hoped for a U.S. Supreme Court nomination so that women could finally break the last gendered barrier to full equality in the courts. Allen wanted an opportunity for greater policy impact, and thus persistently pursued the long shot of a Supreme Court appointment.

8 Shortlisting for the Supreme Court

The year after Allen's appointment to the federal bench, a new U.S. Supreme Court building opened at One First Street in Washington, D.C., under the sign of "Equal Justice Under Law." Yet there were no equal opportunities for women on that Court.[1] Allen was considered for twelve vacancies on the Court by three presidents—Democrats and Republicans. Both parties wanted to win over new women voters after enfranchisement, and a female Justice was one key demand of political women. Allen was the woman mentioned. She was the first woman "shortlisted" repeatedly, appearing on "official lists of possible candidates for appointment" to the most revered court in the nation.[2]

The years in which Allen was a candidate for the Court from 1932 to 1952 produced the appointment of some of the great legal lions of the Supreme Court bench. These prominent Justices included Benjamin Cardozo, Felix Frankfurter, Hugo Black, Robert Jackson, and William O. Douglas. Yet it was also a period when there were many less remarkable appointments, men whose names have been lost to history because they made little impact on the Court beyond the daily routine of adjudication. There had therefore been more than enough room to accommodate the innovation of a woman Justice, especially one with a public reputation and record of judicial achievement like Allen.

Allen met all the basic political, professional, and representational standards for Supreme Court selection, except for her sex.[3] She had significant judicial experience. She had prosecutorial experience. Her intellectual credentials, graduating at the top of her class from the respected law schools of Chicago and NYU, were as good as if not better than those of many appointees. While there were Justices from Harvard and Columbia, where women were officially excluded on the basis of sex, there were also Justices from Alabama, Albany, Colorado, and Kansas City. Three men appointed in this era, Stanley Reed, Robert Jackson, and James Byrnes, had no law degree at all. Allen had several well-placed national political connections in the White House. Geography also helped, identifying her with Utah in the West and Ohio in the Midwest, both desirable constituencies from which to balance out the East Coast Court.[4]

However, as Allen ascended in judicial aspirations, her secret weapon for success—the political power of women's networks—failed.[5] A decade and more after suffrage, women's influence was diluted and Washington no longer feared women's lobbying power. Women were virtually absent in the echelons of national power. Democratic powerhouse Molly Dewson, who had championed Allen, retired and no longer had significant influence, though she wrote a brief personal note to FDR: "Of course if you did appoint Florence Allen it would be STUPENDOUS for us girls."[6] Allen lost her best advocate and campaigner with the death of her partner, Susan Rebhan, in 1935. Friend Harriet Elliott tried to substitute and orchestrate the backdoor lobbying and letter-writing campaign for Allen, using her New Deal connections as one of the few women serving on shadow women's division committees in Washington.[7] Allen tried to raise her visibility by increasing her speaking engagements to women-affiliated organizations, which she had reduced when she took the federal bench. These efforts, however, would not be enough to elevate Allen to the highest office. The political force was still too strong in favor of the traditional male candidate.

REPUBLICAN CONSIDERATION

Allen's name was floated initially for the Supreme Court to two Republican presidents, Calvin Coolidge and Herbert Hoover. In these early days of women's suffrage, presidents were attuned to cultivating the women's vote. A public proposal for women on the Court had been made in 1913 when a Chicago news article, "Women Candidates for Harlan's Seat on the Supreme Bench," argued that "many people will agree that President Taft might—and probably will—do a whole lot worse than to appoint a woman as a justice of the supreme court."[8] The idea began to take shape with the advent of the first woman judge. Allen was considered a moderate, having run for office as a nonpartisan. As one paper noted, "Miss Allen is a progressive judge, but neither a Brandeis nor Taft. She steers the middle course."[9] Her moderation made her eligible for a Republican nomination because presidents of this era sometimes made appointments from the opposite party in a spirit of bipartisanship, to gain political favor, or out of conviction that a balanced Court was important.[10]

Allen first appeared on the radar with recommendations to President Coolidge in 1924 for the one Supreme Court appointment he would make during his tenure. A letter, found in the Coolidge presidential files, from E. L. Kenyon on *St. Joe's Valley News* letterhead from Elkhart, Indiana, recommended her: "If there is a woman in the United States who represents the legal profession and who is qualified to fill the position of a justice of the Supreme Court I believe Miss Allen is that woman."[11] The letter continued: "I feel that as the citizens of the United States now include both men and women and as two states have seen or thought it wise to elect to the Governorships women of their citizens of their state, there certainly should be on the Supreme Court a woman of renown." Kenyon pointed out that "JUSTICE is depicted by a woman holding up the scales. I can not recall of seeing Justice depicted by a man, either in statuary or pictures." A second recommendation was sent to Coolidge by William Hart, the president of the Ohio State Bar Association, commending Allen as "a lady of fine ideals, large ability and accomplishments, great earnestness of purpose," and one who represented the "conviction of womankind" on the subject of international peace.[12] Coolidge did not take the opportunity to break new ground, appointing instead his attorney general and college friend, Harlan Fiske Stone.

Coolidge did, however, appoint the first woman to serve on any federal court, Genevieve Cline to the U.S. Customs Court in 1928, then an Article I court. Cline, like Allen, was from Cleveland, and had graduated from the part-time program at Cleveland Law School. As head of the Ohio Republican women, she had helped win the state for Coolidge. There was immediate opposition to Cline on account of her sex, but the president cited her six years of experience as an appraiser of shipping merchandising in Cleveland, interpreting customs and tariff laws. Cline, upon being sworn in, said, "I do want to say not only for myself but in behalf of my sister members of the bar, I thank you and want to assure you that I shall meet all absolutely fairly as *man to man* in the court."[13]

Allen was next considered by President Hoover. Her name appears in the historical record in connection with Hoover's last appointment in 1932 to fill the position vacated by noted jurist Oliver Wendell Holmes, retiring at age ninety, and filled by New York liberal Benjamin Cardozo. Allen was included on an official White House list of forty possible candidates for the Supreme Court suggested to White House Press Secretary Ted Joslin. Allen's consideration by Hoover is also evidenced in his papers by a one-page "Application for Appointment" for "Associate Justice of the Supreme Court of the U.S." completed with her biographical and professional accomplishments. Hoover had met Allen a few years earlier when they had appeared together at a national conference of the League of Women Voters speaking, and disagreeing, about peace initiatives.[14] Hoover was reportedly open to appointing a woman, still interested in courting the women's vote. The president wrote to his attorney general, William Mitchell, about the possibility of a woman Justice, but Mitchell deflected, saying that "I should like very much to appoint a woman to a distinguished position," but then adding, "if I could find a distinguished woman to appoint," intimating that a such a qualified woman could not be found.[15] Hoover did appoint a woman to the Article I U.S. Board of Tax Appeals, nominating D.C. tax lawyer Annabel Matthews.[16]

Also included in President Hoover's files was an editorial in the *Christian Science Monitor* endorsing two women candidates for Supreme Court nomination, Florence Allen and Mabel Walker Willebrandt.[17] Willebrandt had also been included on the White House list of forty candidates as a progressive Republican who had served two presidents, enforcing Prohibition and arguing many cases as assistant U.S. attorney general before the Supreme Court.[18] But Willebrandt was the "controversial personification of prohibition" and now a pariah with the increasingly unpopular liquor law that destroyed her judicial candidacy.[19] Several years later, Willebrandt sent a four-page letter to President Roosevelt advocating for the appointment of a woman and a "real intellectual liberal."[20] She pleaded that "it will be years and years, if ever, before we have a Chief Executive like you with enough courage and independence to do it." Willebrandt argued that "the major blocs of our people rightfully should be represented on the court," and that women have "a viewpoint that, if expressed by an intelligent womanly woman, would surely only richen the court's interpretative powers." Roosevelt ignored the petition and wrote back to say he had nominated William Douglas.

ROOSEVELT PACKS THE COURT

As Willebrandt had suggested, FDR's administration did indeed present women with one of the best opportunities for a nomination to the Supreme Court. Roosevelt would completely remake the Court with eight appointments, changing its entire political composition.[21] Allen appeared as a possibility for each of these vacancies. However, he would appoint only men from his inner circle—friends, poker cronies, advisors, and political colleagues—to ensure loyalty and presidential allegiance.[22]

Women had a powerful ally in the Roosevelt White House, First Lady Eleanor Roosevelt, and many thought that she would make all the difference. Allen connected with the First Lady through her mentors, New York social feminists Frances Kellor and Mary Drier. The First Lady corresponded with Allen and occasionally featured the first woman judge in her daily news columns.[23] Shortly after FDR was inaugurated, Allen wrote to Eleanor Roosevelt to discuss the president's political appointments of women.[24] She applauded FDR's appointments of "outstanding women in the United States service," noting that as a woman and a Democrat, she was "keenly interested in the advancement of trained and capable women." She added that she knew from her "close connections with the business and professional women, of the resentment that was felt against President Hoover because he did not recognize women."

President Roosevelt was supremely focused on Court appointments in his second term, seeking to shift the archconservativism of the Court, which had been striking down his New Deal legislation for economic recovery. He had no opportunities to appoint a Supreme Court Justice in his first presidential term, as conservative Justices held on to their positions even as they aged into their seventies. These "Nine Old Men" were lampooned in the press and in a popular book of the same name, depicted as elderly Justices who were political, vengeful, and incapable of doing their job.[25] The Justices ranged in age from sixty-one to eighty, six being older than seventy. The conservative Justices had obstructed FDR's plan and promised recovery from the Great Depression. They repeatedly struck down Roosevelt's progressive New Deal legislation regulating commerce and corporations. Criticisms of the Court's reactionary obstruction and judicial activism had been swirling since its *Lochner* decision in 1905, which had used the Substantive Due Process Clause to invalidate state workplace protection laws.[26] The "Four Horsemen"—a nickname the press gave to archconservative Justices Willis Van Devanter, James McReynolds, George Sutherland, and Pierce Butler, conjuring the biblical apocalypse—voted as a bloc to invalidate economic legislation under substantive due process and the exhumed nondelegation doctrine, protecting corporations rather than workers. The liberals on the Court, the famous jurists Holmes, Cardozo, and Louis Brandeis, were repeatedly outvoted by the conservatives. Thus, changing the personnel on the Court became Roosevelt's key goal.[27]

In 1937, Roosevelt proposed legislation for a court-packing plan. He had just won a second term by a landslide, winning every state except Maine and Vermont, and 61 percent of the popular vote, and felt empowered to govern aggressively under that mandate.[28] The proposed Judicial Procedures Reform Bill provided that the president could appoint one Justice for every Justice over the age of seventy, if they had served more than ten years, up to a maximum of fifteen Justices. That would have allowed Roosevelt to appoint six additional Justices, given the ages of the sitting jurists. There was precedent for changing the size of the Court, as it had historically varied from the original six, to five, to ten, to seven, to the nine seats today.

Roosevelt's court-packing plan was controversial, creating a "firestorm."[29] He was not deterred from his plan, believing it critical to the success of his administration. The plan was unpopular among legal elites as threatening the constitutional order and separation of powers, but had strong support from the regular people on work relief. Constitutional crisis was averted when two Justices, independent Chief Justice Charles Hughes and conservative Justice Owen Roberts, began to vote to uphold legislation. Called the "switch in time that saved nine," this shift halted the desperate need for court packing because it broke the deadlock against reform legislation and thus preserved the structural integrity of the Court.[30] Roosevelt then began to get a series of appointments that allowed him to break the judicial impasse.

There was therefore a national spotlight on FDR's first opportunity to appoint a new Justice in August 1937. Roosevelt's approach for selecting candidates was to select those who were personally loyal and to reward those who had supported his policies and legislation. He favored politicians from Congress and the federal executive branch rather than candidates with judicial experience. Roosevelt initially promised the seat to Senate Majority Leader Joe Robinson as payback for his fierce stewardship of the court plan, but Robinson died. The president then chose Senator Hugo Black of Alabama for his first appointment. Black was a political ally who supported most of FDR's New Deal legislation and the court-packing plan, and he brought an important southern state to Roosevelt. But the press called this pick "the worst he could find," claiming it was "blindly partisan" to appoint such an unqualified rural lawyer. This first appointment became a debacle when, one week after the appointment, a newspaper revealed that Black had been a member of the Ku Klux Klan, though he had resigned, and public outrage quickly escalated to calls for his impeachment. Nevertheless, Black remained on the Court and evolved into a fierce defender of civil rights and racial equality.[31]

Florence Allen had been identified as a candidate for this first vacancy. A memorandum for the "Supreme Court Appointments file" was prepared for Roosevelt with a list of possible nominees, including the name of "Judge Florence E. Allen, of Ohio," and "an otherwise unremarkable three-page-list of men."[32] Roosevelt had appointed Allen to the federal appellate court three years before and was familiar with her record. He had also appointed other women judges, including Marion Harron to the Article I Board of Tax Appeals, replacing Annabel Matthews; Ellen Ready as D.C. municipal judge; and Fay Bentley as D.C. juvenile judge. The national press featured

Allen as a top choice on a very short list because she was an "inconspicuous, sound, liberal jurist" with significant judicial experience who came from the desirable Midwest.[33] Yet, they noted practically, it was more likely her real chance would come when and if "Roosevelt had three or four Supreme Court appointments to distribute."[34] Feminist journalist Dorothy Dunbar Bromley championed Allen and encouraged "so good a feminist" as the president to choose the woman whose colleague Judge Will Stephenson endorsed for her "honest, fearless, and outspoken" decisions.[35]

A second vacancy arose a few months later in early 1938 with seventy-five-year-old Justice Sutherland's retirement, giving Roosevelt another quick opportunity for an appointment. Allen recounted in her memoir, "All of a sudden my name was mentioned."[36] Senator Vic Donahey of Ohio had forwarded Allen's name to the president and lobbied four leading unions to endorse her nomination.[37] Allen was optimistic, noting in her diary that she was "nominated @ S.Ct. again," that "More SCt" was happening, as Eleanor Roosevelt commented publicly and the papers amplified her name.[38] Both the *Washington Post* and *Washington Times* reported that the president was "toying with the idea of naming a woman to the high bench" and "anxious to give a woman who has demonstrated her judicial fitness an opportunity to reach the Supreme Court."[39] Allen, "on the list last summer," was "eminently qualified," as Justices should be picked from among lower-court judges who had "proved their judicial talents," because such a "merit system" would produce more capable Justices than "the spoils system."[40] The *Times* recognized, "of course," that "the talk of a woman on the Supreme Court is rattling a lot of dry bones (in the head) and a lot of earnest souls are fearing that this would lead to a woman president some day, at which point the country would explode."[41]

The appointment seemed imminent when Allen was invited to the White House for dinner with the president. In her diary, she characterized it as a "judicial dinner" held "to discuss" the nomination.[42] However, it was an impolitic time for the president to be considering Allen. She was in the middle of writing the final decision in the *TVA* case, critical to sustaining Roosevelt's economic and social agenda. Elevating Allen while the decision was pending looked too obviously like a presidential bribe. After some back-and-forth, Allen declined the dinner invitation, citing the workload of finalizing the opinion and likely appreciating the appearance of conflict.[43] Maybe she should have accepted, for the next day, the national newspapers reported that Allen's name had been eliminated from the Court shortlist, noting however that the Justice Department had emphasized that the removal applied only to this particular vacancy.[44]

President Roosevelt instead nominated Solicitor General Stanley Reed. Allen's fellow judges on the *TVA* panel knew of her hopes for the position and counseled her not to let her emotions show from the bench. On the morning the Reed appointment was announced, Judge John Gore whispered to Allen, "Now smile!," when she entered the courtroom, so that the watching reporters could not see her disappointment. After all, the selection seemed unfair, given that Reed had no judicial experience, had risen to federal service in Republican appointments, and did not have a law degree (though he had studied at Virginia and Columbia). On Reed's retirement, *Time* magazine reported that he was steady, but not "the most brilliant judge," and "through the years he seemed to swing from New Deal–type liberalism to the middle-of-the-road to a form of conservatism."[45]

Despite the missed opportunity of the Reed appointment, Allen was still optimistic and expected an appointment. *Life* magazine published a full-page portrait of Allen in her judicial robes, likely planned as the photo of the first woman Justice and continued as endorsement of her national candidacy. It wrote: "Because of the profound respect which Judge Allen has won by her ability and erudition, wiseacres would not be surprised if the precedent-setting President were to choose her for this supreme distinction."[46]

Allen headed to New York to regroup with mentor Frances Kellor. Allen's partner, Mary Pierce, wrote to a friend that she was planning to retire and move with Florence to Cincinnati, "but with the SC looming up I'll hold off on Cincy a little," joking that "Washington would suit me as well!"[47] They worked to increase Allen's public visibility. Ohio papers ran a coordinated campaign, complimenting her for "thinking as a man" and for "lacking the hard-boiled attitude so often accompanying women successful in competition with men." They reported that "President Roosevelt, sources close to the White House say, has been impressed by the unbroken line of liberal decisions which the Ohio jurist has given since he appointed her," citing the *TVA* case. "Mr. Roosevelt, breaker of precedents, is said to be sold on the idea of a woman on the high court and it is generally conceded that Judge Allen is the outstanding possibility for her sex."[48] Allen raised her Washingtonian profile by speaking at events like the D.C. Women's Bar Association, earning press time in the *Washington Post*.[49] Then Justice Cardozo died and a third vacancy on the Supreme Court was open to Roosevelt. Allen's name again led the public speculation, as papers opined that it "would pay to keep an eye on Judge Allen of Ohio," even if the male lawyers at the annual American Bar Association Convention never mentioned her name among possible candidates.[50]

Roosevelt ignored the public comments and in January 1939 appointed the person he had wanted all along, his friend of thirty years and advisor, Felix Frankfurter. The men were friends from Harvard Club days and regular poker buddies. Frankfurter, a Harvard constitutional law professor, would become one of the greats on the Court, but became conservative over time, favoring judicial restraint and resisting civil liberties reform.[51] He opposed an Equal Rights Amendment, mansplaining to women advocates how it was "fraught with mischief" and would endanger women's protective laws, legislation he had built his career on. He would enshrine the standard of women's difference and inferiority in need of protection in his majority opinion in *Goesaert v. Cleary*, stunting the development of gender equality law.[52] When it was suggested to him that he hire a woman during the labor shortage of World War II, he said, "I won't have a woman law clerk. Can't stand them."[53]

Roosevelt's fourth appointment of a Justice should have been one of Allen's best chances for nomination. The momentum had been building in her favor from the supportive national press and lobbying supporters; she had solidified her New Deal philosophy in the *TVA* decision and others; and the three prior appointments had diluted the controversial impact of a woman Justice.[54] "Now is the time to strike," counseled Allen's friend and advisor, Judge John Martin, with whom she had adjudicated the *TVA* case, because Roosevelt presumably had only one more year in office, and "if Roosevelt didn't appoint her she probably wouldn't get it." He instructed Mary Pierce to "let the women be turned loose now, with insistent demand for her appointment for the next vacancy." In February 1939, Justice Louis Brandeis (then eighty-two years old) resigned, ending his tenure as one of the great liberal minds on the Court. Two days later, Allen's name resurfaced, and the FBI conducted an updated report.[55] The 1939 report prepared by a higher-up in the Bureau expanded beyond her Sixth Circuit investigation and summarized her credentials, while citing the same old criticisms from the past of her inappropriate political ambition and campaigning for Congress while on the state court, and reupping the expressed bias of professional colleagues against the competence of a woman judge.

One month later, FDR announced he had a "surprise" in mind for the Court, and everyone assumed it was a woman.[56] The national papers reported that a "Justice Department's official private list" was down to Allen, William Douglas, and Attorney General Frank Murphy, while some also included D.C. circuit judge Harold Stephens, Allen's childhood friend and reference to the federal bench.[57] An exposé in the *Baltimore Sun* revealed a behind-the-scenes battle between supporters of Douglas, a Columbia law professor and chair of the new Securities and Exchange Commission, and Stephens.[58] Some had their "money on Chairman Douglas" as "a New Dealer without a blemish," though he "never practiced law in any broad sense." Other "influential Administrationists" thought Stephens was in the lead due to his western Utah connections, federal circuit experience, and young age of early fifties—all equally true of Allen. Out of that battle emerged a third choice: Allen, as a pacifying option offered by her "champions" who were "beating the bushes." Indeed, the *Sun* reported, "the woman politicians nearest the 'throne' are pressing for this appointment, on the ground first that Judge Allen's fitness is beyond question and next that her appointment would be the smartest political act of the Roosevelt Administration." The paper noted that her "greatest handicap in the past has been that she is a woman. A lot of people have recoiled from the prospect of a woman on the Supreme Court, to them the thing is almost unthinkable." Yet Allen was "admittedly a competent judge," of "sufficient youth for all practical purposes" at age fifty-four, and "enough of a Westerner to meet geographical requirements."

But then Douglas supporters played dirty. Insiders pressing for Douglas fed false information to the press claiming that Allen had a high reversal rate "worse than any other prominent federal judge," which had eliminated her from Court consideration.[59] These incendiary claims reached forty million people across the country, printed in the syndicated national gossip column "Washington Merry-Go-Round," written by the reporters who had penned the best-selling book *Nine Old Men*. Just a few months before, the reporters had incorrectly and embarrassingly linked her name to a crackpot federal judge who was suing to exempt federal judges' salaries from taxation.[60] Now, the same reporters snidely wrote: "Some of the newshawks who had predicted Judge Florence Allen's appointment to the Supreme Court were left high, dry and gasping when Douglas's name was sent to the Senate." They added: "It was true that for a time President Roosevelt considered the Ohio jurist." But what people didn't know was that "some of those who favored Douglas showed Attorney General Murphy," who was "an avowed advocate of Douglas," the list of her reversed cases that was claimed to be the worst of all federal judges. The attorney general, they reported, "was persuaded to place this record before the President, and that ended the possibility of a woman on the Supreme Court—at least for the time being."[61]

Roosevelt chose Douglas, a young appointee at forty years old and the president's "regular poker-playing companion."[62] He was considered a westerner, raised in Washington state, though he worked most years in New York and D.C. He would be a loud, big personality on the Court who would lead the civil libertarian wing.[63] Douglas also hired the first female law clerk on the Court, Lucile Lomen, during World War II when many men were serving in the military.[64]

Despite the lost opportunity, Allen could not let the attack on her work and reputation linger. She worked to correct the record. Her law clerks carefully researched all of her prior decisions, identifying only one case on the federal court that had been reversed in her five years and more than one hundred decisions.[65] They also found only one authored case from the state court over eleven years that was reversed, in which Justices Holmes and Brandeis agreed with her in dissent.[66] "These dissents," Allen said, "written by such uniformly respected judges, in the opinion of many lawyers would raise a reasonable inference that the case was rightly decided by the Supreme Court of Ohio, and wrongly reversed."[67] Allen's surrogate, former Illinois judge Catharine McCulloch, sent this information directly to Attorney General Murphy to clarify the record and preserve future candidacies.[68] Murphy wrote back directly to Allen, saying he was not aware of the reversals. "No such list as the article speaks of was ever shown to me," he said, "and I am at a loss to know where the report originated." He added, "I have frequently had occasion to express the highest regard for your ability and qualifications for judicial service, and accordingly it distresses me greatly that a statement should be published that does so great an injustice to you."[69]

The media frenzy, Allen realized with a sinking heart, was intended to kill off her nomination efforts forever.[70] The press continued to raise her name, but when Murphy next provided the president with a list of fourteen candidates for the Court, Allen's name was not on the list.[71] Murphy himself became the nominee. The attorney general was a strong favorite for appointment because he met all the presumable qualifications, being an ardent New Dealer, a Catholic (like the previous occupant of the seat being filled), and a "westerner" (from Michigan) to balance the heavy East Coast presence on the Court. He had been mayor of Detroit, an assistant U.S. attorney, and governor of the Philippines before coming to Washington.[72]

On the same day that Murphy wrote to Allen, the same FBI agent who had prepared Allen's updated report filed his memo in a separate FBI investigation into corrupt judges taking bribes that flagged Judge Allen's name.[73] The case involved judges "selling justice" by exchanging judicial favors for financial gain and accused Second Circuit Judge Martin Manton and Third Circuit Judge J. Warren Davis of fraud and bribery. The memo included the statement of a witness who said he paid to have a judge intervene in his case, and also negotiated with the intermediary to "fix another case" pending in front of Judge Fred Raymond in the district court in Michigan. If Raymond couldn't be reached, the intermediary promised, he "could secure a favorable decision" for the witness "in the Circuit Court of Appeals in Cincinnati," which "had a woman judge named Allen, this apparently being Florence E. Allen, in Cincinnati who would take care of the case." The witness said that nothing further came of that overture. Manton was later convicted for taking bribes from wealthy corporate defendants in patent litigation cases to cover significant real estate losses he suffered in the Great Depression.[74] Allen too had suffered great financial loss in the Depression with the million-dollar Alcazar debt, and had developed a particular interest in patent litigation, but there is no evidence that the FBI investigated her any further.

Allen continued to try to rehabilitate her intellectual reputation and emphasize her constitutional experience by writing a book on the

Constitution, aptly titled *This Constitution of Ours* (1940).[75] Several of the successful appointees to the Court had distinguished themselves by legal academic work. Frankfurter, Douglas, Stone, and subsequent appointee Wiley Rutledge were law professors with academic writings.[76] Solicitor General Robert Jackson positioned himself into Court contention by authoring a book, *The Struggle for Judicial Supremacy*, that offered an exhaustive justification of FDR's court-packing plan for public audiences. Allen followed this strategy, writing her book for a general audience by providing a plain account of the framework of liberties of the Constitution. The book, based on a lecture series she gave at Bryn Mawr College, was more inspirational than educational, more Hallmark gift book than scholarly analysis, designed for high school students rather than lawyers. It was also cowritten in large part by her friend Bertha Miller, to whom she assigned part of the royalties. Allen's publisher had balked at the book proposal, wanting instead to publish a promised autobiography by Allen, working with a hired ghostwriter.[77] But Allen vacillated, reluctant to expose herself and her work to public view, even when such notoriety could have helped her Supreme Court chances. Her *Constitution* book was not very good and did not sell well, priced too high for general readers. It received a few polite reviews, more for its author than its content.[78] The *New York Times* criticized Allen's preoccupation with war.[79] Another reviewer wanted more expertise from the judge: "Had Florence Allen drawn on her rich experience in the constitutional law field and written such a book, she undoubtedly would have made a worth-while contribution to legal literature. Whereupon her scholarly tome would have gone on the shelves of a hundred law libraries, to be consulted by lawyers and judges deep in constitutional lore and promptly forgotten by everyone else. Florence Allen did not write such a book."[80] Allen pandered to friends, trying to get them to endorse and publicize her book, but ultimately this attempt at reputation enhancement failed.

One year later, in July 1941, Roosevelt made three Supreme Court nominations. He elevated to Chief Justice Harlan Stone, a Republican associate justice, "in the interest of bipartisanship."[81] He then appointed Senator James Byrnes and Solicitor General Jackson. Byrnes was considered the most influential southern member of Congress, but he would serve on the Court only one year, resigning to go on to bigger things as

"Assistant President" to Roosevelt during the war, secretary of state, and governor of South Carolina.[82] Jackson was a loyal New Dealer, FDR's attorney general and solicitor general, who had actively advocated for the court-packing plan and publicized it to public audiences. He had no law degree, having attended Albany Law School for only one year. Jackson would become one of the Court's great jurists and serve as chief prosecutor of Nazi war criminals in the Nuremberg trials.[83]

The final Court vacancy, opened by Byrnes's resignation, triggered renewed lobbying for Allen, and the press reported that informants confirmed she was under "serious consideration." Stephen Young, Allen's colleague in the Cleveland prosecutor's office and now a congressional representative, urged the appointment of a woman to honor women who were "doing so much and making such great sacrifices" for victory during the second world war.[84] Roosevelt, however, nominated D.C. Circuit Judge Wiley Rutledge as Byrnes's replacement. In the midst of war, Roosevelt was less focused on his Court appointments after having had so many. Rutledge was young for a Justice at age forty-eight and had been a strong public supporter of FDR's New Deal policies and court plan. Rutledge got the nod, Roosevelt said, because he had geography in his favor as a westerner, having worked as a law professor and dean at law schools in Colorado, Missouri, and Iowa. He was the first Roosevelt appointee with federal appellate experience, with four years on the federal appellate court.[85] In an unusual request, the president asked Justices Black, Douglas, and Murphy to weigh in on Rutledge's published opinions. Allen wrote to the new Justice Rutledge about a mutual friend pressuring him to promote her *Constitution* book; he wrote back, graciously, but perturbed by the "presumptuous" and "thoughtless" request that he present her book to a program speaker. He tried to defuse the affront by ending the note by relaying an "Oriental" joke made by an attorney during oral argument.[86] Rutledge would serve only six years on the Court before his death.

As historians have observed, "by the end of Roosevelt's presidency, he had replaced almost every sitting justice on the Court," thoroughly transforming the Court. Yet even with all those opportunities, legal scholars point out, "he never nominated a woman, even though Allen must have been on his mind."[87]

TRUMAN'S POLITICOS

The next president, Democrat Harry Truman, would continue to consider Allen for the Court. In the four appointments he would make, President Truman seriously considered appointing a woman. Allen's name "resurfaced amidst a very long list of men" prepared for Truman by his attorney general, Tom Clark.[88] She tried to keep her profile in front of him, for example noting enthusiastically in her diary that "pres sees me!!!!" when she attended a committee meeting at the White House.[89] Ultimately, though, the four men Truman nominated all shared similar characteristics: "They had all held public office; they were his political, professional, and personal friends; he understood them; he liked them; they liked him; he liked their politics."[90] Truman would rely on cronyism even more than Roosevelt had.

Truman appointed one Chief Justice, Fred Vinson. Vinson had served as representative from Kentucky, where he befriended Truman in Congress, and also served on the D.C. Circuit and as secretary of treasury.[91] Vinson was a close personal friend of the president's. They socialized weekly in D.C. and at the summer White House in Florida, drinking and playing poker. Truman considered Vinson an important advisor and hoped he would provide political leadership and mediation on a contentious Court. Allen vied for this long-shot appointment, but suffragist Carrie Chapman Catt refused to use her capital and support her this time. Catt warned that a failed campaign would cause Allen and the women's movement to lose prestige and she was "afraid to risk it." She explained, "There is a good deal of politics in the wind just now, and it doesn't include giving more places to women, as you know."[92]

The year before, in 1945, Truman had appointed his first Associate Justice, Senator Harold Burton of Ohio, a Republican whom Truman had worked with in the Senate and trusted. Truman nominated Burton to maintain bipartisanship, as the opening had been left by a Republican appointee, Justice Roberts. Burton had been a Cleveland lawyer and reform mayor of that city whom Allen knew and lunched with in Washington. He spent thirteen years on the Court, "characterized by a combination of uncertainty, deliberate caution, independence, and unpredictability," known as a strong supporter of judicial restraint.[93]

Truman next had two appointments in 1949, and Allen and her supporters thought her chances had significantly improved for a nomination. A woman had been elected to the Senate, Margaret Chase Smith, a Republican from Maine, and Allen corresponded with her in hopes she would leverage her influence in that legislative body.[94] Allen supporters were still working their public campaign, orchestrating a testimonial dinner in November 1948 at NYU Law School to boost Allen's visibility for Court consideration. The banquet of one thousand at the Waldorf-Astoria, organized by Judge Dorothy Kenyon, placed Eleanor Roosevelt as honorary chair. Roosevelt could not attend, working abroad for the United Nations, but wrote a tribute explicitly commenting that "if a president of the United States should decide to nominate a woman for the Supreme Court, it should be Judge Allen," given her significant nonpartisan backing of American women.[95]

India Edwards, chair of the Democratic Party Women's Division, had now convinced President Truman to appoint a woman, using her personal connection, political power, and the press. When there was a vacancy on the Court, Edwards said, she "went over and talked to the President about appointing Florence Allen to the Supreme Court and he said, 'Well, I'm willing. I'd be glad to. I think we ought to have a woman.' And he was perfectly sincere."[96] Truman told Edwards he agreed that "it a good idea to have a woman, especially one of 'Sister' Allen's reputation and capability as a Supreme Court Justice."

But first Truman had to consult his personal friend and advisor, Chief Justice Vinson, as to whether the Justices would accept a woman into their group.[97] As regular drinking and poker buddies, the two had developed a social and political connection that by "today's standards may have bordered on the unethical" by compromising the Justice's independence.[98] Vinson reported back to Truman that the Justices said no, the "Justices didn't want a woman." They "would not willingly have a woman as a Justice" because she would make it difficult for them to meet in conference, "to meet informally with robes off," "shoes off, feet up, and shirt sleeves rolled up, in a casual discussion that could not be done in the presence of a woman." Edwards retorted, "They could if they wanted to."[99] She called out this pretext of collegiality for what it was, pure sexism, for the feuds and infighting among the Justices were "public and vicious."[100]

Battles waged between Justices Black and Jackson both personally and philosophically, as they were like "two high school boys bullying each other over perceived threats to their reputations."[101] Justice Frankfurter goaded his colleagues with his professorial air of intellectual superiority, focused particularly on Chief Justice Vinson, who he thought was not very smart.[102] The two literally came to blows when Frankfurter, pontificating in a lecture to his colleagues, questioned Vinson's integrity. Vinson clenched his fist, pushed his chair away from the table, and said, "No son of a bitch can ever say that to Fred Vinson." Vinson, a big man over six feet tall, charged toward the diminutive Frankfurter threatening blows, while other Justices pushed back their chairs to block Vinson's attack.[103]

Twenty years later, it was revealed that Truman also proposed a compromise plan to appoint Allen for just one year. An article in the nationally syndicated weekly *Parade Magazine* reported that Truman had contemplated nominating Allen, "the Justice Holmes of the female judiciary," with "the stipulation that she serve only a year and then resign."[104] It was a "meager offer," the reporter concluded, as her "influence would have been small, since it takes almost a year to learn the ropes as a Supreme Court justice. Florence Allen would have been off the bench almost before she had begun." But the positive benefit would have been that "at least the all-male precedent would have been broken."

Truman did not follow through on the token plan, and instead fell back on his usual approach of appointing his friends. The president's next appointment was Tom Clark, his attorney general (and poker buddy), whom some called "the worst appointment ever made."[105] His appointment was unpopular for its "blatant cronyism," "raw political favoritism," and Clark's apparent "cashing in of political I.O.U.s."[106] He came with scandals that plagued his career, including "irregularities in his early Texas law practice days; his purported role in the unjustified paroling of Al Capone gangsters from a federal penitentiary"; and improper behavior in voting fraud. He had a questionable record toward minorities and oversaw the internment of Japanese Americans, but the NAACP and labor unions still supported him. When Clark betrayed the president's loyalty in ruling against him in the *Youngstown Steel* case and the use of executive power to seize private steel mills in the midst of the Korean War, Truman said Clark was "about the dumbest man I think I've ever run across," and "my biggest mistake."[107]

A few months later, Truman again chose to appoint a trusted friend, Senator Sherman Minton of Indiana. Minton sat next to Truman in Congress when the landslide of 1934 caused the need to add a new row of Democratic seats at the back of the chamber.[108] Allen saved a newsclip from Minton's home state that called the appointment "very mediocre," saying Minton's "seven-year stint on the Court [of Appeals for the Seventh Circuit] has been universally and justly regarded as a failure."[109] On the Supreme Court, the "likeable, witty, popular, tobacco-chewing Minton . . . wrote no opinions of lasting significance" and was conservative on civil liberties, though he supported strong governmental power as a New Dealer.[110] Representative Stephen Young had tried to use this vacancy as an opportunity for Allen, again going to bat for her and proposing her nomination and an expanded Supreme Court of eleven to thirteen Justices to handle the heavy workload of the Court.[111]

India Edwards's lobbying did, however, pay off in securing another historic judicial appointment from Truman: the first woman district court judge. In October 1949, Truman appointed feminist lawyer Burnita Shelton Matthews to the U.S. District Court for the District of Columbia.[112] He also tried, unsuccessfully, to nominate another woman, Frieda Hennock, to the Southern District of New York.[113] Edwards, though, still had "her eye on the Supreme Court," as Allen had "only lost by an eyelash" when Minton was appointed instead of her because there were still "certain Justices who are old fashioned in their views about women."[114]

At the end of Truman's presidency, in April 1952, there were hints of renewed interest in considering Allen as the FBI prepared another, updated report.[115] The timing was puzzling, as there was no immediate Court vacancy, though the investigation happened days after Truman's executive order in the steel case, when he may have been acutely focused on the Court. The 1952 FBI summary repurposed past reports of her qualifications for judicial office, thereby perpetuating old statements based on sex bias and prejudice against women, reminding the White House of the risk of a gendered appointment. The accusation of Allen "being politically ambitious with respect to the Supreme Court" was now underscored in the memo. It corrected the record to negate allegations against Allen about ethical conflicts of campaigning for Congress while in judicial office, accepting Allen's explanation. Truman, however, made no further Supreme Court appointments.

AGED OUT UNDER EISENHOWER

Republican Dwight Eisenhower won the presidency in 1953 and would appoint five Justices to the Court. Allen gained a new generation of supporters from women legal and professional organizations that would lobby for her appointment, emphasizing her three decades of judicial experience.[116] Eisenhower articulated express criteria for his appointees, seeking a "middle-of-the-road" philosophy and a person with the character and ability to command respect and confidence, common sense, high ideals, the "absence of extreme views," and passage of a thorough FBI check.[117] Allen seemed to meet these criteria. But her supporters were told flatly by Senator John Bricker of Ohio that the administration said she was just too old at age seventy-two. Ernestine Powell, chair of the National Woman's Party, was furious, claiming that age was an excuse and that Allen had been blocked by Washington insiders at the Women's Bureau, saying that "those gals sabotaged every woman they could not control."[118] Regardless, a Supreme Court appointment was no longer politically viable.[119] Allen understood that her chances had dimmed, and wrote in her diary that she was "depressed about Supreme Court."[120]

Eisenhower appointed Chief Justice Earl Warren, a liberal Republican and three-term governor of California who would lead the liberal civil rights era on the Court. After that, Eisenhower sought more traditional candidates with judicial experience, nominating John Marshall Harlan II, a well-regarded Second Circuit judge. He next nominated William Brennan, a liberal Democrat, for the designated "Catholic" seat on the Court. Appointed in a bipartisan gesture of good will and neutrality, Brennan would become a leading liberal Justice.[121]

For Eisenhower's fourth appointment, in early 1957, Allen's supporters made one big final push. Women deluged the White House with a coordinated letter-writing campaign, appealed to the press, and provided a comparative report of international women supreme court justices. Big names like Judge Marion Harron, Judge Lorna Lockwood of Arizona, and Viola Smith, the first female foreign services officer, lent their reputation and their connections.[122] Important organizations like the National Association of Women Lawyers and the Business and Professional Women committed to aggressive lobbying for Allen.[123] Representative Frances Bolton of Ohio, one of the few women in Congress, who would serve for decades, appealed directly to the president's chief of staff. She wrote that "this is really a shot in the dark although it may have some very real value," and recommended Allen for the vacancy on the basis of her thirty-six years of judicial experience and authority on constitutional law.[124] "The thought behind this is that perhaps it will be a 'ten strike' to have a woman appointed to the bench and I certainly know of none anywhere with a more fitting background." While Allen was a Democrat, Bolton wrote, "I know the President is more or less alternating his appointments." She added that "she may be over age but that might be an added reason for giving her the appointment at this moment," meaning that she would not serve long. "Heaven knows, the Republican party needs a shot in the arm, and this may draw women." Allen now presented herself as a nonpartisan, emphasizing her Republican connections.[125]

Despite the full-court press, Judge Charles Whittaker got the appointment, which by all accounts was a terrible choice. He had served for one year as a federal appellate judge on the Eighth Circuit, and two years on the district court. But he was nominated because he was a close friend of Eisenhower's brother Arthur in Kansas City. Soon after his appointment, Whittaker called the attorney general, complaining of being overwhelmed by the job and wanting to quit. He stepped down after five years, citing a nervous breakdown and physical exhaustion from the pressure and angst on the Court, returning to private practice with General Motors.[126]

Eisenhower's final appointee was an Ohioan from the Sixth Circuit, Allen's junior colleague Potter Stewart. Stewart was forty-three years old, thirty years younger than Allen. His father, James Garfield Stewart, was a justice on the Ohio Supreme Court and politically as well connected as his son, having been mayor of Cincinnati and a Republican candidate for Ohio governor. Potter Stewart had worked at a big New York law firm and had the support of the bar.[127] Justice Reed rubbed salt in Allen's wounds by writing her shortly after the nomination that "Potter Stewart is doing well here, as all who knew were sure he would."[128] Stewart became famous for legally defining obscenity as "I know it when I see it."[129] He also advocated changing the traditional gendered honorific of "Mr. Justice" to the neutral "Justice," based on his experience sitting with Allen, saying that "sooner or later we were going to have women serving on the Court, and that it would be wise to anticipate that change." The Court voted eight to one to make the change.[130]

Allen's supporters from women lawyers' associations alternatively proposed that Eisenhower appoint her to the United Nations' International Court of Justice, which would have been a fitting place for her interests and skill set, but she lacked the political gravitas or party affiliation for this position.[131] Eisenhower appointed only one woman judge, Mary Donlon, replacing Genevieve Cline on the U.S. Customs Court, restructured in 1956 as the Article III U.S. International Court of Trade. Donlon's announcement appeared in the back "woman's page" of the *New York Times*, next to articles about the latest fall fashion and food-shopping advice; "gallantry" and "chivalry" were cited as the basis for her appointment.[132]

WHY NOT FLORENCE?

Allen was not chosen for the U.S. Supreme Court because she was a woman. Women's lobbying groups had little influence to advance their candidate after their initial legislative success once enfranchised, as their past efforts were overtaken by integration into the main parties. Sexism was strong, as lawyers and judges dismissed women's ability to handle the intellectual difficulty of matters brought before the Court. A few devastating press articles questioned Allen's competence. It was the high mark of cronyism, the old boys' club at its worst, and a woman had no chance with this insiders' club.[133] Allen was criticized for her political ambitions, which violated demure gender norms, even though such ambitions were expected among men candidates. After her confirmation to the Sixth Circuit, when supporters said they hoped to see her on the "Supreme Bench of the U.S.," Allen responded with a reality check. "I know two things," she said. "First, that will never happen to a woman while I am living, and second, that perhaps it is just as well not to mention that possibility at the present time because there is a certain type of lawyer that immediately becomes fighting mad when that possibility is mentioned."[134]

Some also considered Allen too moderate—not liberal enough for the Democrats and too progressive for the Republicans.[135] Allen often ran as a nonpartisan and described herself as a liberal conservative, self-identifying as a moderate despite her Democratic credentials. *Time* magazine called her "middle-of-the roadish," and *News-Week* said her opinions were a mix of both liberalism and conservativism.[136] Labor abandoned its support, believing Allen not zealously liberal enough, though they belatedly realized she was a judicial ally and quietly renewed their support.[137] Roosevelt stated that he wanted an "evangelical" of the New Deal, but the press said Allen's "handicap" was that the president's inner circle wanted a "pronounced liberal."[138] Allen did demonstrate this evangelism for progressive governmental power consistently in her opinions, especially the *TVA* and *Filburn* decisions. She had also demonstrated her Democratic loyalty, running for Congress twice under the party label and delivering a speech in 1932, "I Shall Vote for FDR," that publicly proclaimed her endorsement of Roosevelt and his agenda. Yet Roosevelt, and Truman after him, did not always pick the person with the strongest liberal views, and to the contrary picked candidates from the opposing party and those with moderate views.[139]

The race issue may have also come into play in weighing against Allen's Supreme Court nomination, given that the NAACP had actively opposed her federal appellate court appointment. Opposition by the NAACP and labor unions had previously caused the failure of the nomination of John Parker, a respected Fourth Circuit Court of Appeals judge from North Carolina, suggesting that their opposition to Allen packed significant weight.[140] Following the Hugo Black scandal over his Klan membership, public claims of racism were particularly sensitive.[141] The NAACP continued to aggressively oppose Allen, as it had in her federal appellate appointment, on the basis of her vote on the Ohio Supreme Court in *Weaver v. Ohio State University* refusing to strike down racial segregation in college housing and reinscribing Jim Crow ideas of social segregation. *Weaver* was an important test case for the organization in challenging racial segregation and Judge Allen had failed that test.[142] Her obstinate defense of her decision in *Weaver* on technical legalistic grounds was politically obtuse, even if it appeased some White House concerns.

There were also veiled allegations of communist connections against Allen that may have shadowed her nomination. The file highlighted her radical dissent in *State v. Kassay* in support of the communist defendant, protecting political speech, characterizing it as endorsing an "ultra-radical communistic element" and allowing a threat to "go unpunished."[143] FBI reports identified Allen on a list of members of the American Council Institute of Pacific Relations, an international organization that, according to the FBI, had been "infiltrated by Communists." The Daughters of the American Revolution had identified her as a "Red" for her peace work. It was true that her passionate activism for ending the inhumanity of war was radical, aggressive, and highly visible. The FBI had also flagged her fleeting membership in the "Law and Order" committee of community leaders, prosecutors, and police reacting to the violent Cleveland May Day Riots in 1919, when socialists paraded, protesters shot at police, police resorted to strong tactics, and the city banned protests. Cleveland, like other urban areas at the time, also experienced a flaring of racial violence over the racist film *Birth of a Nation* and attacks on Black children riding in streetcars and swimming in lakes. The Law and Order group tried to mediate this unrest, supporting free speech and public assembly but enforcing the rule of law and avoidance of riots.[144] Allen joined the group in her role as a prosecutor, along with other influential public and religious community officials, including her cousin, medical doctor Jacob Tuckerman, who led the committee.[145] Years later, the FBI cleared any rumors, concluding that "FEA is certainly no communist," calling into question the reliability of the sources, and underscoring that there was "nothing derogatory in our files" about Allen and communism.[146]

Allen's spinster status may also have been suspicious, as papers often highlighted that "she is unmarried."[147] Early on, the "bachelor woman" had been celebrated for her unmarried status as exemplifying her singular dedication to the judicial profession. But during the Depression and the vast loss of jobs, the unmarried working woman became a pariah, a target of social animus for allegedly taking jobs away from those who had a household to support. Further animosity against single women was fueled by the Economy Act of 1932, which prohibited the government from employing both members of a married couple, resulting in loss of married women's jobs, pitting them against unmarried women.[148] Allen stepped into this debate inadvertently by a casual comment during a broadcast speech to professional women that spread among the nation's newspapers. She said that "during this entire period of financial stress the unmarried woman earning her living has stood out like a shining star," and that the "old maid in the family" was the family's "refuge from the problems."[149] Allen's unorthodox position drew public outrage and cast aspersions on her own unmarried status.

In addition, the growing cultural conservativism and the Lavender Scare made any hint of lesbianism a red flag. Allen's public defense of Marion Harron made that connection. She understood the risk of the association, and cautioned Harron against "being too public in her efforts to promote" her Supreme Court appointment, and to remain anonymous in any recommendation letters to protect them both from those who wanted to make trouble by embarrassing them "or worse."[150] Olga Jones, a D.C. reporter and friend from outlawry work, wrote to Allen intimating that this type of sensitive issue lay behind the failed nomination: "As an old newspaper person, I think I know what was back of what happened; but I must not write it. You trust me some time and I shall tell you the whole story as I see it." Jones explained that she was not comfortable sending "this sort of letter" to Allen at her office.[151]

Similar types of rumors of sexual orientation, however, were dismissed by President Roosevelt in his appointment of Justice Frank Murphy. Modern commentators have concluded that Murphy was "a gay main hiding in plain sight."[152] He was a "bachelor," remaining unmarried, but for forty years "was very close to a male companion," Edward Kemp, his Michigan law school classmate with whom he lived and worked. Kemp was Murphy's speechwriter, aid, and roommate and inherited all of Murphy's estate.[153] Murphy's biographers uncovered one letter from a lover, written when Murphy was governor of the Philippines, recounting a gay sexual encounter. Once Murphy was in D.C., during the time of the Lavender Scare, he was often seen with glamorous women on his arm, and he became engaged to a woman, though they never married, and made plans before his death to live in a house with both her and Kemp. Murphy evinced a deep understanding of the harms of discrimination, becoming an "outspoken social justice champion" on the Court, famously casting a dissent in the *Korematsu v. United States* case opposing the internment of Japanese Americans and its "ugly abyss of racism."[154]

While many factors may have contributed to Allen's failed consideration for the U.S. Supreme Court, at the end of the day, she was not appointed because she was a woman. Presidents perceived no value, and feared great risk, from the unprecedented appointment of a female Justice. At this highest level of the judiciary, women had little political influence or leverage by which to force the integration of the highest court. And no women played poker or politics in the backrooms of the Washington boys' clubs. The limits of women's power had been reached.

Epilogue

THE DIFFERENCE OF GENDER

After forty years of judging, Judge Allen retired. In October 1959, the seventy-five-year-old Allen was feted with the customary luncheon and portrait presentation to the court. The event was orchestrated by two women federal judges, tax court judge Marion Harron and Burnita Shelton Matthews of the D.C. district court. Matthews described the "beautiful and brilliant" setting of the walnut-paneled courtroom, filled to capacity, and Allen's portrait decorated with a drape of red velvet next to a large brass bowl of mammoth gold chrysanthemums.[1] The first woman judge was supported by her community of women, partner Mary Pierce, sister Esther, niece Keenie, grandniece and namesake Florence Allen Hill, and friends from the National Association of Women Lawyers. All of Allen's colleagues from the Sixth Circuit attended the presentation, no longer dismissing her as an unwanted guest.

The portrait donation was funded in part by the Cleveland Patent Law Association, claiming Allen as one of their own. The patent bar held a separate event days earlier where Justice Potter Stewart spoke, though he damned her with faint praise, noting only that she was a "helpful teacher," with a "boundless capacity for work," and "sometimes gave the appearance of aloofness."[2] Allen was aggravated by his remarks and wrote a sarcastic thank you back, saying she "had not the slightest conception" that he came to Cleveland "to make such a friendly statement upon the work that I have tried to do in the United States Court of Appeals."[3]

At the court's retirement celebration, Judge Allen spoke briefly, recounting some of her familiar anecdotes from practice while slipping into nostalgia. Chief Judge Thomas McAllister of the Sixth Circuit spoke fondly of Allen, saying the judges of the court were proud of serving with her and thought of her "with affection as a comrade and a friend."[4] "The heart and mind of Florence Allen," he said, "will flame for generations as a beacon for thousands of young women who will take their rightful places in government, in the practice of the law, and in judicial service—and lawyers and judges yet unformed will read the words she has written, in the endless, ever-old and ever-new quest for justice."

Allen was considered a success by all accounts—"a bright star," "elevated to the second highest court in the land," who had "opened up avenues not only to herself, but to other women."[5] As Justice Ruth Bader Ginsburg later explained, Florence Allen made it "less difficult for the rest of us to gain appointment or election to the judiciary, and realistic for legions of women in the future to aspire to—and achieve—a full life in the law."[6] Allen knew this, and said when first elected to the trial court: "It's so worth-while being a judge, because, if I make good, I can help prove that a woman's place is as much on the bench, in city council, or in Congress, as in the home. This entrance of woman into other fields of activity can but demonstrate that her latent capabilities are unmined gold that the world cannot be without."[7] That was Allen's objective for her own legacy: "I have tried with all that is in me to justify the presence of women on the courts."[8]

Allen once said it "was not easy to be a judge," to make life and death decisions; but, she said, "it is a wonderful thing to be a woman and feel the force of awakened womanhood behind you."[9] After retirement, she technically accepted an appointment as senior judge, subject to physician approval, but did not end up hearing cases.[10] Instead, Allen spent her last twenty-five years dedicated to traveling the world to improve the legal rights of women, marrying her faith in international law with her commitment to women's equality. She worked mostly with the International Federation of Women Lawyers, or Federación Internacional de Abogadas, founded in Mexico City in the aftermath of World War II. Women were not welcomed into international bar association meetings at that time, so they created their own space and organization.[11] The Federación adopted a dispersion strategy of sending members around the world to speak out for its aims of family law reform, protecting children through juvenile courts, advancing equal employment for women, suffrage for women in all countries, and passage of equal rights amendments. "Their agenda of ending patriarchy was radical," wrote a legal historian. "These women were trained in the masculine legal profession and experienced at operating in male organizations. They used the language and power of law to give them legitimacy, to give them access to institutional spaces, and to effect change."[12] Allen traveled as part of this dispersion diplomacy, conferring with the supreme court justices of Japan, advising women lawyers in the newly established Republic of Turkey, and challenging Israel's new religious regime on married women's property.[13] She went to Finland, Peru, and Mexico, usually accompanied by Mary Pierce, using her gravitas as the first woman judge in America to advocate equality for her "sisters in the law."[14] Allen won the respect and loyalty of Federación president Rosalind Bates, the Latina leader of the next generation of international women lawyers who became one of Allen's loudest advocates for a Supreme Court nomination.

Allen's closing words in her memoir call women lawyers to action for justice and the rule of law. She was concerned about the loss of women in national leadership, which had deviated from the suffrage promise.[15] While she noted the "great changes in the status of women" that had come about during her time, it was "hardly fitting to satisfy ourselves with the fact that women today may enter lucrative employment in one of the time-honored professions." Instead, the present time called for the need to "raise our sights and reappraise opportunities" for the greater good. The lawyer, through her own integrity and idealism, had to act to teach citizens the meaning of equality, justice, and liberty: "In these days, when we see the ethical basis of law attacked, when we see government of men, not of laws, government which openly repudiates the equality of men before the law, their right to personal freedom, their right to work at whatever calling they choose, when, in a word, the principles of justice are discarded . . . we, as lawyers, face a specific challenge. . . . We have to fight as lawyers against the movement to abolish the conception of right and justice which lies at the basis of civilization."[16]

Allen's story, like the story of women's integration of the law and courts more generally, reveals both the power and limitation of gender. Gender made a difference in the success of Allen's historic election and ascension to the bench. Women in the suffrage movement, both those in the national organization and grassroots activists, were critical to her success. Political connections to Eleanor Roosevelt, Molly Dewson, Bernice Pyke, and India Edwards were instrumental in shepherding her nominations. Personal friends like mentor Frances Kellor and partners Susan Rebhan and Mary Pierce provided the support system to sustain her professional success and personal happiness. Allen paid this forward, endorsing Judges Marion Harron and Mary Grossman, as well as mentoring enumerable women lawyers as she extended the ladder down behind her over the years.

Gender also made a difference in Allen's failures. As women gained suffrage and faced the political need to join the mainstream parties if they were to have any meaningful influence, the assimilation into the male establishment was unwelcome and resisted. In that environment, they lost touch with the female power bases and networks that had "nurtured the personal and public lives of earlier generations of women."[17] Allen's unsuccessful runs for Congress showed this lack of support for women candidates from the partisan male establishment and the aversion of male voters. She was sidelined by male judicial colleagues into limited roles and less influential cases. The sexism she encountered made it more difficult for Allen to do her work fully and effectively. Her gender disqualified her for a U.S. Supreme Court appointment, as she was dismissed by Washingtonians operating under a fraternity of brotherhood and political cronyism.

Gender, however, made little difference to the results or process of Allen's judicial decision-making. Modern scholars have obsessed over the question of whether women judges judge differently.[18] The assumption is that women must offer something distinctive or advantageous to justify their selection over the default choice of a man. Allen's judicial record confirms the results of modern studies, which almost uniformly conclude that women judges do not judge substantively differently than men. To the contrary, these studies show that the outcomes of decisions are driven by the same array of political, moral, jurisprudential, and experiential influences.[19] One key explanation for this similarity is judicial assimilation; as one legal scholar has written, the law and process to become a judge "suppresses gender-based differences in behavior," as "women must act like men to gain acceptance into the male-dominated judicial sphere and then are expected to apply precedent that has been overwhelmingly decided by men."[20] Allen did not utilize a feminine decision-making style like problem solving or social welfare, instead adopting a masculine mantra—"to do justly"—emphasizing the traditional command of justice as judgment.[21]

Gender may have made a small difference at the margins of Allen's cases involving women parties. Allen said that women brought a social consciousness and moral authority that helped them understand a broader scope of issues impacting women.[22] Some modern studies suggest that women judges show more affinity for female victims in sex discrimination cases.[23] The explanation offered is that women judges have a different perspective, derived from their own social experiences and those of other women, from which to better understand the problem and gendered realities of a female party.[24] Indeed, this assumption is so strong that other first women judges like Constance Baker Motley and Ann Aldrich (first woman district judge in the Northern District of Ohio) were asked to recuse in sex discrimination cases because they would identify too much with the female plaintiff; both Motley and Aldrich refused.[25] Allen showed this type of feminist affinity for women in many of her routine cases of employment, wills, property, and family law, seeming to appreciate the way in which women had been subordinated and negatively impacted by the operation of the law.[26] However, in the few cases that came before her directly presenting issues of gendered harm in juries, employment, or prison sentences, Allen seemed to take a back seat, using anonymity or deference to male colleagues rather than promoting her own female perspective. Studies have shown that "judicial decisions were perceived as more authoritative" when written by a man. Behind the scenes, though, Allen may have been exercising what studies have called "panel effects," where the presence of a woman on a judicial panel helps her colleagues better understand the gendered problem and its consequences.[27]

Gender could have made a difference if Allen had been appointed to the U.S. Supreme Court. In the years when she could have been nominated, the Court heard cases of gender discrimination in the contexts of labor, employment, voting, and jury service—cases where a Justice Allen might have cast a counter vote and influenced the deliberations at conference.[28]

Particularly in the series of jury cases chipping away at all-male juries, where the Court grasped for legal justifications, it could have used a woman Justice like Allen who understood the sex equality theory supporting the jury right.[29] Indeed, it would take the advent of the first woman Justice, Sandra Day O'Connor, forty years later to clarify the gender equality right to jury service.[30] A Justice Allen also could have weighed in on one of the first cases of gender discrimination under the Equal Protection Clause, *Goesaert v. Cleary*. The case set women's antidiscrimination law back thirty years as the Supreme Court developed a low, rational basis standard to assess sex-based classifications.[31] Justice Frankfurter and the majority easily upheld a state law prohibiting women from working as bartenders, concluding it was rational to assume that women had physical, moral, and social weaknesses needing protection. He included a lewd anecdote of the Shakespearian "alewife, sprightly and ribald," joking about the absurdity of women bartenders.

Looking at the big picture, it is clear that gender and the advent of the first woman judge made a "profound change in the status of women and a radical departure in the conception and work of the courts."[32] Allen's gender made a tremendous difference in her symbolic role in shattering the glass ceiling of the judiciary, thereby enhancing the legitimacy of the courts. She was a powerful, nationally visible role model of "what a judge looks and sounds like" for women, lawyers, judges, politicians, and the general public, displaying how women could effectively govern in judicial roles.[33] As Allen explained, her breakthrough also empowered all women, for "when women sit in government, women as a whole become conscious of their individual interest and ownership in government."[34] Diversifying the bench to include women improved the legitimacy of the courts by ending the systemic discrimination the law itself created and enforced. As Allen said, since women are litigants, citizens, and persons in the courts, "they are entitled to play their parts equally with men in the administration of justice."[35] It is important, she said, that courts, as defenders of the rule of law, not be seen as systems of exclusion and oppression. Thus, it was justice simply to no longer exclude one-half of the human race from judicial office.

Women on the bench also critically enhance the representational role of the courts as impartial tribunals by expanding the diversity of arbiters to include a broader portion of the polity. This representation functions to improve people's trust in the decisions of the courts, with judges democratically reflecting the populace as a nonexclusionary body.[36] Integrating the bench to include women makes for a "fairer legal system" beyond mere "window dressing or political correctness," by more inclusively reflecting the norms of a wider and more representative community.[37] Allen explained how women judges recalibrated the court's structural impartiality by centering women's experience and by negating stereotypes of women in the legal system that unfairly disadvantage litigants, witnesses, attorneys, and jurors.[38]

Gender, however, in the context of Allen's historic first appointments, operated as tokenism, delaying rather than accelerating the advent of women judges. In the long run, Allen's legacy won out, but it was muted by the glacial pace of appointing women judges. In the short term, Allen's influence was silenced by subsequent conservative appointments that replaced her individual contributions. Her immediate successor on the Sixth Circuit, appointed by President Eisenhower, was conservative Paul Weick, a federal district judge who had been a personal injury and corporate lawyer in Akron and an advisor to the Republican Party. A "lawyer's lawyer" embraced by the fraternity of male lawyers as president of the bar association, he was known for ending school desegregation remedies and ruling against recovery for the students killed in the Kent State shooting by the Ohio National Guard.[39]

The next woman appointed to the Sixth Circuit, by President Jimmy Carter in 1979, twenty years after Allen's retirement, was conservative Michigan jurist Cornelia Kennedy, initially nominated to the district court by President Richard Nixon. Judge Kennedy ruled against women in a ban on coed sports, upheld the right of voters to restrict civil rights for LGBTQ people, vacated Detroit school desegregation remedies, ruled against Black plaintiffs in most race-based cases against the police or prisons, and ruled against the plaintiff in a sexual harassment case, writing that "civil rights law did not protect a woman from a boss's obnoxious or suggestive words." Kennedy had been the first woman law clerk on the D.C. Circuit, hired by Allen's good friend Harold Stephens, who seemed to have absorbed some of the ideals of women's equality from Allen. Kennedy, however, faced sexism similar to that experienced by Allen and other women judges, with the American Bar Association questioning her qualifications and competence even after nine years as a federal district judge and several more on the state court.[40]

Beyond the Sixth Circuit, it would take decades before Allen's famous first triggered second and third appointments of women. It would be sixty years, over half a century, before a woman was appointed to the U.S. Supreme Court. It was not until 1981 that Ronald Reagan, faced with a demonstrable gender gap, wooed women voters by making a campaign promise to appoint the first woman Justice, which he did in nominating Sandra Day O'Connor, an Arizona jurist and legislator.[41] It would also take sixty years before another woman served on the Ohio Supreme Court. Blanche Krupansky was temporarily appointed by a Republican governor in 1981, and Alice Robie Resnick was elected in 1989.[42] It would be almost forty years after Allen's first before a woman served on the highest court of any state, with the ascension of Rhoda Lewis in Hawaii and Lorna Lockwood in Arizona.[43] And it would be thirty years before a woman was appointed to any federal appellate court, as it was not until 1968 that President Lyndon Johnson nominated Shirley Hufstedler to the Ninth Circuit.[44]

As scholars have explained, although token women like Allen "in a highly visible and powerful office may provide a 'role model' for women, they do not automatically trigger an increase in appointments," because tokenism can operate in the opposite way, restricting rather than expanding opportunities due to the "mistaken belief that inequality has been eradicated."[45] It would take a systemic disruption to change this status quo and include women in meaningful numbers. That disruption came at the federal level in the form of President Carter's 1977 executive order changing the process for nomination of federal judges and prioritizing the recruitment of women and racial minorities.[46] The new process deemphasized the practice of senators recommending political candidates and created mandatory nominating commissions composed of diverse lawyers and leaders, including women, to generate a merit-based list of candidates that included certain numbers of women and people of color. Women now had meaningful opportunities for judicial appointment, even though they were still asked sexist questions like whether their "husbands would be jealous if they were appointed, whether they would be able to sentence criminals to jail, whether they could handle the workload, and who would take care of their children."[47]

One hundred years after Allen's historic first, there is still a recognized "gavel gap"—a disconnect between the 33 percent representation of women on the bench, but the 52 percent representation of women in society and the 57 percent representation of women in law schools seeking entry to the legal profession.[48] Women continue to demand equal representation and power in the critical lawmaking venues of society. And there have been successes. As of May 2024, seventeen states had female majorities on their supreme courts, although five states had only one woman justice.[49] Allen's Ohio Supreme Court was majority women in 2014, and close to equal with three of seven justices in 2025. In Allen's Northeast Ohio, the Summit County Common Pleas bench of ten judges was all women in 2026, as it had been since 2019.[50] The face of justice can be female.

Judge Florence Allen died at age eighty-two on September 12, 1966, weakened after a fall the year before in which she broke a hip.[51] The *Washington Post* memorialized her as a "champion of women's rights" who was known to her associates as a "two-fisted woman"—a strong, tough, aggressive, hard-hitting woman who was a "fighter for principles."[52] Judge Marion Harron, colleague, protégé, and friend, wrote Allen's eulogy.[53] Harron highlighted the way in which Allen embodied women's broader transformation of the law: "The unique and remarkable fact in the life and career of Judge Allen is that during her life-span she herself did and achieved outstanding things that in themselves constituted the great changes in the status of women in the United States and the world: she accomplished those things which meant that womenhood attained the rights of full citizenship, the right to enter the learned professions, the right to stand for elective office, and the right to take their places in government and in judicial service." In her early years, Harron recounted, Allen worked for the attainment of women's rights and human rights through suffrage and international peace activism. "When some of those rights had been won, Judge Allen then went to do the things which women had claimed they could and were entitled to do; she accepted the heavy responsibilities of those rights and by her hard and brilliant work, she entered the highest judicial services as a judge." That Allen did not serve as a Justice of the Supreme Court of the United States, Judge Harron concluded, "is our Nation's loss."

Acknowledgments

While writing and research is an individual journey, it takes a village to bring the work to fruition. I am grateful to the University of Akron School of Law for supporting this work through a sabbatical and financial research assistance through the Center for Constitutional Law at Akron. A special thank you to my editor, Maura Roessner, for her wisdom and enthusiasm for this project. I am grateful for the outstanding work of copyeditor Richard Earles. And I am thankful for the publicity efforts of Michelle Blankenship, helping others know about the first woman judge.

My thanks to Dean Richard Aynes, who first introduced me to Florence Allen in the hallways of the law school. And to Joan "Punky" Organ for friendship and partnership on our path to finding Florence Allen; your dedication, incomparable detective work, and conversation have made all the difference to Florence's legacy. Thanks also to Richard Dana, for sharing your research and thoughts on Florence and her family.

I am indebted to all those who read the manuscript and provided thoughtful feedback, including Steve Funk, lawyer and spouse, who read every word—more than once—and spent many dinners listening to thoughts about Florence. Special appreciation goes out to Professor Martin Siegel for your heavy lifting of reading the entire manuscript and your deep engagement with its ideas. Thanks to Professor Sally Kenney for your thoughtful suggestions, and to Professor Ryan Vacca for your expert insights on patent law. And a heartfelt thanks to my Akron Law colleagues who read chapters and joined in discussions along the way, including

Michael Gentithes, Vera Korzun, Charlie Oldfield, and Heather Zirke. I appreciate the help with resources from fellow historians Anya Jabour and Hannah Brenner Johnson. I want to thank as well the many student research assistants who provided help at all phases of this project, including Karen Annarumo, Robert Barrett, Ashley Bierman, Dominie Burwell, Kendra Colby, Mitchell Crawford, Amy Day, Kyle Fuller, Carrie Hill, William Huff, Taylor King, Kara Marlin, Morgan Mayer, Jeanette Meisel, Heather Melena, Nick Moglia, Jenna Poleykett, Dominick Sawaya, Danielle Schantz, Marc Scolnik, Skylar Sluzewski, and Rebekah Sullivan, with a special thanks to Kathy Ainsworth. A shout out as well to Bettina Elias Siegel for book talk and your gift of author websites.

I am immensely grateful for the dedication and assistance of the librarians who make legal research possible, with a special appreciation for those innovators who have digitized collections and revolutionized a whole new world of research. Thanks to Sarah Starnes, Sue Altmeyer, and Tiffanie Nevins at the University of Akron School of Law Library for your help with my many questions and requests to find needles in the haystack. A special thanks goes to Ann Sindelar at the Western Reserve Historical Society as the custodian of Allen's donated papers. My gratitude also for the help of librarians at the Library of Congress, Schlesinger Library at Harvard, University of Chicago Library, Western Reserve Academy, New York University Special Collections, Ohio Supreme Court Law Library, Sixth Circuit Library, and Bowling Green State University, who all responded to requests with diligence and interest. Your role in preserving our collective historical legacy and facilitating its access is an important one.

Notes

Some of the research in this book was previously published in Tracy A. Thomas, "The Jurisprudence of the First Woman Judge, Florence Allen: Challenging the Myth of Women Judging Differently," *William & Mary Journal of Race, Gender, and Social Justice* 27, no. 2 (2021): 293–349.

Unless otherwise noted, all letters, diaries, speeches, newsletters, newsclips, and other primary documents cited in this book are located in the Florence Ellinwood Allen Papers, Western Reserve Historical Society, Cleveland, Ohio.

INTRODUCTION

1. Allan Harding, "The First Woman to Sit on a Supreme Court Bench," *American Magazine*, Apr. 19, 1923, 19, 198–202; "Ohio Woman Judge Was News Writer: Miss Florence Allen Is First of Her Sex to Be Elected," *Washington Post*, Nov. 11, 1922, 4; "First Woman Judge Voices Thanks: Florence Allen, Appointed by Roosevelt, Urges Feminist Cause," *Washington Post*, Mar. 8, 1934, 13.

2. Katz, "'May It Please Her Honor,'" 1732–36; Morello, *Invisible Bar*, 217–31.

3. Tuve, *First Lady*, 126; *Time*, Mar. 19, 1934, Florence Ellinwood Allen Papers, Library of Congress [hereafter LOC Papers]; "Taft Court Room Gets Judge Allen," *Plain Dealer*, Apr. 10, 1934, LOC Papers.

4. Allen, *Justly*, 95.

5. Jefferson and Johnson, *Shortlisted*, 16, 31, 72; Tuve, *First Lady*, 161–67.

6. Telegram, President and Mrs. Roosevelt to Florence E. Allen [hereafter FEA], Jan. 14, 1938; Cook, "First Woman Candidate," 27.

7. Drew Pearson and Robert S. Allen, "Washington Merry-Go-Round: Florence Allen Eliminated by Long Record of Reversals by Higher Courts," United Feature Syndicate, Mar. 24, 1939.

8. Memorandum, "Reversals of Decisions of Judge Florence Allen" [ca. 1939]; Allen, *Justly*, 112.

9. Catharine McCulloch to Frank Murphy, Apr. 17, 1939.

10. Allen, *Justly*, 112–13.

11. "Judge Allen First Choice of Women," *Cincinnati Enquirer*, July 21, 1949.

12. Edwards, *Pulling No Punches*, 171–72; Edwards, "Oral History Interview," 84–85.

13. Edwards, *Pulling No Punches*, 171–72.

14. Sloan, *Court at War*, 13–15.

15. Jefferson and Johnson, *Shortlisted*, 72; St. Clair and Gugin, *Vinson*, 156–61, 176, 190; Abraham, *Justices and Presidents*, 232, 240, 251; Sloan, *Court at War*, 87; Murphy, *Wild Bill*, 101; Clark, "One Man's Token," 504.

16. Edwards, *Pulling No Punches*, 171–72.

17. Philip Hoffman, "Does the U.S. Supreme Court Need a Woman Justice?," *Parade Magazine* (*Oakland Tribune*), Dec. 11, 1966; Mary McLeod, "NAWL President's Letter," Jan. 1967.

18. Abraham, *Justices and Presidents*, 232, 240, 251.

19. Edwards, *Pulling No Punches*, 171–72.

20. Brown-Nagin, *Civil Rights Queen*, 259.

21. E. A. Tamm, FBI Memorandum to the Director Re: Florence Ellinwood Allen, Feb. 15, 1939 (including R. C. Chapman, FBI Investigative Report Regarding Hon. Florence E. Allen, Jan. 20, 1934).

22. *Plain Dealer*, Jan. 19, 1934, 8; "Judge Allen Prepares to Take Post Here," newsclip, n.d., LOC Papers.

23. "Woman Judge: Federal Court Post Goes to Florence Allen," *News-Week*, Mar. 17, 1934, 9.

24. "Oh, Look, Your Honors, a Skirt!," *Cincinnati Times Star*, Apr. 10, 1934.

25. "Judge Allen as Kate Carter Sees Her," newsclip, Nov. 2 [1922].

26. FEA, Diary [hereafter Diary], July 19, 1916; "Ohio's Woman Judge an Imposing Figure," *New York Times*, Dec. 3, 1922.

27. Newsclip, *Washington Post*, Apr. 28, 1934.

28. Organ, "Sexuality as a Category," 105, 148; Diary, Jan. 6, 1919; June 4, 1920; Nov. 30, 1923.

29. Drachman, *Sisters in Law*, 98–99; Cott, *Grounding*, 182.

30. Organ, "Sexuality as a Category," 93; Diary, Dec. 10, 1912; Mar. 29, 1913; June 16–18, 1913; Nov. 25, 1913; Feb. 14, 1915; Jan. 16, 1916; Nov. 20, 1923; June 4, 1920.

31. Diary, Jan. 6, 1919; June 4, 1920; Organ, "Sexuality as a Category," 146–48.

32. Beachy, *Gay Berlin*, xvii–xix, 85–87; Leng, *Sexual Politics and Feminist Science*, 117–26, 134–39.

33. Tuve, *First Lady*, 17; Diary, Aug. 29, 1904.

34. Diary, July 13, 1905.

35. Schwarz, *Radical Feminists*, 1, 36, 75, 86–89; Scutts, *Hotbed*, 6, 8, 151–56; Diary, Feb. 9, 28, 1912; Mar. 1, 1912; Dec. 29, 1912; June 26, 1913.

36. Organ, "Sexuality as a Category," 16–17, 146, 210; Faderman, *To Believe*, 137–38, 529–32; Faderman, *Odd Girls*, 16, 25; Ware, *Partner*, xv; Rouse, *Public Faces*, 8.

37. Faderman, *Odd Girls*, 2–6, 15, 19; Faderman, *To Believe*, 25–26, 199–200, 269–70.

38. Jefferson and Johnson, *Shortlisted*, 157.

39. Organ, "Sexuality as a Category," 11–12; Faderman, *To Believe*, 20–21; Kenney, "Stupendous," 214–15; Jefferson and Johnson, *Shortlisted*, 154, 157; O'Connor and Yanus, "Women as Leaders," 245–47.

40. Salmon Levinson to FEA, Jan. 27, 1927, Salmon Levinson Papers, Hanna Holborn Gray Special Collections, University of Chicago.

41. "Woman Justice from Ohio Rates Portia Great Judge," Portland, Oregon, newsclip, 1923; "Cleveland Outside the Spotlight," *Plain Dealer*, Mar. 11, 1934; "Judge to Be Here," *Edwardsville (IL) Intelligencer*, Nov. 10, 1922; newsclip, *Chronicle Telegram* (Elyria, Ohio), Sept. 13, 1935.

42. "Her Legal Vigor Woven at Blackboard and Plow," *Plain Dealer*, Feb. 23, 1930.

43. Tuve, *First Lady*, 63, 80, 93; Allen, *Justly*, 65, 71; Organ, "Sexuality as a Category," 175 n.59; "Gets Lady Manager for Senate Fight," *Appleton (WI) Post Crescent*, June 1, 1926; "Columbus Woman Heads 244 Who Passed Ohio's Bar Test," *Bellefontaine Examiner*, Dec. 23, 1926; Tuve, *First Lady*, 93; Breckinridge, *Twentieth Century*, 333.

44. Organ, "Sexuality as a Category," 149–50, 184; "Prominent Ohio Women Are Spending Month in Estes Park," *Estes Park Trail*, Aug. 9, 1929; Joan Organ, "Imagine My Surprise—or Not," Estes Park Museum Program, Oct. 22, 2022.

45. Tuve, *First Lady*, 134; obituary, Susan Rebhan, "Death Ends Career," *Plain Dealer*, Sept. 13, 1935.

46. Faderman, *To Believe*, 20–21; Organ, "Sexuality as a Category," 11–12; Jefferson and Johnson, *Shortlisted*, 154, 157; Kenney, "Stupendous," 214–15.

47. Helen Allen Shockey to FEA [ca. 1920s]; FEA to Anna Brenna Meyers, July 17, 1962, LOC Papers; New Year's card to FEA from the Hentels, n.d.; Shelia Wylie to "Cap and Mary," May 24, 1962, LOC Papers.

48. Telegram, Lyndon Johnson to Mary Pierce, Sept. 14, 1966; Telegram, Dorothy Kenyon to Mary Pierce, Sept. 14, 1966.

49. Thomas, "More Than the Vote," 361–66; DeWolf, *Gendered Citizenship*, 15, 39.

50. FEA, speech, "The Battlefield of Thought," 1926.

51. Stansell, *American Moderns*, 1; Brown, *Setting the Course*, 1–5.

52. Diner, *Very Different Age*, 3–13; Flanagan, *America Reformed*, vi–viii, 9; Painter, *Standing at Armageddon*, 35–39.

53. Stansell, *American Moderns*, 7.

54. Cott, *Grounding*, 4–5, 14, 17, 35; Thomas, "Long History of Feminist Legal Theory," 1, 10–12.

55. Stansell, *American Moderns*, 227–31; Sochen, *New Woman*, ix–x.

56. Tuttle, *Race Riot*, 14.

57. Burns, *1920*, 24–26, 125–26; Pietrusza, *1920*, 158.

58. FEA, typescript, "How Did I Come to Be a Judge?" [ca. 1922], 1; Allen, *Justly*, 24; Diary, Apr. 5, 1920.

59. Dorothy Dunbar Bromley, "Woman Is Worthy of High Court," *New-York Telegram*, Jan. 4, 1937.

60. 306 U.S. 118 (1939); 317 U.S. 111 (1942).

61. 17 F. Supp. 308 (S.D. Ohio 1936).

62. 349 U.S. 294, 301 (1955).

63. 126 Ohio St. 290 (1933).

64. "Ohio Woman Jurist Speaks at Banquet," *Washington Post*, Dec. 4, 1927.

65. FEA, "Come to Be a Judge," 17.

66. "Florence E. Allen Named Federal Judge," *New York Times*, Mar. 7, 1934, 9.

67. Eskridge and Frickey, "Making of the Legal Process School," 2031–55.

68. Schreiner, *Dreams*, 68–85; FEA, speech, "Civilized World," Feb. 21, 1955.

1. INTEGRATING THE LEGAL PROFESSION

1. FEA, speech at presentation of the Suffrage Tablet, Ohio State House [1933].

2. FEA, typescript, "Abstract of Speech at General Federation," given to General Federation of Women's Clubs, June 13, 1960.

3. Drachman, *Sisters in Law*, 2.

4. Drachman, *Sisters in Law*, 2; Doerschuk, *Women in the Law*, 115.

5. Grossberg, "Masculinity," 145; Morello, *Invisible Bar*, 173.

6. Grossberg, "Masculinity," 137–38.

7. Grossberg, "Masculinity," 134–36; Bennett, *Lawyer's Myth*, 94–95.

8. Drew, "Women and the Law," 21.

9. 83 U.S. (16 Wall.) 130, 138–39 (1873); Friedman, *First Woman Lawyer*, 25–26; Drachman, *Sisters in Law*, 17.

10. *In re* Lockwood, 154 U.S. 116 (1894); Norgren, *Belva Lockwood*, 49.

11. Resnick, "Representing What?," 16.

12. Landever, "Four Remarkable," 1–15, 44–45; Kennedy and Day, *Bench and Bar*, 124–25; Jesse Bethea, "Daisy's Way: The Wild and Tragic Career of Ohio's First Black Woman Lawyer—Part 4," *Columbus Underground*, Feb. 22, 2025.

13. Diary, Jan. 6, 16, 20, 1916.

14. Cott, *Grounding*, 4, 49, 117; Thomas, "Long History of Feminist Legal Theory," 11.

15. FEA, speech, "A Vision of Women of the Future," delivered to Cleveland Trust Company, n.d.

16. Allen, *Justly*, 23; Constance Marshall, "Judge Allen, Pioneer," *Woman Citizen* 11 (June 1926): 1, 6.

17. Tuve, *First Lady*, 9; Allen, *Justly*, 7–10.

18. Tuve, *First Lady*, 9; Allen, *Justly*, 2; Marshall, "Pioneer," 6.

19. Gordon, *Mormon Question*, 22–29; Iversen, *Antipolygamy Controversy*, 21–22.

20. Elizabeth J. Hauser, "Florence E. Allen—Lawyer," *Woman Citizen* [1919]; *Encyclopedia of Cleveland History*, https://www.case.edu.

21. Iversen, *Antipolygamy Controversy*, 247.

22. Iversen, "Corinne Allen," 111; Tuve, *First Lady*, 3, 7–8; Smith College obituary, Corinne Allen, 1931.

23. Iversen, *Antipolygamy Controversy*, 248–49, 252; Mrs. Clarence E. Allen, "Have You Taught Your Child to Be a Monogamist?," *Child Welfare Magazine*, Feb. 1916, 10.

24. Iversen, "Corinne Allen," 111; FEA, typescript, "How Did I Come to Be a Judge?" [ca. 1922], 2.

25. "Death Claims Pioneer Solon, Clarence Emer [*sic*] Allen," newsclip, n.d.; Clarence Emir Allen, in *Biographical Directory American Congress*, LOC Papers.

26. Iversen, *Antipolygamy Controversy*, 214–25, 222.

27. "Death Claims Pioneer"; C. E. Allen to Hon. R. N. Baskin, Dec. 6, 1911.

28. "Florence Allen Is Truly a Product of Ohio," *Youngstown Vindicator*, Oct. 28, 1928; Tuve, *First Lady*, 3–6.

29. "Baseball Curve First Used by Reserve Men," *Kent Courier*, June 22, 1926.

30. Allen, *Justly*, 17.

31. Tuve, *First Lady*, 8, 20.

32. Tuve, *First Lady*, 10–12; Allen, *Justly*, 18–21.

33. Charles Thwing to FEA, May 13, 1904.

34. Tuve, *First Lady*, 15; Organ, "Sexuality as a Category," 220; Iversen, *Antipolygamy Controversy*, 221; FEA, "Come to Be a Judge," 6; "Former Mills Dean Dr. Gaw," *San Francisco Examiner*, Dec. 30, 1973.

35. Allen, *Justly*, 21–22; Tuve, *First Lady*, 16–17.

36. "The Poems of Florence E. Allen," newsclip [ca. 1908].

37. FEA, music review, "Bohemian Girl, Second Night," *Plain Dealer*, Oct. 14, 1908.

38. Tuve, *First Lady*, 21; FEA to "Mamma," Oct. 1, 1906.

39. Tuve, *First Lady*, 21; Diary, Jan. 2, 1907; Allen, *Justly*, 24; Betty Browning, "Interview with a Feminist—Florence Allen," *Chicago Daily Tribune*, Sept. 17, 1939, G3; FEA, "Come to Be a Judge," 7.

40. Grossberg, "Masculinity," 143.

41. Garner, "Socratic Misogyny," 1597, 1602–7, 1612–29; Abrams, "Feminism's Transformation," 502.

42. Drachman, *Sisters in Law*, 37–38, 41, 64, 70.

43. Drachman, *Sisters in Law*, 150–67; Epstein, *Women in Law*, 49–50; Morello, *Invisible Bar*, 76.

44. Drachman, *Sisters in Law*, 149; Clark, "Founding," 613.

45. Abrams, "Feminism's Transformation," 497; Katcher, "Legal Training," 335, 363, 367.

46. Abrams, "Feminism's Transformation," 504.

47. Kohn, "Cambridge Law School," 120–21, 150.

48. Diary, Oct. 26, 1915; Dec. 5, 12, 1915; Charles F. Thwing to FEA, Apr. 17, 1917.

49. Landever, "Four Remarkable," 44.

50. Diary, Mar. 22, 1909; "Music and Musicians," *Deseret News*, May 29, 1909, 17.

51. Brown, *Setting the Course*, 34–35.

52. Brown, *Setting the Course*, 34.

53. Rosenberg, *Beyond Separate Spheres*, 28, 30–31, 43–44; Drachman, *Sisters in Law*, 144, 256.

54. Jabour, *Breckinridge*, 79, 144.

55. Allen, *Justly*, 24.

56. Abrams, "Feminism's Transformation," 500; Marshall, "Pioneer," 7.

57. FEA, speech, "The Business Woman of Tomorrow," July 12, 1939.

58. Tuve, *First Lady*, 22; Allen, *Justly*, 24.

59. Allen, *Justly*, 24.

60. Allen, *Justly*, 49.

61. Tuve, *First Lady*, 23; Eckhaus, "Restless Women," 1996.

62. Eckhaus, "Restless Women," 1998.

63. Drachman, *Sisters in Law*, 143, 145; Morello, *Invisible Bar*, 95–96.

64. Allen, *Justly*, 25, 28; FEA Response to Bureau of Vocational Information Questionnaire [hereafter BVI Response], Mar. 12, 1920; Drachman, *Sisters in Law*, 131; FEA, speech at banquet of NYU Law School, Apr. 17, 1963.

65. Drachman, *Sisters in Law*, 120–21.

66. Zouch v. Parsons (1765) 97 Eng. Rep. 1103 (K.B.); 3 Burr. 1794.

67. Diary, Feb. 20, 1912; Dec. 17, 1912.

68. Diary, Jan. 16, 30, 1912; Mar. 13, 1913; Nov. 12, 19, 1912; Dec. 23, 1912; Patten v. Poulton, 161 Eng. Rep. 626 (Ecc. Court 1858).

69. Allen, *Justly*, 28; "Second in Her Law Class Is the Cleveland Woman," newsclip, n.d.

70. Allen, *Justly*, 143–44; telegram, Frank Sommer to FEA, Apr. 30, 1941.

71. Tuve, *First Lady*, 25.

72. Allen, *Justly*, 27; Drachman, *Sisters in Law*, 147–48; Diary, Dec. 15, 1911; Jan. 4, 12, 15, 19, 1912; Feb. 19, 1912.

73. Allen, *Justly*, 26–27; Diary, Dec. 11–15, 19–21, 29, 1911; Jan. 1, 3, 6, 7, 11, 12, 15, 17, 18, 21, 23, 25, 1912; Feb. 2, 4–6, 1912; Apr. 25, 29, 1912, Dec. 30, 1912.

74. Thomas, "Long History of Feminist Legal Theory," 3–6, 11; Cott, *Grounding*, 5.

75. Diary, Apr. 28, 1912; FEA, address at Jane Addams Memorial, Sept. 6, 1939; Brown, "Jane Addams," 484, 492.

76. Ladd-Taylor, *Mother-Work*, 116; Brown, "Jane Addams," 484–88, 511; Lemons, *Woman Citizen*, ix–x.

77. Batlan, *Justice for the Poor*, 180–81; Lemon, *Woman Citizen*, 145.

78. Allen, *Justly*, 24; FEA, "Come to Be a Judge," 7.

79. Allen, *Justly*, 24; "Women and Their Work: Miss Florence E. Allen," *Plain Dealer*, Aug. 21, 1910.

80. Tuve, *First Lady*, 23; Organ, "Sexuality as a Category," 17.

81. Press, *Founding Mother*, iii–viii; FEA, memorial address for Frances Kellor Hall, Nov. 19, 1953.

82. Von Drehle, *Triangle*, 26–64, 101–2, 240, 313–15, 323–27; Orleck, *Common Sense*, 5–6, 57.

83. Diary, Feb. 1, 1912.

84. Orleck, *Common Sense*, 5–6, 57.

85. Tuve, *First Lady*, 23.

86. Tuve, *First Lady*, 28.

87. Allen, *Justly*, 26–27.

88. Cott, *Grounding*, 39.

89. Schwarz, *Heterodoxy*, i; Cott, *Grounding*, 12, 38–39; Scutts, *Hotbed*, 2–8; Stansell, *American Moderns*, 89–90; Lopach and Lukowski, *Jeannette Rankin*, 45; Organ, "Sexuality as a Category," 74–75; Diary, Feb. 9, 28, 1912; Mar. 1, 1912; Dec. 29, 1912; June 26, 1913.

90. Diary, June 9, 1913.

91. N. R. Howard, "Miss Allen Talks of Women's Gains," *New York Times*, Mar. 25, 1934.

92. "Second in Her Law Class."

93. FEA, essay for *The Independent Woman*, n.d.

94. Diary, June 9, 26, 30, 1913; July 24–31, 1913; Aug. 8, 13, 25, 30, 1913; Sept. 2, 11, 19, 1913; Oct. 29, 1913; Mar. 17, 1914.

95. Diary, Jan. 5, 18, 1914; Apr. 3, 9, 14, 21, 1914; May 17, 18, 28, 1914; June 2–3, 20, 1914; July 4, 1914.

96. FEA, "Come to Be a Judge," 7.

97. FEA, "Come to Be a Judge," 7; Marshall, "Pioneer," 7.

98. Diary, Nov. 4, 7, 13, 18, 1914; Marshall, "Pioneer," 7.

99. "Spinster Breadwinner Hailed as Heroine by Woman Judge," *Washington Post*, Mar. 10, 1934, 11.

100. Diary, Jan. 21, 26, 1915; Feb. 3, 1915; Apr. 14, 1915; Nov. 19, 1914; Hauser, "Allen—Lawyer."

101. Tuve, "First Woman State Supreme Court Judge," 54; Diary, Feb. 9, 1915; Aug. 19, 23, 1915.

102. BVI Response, Feb. 13, 1918; BVI Response, Mar. 12, 1920.

103. Diary, Jan. 16, 22, 1915; Apr. 21, 1915.

104. FEA, "Come to Be a Judge," 8; Diary, Nov. 18, 26, 1915; June 8, 1916.

105. Diary, Aug. 3, 5, 1915; Nov. 5, 1915; June 2, 13, 1916.

106. Tuve, "First Woman State Supreme Court Judge," 54; Diary, Feb. 9, 1915; Aug. 19, 23, 1915.

107. Diary, Nov. 4, 7, 13, 18, 1914; Marshall, "Pioneer," 7.

108. "The First Woman to Sit on a Supreme Court Bench," *American Magazine* 95 (Apr. 1923): 18–19, 198–202.

109. Diary, Nov. 30, 1914; Dec. 2, 13, 17, 1914.

110. FEA, "Come to Be a Judge," 8; Diary, Nov. 13, 18, 21, 28, 1914; Dec. 14, 1914.

111. BVI Response, Feb. 13, 1918.

112. FEA, "Come to Be a Judge," 8.

113. Diary, Mar. 30, 1915; May 19, 1916; Sept. 21, 22, 1916.

114. Diary, June 19, 1916.

115. Diary, Mar. 8, 1917; Price, *Mafia Cop Killers*, 19.

116. Burton v. Greif, 11 Ohio App. 102 (1919).

117. Taylor v. French, 117 N.E. 173, 177 (Ohio 1917); Petition in Mandamus, Ohio v. Fulton (Ohio Sept. 1917).

118. "Women Flay Bill to Check Divorce Cleveland," *Plain Dealer*, Apr. 1, 1915, 5.

119. Diary, Mar. 16, 17, 1916; Apr. 5, 7, 8, 1916.

120. *In re* Employees, N.W.L.B., No. 491 (Dec. 3, 1918), *rev'd after rehearing*, *In re* Employees v. Cleveland Railway Co., N.W.L.B., No. 491 (Mar. 17, 1919).

121. FEA, "The Women Conductors," *Plain Dealer*, Dec. 5, 1918.

122. "Requests U.S. to Explain Car Rule," *Plain Dealer*, Sept. 26, 1918; "Will Reopen Case for Conductorets," *Plain Dealer*, Oct. 25, 1918; "Car Women Look for Victory Soon," *Plain Dealer*, Nov. 2, 1918.

123. Diary, Oct. 2, 14–18, 23, 29, 1918; "Isolation Will Be Used in Flu Fight," *Plain Dealer*, Oct. 5, 1918, 1.

124. Conner, *Labor Board*, 150–51; Snyder, *Democratic Justice*, 127.

125. Hauser, "Allen—Lawyer."

126. *In re* Employees, N.W.L.B., No. 491 (Dec. 3, 1918).

127. "Conductorets Vote to Quit," *Cleveland News*, Dec. 7, 1918; "Strike Ends as Men Vote 595 to 583 to Accept Compromise," newsclip, n.d.

128. "Judge Holds Quiz over Car Decision," newsclip, n.d.

129. *In re* Employees, N.W.L.B., No. 491 (Mar. 17, 1919).

130. Conner, *Labor Board*, 156; Tuve, *First Lady*, 49.

131. "City Transit to Hire Women Crews," *Plain Dealer*, Feb. 12, 1943.

132. "Sees Victory for Women," *Plain Dealer*, Mar. 25, 1919.

133. "Not Even the Law Is Immune April 1," *Plain Dealer*, Apr. 2, 1919.

134. Diary, Mar. 20, 24, 25, 1919.

135. Porter, *Cleveland*, 76–79; "Bernice Pyke, 84, Suffrage Leader," *New York Times*, May 13, 1964.

136. BVI Response, Mar. 12, 1920.

137. Tuve, *First Lady*, 53; "Cleveland's New City Prosecutor Has Friends Here," Apr. 25, 1918.

138. Bragg, "Judge Whitehead," 151–52; Babcock, *Woman Lawyer*, 215–16.

139. "Prosecutor Has Friends"; "Sees Victory."

140. Samuel Doerfler, "Men Pleased Too," newsclip, Apr, 17, 1919.

141. "Sees Victory."

142. Newsclip, FEA scrapbook [ca. Mar. 1919].

143. Drachman, *Sisters in Law*, 207–8.

144. FEA, speech at retirement luncheon, Oct. 14, 1959.

145. Diary, Apr. 1, 1919.

146. FEA, "Governmental Task," 163.

147. "Prosecutress Wins First Case Alone," newsclip, FEA scrapbook [ca. Apr. 1919].

148. Diary, May 1, 5, 8, 15, 1919; Feb. 10, 17, 1920; Mar. 7, 1920; May 18, 1920.

149. Diary, Apr. 18, 19, 28, 1919.

150. Diary, June 18, 1919; May 11, 1920.

151. "Miss Allen Gets New Job," *Plain Dealer*, Aug. 24, 1919; BVI Response, Mar. 12, 1920.

152. "Judge Allen Honored by Lawyers," *Plain Dealer*, Oct. 11, 1959.

153. FEA, "Come to Be a Judge," 12; FEA, radio speech, "Personal View," for BBC Home Service Program, Aug. 9, 1950.

154. FEA, "Come to Be a Judge," 11.
155. Tuve, *First Lady*, 53.
156. FEA, "Come to Be a Judge," 11–12.
157. Doerschuk, *Women in the Law*, 9–10, 39–46, 103; Drachman, *Sisters in Law*, 168–72, 187–89, 265–66.
158. BVI Response, Feb. 13, 1918; BVI Response, Mar. 12, 1920; "Women on Juries Is New Move," newsclip, FEA scrapbook [ca. Mar. 1919].
159. "Ask More from Girl Than a Man," *Akron Press*, June 8, 1926; "Forget You're Feminine, Says Woman Judge," *Cleveland Press*, June 16, 1926.
160. "Women's Clubs Make Gains During Year Just Passed," *Plain Dealer*, Jan. 4, 1920; "Current Events at the Central YWCA," *Plain Dealer*, Jan. 8, 1920.
161. FEA, "Address to International Federation of Business and Professional Women," London, Aug. 1950; FEA, speech in honor of Mary Zimmerman, Apr. 17, 1952.
162. FEA, speech, "The Effect of Women upon the Administration of Justice" [ca. 1930], LOC Papers.

2. DEMANDING SUFFRAGE AND CITIZENSHIP

1. Elizabeth J. Hauser, "Florence E. Allen—Lawyer," *Woman Citizen* 4, no. 14 (Sept. 6, 1919), 347.
2. Danae King, "Park Honors Social Justice Pioneers," *Columbus Dispatch*, Oct. 28, 2018.
3. Keyssar, *Right to Vote*, 186, tab. A.17, A.18; McCammon and Campbell, "Winning the Vote," 64–66; Catt and Shuler, *Woman Suffrage*, 180, 216.
4. 88 U.S. 162, 165, 169–70 (1874).
5. Isenberg, *Sex and Citizenship*, xii–xiv, 6; Kerber, *Women of the Republic*, 235–36; DeWolf, *Gendered Citizenship*, 16.
6. Thomas, "More Than the Vote," 350, 355–58; Isenberg, *Sex and Citizenship*, ix–xv; Kerber, *Women of the Republic*, 235–37; DeWolf, *Gendered Citizenship*, 16; DuBois, *Feminism and Suffrage*, 54; Ritter, *Social Design*, 6, 35.
7. DuBois, *Suffrage*, 119; Iversen, *Antipolygamy Controversy*, 4, 25; Gordon, *Mormon Question*, 66–68.
8. "Florence E. Allen Dies," *Washington Post*, Sept. 14, 1966.
9. FEA, address at Radcliffe College honoring Maud Wood Park, Nov. 10, 1960.
10. Iversen, *Antipolygamy Controversy*, 246–48; Diary, Dec. 13, 1911; FEA to Corinne Allen, Postcard, Mar. 20, 1911; "Talks Here on Utah Suffrage," *Plain Dealer*, Oct. 15, 1913; "Tells of Utah's Woman-Made Law," *Plain Dealer*, Oct. 16, 1913.

11. Tuve, *First Lady*, 15.

12. Iversen, "Corinne Allen," 117.

13. Iversen, *Antipolygamy Controversy*, 176, 246–52; Iversen, "Corinne Allen," 129–39; Tuve, *First Lady*, 7; "Mrs. Allen Is No Friend of Roberts, the Polygamist," *Indianapolis Sun*, Nov. 4, 1899.

14. Iversen, "Corinne Allen," 114; Kraditor, *Ideas*, 10–25, 33; Isenberg, *Sex and Citizenship*, 38–39; Marilley, *Woman Suffrage*, 100–114; Ladd-Taylor, *Mother-Work*, 110; Clapp, *Mothers*, 3–5.

15. FEA, manuscript, "The Rural Home and the Courts"; FEA, "Christianity and Government," *Moral Welfare* 22, no. 4 (Jan. 1931); FEA, speech, "The Home and Sense of Partnership," Michigan State College, May 3, 1947; FEA, manuscript, "Home," Aug. 9, 1950.

16. FEA, Radcliffe address.

17. "Women's Influence Wanes: Judge Allen Warns of Slacking," *Christian Science Monitor*, Nov. 14, 1960.

18. Marino, *Votes for College Women*, 1–8.

19. Cott, *Grounding*, 36; "What Will New York Do with Mrs. Pankhurst?," *New York Times*, Sept. 13, 1913; Diary, Dec. 22, 1911; Jan. 5, 1912; Dec. 15, 1912; Oct. 25, 1913.

20. FEA Cartoon Collection, LOC Papers.

21. Diary, Jan. 4, 1912; Nov. 7, 23–25, 1912; Apr. 20, 1915; Ethel Pfeiffer Harris to FEA, Dec. 13, 1916.

22. Isenberg, *Sex and Citizenship*, 21; Thomas, *Elizabeth Cady Stanton*, 20–22; Kraditor, *Ideas*, 42–52; Marilley, *Woman Suffrage*, 189.

23. DuBois, *Blatch*, 141.

24. DuBois, *Blatch*, 140–43; Diary, May 4, 5, 1912.

25. "Ohio Women May Hike," *Plain Dealer*, Feb. 19, 1913; Jack, *Rosalie Gardiner Jones*, 10, 121, 224; "General Lets Hikers Accept Lift on Road," *Baltimore News*, Feb. 15, 1913, 1.

26. "Suffrage Army, 5,000 Strong, Ready for Big Parade Today," *Plain Dealer*, Mar. 3, 1913; "Parade Sidelights," *Plain Dealer*, Mar. 4, 1913.

27. DuBois, *Suffrage*, 191–92; Zahniser and Fry, *Alice Paul*, 137, 145.

28. "Ohio Boy to Carry Banner in Parade of Suffragists Monday," *Plain Dealer*, Mar. 1, 1913; "Suffrage Army, 5,000 Strong, Ready for Big Parade Today," *Plain Dealer*, Mar. 3, 1913; "Parade Sidelights," *Plain Dealer*, Mar. 4, 1913.

29. Jones, *Vanguard*, 163–65.

30. Zahniser and Fry, *Alice Paul*, 146–48; Hamlin, *Free Thinker*, 205.

31. Upton, "Woman Suffrage Movement," 329.

32. McClain, "What Becomes," 1755; Painter, *Sojourner Truth*, 334.

33. Allen and Welles, *Ohio Woman Suffrage*, 38–39.

34. Capuzza, *Fifth Star*, 5, 7, 20, 51, 66; Tuve, *First Lady*, 26, 30–32; Allen, *Justly*, 29; Hauser, "Allen—Lawyer."

35. Capuzza, *Fifth Star*, 185–203; Allen and Welles, *Ohio Woman Suffrage*, 41; Katz, "Sex, Suffrage," 350–52; "Suffragists Fill Capital Streets Three Thousand," *Plain Dealer*, Aug. 28, 1912, 1, 2.

36. Allen, *Justly*, 32; Diary, Sept. 8, 1912; A. E. McKee, "Suffragists Fill Capital Streets," *Plain Dealer*, Aug. 28, 1912; "Motormen Curse, Schedules Smash—Suffragets Start Campaign, *Cleveland Press*, newsclip, n.d.

37. Tuve, *First Lady*, 32–33; Diary, July 1912; Allen, *Justly*, 34; "Suffragists Plan Trip," *Plain Dealer*, June 22, 1912; "Suffragists Post Bills," *Plain Dealer*, June 23, 1912; "Travel Lunchless to Talk Suffrage," *Plain Dealer*, June 25, 1912; Abbott, *History of Woman Suffrage*, 18–19.

38. "Suffragists in Films," *Plain Dealer*, June 20, 1912.

39. Katz, "Hold Public Office in Ohio," 352; Diary, Sept. 23, 1912.

40. Allen and Welles, *Ohio Woman Suffrage*, 46; Capuzza, *Fifth Star*, 218–26.

41. Diary, June and July 1914; Hauser, "Allen—Lawyer"; Tuve, *First Lady*, 36.

42. Allen and Welles, *Ohio Woman Suffrage*, 46; Tuve, *First Lady*, 37–39.

43. Allen and Welles, *Ohio Woman Suffrage*, 46.

44. Allen, *Justly*, 33–35; *Plain Dealer*, Oct. 29, 1914, 10; Abbott, *History of Woman Suffrage*, 32–22; Diary, Oct. 10, 24, 28, 30, 1914; "Statement by Miss Allen," *Plain Dealer*, Oct. 31, 1914.

45. "Van Deman Heads Bar Association," newsclip, July 9, 1914.

46. Diary, June 8, 25, 1914; July 1, 1914; Aug. 22, 31, 1914; Sept. 21, 1914; Nov. 4, 1914.

47. Diary, July 31, 1914; Aug. 1, 1914.

48. "Predicts Women Win," *Plain Dealer*, Oct. 10, 1914; Capuzza, *Fifth Star*, 223–25.

49. Upton, "Woman Suffrage," 333–34.

50. Wheeler, "Short History," 9, 17; DuBois, *Feminism*, 237; Zahniser and Fry, *Alice Paul*, 215; DuBois, *Blatch*, 3, 94.

51. "Women Can Win Despite Congress," *Plain Dealer*, Oct. 31, 1915; "Suffragists and Club Women to Factor in Expo's Success," *Plain Dealer*, Mar. 5, 1916.

52. Allen and Welles, *Ohio Woman Suffrage*, 48–49.

53. Catt and Shuler, *Woman Suffrage*, 180; Keyssar, *Right to Vote*, 186.

54. Coffin v. Bd. of Election, 56 N.W. 567, 569 (Mich. 1893).

55. Scown v. Czarnecki, 106 N.E. 276, 277, 302 (Ill. 1914); Catt and Shuler, *Woman Suffrage*, 180–82.

56. Keyssar, *Right to Vote*, tab. A.18.

57. Capuzza, *Fifth Star*, 146–47.

58. 6 Ohio Cir. Dec. 36, 38 (Ohio App), *aff'd without decision*, 47 N.E. 1114 (Ohio 1896).

59. Capuzza, *Fifth Star*, 146–47; Allen and Welles, *Ohio Woman Suffrage*, 35–37.

60. Grace Treat to FEA, Feb. 17, 1916.

61. FEA, typescript, "How Did I Come to Be a Judge?" [ca. 1922], 9.

62. "Charter Meeting Ends with Snarl," newsclip, Feb. 5, 1916; "Women Gain Big Point in Getting Suffrage Rights," *Plain Dealer*, Feb. 5, 1916.

63. FEA, presentation to Charter Commission of East Cleveland, n.d., LOC Papers; FEA to Dr. Blanche Haines, July 7, 1916; Tuve, *First Lady*, 42, 46 n.54; Diary, Dec. 21, 1915; Jan. 3–18, 1916; Feb. 1–14, 1916.

64. FEA to Mrs. Orton (Nelli) Clark, July 3, 1916.

65. Brief and Reply Brief of Relator, Taylor v. French, 117 N.E. 173 (Ohio 1917).

66. Allen, *Justly*, 93; Cobble, *For the Many*, 3.

67. Lopach and Lukowski, *Jeannette Rankin*, 1–4.

68. Allen, *Justly*, 36–37; Diary, Oct. 25, 26, 1916.

69. Kohn, "Cambridge Law School," 120–21, 155.

70. 117 N.E. 173, 177 (Ohio 1917).

71. Brief, *Taylor*, 4, 7, 10.

72. Brief, *Taylor*, 10–15.

73. "Scope of Home Rule Amendment," *Harvard Law Review* 31 (1918), 653.

74. *Taylor*, 117 N.E. at 177.

75. FEA to Mrs. Wilber Brotherton, July 3, 1916; "Lakewood Suffrage Head Plans School in Citizenship for New Women Voters," *Plain Dealer*, Feb. 24, 1918; Allen, *Justly*, 37.

76. Cott, *Grounding*, 105–6.

77. FEA to Blanche M. Haines, July 9, 1916; Nelli Sawyer Clark to FEA, June 29, 1916; FEA to Clark, July 3, 1916; Haines to FEA, July 2, 1916.

78. Diary, Nov. 20–22, 1916; "Suffragists Seek Presidential Vote," *Plain Dealer*, Dec. 10, 1916.

79. Keyssar, *Right to Vote*, tab. A.19; see *Scown*, 106 N.E. at 277.

80. Keyssar, *Right to Vote*, tab. A.19.

81. Allen and Welles, *Ohio Woman Suffrage*, 50–51; "Ohio Women Open Big Fight to Get Presidential Vote," *Plain Dealer*, Jan. 4, 1917, 1, 4; "Cleveland Women Plead Vote Case," *Plain Dealer*, Jan. 26, 1917.

82. Allen, *Justly*, 37.

83. Hauser, "Allen—Lawyer"; Mary Pollard Clarke to FEA, Feb. 3, 1917; FEA to Mrs. G. Harvey Clarke, Feb. 5, 1917.

84. Allen and Welles, *Ohio Woman Suffrage*, 51; "Ohio House Passes Suffrage Measure Votes 72 to 50," *Plain Dealer*, Feb. 2, 1917, 1, 8.

85. Allen and Welles, *Ohio Woman Suffrage*, 51.

86. "Rules on Women's Vote," *Plain Dealer*, Apr. 1, 1917.

87. Telegram, Harriet Taylor Upton to Newton Baker, Oct. 29, 1917; Elizabeth Hauser to FEA, Oct. 30, 1917.

88. "Suffragists Hurl New Bomb at Antis," *Plain Dealer*, Sept. 21, 1917; "Anti-Suffragist Petitions Held Up by Court Ruling," *Plain Dealer*, Sept. 22, 1917; FEA to Attorney C. A. Sorenson, Jan. 23, 1918; FEA to Editor of *New York Evening Post*, Oct. 30, 1917.

89. "High Court Will Settle Vote Fight," *Plain Dealer*, Sept. 25, 1917; "File New Suit in Referendum Fight," *Plain Dealer*, Sept. 26, 1917; "Continue Fight on Referendum," *Plain Dealer*, Sept. 28, 1917; draft, Petition in Mandamus, Ohio v. Fulton (Ohio S.Ct., Sept. 1917).

90. W. S. Buel, "Refuses to Enjoin Vote Referendum," *Plain Dealer*, Sept. 27, 1917; "Ohio Is Assured Vote on Suffrage," *Plain Dealer*, Oct. 24, 1917.

91. Frank Davis to FEA, Oct. 23, 1917; Davis to Harriet Taylor Upton, Oct. 12, 1917.

92. Elizabeth Hauser to FEA, Nov. 15, 1917.

93. Capuzza, *Fifth Star*, 90–91, 181–82; Thurner, "Better Citizens," 203, 204–5.

94. Dudden, *Fighting Chance*, 92–93, 232.

95. Diary, Apr. 9, 1920; "Miss Gail Laughlin, a Suffrage Pioneer," *New York Times*, Mar. 14, 1952.

96. FEA, Radcliffe address, 5–6; Park, *Front Door Lobby*, 14; Hamlin, *Free Thinker*, 237, 254.

97. Woodrow Wilson to Carrie Catt, June 13, 1918, LOC Papers; DuBois, *Suffrage*, 151–54, 187–88; DuBois, *Blatch*, 4; Kraditor, *Ideas*, 163–73; Elizabeth Hauser to FEA, Nov. 15, 1917; Allen and Welles, *Ohio Woman Suffrage*, 52, 57; McDonaugh and Price, "Woman Suffrage," 426–28; Hamlin, *Free Thinker*, 104, 222, 237, 254.

98. Henry Emerson (R-Ohio) to FEA, Jan. 23, 1918; Robert Crosser (D-Ohio) to FEA, Feb. 5, 1918.

99. Catt and Shuler, *Woman Suffrage*, 334–51.

100. "Women's 1920 Vote Depends on Ohio Case," *Plain Dealer*, Feb. 13, 1920; "Arguments Heard in Ohio Cases," *Plain Dealer*, Apr. 24, 1920.

101. Frank Davis, memorandum, "The Action of a State Legislature in Ratifying or Refusing to Ratify a Federal Amendment," Mar. 5, 1918.

102. FEA to Elizabeth Hauser, Mar. 14, 1918.

103. 253 U.S. 221, 231 (1920); James Rice to Harriet Taylor Upton, Feb. 19, 1918; Upton to Political Committee, Feb. 23, 1918; Frank Davis to Upton, Mar. 1, 1918; FEA to Upton, Mar. 9, 1918; Charlotte Jordan to FEA, Feb. 16, 1918.

104. DuBois, *Suffrage*, 273–76; Weiss, *Woman's Hour*, 312–18.

105. Jessie Glasier, "Many Women's Clubs Planting Memorial Trees for War Dead," *Plain Dealer*, Aug. 23, 1920.

106. "Women to Bring Out New Voters," *Plain Dealer*, Oct. 10, 1920, 20A; "Jewish Council Is to Present Program," *Plain Dealer*, Oct. 17, 1920, 66.

107. Fairchild v. Hughes, 258 U.S. 126 (1922); Leser v. Garnett, 258 U.S. 130 (1922).

108. Monopoli, *Constitutional Orphan*, 1–2, 43–67; Cahill, *Recasting the Vote*, 7; Jones, *Vanguard*, 175, 190.

109. Monopoli, *Constitutional Orphan*, 1–2, 43–67.

110. Allen and Welles, *Ohio Woman Suffrage*, 5.

3. JUDGING THE TRIAL COURT

1. "Invites Women Voters," *Plain Dealer*, Aug. 30, 1920; Diary, Aug. 27, 1920.

2. Katz, "Hold Public Office in Ohio," 315; Kenney, *Gender and Justice*, 2; Morello, *Invisible Bar*, 224–25; Ritter, *Social Design*, 111–12.

3. Stanton, Anthony, and Gage, *History of Woman Suffrage*, vol. 1, 523–24.

4. "Ohio's Woman Judge Is Imposing Figure," *New York Times*, Dec. 3, 1922, A110.

5. Burns, *1920*, 19–20; (F. L.) Allen, *Only Yesterday*, 13, 36–37.

6. Burns, *1920*, 200–2; Lemons, *Woman Citizen*, 89; Cott, *Grounding*, 73.

7. Monopoli, *Constitutional Orphan*, 115–26; Katz, "Sex, Suffrage," 118.

8. Katz, "Hold Public Office in Ohio," 350–53; People v. Patterson, 183 N.W. 28 (Mich. 1921).

9. Monopoli, *Constitutional Orphan*, 102–11, 116–26; Katz, "Sex, Suffrage," 156–59; e.g., *In re* Opinion of Justices, 135 N.E. 173 (Mass. 1922).

10. Katz, "Sex, Suffrage," 186–87, 190.

11. "Slow Full Suffrage," *New York Times*, July 31, 1921, E26.

12. Katz, "'May It Please Her Honor,'" 1732–36, 1750–54, 1769, 1789–95.

13. "Woman Is Held Own 'Property,'" *Detroit Free Press*, Dec. 18, 1920, 1, 3.

14. Morello, *Invisible Bar*, 219–21; Karin, "Esther Morris," 320–33.

15. Ryder, "Clearing the Bar," 6; Katz, "'May It Please Her Honor,'" 1732–33.

16. Bragg, "Judge Whitehead," 152–54.

17. Drachman, *Sisters in Law*, 229–33.

18. Glasbeek, *Feminized Justice*, 1–2, 11, 18, 28, 33, 50; Morello, *Invisible Bar*, 227–28; Quinn, "Fallen Woman," 451.

19. Katz, "'May It Please Her Honor,'" 1739; Greene and Renberg, "Judging Without a J.D.," 1287; Willrich, *City of Courts*, xxi–xxv, 10.

20. Morello, *Invisible Bar*, 224–27; Cook, "Moral Authority," 144–46; Drachman, *Sisters in Law*, 229–34.

21. Katz, "'May It Please Her Honor,'" 1770.

22. Freedman, *Maternal Justice*, 83, 104, 106.

23. Cook, "Moral Authority," 156.

24. "Mrs. Jean H. Norris Appointed to Bench," *New York Times*, Oct. 28, 1919; Quinn, "Fallen Woman," 476; Quinn, "Home Term Part," 736–40.

25. Drachman, *Sisters in Law*, 229–34; Cook, "Moral Authority," 156.

26. Diary, Aug. 16, 17, 18, 1920.

27. McLeod, *Judge Jane Bolin*, 36, 39, 44, 47; Katz, "'May It Please Her Honor,'" 1736.

28. Epstein, *Women in Law*, 238; Morello, *Invisible Bar*, 218.

29. Drachman, *Sisters in Law*, 181, 229–33.

30. Grossberg, "Masculinity," 139–41.

31. Letter from Judge Frank Stevens, Sept. 2, 1920; letter from Judge Vickery [ca. Sept. 1920]; "Ohio Jurist Dies," *New York Times*, Sept. 27, 1932, 21.

32. Letter from Frank Davis, U.S. Assistant Attorney General, Sept. 4, 1920; manuscript, "Qualifications of Florence E. Allen for Common Pleas Judge."

33. "Elect Miss Allen," *Plain Dealer*, Aug. 28, 1920.

34. Editorial, "Florence E. Allen," *Plain Dealer*, Oct. 28, 1920.

35. "Florence E. Allen," *Cleveland News*, Sept. 6, 1920.

36. FEA, typescript, "How Did I Come to Be a Judge?" [ca. 1922], 14; Diary, Feb. 7, 13, 19, 21, 1920.

37. "Florence Allen Endorsed for Judge," *Youngstown Vindicator*, Feb. 7, 1920, 64; Diary, Feb. 7, 13, 19, 21, 1920; Tuve, *First Lady*, 52; Abbott, *History of Woman Suffrage*, 75.

38. Tuve, *First Lady*, 52.

39. [Signature illegible] at Ohio Executive Department to Elizabeth Hauser, Feb. 28, 1920.

40. Allen, *Justly*, 43.

41. "2000 Nominate Woman Judge," *New York Times*, Sept. 4, 1920.

42. Diary, Sept. 10, 1920; Oct. 7, 1920.

43. "Bernice Pyke, 84, Suffrage Leader; Ohio Democrat First Woman Convention Delegate, Dies," *New York Times*, May 13, 1964; Porter, *Cleveland*, 63.

44. FEA to Homer Cummings, Sept. 24, 1919; newsclip, "Woman Objects to Service Bill," Oct. 14, 1919; *Columbus State Journal*, Oct. 16, 1919; "Balks at Baker's Bill," Nov. 16, 1919.

45. *Cincinnati Enquirer*, Sept. 28, 1919.

46. Allen, *Justly*, 41–42; FEA, untitled speech, Detroit, 1946.

47. Steinglass and Scarselli, *Ohio State Constitution*, 89–90.

48. "Women Voters, Read!," *Cleveland Press*, Feb. 4, 1921.

49. Lemons, *Woman Citizen*, 89; Cott, *Grounding*, 73.

50. Ritter, *Social Design*, 42, 54–55; Lemons, *Woman Citizen*, 85; DuBois, *Blatch*, 124–25.

51. FEA, "The First Ten Years," *Woman's Journal*, Aug. 1930, 5; FEA, address, "Women and Citizenship," delivered to Philadelphia Society for Ethical Culture, Nov. 27, 1921.

52. Allen, "Governmental Task," 162.

53. Katz, "'May It Please Her Honor,'" 1776.

54. "Florence E. Allen," *Plain Dealer*, Oct. 28, 1920.

55. FEA, statement of expenses, Oct. 12, 1920; "Woman Pays $318.16 to Get Herself Elected," newsclip, Dec. 1, 1920.

56. Diary, Oct. 1920.

57. FEA, speech, "Separate Judicial Belief" [ca. 1920].

58. Allen, *Justly*, 41–44; Diary, Oct. 2, 1920; FEA, Detroit speech, 2; Tuve, *First Lady*, 54–55.

59. Allen, *Justly*, 43, 50–51; "Tis Judge Allen," *Cleveland Press*, Nov. 3, 1920.

60. FEA, Detroit speech; Diary, Aug. 31, 1920; Sept. 2, 10, 1920.

61. Allen, *Justly*, 44; FEA, "Tried and Approved—the Woman Juror," *Woman Citizen*, June 4, 1921.

62. Frankfurter and Pound, *Criminal Justice in Cleveland*, 266.

63. Corder and Wolbrecht, *Counting Women's Ballots*, 153–54.

64. Katz, "Sex, Suffrage," 119, 136, 144–45, 152, 155; Katz, "Hold Public Office in Ohio," 315–16.

65. Scharf, "Women's Movement," 68–82; Barber, *Proportional Representation*, 3, 121; Lemons, *Woman Citizen*, 125; Warner, *Progressivism in Ohio*, vii–ix, 70–77; Tuve, *First Lady*, 2, 35.

66. Barber, *Right to Representation*, 27, 32, 60, 62–63, 65, 163; Moley, "Proportional Representation," 652–69.

67. "Cautions Voters Against 'Plunking,'" *Plain Dealer*, Sept. 18, 1923, 19.

68. Allen, *Justly*, 49.

69. Lemons, *Woman Citizen*, 125–26.

70. Tuve, *First Lady*, 52, 92–93; FEA, YWCA lecture, Nov. 17, 1919; Barber, *Right to Representation*, 33, 52; Barber, *Proportional Representation*, 59, 63, 122.

71. Tuve, *First Lady*, 51, 70, 92–93; Tani, "Portia's Deal," 560–61; Barber, *Proportional Representation*, 145.

72. 141 N.E. 27 (Ohio 1923).

73. Allen, *Justly*, 81.

74. Hile v. City of Cleveland, 141 N.E. 35 (Ohio 1923), *cert. denied*, 266 U.S. 582 (1924).

75. Haley BeMiller, "Ohio Gov. Mike DeWine Signs Bill to Crack Down on Ranked Choice Voting," *Columbus Dispatch*, Mar. 17, 2026.

76. "It's Busy Life," *Cleveland Press*, Jan. 11, 1921.

77. Allan Harding, "The First Woman to Sit on a Supreme Court," *American Magazine*, 1922, 19, 198–202.

78. Randolph, "Judge Florence Allen," 15, 17; Annabel Lee, "Her Honor, Judge Allen," *National Business Woman*, Dec. 1939, at 385.

79. Tuve, *First Lady*, 65.

80. FEA, "Come to Be a Judge," 1.

81. FEA to Lorena Hickok, Sept. 16, 1952.

82. Bennett, *Lawyer's Myth*, 98; Menkel-Meadow, "Feminization of the Legal Profession," 289–93, 298.

83. FEA, "Come to Be a Judge," 1; Constance Marshall, "Judge Allen, Pioneer," *Woman Citizen* 11 (June 1926), 5.

84. Allen, *Justly*, 51–52; FEA, "Come to Be a Judge," 16.

85. Allen, *Justly*, 45; FEA, "Come to Be a Judge," 15; Marshall and May, *Divorce Court*, 234.

86. Diary, Nov. 9, 1920.

87. Allen, *Justly*, 45–46.

88. "Justice Reform, Judge Florence Ellinwood Allen is Promoting It," *Cleveland Press*, Jan. 5, 1921.

89. Allen, *Justly*, 69.

90. FEA, "Come to Be a Judge," 15–16.

91. "Gives Rules for Happy Marriage," newsclip, Apr. 26, 1922.

92. "Cuyahoga County Domestic Relations Court," *Encyclopedia of Cleveland History*, https://www.case.edu.

93. "Entire Bench Aids in Divorce Check," *Plain Dealer*, May 22, 1920; Marshall and May, *Divorce Court*, 57–58, 81.

94. Diary, Jan. 6, 1921; Feb. 21, 1921.

95. "Woman Jurist Is Now on the Bench," newsclip, Jan. 4, 1920.

96. Campaign card (June 14, 1922); manuscript, "Quotes on Judicial Platform," n.d.; Allen, *Justly*, 45; "Asks for Higher Moral Code in Public Officers," *Plain Dealer*, June 30, 1922.

97. FEA, "Come to Be a Judge," 16.

98. "The First Woman Judge of a Court of Common Pleas Believes in 'Speeding Up Justice,'" newsclip, Oct. 1921.

99. Allen, *Justly*, 49; *Cleveland Press*, Sept. 9, 1920; Allen, "Governmental Task," 7.

100. "A Woman Talks to Women—and Men, Dearborn Independent," newsclip, n.d.; FEA, speech, Women's City Club of Cleveland, Mar. 21, 1960.

101. Allen, *Justly*, 47–52.

102. Allen, *Justly*, 50–51.

103. "Woman Jurist Is for Political Pep," newsclip, Sept. 13 [1922].

104. Allen, *Justly*, 50–51.

105. Frankfurter and Pound, *Criminal Justice in Cleveland*, v; Allen, *Justly*, 48; "Cleveland Survey of Criminal Justice," *Encyclopedia of Cleveland History*, https://www.case.edu.

106. "Justice Broken Down, Survey Shows," *Plain Dealer*, Sept. 14, 1921; Frankfurter and Pound, *Criminal Justice in Cleveland*, 297–303; "Law," *Encyclopedia of Cleveland History*, https://www.case.edu.

107. "Prosecutor Praises Ohio Woman Judge," newsclip, Jan. 25, 1921.

108. Epstein, *Women in Law*, 279–80.

109. "Raps Courts That Women Can Sway," *Plain Dealer*, Sept. 22, 1920; "Hits 'Masculine' Courts as Weak," *Plain Dealer*, Mar. 21, 1921.

110. "1921: Women's Court: In Our Pages 75 Years Ago," *International Herald Tribune*, Jan. 18, 1996.

111. "Prosecutor Praises Ohio Woman Judge," newsclip, Jan. 25, 1921.

112. FEA, notes from testimony in Common Pleas Court, 1921.

113. Diary, Jan. 13, 26, 27, 1921; Mar. 22, 1921; Apr. 5, 1921.

114. Diary, Apr. 4, 1921; Oct. 31, 1921.

115. "Woman Swoons at Murder Trial," *Plain Dealer*, Mar. 16, 1921; "Woman's Swoons Halt Murder Case," newsclip [1921].

116. "Bride Hears Plea for Jailed Groom," *Plain Dealer*, Aug. 2, 1922; "Leave Bride to Start Sentence," *Plain Dealer*, Aug. 10, 1922.

117. "Seeks Leniency, Gets the Limit," newsclip, n.d.; "Wrong Man in Dock at Trial," *Plain Dealer*, May 24, 1921.

118. May, *Sly-Fanner Murders*, 86–90, 114–15, 117; "Eyewitnesses Accuse Motto in Slaying," *Plain Dealer*, May 3, 1921, 1.

119. "Last Life Plea Is Denied Motto by Judge Allen," *Plain Dealer*, Aug. 28, 1921.

120. "12 Tentatively Accepted for Motto Jury," *Plain Dealer*, May 12, 1921; "Highest Court Denies Motto's Plea for Life," *Plain Dealer*, Aug. 27, 1921, 1; Allen, *Justly*, 56–57; FEA, speech "The Effect of Women upon the Administration of Justice" [ca. 1932], LOC Papers.

121. FEA, "Come to Be a Judge," 13.

122. Benjamin S. Hubbell to FEA, May 16, 1921.

123. "M'Gannon Guilty of Perjury," *Plain Dealer*, June 26, 1921, 1; Tuve, *First Lady*, 59; "McGannon Found Guilty," *New York Tribune*, June 26, 1921, 7.

124. Don Robertson, "The McGannon Case," *Plain Dealer Magazine*, May 20, 1954, 26, 27.

125. Frankfurter and Pound, *Criminal Justice in Cleveland*, 169, 216–17, 337; "Joyce Swears M'Gannon Was on Death Spot," *Plain Dealer*, June 17, 1921; "McGannon to Testify," *New York Times*, Dec. 27, 1920.

126. "Ban Woman Bailiff from Court Duties," newsclip, n.d.; "Travesty on Justice," newsclip, May 7, 1921; "Woman Juror Jailed, Fined for Contempt," *Columbus State Journal*, May 26, 1921, LOC Papers.

127. "Jurors Tell of Battle to Get Verdict," newsclip, n.d., LOC Papers.

128. "Sentenced to 10 Years," newsclip, LOC Papers.

129. "Guilty of Perjury."

130. FEA, notes on *McGannon* case, LOC Papers; Charge, *McGannon*, June 24, 1921, 7; "Court's Doctors Visit M'Gannon," *Plain Dealer*, May 10, 1921, 1; "To Use Care with M'Gannon Jurors," *Plain Dealer*, June 13, 1921, 19; "M'Gannon Freed After Re-Arrest," *Plain Dealer*, June 18, 1921; "To Recall Miss Neely to Stand," *Plain Dealer*, June 19, 1921; "Jury Locked Up in Trial of

M'Gannon," *Plain Dealer*, June 25, 1921, 1; "McGannon Is Sick in Court," *Plain Dealer*, Sept. 20, 1921, 1; "M'Gannon Ready to Go to Prison," *Plain Dealer*, May 24, 1922, 13; N. R. Howard to FEA, Feb. 9, 1962.

131. "M'Gannon Is Given Freedom," *Plain Dealer*, Jan. 6, 1924; Robertson, "McGannon Case," 27.

132. "Frees Man, Raps Patrol Man," *Plain Dealer*, Jan. 22, 1921; "Compromise on Gas Hit," *Cleveland Press*, Jan. 21, 1921.

133. "Murder Jury Out for Record Stay," *Plain Dealer*, Feb. 14, 1921; Diary, Feb. 14, 15, 1921; Apr. 19, 1921; "Grants Habig New Trial for Murder," *Plain Dealer*, Dec. 17, 1921, 1, 3.

134. "Judge Allen's Record," newsclip, Oct. 20 [1922].

135. Allen, *Justly*, 53–54; "Long Given 5 Days in Contempt Case," *Plain Dealer*, Nov. 3, 1921; "Long's Jail Sentence Stands," *Plain Dealer*, Nov. 15, 1921.

136. Diary, Oct. 21, 24, 25, 27, 31, 1921.

137. Thomas, *Elizabeth Cady Stanton*, 182–83.

138. Weisbrod, "Woman Juror," 60 n.3, 71–73; Ritter, *Social Design*, 110–12, 119; Lemons, *Woman Citizen*, 71–72.

139. Browning v. State, 120 Ohio St. 62 (1929); Thatcher v. Pennsylvania O. & D.R. Co., 121 Ohio St. 205 (1929).

140. Monopoli, *Constitutional Orphan*, 90–95; Ritter, *Social Design*, 100–101, 120; Commonwealth v. Welosky, 177 N.E. 656 (Mass. 1931), *cert. denied*, 284 U.S. 684 (1932).

141. Hoyt v. Florida, 368 U.S. 57 (1961); Taylor v. Louisiana, 419 U.S. 522, 535–37 (1975).

142. FEA, "Tried and Approved," 8; jury letter to Judge Allen, Jan. 14, 1921.

143. "Locks Up Jurors Hearing Trial of Ex-Railway Guard," Dec. 7, 1922; FEA, "Come to Be a Judge"; FEA, "Tried and Approved."

144. FEA, "Tried and Approved."

145. FEA, "Tried and Approved"; FEA, "Come to Be a Judge"; FEA, "Woman Judge Approves Mixed Juries," newsclip [ca. 1921]; "Urges Activity of Women in Government," *Plain Dealer*, July 21, 1922; FEA, "Effect of Women"; FEA, Radio address, "The Jury—a Bulwark of Human Freedom," Jan. 10, 1930.

146. "Where Women Serve on Juries," National League of Women Voters, Apr. 1929.

147. FEA, "Effect of Women"; FEA, "Bulwark of Human Freedom"; FEA, "Governmental Task."

148. Diary, May 6, 10, 12, 13, 21, 1947; July 21, 1947.

149. 329 U.S. 187 (1946).

150. McCammon, *Women's Jury*, 49, 165.

151. "'Conspiracy' Gives Judge Last Case," *Plain Dealer*, Dec. 15, 1922, 22.

152. "Boosting Judge Allen," *Plain Dealer*, Sept. 1, 1922.

4. BATTLING FOR PROGRESSIVE REFORM ON THE STATE SUPREME COURT

1. FEA, typescript, "How Did I Come to Be a Judge?" [ca. 1922], 17.

2. Ohio Const. art. IV, sec. 2; Marshall, *Courts and Lawyers of Ohio*, 226–27.

3. "Florence E. Allen, Ohio's First Woman Supreme Judge, Takes Place on Bench," *Columbus Dispatch*, Jan. 2, 1923, 3.

4. Tuve, *First Lady*, 92; "Justices 1803 to Present," Supreme Court of Ohio, https://www.supremecourt.ohio.gov.

5. "Judge Allen," *Akron Beacon Journal*, newsclip [1922].

6. Tuve, *First Lady*, 92 (citing *Akron Beacon Journal*, Sept. 19, 1922).

7. Steinglass and Scarselli, *Ohio State Constitution*, 54–62, app. B.

8. "Judge Allen."

9. Judicial Platform of Florence E. Allen.

10. Quotes on Judicial Platform.

11. "Record Set by Judge Allen," *Youngstown Telegram*, Oct. 20, 1922; "Woman Judge Sets Record: Battles Perjury," newsclip, n.d.; "From Donald C. Doughtery," manuscript, campaign news [1922].

12. Tuve, *First Lady*, 63.

13. "Judge Allen Is Candidate for Supreme Bench," June 13, 1922; "Nonpartisan Clubs Boost Judge Allen," *Ohio State Journal*, Oct. 22 [1922]; "Organize Judge Allen Clubs in 12 Counties," *Plain Dealer*, Oct. 6, 1922.

14. Newsclip, *Salt Lake Telegram*, Jan. 7, 1923.

15. W. C. Howells, "Women Assured Place on Ballot," *Plain Dealer*, Sept. 12, 1922; "Over 43,000 Sign Petition of Judge Florence Allen," *Youngstown Vindicator*, Sept. 7, 1922.

16. Allen, "Women in Public Office."

17. Tuve, *First Lady*, 65, 80.

18. "'More Justice and Less Politics Are Needed in Our Courts,' Says Miss Allen," *Ohio State Pioneer*, newsclip [1922].

19. "From Donald Doughtery."

20. Diary, Jan. 11, 1922; May 19, 1922; Sept. 9, 19, 1922.

21. Newsclip, *Plain Dealer*, June 14, 1922.

22. "Weekly News Letter from Judge Florence Allen's Campaign Headquarters," Oct. 16, 1922.

23. Tuve, *First Lady*, 66–67.

24. Telegram, FEA to Robert Keefer, July 14, 1922, LOC Papers.

25. Allen, *Justly*, 66; Brown, *Willebrandt*, 47–49.

26. "Republican Women Oppose Judge Allen's Candidacy," newsclip, Oct. 14 [1922]; "Miss Allen to Be Opposed by Women of G.O.P., newsclip, *Columbus Dispatch*, Oct. 24 [1922].

27. "Cleveland Woman to Support Judge Allen," newsclip, Oct. 18 [1922]; "Women Favor Judge Allen," newsclip, Oct. 26 [1922]; Lemons, *Woman Citizen*, 105.

28. Tuve, *First Lady*, 64.

29. Statement of Expenses, 1922, LOC Papers; Tuve, *First Lady*, 73 n.13.

30. Tuve, *First Lady*, 64–65; John T. Burke, "18,000 Here Sign for Judge Allen for High Court," newsclip, Sept. 1, 1922.

31. "Candidate for Supreme Bench," *Ohio State Grange Monthly*, Sept. 1922.

32. "Judge Allen to Deliver Address Here Thursday," newsclip [1922].

33. Lillian Wald to FEA, Nov. 4, 1922, LOC Papers.

34. "Rivals for High Court Give Views," *Plain Dealer*, Oct. 19, 1922.

35. Campaign manuscript, quotes of endorsements [ca. 1922].

36. Obituary, "Judge Robert Day Dies in Columbus," *New York Times*, Sept. 30, 1933.

37. "Says Miss Allen Can't Be Judge," *Youngstown Vindicator*, Nov. 25, 1922.

38. Tuve, *First Lady*, 66; Diary, Sept. 17, 1918; Apr. 20, 1921; May 6, 1921.

39. "Ohio Woman Judge Was News Writer," *Washington Post*, Nov. 11, 1922.

40. "Ohio Judges Are Sworn in Jointly," *Mt. Vernon Banner*, Dec. 16, 1922; "Allen Will Not Wait on Donahey," *Plain Dealer*, Nov. 28, 1922, 5.

41. "Four Justices Fail to Greet Recruit," *Cincinnati Enquirer*, Nov. 13, 1922.

42. Charles W. Wood, "A Portia Come to Judgment," newsclip, June 16, 1923; "Woman Justice from Ohio Rates Portia Great Judge," Portland, Oregon, newsclip, 1923.

43. Tuve, *First Lady*, 66.

44. "Odd Mail Comes to Woman Judge," *Plain Dealer*, Dec. 10, 1922.

45. "Judge Allen Is Candidate for Supreme Bench," June 13, 1922; "Miss Rebhan Says People Want Woman Supreme Judge," *Youngstown Vindicator*, June 14, 1922.

46. Frances Parkinson Keyes, "Homes of Outstanding American Women," *Better Homes and Gardens*, June 1928, 12.

47. "New Dean of Women Enthusiastic About Work at Ohio State," *Lantern*, July 29, 1927.

48. Tuve, *First Lady*, 136–37; newsclip, *Chicago Daily Tribune*, July 13, 1933; "Judge Florence Allen Defends Maiden Class," *Fremont Messenger*, Sept. 20, 1933, LOC Papers.

49. "Ohio History Made by Woman Jurist," *Toledo Blade*, Jan. 3, 1923; "Woman Assumes High Post," *Washington Post*, Jan. 3, 1923, 6; "Woman Takes Oath as Supreme Court Judge," *Baltimore Sun*, Dec. 17, 1922.

50. First Report of the Judicial Council of Ohio to the General Assembly (Dec. 1930); Marshall, *Courts and Lawyers of Ohio*, 226–27; Ohio General Statistics for 1924, Secretary of State, vol. 9.

51. For example, United Fuel Gas v. Ironton, 107 Ohio St. 173 (1923); Metropolitan Sec. Co. v. Orlow, 107 Ohio St. 583 (1923); Brown v. Brown, 107 Ohio St. 228 (1923); Scott v. State, 107 Ohio St. 475 (1923); White v. Findlay, 108 Ohio St. 475 (1923); Hamilton v. Board of Commissioners, 108 Ohio St. 566 (1923).

52. Bertha A. Miller, "Career of Florence Allen Trail of Broken Precedents," *New York Evening Post*, newsclip, Mar. 1934.

53. Kennedy v. Byers, 107 Ohio St. 90 (1923).

54. Ohio Const. art. I, sec. 19a.

55. Reutener v. City of Cleveland, 141 N.E. 27 (Ohio 1923).

56. Allen, *Justly*, 80–81.

57. Noctor v. State *ex rel.* Linehan, 108 Ohio St. 404, 405 (1923) (Allen, J., dissenting).

58. Allen, *Justly*, 82–83; e.g., Masters v. Beamer Bd. Educ., 109 Ohio St, 133 (1923).

59. *Miller*, 140 N.E. 773 (Ohio 1923); *DeRolph*, 78 Ohio St.3d 193 (1997).

60. Retirement Bd. of Teachers' Retirement System v. Kurtz, 110 Ohio St. 332 (1924); Sommers v. Bd. of Educ., 113 Ohio St. 177, 184 (1925).

61. 108 Ohio St. 61 (1923).

62. *Fender*, 108 Ohio St. 149 (1923).

63. Allen, *Justly*, 82, 86.

64. Norris v. Jones, 110 Ohio St 598 (1924); Drew v. Goss, 112 Ohio St. 485 (1925); Cincinnati Baseball v. Eno, 112 Ohio St. 175 (1925).

65. For example, Columbus Ry. Power & Light Co. v. Public Utilities Comm'n, 113 Ohio St. 634 (1925); Lima-Toledo R. Co. v. Public Utilities Comm'n, 121 Ohio St. 421 (1929); New York C.R. Co. v. Public Utilities Comm'n, 121 Ohio St. 588 (1929).

66. Allen, *Justly*, 79–80; Fisher Bros. v. Brown, 111 Ohio St. 602 (1924).

67. Bettman v. Court of Common Pleas of Franklin County, 124 Ohio St 269, 293 (1931) (Allen, J., dissenting); *Ex Parte* Thayer, 150 N.E. 735 (Ohio 1926); State v. Boyatt, 114 Ohio St. 397 (1926); Scott v. State, 111 Ohio St. 178 (1924); Crabbe v. Municipal Savings and Loan Co., 111 Ohio St. 178 (1924); Hamilton v. Bd. of Commissioners, 108 Ohio St. 566 (1923).

68. "Trail of Broken Precedents"; Hoare v. City of Cleveland, 126 Ohio St. 625 (1933); Hardin-Wyandot Lighting Co. v. Public Utilities Comm'n, 118 Ohio St. 592 (1928); Portsmouth Gas Co. v. Public Utilities Comm'n, 119 Ohio St. 24 (1928); City of Cincinnati v. Public Utilities Comm'n, 113 Ohio St. 259 (1925).

69. Baer v. Stanton, 111 Ohio St. 327 (1924).

70. First Report of the Judicial Council of Ohio to the General Assembly of Ohio (Jan. 5, 1931).

71. Browning v. State, 120 Ohio St. 62 (1929); Thatcher v. Pennsylvania O. & D.R. Co., 121 Ohio St. 205 (1929).

72. 116 Ohio St 512 (1927).

73. Feinman, "Historical Overview," 14.
74. Diary, May 3, 5, 7, 10, 11, 17, 1927.
75. 110 Ohio St. 350, 358–59 (1924).
76. Hessick, "Race and Gender," 127, 135–36.
77. 111 Ohio St. 225 (1924).
78. Allen, *Justly*, 87–88.
79. Scott v. City of Columbus, 142 N.E. 25 (1923); Schneiderman v. Sesanstein, 121 Ohio St. 80, 92 (1929) (Allen, J., dissenting).
80. State *ex rel.* Bryant v. Akron Metropolitan Park, 120 Ohio St. 464 (1929), *aff'd*, 281 U.S. 74 (1930).
81. 112 Ohio St. 628 (1925); City of Youngstown v. Kahn Bros Building Co., 112 Ohio St. 654 (1925).
82. 272 US 365 (1926).
83. Automatic Machine Registering Co. v. Green, 121 Ohio St. 301 (1929); Jackson v. Board of County Comm'rs, 122 Ohio St. 456, 459 (1930).
84. Smith v. City of Fremont, 116 Ohio St. 469 (1927); "Trail of Broken Precedents."
85. Wing v. Farrell, 111 Ohio St. 353, 360 (1924) (Allen, J., dissenting).
86. Sullivan v. State, 125 Ohio St. 388, 395 (1932) (Allen, J., dissenting).
87. *Sullivan*, 125 Ohio St. at 395.
88. Decker v. State, 113 Ohio St 512 (1925).
89. Thomas v. Mills, 117 Ohio St. 114, 125 (1927).
90. Evans v. State, 123 Ohio St. 132 (1930); *see also* Lowe v. Union Trust Co., 124 Ohio St. 302 (1931).
91. *Evans*, 123 Ohio St. 132.
92. 121 Ohio St. 280 (1929).
93. "Judge Allen Admits Carrying Gun in Car," *Youngstown Vindicator*, Mar. 16, 1929.
94. F. Kuznik, "The Golden Era of the Cleveland Mob," *Cleveland Magazine*, Aug. 1, 1978; Porrello, *Rise and Fall*, 176–81.
95. 119 Ohio St. 166, 181–83 (1928) (Allen, J., dissenting); Diary, May 31, 1928; June 14, 1928.
96. Abbott, *Ghosts of Eden Park*, 5, 26, 38.
97. Brown, *Willebrandt*, 64–65.
98. Abbott, *Ghosts of Eden Park*, 28, 42, 155, 165–82, 203, 233, 246, 260–63.
99. Abbott, *Ghosts of Eden Park*, 372–74, 386; Ron Hogan, "Rich Bootlegger George Remus Killed His Wife—and Got Away with It," *New York Post*, Aug. 17, 2019.
100. "Re-Elect Judge Allen," *Plain Dealer*, Oct. 6, 1928; Bromley, "Woman Is Worthy of High Court," *New York Telegram*, Jan. 4, 1937.
101. Tuve, *First Lady*, 78–82.

102. Newsclip, *Youngstown Vindicator*, Nov. 4, 1928.

103. Press release [1928].

104. Memo, "Relevant Opinions," ca. 1928; FEA, speech to Brotherhood of Railroad Trainmen, Chittenden Hotel, Sept. 28, 1928; "Re-Elect Florence Allen."

105. "Green Is Heard by Millions," *Plain Dealer*, Sept. 4, 1928.

106. "Judge Allen—Leader," *Cleveland Press*, Aug. 28, 1928.

107. Campaign card, "Re-Elect Judge Florence Allen for a Second Term to Supreme Court, 1928."

108. Press release, "Judge Allen Advocates Non-Partisan Bench," 1928.

109. "Judge Allen—Leader."

110. "Judge Florence E. Allen," *Youngstown Vindicator*, Oct. 14, 1928.

111. Carol Willis Hyatt, "Why Women Call Her Great," newsclip, May 1, 1929.

112. "As a Distinguished Citizen," *Plain Dealer*, newsclip, Aug. 31 [1923].

113. E. A. Tamm, FBI Memorandum to the Director Re: Florence Ellinwood Allen, Feb. 15, 1939; memo, "Record of Judge Florence E. Allen in labor cases and in the Weaver case," n.d., in Franklin D. Roosevelt Presidential Library.

114. 126 Ohio St. 177 (1932).

115. FBI Memo, Feb. 15, 1939; "Criminal Syndicalism Law of Ohio Is Upheld," *Cincinnati Times Star*, Dec. 21, 1932, 28.

116. 126 Ohio St. at 196 (Allen, J., dissenting).

117. 395 US 444 (1969).

118. 124 Ohio St. 413 (1931).

119. 125 Ohio St. 301 (1932).

120. Allen, *Justly*, 92; "Record of Judge Florence E. Allen."

121. 126 Ohio St. 290, 185 N.E. 196 (1933).

122. Diary, Jan. 31, 1933; Feb. 1, 9, 1933; Mar. 13, 1933; Steward, "Time Not Ripe," 30.

123. "Weighs Weaver Appeal," *Plain Dealer*, Feb. 18, 1933.

124. Pritchard, "Negro Experience," 120–22.

125. Steward, "Time Not Ripe," 27; Pritchard, "Negro Experience," 129–32.

126. Steward, "Time Not Ripe," 11, 14, 19, 30; Pritchard, "Negro Experience," 128–34; "Roosevelt Sweep May Put Davey In," *Plain Dealer*, Nov. 4, 1936.

127. Steward, "Time Not Ripe," 5.

128. *Weaver*, 126 Ohio St. at 296.

129. Steward, "Time Not Ripe," 16, 20.

130. 163 U.S. 587 (1896).

131. 126 Ohio St. 290 (1933); "Negro Co-Ed Loses Her Fight at O.S.U.," *Plain Dealer*, Mar. 16, 1933.

132. FEA to Walter White, Secretary, NAACP, Mar. 22, 1934.

133. "Criticizes Faculty in Weaver Case," *Plain Dealer*, Mar. 27, 1933.

134. Clayborne George and Chester E. Gillespie, Legal Defense Committee, Cleveland NAACP, to Senator (OH) Robert Bulkley, Feb. 12, 1934.

135. Steward, "Time Not Ripe," 21; "Segregation—a Symposium," *The Crisis*, Mar. 1934; "Race Issue Bobs Up in Davey Talk," *Plain Dealer*, Nov. 2, 1936.

136. Cook, "Women as Judges: End of Tokenism," 10; Allen, *Justly*, 93.

5. LEGISLATING FOR PEACE AND WELFARE

1. Sklar, "Historical Foundations," 76.

2. Helen Jordan, Campaign Manager, "A Message to Our Friends," Oct. 14, 1932, LOC Papers.

3. Tuve, *First Lady*, 63, 65; *Dayton News*, Nov. 25, 1922; Diary, May 18, 23, 1922.

4. Lemons, *Woman Citizen*, 89; Ambrose, *Liberated Spirits*, 11; Andersen, *After Suffrage*, 27, 37.

5. Ladd-Taylor, "'Agony and Grief,'" 321–23, 328; Ladd-Taylor, *Mother-Work*, 257–71; Lemons, *Woman Citizen*, 145, 158–67.

6. Brown, *Setting the Course*, 52.

7. Wilson, *Women's Joint Congressional Committee*, 19; Lemons, *Woman Citizen*, 55–56; Breckinridge, *Twentieth Century*, 259–60; Bredbenner, *Nationality*, 86; Brown, *Willebrandt*, 8; Cott, *Grounding*, 97; Ladd-Taylor, "'Agony and Grief,'" 328.

8. Ritter, *Social Design*, 58–62; Andersen, *After Suffrage*, 30, 53, 69, 143.

9. Andersen, *After Suffrage*, 1–2, 55; Lemons, *Woman Citizen*, 57, 89; Ritter, *Social Design*, 56–57; Corder and Wolbrecht, *Counting Women's Ballots*, 51; Breckinridge, *Twentieth Century*, 268.

10. FEA, "The First Ten Years," *Woman's Journal*, Aug. 5, 1930, 5; Allen, "Participation of Women," 94.

11. Allen, "First Ten Years"; Allen, "Participation of Women."

12. "Women Members by Congress," *United States House of Representatives: History, Art and Archives*, https://history.house.gov; "Women Senators," *United States Senate*, https://senate.gov.

13. Katz, "Sex, Suffrage," 179.

14. Lopach and Lukowski, *Jeannette Rankin*, 4–10; Lemons, *Woman Citizen*, 103; Breckinridge, *Twentieth Century*, 296.

15. Lemons, *Woman Citizen*, 103, 157–58.

16. Andersen, *After Suffrage*, 113; Becker, *Origins*, 22; Cott, *Grounding*, 321 n.38.

17. Breckinridge, *Twentieth Century*, 300, 322–26; Allen, "Participation of Women," 96.

18. Ritter, *Social Design*, 80–81.

19. Manuscript, "Pledge to Democratic Platform" [1932]; Lemons, *Woman Citizen*, 191.

20. Allen, "First Ten Years"; Allen, "Participation of Women."

21. FEA, radio address, Cleveland, Oct. 31, 1932, LOC Papers.

22. "Famous Jurist Is Easily 'Best Man' in Senate Contest," *Labor*, July 31, 1926; "Voters of Ohio, Send Florence Allen to U.S. Senate," *Labor*, July 31, 1926; Tuve, *First Lady*, 76–78.

23. FEA, *Justly*, 73; Diary, May 13, 14, 19, 1915; June 4, 1915.

24. FEA, "Women and Court Congress," *Plain Dealer*, June 3, 1915.

25. Alonso, *Women's Peace Union*, xxii–xxiv, 1, 25–26; Cott, *Grounding*, 254.

26. FEA, speech, "Outlawry of War," Conference on Causes and Cure of War, Jan. 18, 1925, LOC Papers; Alonso, *Women's Peace Union*, 9; Cott, *Grounding*, 243–44.

27. FEA, "Outlawry of War"; "The Trend of Events," *Herald of Gospel Liberty*, May 3, 1923; "Outlaw All War, Says Woman Judge," *New York Herald*, Feb. 1924.

28. Tuve, *First Lady*, 47–48; "Brothers Sacrificed to Mars, Miss Allen Knows Cost of War," *Labor*, July 31, 1926, LOC Papers.

29. FEA, *Justly*, 73–74; Tuve, *First Lady*, 48, 79; Diary, July 20, 1918; Sept. 28, 1918; Dec. 20–25, 1918; Oct. 2, 3, 1924.

30. "She's in on Politics, Not as Mere Visitor," *Daily News*, May 29, 1919.

31. FEA to Homer Cummings, Sept. 24, 1919; "Miss Allen Quits Democratic Post," *Plain Dealer*, Sept. 24, 1919; "Quits as Protest on Army Plan," *Columbus Dispatch*, Sept. 24, 1919.

32. "Woman Objects to Service Bill," Oct. 14, 1919; "Woman Democrat Balks at Baker's Bill," newsclip [1919]; *Cincinnati Enquirer*, Sept. 18, 1919; Carl D. Ruth, "Dems Shiver in Fear They'll Lose Votes of Women," newsclip [1919].

33. "Woman Democrat Still Balks at Baker's Army Bill," newsclip, Nov. 15, 1919.

34. Allen, *Justly*, 20, 42–43.

35. Gara v. United States, 178 F.2d 38 (6th Cir. 1949).

36. Salmon Levinson to FEA, Feb. 18, 1922; FEA to Levinson, Mar. 19, 1923, Salmon Levinson Papers, Hanna Holborn Gray Special Collections, University of Chicago.

37. Allen, *Justly*, 73.

38. FEA, speech "Women's Obligation for Peace," to National Business and Professional Women, July 1946.

39. FEA, speech manuscript, "Declaration of Independence Against War," 8, 10–11; FEA, speech, "The Establishment of World Peace in Its Relation to the Church," Nov. 13, 1925; "America Must Outlaw War Says Judge Allen," *Salem Daily News*, Mar. 16, 1925; "Christianity and International Relations," *Ohio Christian News*, Dec. 1925.

40. Allen, "Participation of Women," 102–3; FEA, "Outlawry of War"; Press, *Kellor*, 292.

41. FEA to Professor Manley Hudson, Harvard, June 6, 1923; FEA to Senator Arthur Capper, May 25, 1923; "Outlaw All War"; FEA, speech, "Women and the Present Crisis," Detroit, ca. 1945.

42. Newsclip, *Akron Beacon Journal*, n.d., LOC Papers.

43. FEA, "A Charge to Women Voters," *Good Housekeeping*, Oct. 1925, 186; "Prominent Woman Judge to Talk Here," *Baltimore Sun*, Mar. 21, 1925.

44. Abbott, *History of Woman Suffrage*, 78–91; "Ohio Women Stage Demonstration for Peace," *Capitol News Bureau*, May 21, 1924.

45. "Hoover Opens Fight of Administration for World Court," *New York Times*, Apr. 12, 1923; FEA, "Outlawry of War."

46. Alonso, *Women's Peace Union*, xxii.

47. Hathaway and Shapiro, *Internationalists*, intro.

48. Allen, "Nuremberg Trial" (1947), 389; Allen, "Nuremberg Trial" (1948), 6; Bernice Cross, "Jurist Hails Nuremberg Trials," *Champaign-Urbana Courier*, newsclip, n.d.

49. FEA, "Back to the American Standards," *Cleveland Club Woman*, May 1928; Allen, "Participation of Women"; FEA, "Women's Obligation for Peace"; FEA, address at Radcliffe College honoring Maud Wood Park, Nov. 10, 1960.

50. FEA, speech, "Human Rights and the International Court," Sixth Inter-American Bar Association Meeting, Detroit, May 26; FEA, World Alliance for Friendship address, 1931; "Scores Policy in Mexico," *New York Times*, Mar. 14, 1927; "A Women's Symposium Against War: Why Wars Must Cease," *New York Times*, Jan. 20, 1935.

51. FEA, speech, "Peace Through Justice," The Hague, Aug. 16, 1948.

52. Allen, *Treaty as an Instrument*; Allen, *Justly*, 133–42; Ruth E. Riddell, "Judge Allen's Book on Treaties," *Women Lawyers Journal*, n.d.

53. Allen, *Justly*, 73–78, 153; Doris Greenberg, "People Put First in Keeping Peace," *New York Times*, July 12, 1946, 20.

54. "Women Assured Place on the Ballot," *Plain Dealer*, Sept. 16, 1922; "Two Women Seek Election on State Ticket in Ohio," *Associated Press*, newsclip, Oct. 4, 1922.

55. Diary, Mar. 6, 1925.

56. Allen, *Justly*, 76–77.

57. "Scores Pomerene Suffrage Stand," *Plain Dealer*, June 5, 1918; "Suffragists Seek Pomerene's Scalp," *Plain Dealer*, Jan. 26, 1919.

58. Diary, Jan. 23, 28, 1926; Feb. 4, 8, 20, 1926; May 19, 1926; Sept. 9, 1926; "Weekly Club Calendar," *Plain Dealer*, July 24, 1932.

59. "Pomerene Yields to Pleas," *New York Times*, Jun. 7, 1926, 3; "Declaration Is Filed by Judge Allen," newsclip, June 10 [1926]; Diary, Feb. 8, 1925; Mar. 7, 10, 1925; Apr. 25, 1925; May 28, 1925; June 28, 1925; Aug. 11, 28, 30, 1925; Sept. 6, 1925.

60. Newton Baker to Florence Allen Committee, Aug. 3, 1926; newsclip, *Ohio State Journal*, Aug. 5, 1926.

61. Newton Baker to FEA, Feb. 15, 1926.

62. Newton Baker to FEA, Feb. 9, 1926.

63. Oldfather, *Judges, Judging*, 92–93.

64. Allen, *Justly*, 76; Diary, Feb. 10, 1926; Tuve, *First Lady*, 67, 75; Newton Baker to FEA, Feb. 9, 1926; newsclip, *Columbus Ohio State Journal*, Aug. 5, 1926.

65. "Women to Back Justice Allen," *Lorain Herald*, Feb. 26, 1926.

66. FEA, "Back to the Constitution," *Dayton Forum*, Aug. 4, 1926.

67. FEA, "Back to the Constitution"; "Back to Home Life, Says Florence Allen," *Mansfield News*, June 16, 1926; "Back to Fathers Is Plea of Judge," newsclip, June 16 [1926]; "Judge Allen Opposes 'Whitewashes,'" newsclip [1926].

68. Ida Clyde Clarke, "A Woman for the Senate," *Century Magazine*, June 1926, 112.

69. FEA, speech, "Why Should a Woman Be Elected to the Senate?" [1926].

70. Allen, "First Ten Years"; FEA, address, "Women and Citizenship," delivered to Philadelphia Society for Ethical Culture, Nov. 27, 1921; FEA, speech in Detroit, 1946.

71. Clarke, "Woman for the Senate," 131.

72. C. B. Gohdes, "Why Florence E. Allen Impresses Me," newsclip, n.d.

73. Tuve, *First Lady*, 78.

74. Diary, Mar. 21, 1926; Apr. 19, 1927.

75. Cott, *Grounding*, 255; Nielsen, *Un-American Womanhood*, 1, 5, 50; Lemons, *Woman Citizen*, 58, 111, 209, 215.

76. Tuve, *First Lady*, 50; Tuve, "First Woman."

77. "No Blacklist Received Here," *Youngstown Vindicator*, Apr. 8, 1928, 17.

78. Tuve, *First Lady*, 87; Nielsen, *Un-American Womanhood*, 57–59, 73, 126; Lemons, *Woman Citizen*, 123–24, 223.

79. Jack Cejnar, "Light Vote Expected Today," *Coshocton Tribune*, Aug. 10, 1926.

80. Breckinridge, *Twentieth Century*, 303–4.

81. "Judge Allen's Glorious Defeat," *Woman Citizen*, Oct. 1926, 10.

82. Allen, *Justly*, 77.

83. Diary, Jan. 28, 1932.

84. Ware, *Partner*, 146.

85. "Judge Allen Will Not Quit Court Post," *Columbus Dispatch*, Mar. 22, 1932; "Judge Allen Won't Quit," *Ironton (OH) News*, Mar. 25, 1932.

86. FEA, "Statement of Keeping Judicial Office," typescript, 1931; "Judge Allen Will Not Quit"; "Judge Allen Won't Quit"; Tuve, *First Lady*, 103–6, 112.

87. James G. Monnett Jr., "Alcazar Hotel on Heights Sold," *Plain Dealer*, June 7, 1929, 8.

88. Evelyn Theiss, "Cleveland Heights Alcazar Exudes Exotic Style and Grace in Any Age," *Plain Dealer*, Oct. 12, 2008.

89. Allen, *Justly*, 78.

90. Organ, "Sexuality as a Category," 148–49.

91. Tuve, *First Lady*, 134–35; Organ, "Sexuality as a Category," 147 n.80, 177; Diary, Dec. 6, 1931; Mar. 17, 1938; Apr. 3, 30, 1938; Nov. 2, 1938; Sept. 11, 1939.

92. Allen, *Justly*, 78; James G. Monnett Jr., "Commodore and Alcazar in Deals," *Plain Dealer*, July 7, 1936, 22.

93. Allen, "Governmental Task," 14.

94. Helen Jordan, "Notice," Oct. 18, 1932, LOC Papers.

95. Jordan, "Message."

96. FEA, radio address.

97. "Pledge to Democratic Platform."

98. FEA, speech, "Running for Congress" [1932]; Allen, "Governmental Task"; FEA, "First Ten Years."

99. "Dual Dry Poll Looms in Ohio," *Washington Times*, June 14, 1926; "Wet and Dry Fight," *Ashtabula Beacon*, June 16, 1926.

100. "Judge Allen Is Dry Candidate," *Hamilton News*, June 11, 1926; "Judge Allen Says Modern Girl's O.K.," *Plain Dealer*, Apr. 24, 1926.

101. FEA, address to Anti-Saloon League, Detroit Statler Hotel, Jan. 18, 1930; "Not the Only Law," newsclip [Jan. 26, 1930]; Rose, *Repeal of Prohibition*, 160–70.

102. Tuve, *First Lady*, 103–5; FEA, "Statement on Prohibition"; FEA to Woman's Christian Temperance Union, Apr. 7, 1932; Rose, *Repeal of Prohibition*, 171–78, 204–9; FEA, "Running for Congress."

103. FEA, address to Anti-Saloon League.

104. Diary, Aug. 20, 1920; Nov. 26, 1920; Dec. 14, 1920; Apr. 4, 1926.

105. Krusoczky v. State, 140 N.E. 614 (Ohio 1923); White v. Findlay, 141 N.E. 219 (Ohio 1923); Decker v. State, 150 N.E. 74, 74 (Ohio 1925).

106. Tumey v. Ohio, 115 Ohio St. 701 (1926), *rev'd*, 273 U.S. 510 (1927); "Ohio Liquor Courts Declared Illegal," *New York Times*, Mar. 8, 1927, 3.

107. Rose, *Repeal of Prohibition*, 210–12, 230; Monopoli, "Situating *Dobbs*," 53–54; Suk, *After Misogyny*, 123–51.

108. Brown, *Willebrandt*, 51, 53, 55, 79; Okrent, *Last Call*, 13–18, 49.

109. Monopoli, "Situating *Dobbs*," 53–54; Suk, *After Misogyny*, 147.

110. Suk, *After Misogyny*, 126, 147.

111. Monopoli, "Situating *Dobbs*," 53; Brown, *Willebrandt*, 50; Ambrose, *Liberated Spirits*, 12–14.

112. Brown, *Willebrandt*, 55, 75, 78; Ambrose, *Liberated Spirits*, 69.

113. Suk, *After Misogyny*, 149–51; Ambrose, *Liberated Spirits*, 233–34; Rose, *Repeal of Prohibition*, 30.

114. “Members of Congress,” *Plain Dealer*, Oct. 11, 1932, 8.

115. Brown, *Willebrandt*, 79; Rose, *Repeal of Prohibition*, 20–23, 30–31, 88–91, 103, 117–19, 129–30, 137, 168–70.

116. Monopoli, “Situating *Dobbs*,” 53.

117. Andersen, *After Suffrage*, 25, 114.

118. Tuve, *First Lady*, 107, 112; Diary, Nov. 20, 1932; FEA to Farley, Nov. 30, 1932; newsclip, *Cincinnati Enquirer*, Apr. 1, 1934.

6. CHALLENGING THE BRETHREN

1. Allen, *Justly*, 95; “In Honor of Judge Allen,” *Cincinnati Enquirer*, Apr. 10, 1934, LOC Papers.

2. “Miss Florence Allen Takes Oath as First Woman Federal Judge,” *Cincinnati Post*, Apr. 9, 1934; “Woman Judge on Federal Bench,” newsclip, Apr. 9, 1934.

3. “Takes Oath”; “Club Women Will Honor Judge Allen,” *Cincinnati Times Star*, Apr. 4, 1934.

4. Newsclip, *Cincinnati Times Star*, Apr. 12, 1934.

5. “Judge Allen Bench Nomination Okehed,” newsclip, Mar. 14, 1934.

6. “Judge Allen,” *Cincinnati Post*, Apr. 10, 1934.

7. “Judge Allen Prepares to Take Post,” newsclip, Apr. 1934, LOC Papers.

8. “First Woman Takes Oath of Office,” *Cincinnati Enquirer*, Apr. 10, 1934; “Taft Court Room Gets Judge Allen,” *Plain Dealer*, Apr. 10, 1934.

9. “Ohio’s Woman Judge an Imposing Figure,” *New York Times*, Dec. 3, 1922, A110.

10. Tuve, *First Lady*, 110; newsclip, *Youngstown Vindicator*, Mar. 24, 1934.

11. Epstein, *Women in Law*, 244, 265–66.

12. Tuve, *First Lady*, 92, 101 n.4; Williams et al., “You Can’t Change,” 8, 24.

13. Cook, “Supreme Court Candidates,” 318.

14. Constance Marshall, “Judge Allen, Pioneer,” *Woman Citizen* 11 (June 1926).

15. Suk, *After Misogyny*, 2–3.

16. “Four Justices,” *Cincinnati Enquirer*, Nov. 13, 1922.

17. News photo, *Plain Dealer*, Jan. 21, 1923; Diary, Jan. 8, 1923.

18. Diary, Jan. 8, 26, 1923; Feb. 6, 1923; Jan. 28, 1926; “Society Page,” *Columbus Dispatch*, Jan. 21, 1923, 17.

19. Diary, Mar. 26, 1925.

20. Allen, *Justly*, 79.

21. Diary, Jan. 3, 1923; Mar. 5, 1923.

22. “Florence E. Allen, Ohio’s First Woman Supreme Judge, Takes Place on Bench,” *Columbus Dispatch*, Jan. 2, 1923, 3.

23. Diary, Jan. 11, 12, 1923; Jan. 24, 1924; Jan. 11, 20, 1925.

24. Diary, Jan. 5, 6, 20, 1923.

25. Diary, Jan. 9, 10, 14, 1924; Feb. 27, 1924; Jan. 22, 1925; Feb. 10, 1925; Mar. 5, 12, 13, 24, 27, 1925.

26. Diary, Feb. 27, 28, 1923; Mar. 13, 1925; Mar. 7, 11, 26, 1926.

27. Diary, Feb. 6, 1923.

28. Obituary, "Ohio Jurist Killed by Leap at Hospital," *New York Times*, June 19, 1924, 22.

29. Nathaniel M. Fouch, "Remembering Judge R. M. Wanamaker on the Centenary of His Death," *Ohio Lawyer*, June 24, 2024.

30. Allen, *Justly*, 70, 79.

31. Memorial, James E. Robinson, 124 Ohio St. lxxiii (1932); "James E. Robinson, Ohio Jurist, Dies," *New York Times*, Jan. 28, 1932.

32. Brotherhood of Locomotive Firemen and Enginemen v. Public Utilities Comm'n, 123 Ohio St. 336, 342 (Robinson, J., concurring).

33. Hawke v. Smith, 126 N.E. 400 (Ohio 1919), *rev'd*, 253 U.S. 221 (1920); Browning v. State, 120 Ohio St. 62 (1929).

34. Diary, Oct. 1, 1929; "Judge Allen Wears Boyish Bob, Crystal Beads," newsclip, n.d., LOC Papers; "Bobbed Hair Is Final Decision of Judge Allen," *Troy Daily News*, Sept. 19, 1929; "Bobbed Locks Finally Win Judge Allen," newsclip, Dec. 22, 1929.

35. "Woman Judge Defies All Claim to Vanity," newsclip, Aug. 11, 1922.

36. Diary, Jan. 26, 1927; May 12, 17, 1927.

37. Tuve, *First Lady*, 136–37; "Judge Florence Allen Defends Maiden Class," *Fremont Messenger*, Sept. 20, 1933, LOC Papers.

38. Steinglass and Scarselli, *Ohio State Constitution*, 57.

39. Michael Meckler, "Forgotten Ohio Chief Justice Died 60 Years Ago Today," *Columbus Dispatch*, June 28, 2018.

40. "Supreme Court Trims Chief Justice's Power," *Cincinnati Times Star*, Mar. 16, 1932, 9.

41. 176 N.E. 454, 455 (Ohio 1931).

42. Allen, *Justly*, 88–90.

43. 124 Ohio Stat. 174, 206–7 (1931) (Allen, J., dissenting), *cert. denied*, 286 U.S. 526 (1932); Allen, *Justly*, 90–91; "Ohio Ruling Reversed in Sewer Bond Case," *New York Times*, June 18, 1931.

44. Taylor v. French, 96 Ohio St. 172, 185 (1917) (Jones, J., dissenting).

45. "Supreme Court Trims."

46. "Supreme Court Trims."

47. "Takes Place on Bench"; Diary, Mar. 8, 1923.

48. *Cincinnati Times Star*, Mar. 16, 1932; Tuve, *First Lady*, 103, 108; Diary, Dec. 10, 1932.

49. Boyd, Collins, and Highland, *Supreme Bias*, 95.

50. "Supreme Court Trims"; "Marshall Says Disarmament Is Fanatical Idea," *OSU Lantern*, Jan. 25, 1932.

51. 125 Ohio St. 301 (1932); "Rules Union Labor Not Issue in Bids," *Plain Dealer*, Mar. 24, 1932.

52. "Judicial Candidates," *Cincinnati Times Star*, Oct. 24, 1932, 6; "Supreme Court Trims."

53. Marshall, "Pioneer."

54. "Florence E. Allen Named Federal Judge," *New York Times*, Mar. 7, 1934; Bertha A. Miller, "Career of Florence Allen a Trail of Broken Precedents," *New York Evening Post*, Mar. 7, 1934.

55. Carrie Chapman Catt to Mary (Molly) Dewson, Dec. 26, 1933; Organ, "Sexuality as a Category," 160.

56. Tuve, *First Lady*, 108; Cook, "First Woman Candidate," 26; Roosevelt and Hickok, *Ladies of Courage*, 11, 15.

57. Organ, "Sexuality as a Category," 160; Tuve, *First Lady*, 108 (citing FEA to Molly Dewson, Dec. 4, 1959).

58. Senator Simon Fess to Amy Maher, Mar. 15, 1934.

59. Tuve, *First Lady*, 109; Judge Harold N. Stephens, "Address at Testimonial Dinner for Judge Florence E. Allen," Nov. 8, 1948.

60. FEA to President Franklin D. Roosevelt, 1933.

61. Cook, "First Woman Candidate," 26; Jefferson and Johnson, *Shortlisted*, 23, 29–30; Tuve, *First Lady*, 122; Eleanor Roosevelt, "What Ten Million Women Want," *Home Magazine*, Mar. 1932, 5; Eleanor Roosevelt, "My Day," June 27, 1938, Nov. 17, 1948; FEA to Eleanor Roosevelt: May 1, 1933, Oct. 2, 1933, Oct. 10, 1933, Feb. 12, 1935, Feb. 2, 1936, Sept. 23, 1938, Dec. 7, 1938, Sept. 12, 1939, Nov. 10, 1944, Apr. 16, 1954; Eleanor Roosevelt to FEA: May 5, 1933, Oct. 6, 1933, Jan. 4, 1935, Feb. 19, 1935, Nov. 9, 1936, Mar. 20, 1940; Roosevelt and Hickok, *Ladies of Courage*, 195–98.

62. Mrs. Roosevelt, "Tribute to a Judge" [Nov. 1948], LOC Papers.

63. Diary, Dec. 23, 1933; Tuve, *First Lady*, 114 (citing letters of Molly Dewson to Eleanor Roosevelt, Jan. 24, 1934, and Eleanor Roosevelt to FDR, Jan. 29, 1934, Franklin D. Roosevelt Presidential Library); H. C. Pontius to Rebhan, Feb. 5, 1934.

64. Harold Stephens to FEA, Jan. 25, 1934.

65. "Broken Precedents"; Allen, *Justly*, 95; Carl Weygandt to Attorney General Homer Commings, Dec. 27, 1933.

66. John Clarke to FEA, Jan. 9, 1934; Tuve, *First Lady*, 108–11.

67. E. A. Tamm, FBI Memorandum to the Director Re: Florence Ellinwood Allen, Feb. 15, 1939 (including R. C. Chapman, FBI Investigative Report Regarding Hon. Florence E. Allen, Jan. 20, 1934).

68. Tuve, *First Lady*, 109.

69. Newton Baker to FEA, Jan. 23, 1934.

70. Allen, *Justly*, 92; Tuve, *First Lady*, 109–10.

71. "Record of Judge Florence E. Allen in Labor Cases and in the Weaver Case," n.d., Franklin D. Roosevelt Presidential Library.

72. Telegram, L. W. Adams to Senator Robert Bulkley, Feb. 27, 1934.

73. Steward, "Time Not Ripe," 32; Pritchard, "Negro Experience," 133.

74. Clayborne George and Chester E. Gillespie, Legal Defense Committee, Cleveland NAACP, to Senator (OH) Robert Bulkley, Feb. 12, 1934.

75. Diary, Feb. 14, 1934; Mar. 11, 1934.

76. FEA to Walter White, Secretary, NAACP, Mar. 22, 1934.

77. Allen, *Justly*, 92.

78. Memorandum, "Cases Showing the Attitude of the Supreme Court of Ohio with Reference to Race Discrimination," n.d.

79. Board of Education of Dayton v. State *ex rel.* Reese, 114 Ohio St. 188 (1926); Epoch Producing Corp. v. Riegel, 113 Ohio St. 697 (1925).

80. Diary, Mar. 23–25, 1915; "'Birth of a Nation' May Yet Be Seen Here," *Plain Dealer*, Oct. 10, 1915.

81. Eva Epstein Shaw to Mrs. Jesse Heslip, Mar. 13, 1934; Shaw to Heslip, Mar. 13, 1933.

82. "Record of Judge Florence E. Allen."

83. FBI Memorandum, 1939.

84. "The Learned Sixth: New Paper Reexamines Judge Florence Allen, Sixth Circuit Trailblazer," *Sixth Circuit Blog*, Aug. 5, 2020.

85. "Charles Moorman, a Federal Jurist," *New York Times*, Jan. 27, 1938, 21; "Judge Charles Simons, 87, of Michigan Appeals Court," *New York Times*, Feb. 3, 1964, 27; "Xen Hicks," 127.

86. Allen, *Justly*, 95–97.

87. Allen, *Justly*, 95–97.

88. Allen, *Justly*, 98.

89. Epstein, *Women in Law*, 283, 286; Tuve, *First Lady*, 133.

90. Allen, *Justly*, 133; Jefferson and Johnson, *Shortlisted*, 70; Batchelder, "In Memoriam of Judge Kennedy," 1016; Douglas Martin, "Cornelia G. Kennedy, a Pioneering Federal Judge, Dies at 90," *New York Times*, May 23, 2014.

91. William Safire, "Goodbye, Mr. Justice," *New York Times*, Oct. 11, 1981.

92. Diary, Jan. 1, 3, 4, 9, 15, 24, 1936.

93. Allen, *Justly*, 102–3.

94. For example, Great Lakes Equipment Co. v. Fluid Systems Inc., 217 F.2d 613 (1955); Cold Metal Process Company v. Republic Steel Corp., 233 F.2d 828 (1956).

95. "Judge Allen Honored by Lawyers," *Plain Dealer*, Oct. 11, 1959, 33; Tuve, *First Lady*, 156–58.

96. Judge Charles Simons to FEA, June 15, 1959.

97. FEA to Judge Charles Simons, June 17, 1959.

98. Cook, "Supreme Court Candidates," 314–26; Haire, "Rating the Ratings," 1; Susan Ness, "A Sexist Selection Process Keeps Qualified Women off the Bench," *Washington Post*, Mar. 26, 1978.

99. Organ, "Sexuality as a Category," 162, 223–24; Quinn, *Eleanor and Hick*.

100. Organ, "Sexuality as a Category," 25, 207, 221–22.

101. FEA to "The Girls," June 20, 1955.

102. Johnson, *Lavender Scare*, 1–9.

103. Faderman, *Odd Girls*, 93, 99.

104. Johnson, *Lavender Scare*, 1.

105. Johnson, *Lavender Scare*, 101–18.

106. Adkins, "'These People.'"

107. "Employment of Homosexuals and Sex Perverts in Government," Interim Report, Committee on Expenditures in Executive Government, Dec. 15, 1950, at 4.

108. Canaday, *Queer Career*, 36, 209; Johnson, *Lavender Scare*, 190; Faderman, *Odd Girls*, 143.

109. Edwards, *Pulling No Punches*, 188.

110. "Nomination of Marion J. Harron, Hearing Before the Senate Committee on Finance," 81st Congress, Apr.–June 1949, at 31, 35–36.

111. Letter from Judge Florence Allen, Harron Hearing, 31, 35, 154; Tuve, *First Lady*, 165–67.

112. J. Edgar Hoover to FEA, Jan. 10, 1949; Hoover to FEA, Jan. 18, 1949; Hoover to FEA, Mar. 16, 1949; FEA to Hoover, Mar. 22, 1949; FBI Investigative Report to Director, Jan. 10, 1949; SAC, Cincinnati to Director FBI, "Office Memo: Sixth Circuit Conference," Apr. 30, 1959.

113. FEA to Marion Harron, May 1957; Organ, "Sexuality as a Category," 242.

114. Brinson, *Personal and Public Interests*, 150–59; "Glamour at the Inquiry," *New York Times*, Apr. 4, 1958; "Frieda Hennock Simons Dead," *New York Times*, June 21, 1960, 33.

115. Brown-Nagin, *Civil Rights Queen*, 259.

116. Boyd, Collins, and Highland, *Supreme Bias*, 92, 94.

117. Mildred Adams, "Can Women Make Good as Judges," *Christian Advocate*, Dec. 10, 1925.

118. Allen, *Justly*, 52.

119. FEA to President Dwight Eisenhower, June 4, 1959.

120. Allen, "Women in Public Office," 22.

7. RESHAPING FEDERAL LAW FOR ECONOMIC AND SOCIAL JUSTICE

1. Telegram, FEA to Frances Kellor, Mar. 15, 1934.

2. Banner, *Most Powerful Court*, 278–310.

3. Tushnet, *History of the Supreme Court*, 39–40, 260–61.

4. Tushnet, *History of the Supreme Court*, 2–3; Sloan, *Court at War*, 15, 397; Banner, *Most Powerful Court*, 339–72.

5. Fleisher v. U.S., 91 F.2d 404 (1937), *rev'd*, 302 U.S. 218 (1937); Detrola Radio & Television Corporation v. Hazeltine Corp., 117 F.2d 238 (6th Cir. 1940), *rev'd*, 313 U.S. 259 (1941); Great Atlantic & Pacific Tea Co. v. Supermarket Equipment, 179 F.2d 636 (6th Cir. 1950), *rev'd*, 340 U.S. 147 (1951); Huffman v. Ford Motor Co., 195 F.2d 170 (6th Cir. 1952), *rev'd*, 345 U.S. 330 (1953); NLRB v. Bill Daniels, Inc., 202 F.2d 579 (6th Cir. 1953), *rev'd*, 346 U.S. 918 (1954).

6. 28 U.S.C. § 2281 (formerly 28 U.S.C. §§ 380 & 380a); 28 U.S.C. § 1253; Solimine and Walker, "Strange Career," 912–13.

7. *Columbus Citizen*, June 2, 1924.

8. Diary, May 11, 14, 1927; Dec. 12, 1937; "Woman Judge on Federal Bench," newsclip, Apr. 9, 1934; Tuve, *First Lady*, 153.

9. Tuve, *First Lady*, 116, 132, 153.

10. Peppers, "Thoughts on Law Clerk Diversity," 115–21.

11. Tuve, *First Lady*, 153.

12. Central Storage Warehouse Co. v. Pickering, 114 Ohio St. 76, 91–94 (Allen, J., dissenting).

13. Boyd, Collins, and Highland, *Supreme Bias*, 90; Moyer et al., "'All Eyes,'" 464; Gomez, "Female-Neutrality Paradox," 113.

14. Judge Thomas McAllister to FEA, Jan 6, 1966.

15. Farhang, Kastellac, and Wawro, "Politics of Opinion Assignment."

16. Varsava, "Opinion Authorship," 1609–10; Livermore et al., "Gendered Judicial Opinions," 134; Farhang, Kastellac, and Wawro, "Politics of Opinion Assignment," S59, S60, S63.

17. Thomas, "Struggle for Gender Equality," 145.

18. For example, Goesaert v. Cleary, 335 U.S. 464 (1948); People v. Jemnez, 121 P.2d 543 (Cal. App. 1942); Greco v. Roper, 145 Ohio St. 243 (1945); State *ex rel.* Hundley v. McCune, 27 Ohio N.P. 77 (C.C.P. Franklin Cty. 1928); Thatcher v. Pennsylvania O.R., 121 Ohio St. 205 (1929); Davis v. U.S., 62 F.2d 473 (6th Cir. 1933); Hunter, "Century Since Suffrage," 125–35.

19. NLRB v. Brown-Brockmeyer Co., 143 F.2d 537 (6th Cir. 1944).

20. 17 F. Supp. 308 (S.D. Ohio 1936).

21. "Fate of Minimum Wage Legislation May Hinge on Federal Court Ruling in Ohio Women's Pay Act," *Evening Huronite* (SD), Aug. 6, 1936, 13.

22. "Court Keeps Ohio on Minimum Wage," *Plain Dealer*, June 27, 1936; "Ohio's Wage Law Upheld by U.S. Court," *Syracuse Herald*, Nov. 20, 1936, 90.

23. "Ohio Wage Law Faces New Fight," *Plain Dealer*, Nov. 21, 1936; "Ohio Wage Act Held Legal Is U.S. Court," *East Liverpool Review*, Nov. 20, 1936.

24. FEA to Josephus Daniels, Dec. 8, 1936.

25. 17 F. Supp. at 309.

26. 261 U.S. 525 (1923); Snyder, *Democratic Justice*, 127–33.
27. Boisseau and Thomas, "After Suffrage," 235–36.
28. *Adkins*, 261 U.S. at 553.
29. Bernstein, "Feminist 'Horseman,'" 379; Zimmerman, "Jurisprudence of Equality," 211–21.
30. 264 U.S. 292 (1924).
31. 208 U.S. 412 (1908); 198 U.S. 45 (1905).
32. 298 U.S. 587 (1936).
33. 298 U.S. at 618–22 (Hughes, J., dissenting).
34. 298 U.S. at 631 (Stone, J., dissenting).
35. 17 F. Supp. 308.
36. 17 F. Supp. at 311.
37. 300 U.S. 379 (1937).
38. Cushman, *Rethinking the New Deal Court*, 7–18.
39. *Columbus Citizen*, Nov. 20, 1936, 1, LOC Papers; FEA to Josephus Daniels, Dec. 8, 1936.
40. Aronson, *Crystal Eastman*, 237; Boisseau and Thomas, "After Suffrage," 231.
41. Zimmerman, "Jurisprudence of Equality," 220–21; Ware, *Partner*, 98, 101.
42. 21 F. Supp. 947 (E.D. Tenn. 1938), *aff'd*, 306 U.S. 118 (1939); Allen, *Justly*, 105
43. 21 F. Supp. 947 (E.D. Tenn. 1938).
44. 306 U.S. 118 (1939).
45. Russell Porter, "TVA Called Invalid as Trial of 18 Suits to Curb It Is Begun," *New York Times*, Nov. 16, 1937, 1.
46. "The TVA in Court," *Chattanooga Times*, Nov. 15, 1937; Fred Hixon, "Three Judges Open Momentous Trial," *Chattanooga Times*, 1937.
47. "TVA Goes on Trial for Its Life," *Life*, Nov. 29, 1937.
48. Lemons, *Woman Citizen*, 131–32; Hubbard, *Origins of the TVA*, 20, 234.
49. 16 U.S.C. § 831l; Bennett, "Roosevelt, Willkie, and the TVA," 392.
50. Ashwander v. TVA, 9 F. Supp. 965 (N.D. Ala. 1935), *rev'd*, 78 F.2d 578 (5th Cir. 1935), *aff'd*, 297 U.S. 288 (1936).
51. Alabama Power Co. v. Ickes, 302 U.S. 464 (1938).
52. "TVA Called Invalid"; Allen, *Justly*, 105.
53. "Asks Impeaching of Judge over TVA," *New York Times*, Jan. 15, 1937, 10.
54. TVA v. Tennessee Electric Power, 90 F.2d 885 (6th Cir. 1937).
55. "'Go Ahead' Is Word to TVA," *Cincinnati Enquirer*, May 15, 1937.
56. Allen, *Justly*, 106–7; "Court Test," *Newsweek*, Nov. 29, 1937, 36.
57. "Fishing, Fractures Ankle: Judge Florence Allen in Colorado Hospital," *Herald Tribune*, July 18, 1937.
58. Allen, *Justly*, 107; Tuve, *First Lady*, 119; Diary, Sept. 10–27, 1937.

59. Organ, "Sexuality as a Category," 203 (citing FEA to Harriet Elliott, Jan. 17, 1938).

60. Diary, Nov. 13, 1937; "Justice Here Means Share and Share Alike," *Commercial Appeal* (Memphis), Dec. 1937.

61. Mark Dudney, "John Jordan Gore: Middle Tennessee's First Federal Trial Judge," *Herald-Citizen* (Cookeville, TN), Aug. 14, 2011; Dudney, *Sons of the Cumberland.*

62. Hixon, "Three Judges Open."

63. "Legal Talent Arrayed for Lengthy Court Fight over Validity of TVA Act," *Chattanooga Times*, Nov. 16, 1937; Bennett, "Roosevelt, Willkie, and the TVA," 388–92; "Takes Baker's Place," *Chattanooga Times*, Nov. 23, 1937; Trestman, *Fair Labor Lawyer*, 77, 83, 100.

64. Drew Pearson and Robert S. Allen, "Washington Merry-Go-Round," *Washington Daily*, Feb. 8, 1938.

65. Allen, *Justly*, 107–9; "Judge Allen Orders Every Minute Utilized," newsclip, Nov. 11, 1937; "Candid View of Decorum," newsclip, 1937; Fred Hixon, "Judges Admit TVA Testimony into Records," newsclip, n.d.; Fred Hixon, "TVA Asks to Debate on PWA," newsclip, Nov. 19, 1937; "Witnesses for TVA Go on Stand Monday," newsclip, 1937; "TVA Opponents State Facilities State Facilities Ample for Need," *Chattanooga Times*, Nov. 17, 1937; "Opponents Denied TVA Board Record," newsclip, Nov. 12, 1937; "Plaintiffs Renew Rate Data Motion," newsclip, Nov. 23, 1937.

66. 306 U.S. 118 (1939).

67. Chief Judge Charles Moorman to FEA, Dec. 3, 1937.

68. Diary, Jan. 21, 24, 1938.

69. "18 Utility Companies to Appeal," *Plain Dealer*, Jan. 22, 1938.

70. Allen, *Justly*, 111; Diary, Dec. 8, 1937; "TVA: Defeat of Utilities," *Newsweek*, Jan. 31, 1938.

71. 302 U.S. 464 (1938).

72. *TVA*, 21 F. Supp. 947 (E.D. Tenn. 1937); "TVA Says Powers of U.S. Are Issue," *Chattanooga Times*, newsclip [1937].

73. 306 U.S. 118 (1939).

74. Tuve, *First Lady*, 159.

75. For example, Midland Steel Products Co v. NLRB, 113 F.2d 800 (6th Cir. 1940); NLRB v. Packard Motor Co., 157 F.2d 80 (1946); NLRB v. Hoper Mfg. Co., 170 F.2d 692 (6th Cir. 1948); NLRB v. Salant and Salant, 183 F.2d 462 (6th Cir. 1950); Ohio Power Co. v. NLRB, 176 F.2d 385 (1949); Emulsified Asphalt Products Co. v. Mitchell, 222 F.2d 913 (6th Cir. 1955); Stanley v. U.S., 245 F.2d 427, 433 (6th Cir. 1957); NLRB v. Pittsburgh Steamship Co., 180 F.2d 731 (1950), *aff'd*, 340 U.S. 498 (1951).

76. 78 F.2d 684 (6th Cir. 1935).

77. "Title II: Appeals Court Hits PWA Slum Clearance Projects," *News-Week*, July 20, 1935; Kalman, *FDR's Gambit*, 51.

78. Chen, "Story of *Wickard*," 83; Chen, "*Filburn*'s Legacy," 1737.

79. Chen, "*Filburn*'s Legacy," 1739.

80. 43 F. Supp. 1017, 1020 (S.D. Ohio 1942) (Allen, J., dissenting), *rev'd*, 317 U.S. 111 (1942).

81. Walling v. Sanders, 136 F.2d 78 (6th Cir. 1943); Trestman, *Fair Labor Lawyer*, 101–2.

82. For example, Deupree v. Levinson, 186 F.2d 297 (6th Cir. 1950); Brown & Williamson Tobacco v. U.S., 201 F.2d 819 (6th Cir. 1953); Poliafico v. U.S., 237 F.2d 97 (6th Cir. 1956); Niepert v. Cleveland Illumination Co., 241 F.2d 916 (6th Cir. 1957); Miller v. Hocking Glass Co., 80 F.2d 436 (6th Cir. 1935); Wexler v. IRS, 241 F.2d 304 (6th Cir. 1957); Auto Club of Michigan v. IRS; McInerney v. Comm'r IRS, 82 F.2d 665 (6th Cir. 1936); Rudolph Wurlitzer Co. v. Comm'r, 81 F.2d 971 (6th Cir. 1936); Pogers v. Comm'r IRS, 111 F.2d 987 (6th Cir. 1940).

83. Allen, *Justly*, 99–101; Kock v. FTC, 206 F.2d 322 (6th Cir. 1953); Cardinal v. U.S., 79 F.2d 825 (6th Cir. 1935); Devine v. Patterson, 242 F.2d 828 (6th Cir. 1957).

84. Tuve, *First Lady*, 157; "Judge Allen Honored by Lawyers," *Plain Dealer*, Oct. 11, 1959, 33.

85. A. O. Smith Corp. v. Petroleum Iron Works Co., 73 F.2d 531 (6th Cir. 1936) (Allen, J., dissenting).

86. Detrola Radio & Television Corporation v. Hazeltine Corp., 117 F.2d 238 (6th Cir. 1940), *rev'd*, 313 U.S. 259 (1941); Dow Chemical Co. v. Halliburton Oil Well Cementing Co., 139 F.2d 473 (6th Cir. 1943), *aff'd*, 324 U.S. 320 (1945); *Great Atlantic*, 179 F.3d 636 (6th Cir. 1950), *rev'd*, 340 U.S. 147 (1951).

87. *Great Atlantic*, 340 U.S. 147 (1951).

88. Paine & Williams Co. v. Baldwin Rubber Co., 113 F.2d 840 (6th Cir. 1940); Rice v. Nash-Kelvinator Corp., 150 F.2d 457 (6th Cir. 1945); Royal Patent Corp. v. Monarch Tool & Mfg. Co., 203 F.2d 299 (6th Cir. 1953).

89. Allen, "Invention American Style," 312.

90. 234 F.2d 140 (6th Cir. 1956).

91. 234 F.2d at 146; FEA to Judge Learned Hand, May 27, 1940; FEA to Hand, Mar. 13, 1959; Hand to FEA, Mar. 15, 1959.

92. 356 U.S. 148 (1958).

93. Yates v. United States, 354 U.S. 298 (1957).

94. 126 Ohio St. 177 (1932) (Allen, J., dissenting).

95. 161 F.2d 113 (6th Cir 1947).

96. "FBI Reveals Names of 2 Seized as Spies," *New York Times*, Aug. 27, 1943, 18; "8 Named as Spies by Jury in Detroit," *New York Times*, Sept. 18, 1943, 7.

97. 332 U.S. 708 (1948); "Countess Convicted as Spy Wins Retrial," *New York Times*, Jan. 20, 1948, 6; "Woman Wins 2d Hearing as Spy," *New York Times*, Oct. 9, 1951, 14; "Von Moltke Plea Made," *New York Times*, June 12, 1951, 14; "High Court Upholds Nazi Spy's Sentence," *New York Times*, Apr. 22, 1952.

98. 347 U.S. 483 (1954), *further relief ordered*, 349 U.S. 294 (1955).

99. 226 F.2d 180 (6th Cir. 1955); "US Court Rules Out Color Line in Housing," *Cleveland News*, Oct. 27, 1955.

100. 151 N.E. 39 (Ohio 1926).

101. 228 F.2d 853 (6th Cir. 1956).

102. Booker v. State of Tennessee Bd. of Educ., 240 F.2d 689 (6th Cir. 1957).

103. 240 F.2d 689.

104. Bullock v. U.S., 265 F.2d 683 (6th Cir. 1959).

105. Louis Menand, "The Civil-Rights Showdown Nobody Remembers," *New Yorker*, July 31, 2023; Martins, *Most Tolerant Little Town*.

106. McSwain v. County Bd. of Education of Anderson County, 138 F. Supp. 570 (E.D. Tenn. 1956).

107. Menand, "Civil-Rights Showdown."

108. *Bullock*, 265 F.2d 683; FEA, notes, "Court Record 1958–59."

109. Kelley v. Bd. of Educ. City of Nashville, 270 F.2d 209 (6th Cir. 1959), *cert. denied*, 361 U.S. 924 (1959); FEA, "Court Record."

110. *Kelley*, 270 F.2d at 211; Egerton, "Walking into History."

111. Brief for Appellants, Kelley v. Bd. of Educ., 19.

112. Kelley v. Metropolitan County Bd. of Educ., 436 F.2d 856 (6th Cir. 1970).

113. FEA to "The Girls," June 22, 1957.

8. SHORTLISTING FOR THE SUPREME COURT

1. Resnick, "Representing What?," 1.

2. Jefferson and Johnson, *Shortlisted*, 16.

3. Cook, "First Woman Candidate," 22.

4. A. Viola Smith, "Judge Florence Ellinwood Allen," 1956, LOC Papers; Cook, "First Woman Candidate," 22.

5. Organ, "Sexuality as a Category," 60.

6. Tuve, *First Lady*, 141; Cook, "First Woman Candidate," 26 (citing Molly Dewson to FDR, Mar. 16, 1939, Franklin D. Roosevelt Presidential Library).

7. Organ, "Sexuality as a Category," 21–22, 179–80, 209.

8. *Day Book*, Feb. 12, 1913.

9. "Woman Justice from Ohio Rates Portia a Great Judge," Portland, Oregon, newsclip, 1923.

10. Abraham, *Justices and Presidents*, 175–239.

11. Jefferson and Johnson, *Shortlisted*, 232 (citing E. L. Kenyon to Calvin Coolidge, Dec. 27, 1924).

12. William Hart to President Calvin Coolidge, Jan. 21, 1934.

13. Morello, *Invisible Bar*, 231.

14. "Hoover Opens Fight of Administration for World Court," *New York Times*, Apr. 12, 1923.

15. Brown, *Willebrandt*, 216 (citing William D. Mitchell to Mark Sullivan, July 6, 1934); Cook, "First Woman Candidate," 125 (citing William Mitchell to Herbert Hoover, Aug. 5, 1929).

16. Jefferson and Johnson, *Shortlisted*, 16–17.

17. Jefferson and Johnson, *Shortlisted*, 16–17; "A Woman on the Supreme Bench?," *Christian Science Monitor*, Mar. 12, 1930.

18. Brown, *Willebrandt*, xi, 34, 43, 50, 75, 109, 216.

19. "Woman on the Supreme Bench?"; "Worker Willebrandt," *Time*, Oct. 8, 1928; Brown, *Willebrandt*, 216; Jefferson and Johnson, *Shortlisted*, 16–17; "Mabel Walker Willebrandt Dies," *New York Times*, Apr. 9, 1963.

20. Brown, *Willebrandt*, 217–18.

21. Feldman, *Scorpions*, v; Sloan, *Court at War*, 12.

22. Sloan, *Court at War*, 13, 23.

23. Tuve, *First Lady*, 123; Jefferson and Johnson, *Shortlisted*; Eleanor Roosevelt, "My Day," June 27, 1938; Eleanor Roosevelt, "My Day," Nov. 17, 1948; Frances Kellor to FEA, 1938; FEA to Eleanor Roosevelt, Feb. 12, 1935.

24. Organ, "Sexuality as a Category," 182–83 (citing FEA to Eleanor Roosevelt, May 1, 1933, Franklin D. Roosevelt Presidential Library).

25. Pearson and Allen, *Nine Old Men*.

26. 198 U.S. 45 (1905); Kalman, *FDR's Gambit*, 23, 84; Banner, *Most Powerful Court*, 245, 265.

27. Kalman, *FDR's Gambit*, x, 1, 23, 63.

28. Kalman, *FDR's Gambit*, ix, 61.

29. Kalman, *FDR's Gambit*, ix–x, 105, 168; Abraham, *Justices and Presidents*, 209–10.

30. Cushman, *Rethinking the New Deal Court*, 7–18; Banner, *Most Powerful Court*, 310–11; Kalman, *FDR's Gambit*, x, 297–98.

31. Feldman, *Scorpions*, 131; Abraham, *Justices and Presidents*, 211–23.

32. Jefferson and Johnson, *Shortlisted*, 26–27.

33. "East Ignored for Court Post," newsclip, Aug. 4, 1937; Turner Catledge, "A New Deal Foe: Conservative Writes to President He Will Quit June 2, End of Term," *New York Times*, May 19, 1937; "Roosevelt: One Conservative Retires," *Newsweek*, May 29, 1937.

34. "Supreme Court Job for Woman Hinted Possible," *Washington Post*, Feb. 15, 1937.

35. Dorothy Dunbar Bromley, "Woman Is Worthy of High Court," *New York Telegram*, Jan. 4, 1937.

36. Allen, *Justly*, 110; "High Court in Command of Liberals," *Plain Dealer*, Jan. 6, 1938; "F.R. May Put Woman on High Court," Boston newsclip, Jan. 5, 1938; "FDR Considers Woman for Supreme Court Seat," *Columbus Citizen*, Jan. 10, 1938; "Roosevelt Considers Woman for High Court," newsclip, Jan. 10, 1938.

37. Senator Vic Donahey to FEA, Jan. 13, 1938.

38. Diary, Jan. 5, 10, 11, 13, 19, 1938.

39. Newsclip, *Washington Times*, Jan. 14, 1938; "Sex No Barrier to Court Post," newsclip, n.d.

40. "Mr. Justice Florence Allen for The Supreme Court," *Washington Times*, Jan. 12, 1938, 6; "Governor Murphy, Florence Allen Held Leading for Court Post," *Washington Post*, Jan. 13, 1938.

41. "Mr. Justice," 6.

42. Diary, Jan. 10, 12, 14, 1938; telegram, Roosevelts to FEA, Jan. 14, 1938.

43. Allen, *Justly*, 110–12; Cook, "First Woman Candidate," 27; Diary, Jan. 5, 14, 17, 19, 1938.

44. "Court List Omits Florence Allen," *Plain Dealer*, Jan. 14, 1938; "Mr. Justice."

45. Allen, *Justly*, 110; "Supreme Court: Reed Steps Down," *Time*, Feb. 11, 1957; Abraham, *Justices and Presidents*, 216–17, 265–66.

46. "An Able Woman Pioneer Makes Constitutional History," *Life*, Jan. 24, 1938, 21.

47. Organ, "Sexuality as a Category," 202–3 (citing Mary Pierce to Harriet Elliott, Jan. 17, 1938).

48. Newsclip, *Cleveland Press*, Jan. 15, 1938; "This Able Jurist Deserves Supreme Court Post!," newsclip. Jan. 14, 1938; Frederick W. Fray to Franklin D. Roosevelt, Jan. 18, 1939, LOC Papers; Ned Brooks and Charles T. Lucey, "Ohioans in Washington: Judge Allen Spanks a Lawyer," *Columbus Citizen*, Jan. 15, 1938.

49. "Courts Nearing Ideal of Justice, Parley Is Told: Judge Florence E. Allen Talks at Dinner of Women's Bar," *Washington Post*, Mar. 27, 1938, M14; "Judge Florence Allen Honored by D.C. Kappa Beta Pi," *Washington Post*, Mar. 27, 1938.

50. Drew Pearson and Robert S. Allen, "Washington Merry-Go-Round," United Feature Syndicate Aug. 4, 1938; "In Cardozo's Place," *Plain Dealer*, July 12, 1938.

51. Snyder, *Democratic Justice*, 5, 330, 530; Feldman, *Scorpions*, 252.

52. 335 U.S. 464 (1948); Snyder, *Democratic Justice*, 504; Abraham, *Justices and Presidents*, 217–20.

53. Sloan, *Court at War*, 522 n.15.

54. Newsclip, *Washington Times-Herald*, Mar. 14, 1939, 2.

55. E. A. Tamm, "FBI Memorandum to the Director Re: Florence Ellinwood Allen," Feb. 15, 1939.

56. Albert L. Warner, "Florence Allen Still in Race for Supreme Court," *New York Herald Tribune*, Mar. 14, 1939; "Roosevelt Hints at Court Post Surprise," *Baltimore Sun*, Mar. 12, 1939; "Florence Allen," *Columbus Dispatch*, Mar. 24, 1939.

57. Paul Mallon, "News Behind the National News," *Plain Dealer*, Mar. 18, 1939.

58. J. Fred Essary, "Roosevelt Hints at Court Post Surprise: Judge Florence E. Allen May Be Choice He Has in Mind," *Baltimore Sun*, Mar. 12, 1939, 1; see also J. Fred Essary, "Utah Jurist May Be Given Cardozo Post," *Baltimore Sun*, Dec. 10, 1938.

59. Drew Pearson and Robert S. Allen, "Washington Merry-Go-Round: Florence Allen," *Columbus Dispatch*, Mar. 24, 1939.

60. Drew Pearson and Robert S. Allen, "Washington Merry-Go-Round," United Feature Syndicate, Nov. 21, 1938; "National Whirligig," *Detroit Free Press*, Dec. 6, 1938; FEA to Eleanor Roosevelt, Dec. 7, 1938; John Martin to FEA, Dec. 17, 1938.

61. Pearson and Allen, "Washington Merry-Go-Round," Mar. 24, 1939.

62. Feldman, *Scorpions*, 258.

63. Abraham, *Justices and Presidents*, 222; Murphy, *Wild Bill*, xii–xvi.

64. Chandra, "Lucile Lomen."

65. Memorandum, "Reversals of Decisions of Judge Florence Allen" [ca. Mar. 1939]; Allen, *Justly*, 112; Fleisher v. U.S., 91 F.2d. 404 (6th Cir. 1937), *rev'd*, 302 U.S. 218.

66. Ohio Public Service Co. v State, 115 Ohio St. 325, *rev'd*, 274 U.8. 12.

67. Allen, *Justly*, 112.

68. Catharine McCulloch to Frank Murphy, Apr. 17, 1939.

69. Frank Murphy to FEA, May 5, 1939.

70. Allen, *Justly*, 112–13.

71. "Court Vacancy," *Newsweek*, Nov. 27, 1939, 13; Cook, "First Woman Candidate," 28–29.

72. Abraham, *Justices and Presidents*, 225–26; Allen, *Justly*, 112.

73. E. A. Tamm, "FBI Memorandum to the Director Re: Judicial Investigation," May 5, 1939.

74. "Ex-Judge Manton of U.S. Bench Here," *New York Times*, Nov. 18, 1946; Stein, *Justice for Sale*.

75. Cook, "First Woman Candidate," 25–26; Allen, *This Constitution of Ours*; Tuve, *First Lady*, 145–50.

76. Sloan, *Court at War*, 8.

77. Tuve, *First Lady*, 146; "Memorandum of Agreement for Autobiography and This Constitution of Ours," Feb. 10, 1939.

78. "Gives Fascination to Constitution," *Plain Dealer*, Feb. 19, 1940; Prof. Harlan Hatcher, "Book Review," *Columbus Citizen*, Feb. 18, 1940; Eleanor Roosevelt to FEA, Mar. 20, 1940.

79. John Corbin, "Judge Allen Interprets the Constitution," *New York Times*, Feb. 18, 1940, BR2.

80. Billig, "Book Review."

81. Sloan, *Court at War*, 19.

82. Sloan, *Court at War*, 8.

83. Feldman, *Scorpions*, 97, 275.

84. "Florence E. Allen Being Considered for Place on U.S. Supreme Court," *New York Times*, Oct. 20, 1942.

85. Sloan, *Court at War*, 153–54.

86. Justice Wiley Rutledge to FEA, Jan. 17, 1944.

87. Jefferson and Johnson, *Shortlisted*, 28–29; Abraham, *Justices and Presidents*, 230–34; Cook, "First Woman Candidate," 29.

88. Abraham, *Justices and Presidents*, 162, 237, 239; Jefferson and Johnson, *Shortlisted*, 32.

89. Diary, Jan. 19, 1948.

90. Abraham, *Justices and Presidents*.

91. St. Clair and Gugin, *Vinson*, 163.

92. Carrie Chapman Catt to FEA, May 10, 1946.

93. Abraham, *Justices and Presidents*, 243.

94. Margaret Chase Smith to FEA, Jan. 11, 1949.

95. Allen, *Justly*, 143–45; ER, "A Tribute to a Judge," 1948, LOC Papers; Brinkley, *Justice Was Her Calling*.

96. Edwards, *Pulling No Punches*, 171–72; Edwards, "Oral History Interview," 84–85.

97. Edwards, *Pulling No Punches*, 171–72; Edwards, "Oral History Interview," 84–85; St. Clair and Gugin, *Vinson*, 156–63, 190–91.

98. St. Clair and Gugin, *Vinson*, 156.

99. Edwards, *Pulling No Punches*, 171–72; Edwards, "Oral History Interview."

100. Sloan, *Court at War*, 13–15.

101. St. Clair and Gugin, *Vinson*, 159.

102. Abraham, *Justices and Presidents*, 232, 240; Sloan, *Court at War*, 87; St. Clair and Gugin, *Vinson*, 156, 161, 190.

103. Abraham, *Justices and Presidents*, 251; St. Clair and Gugin, *Vinson*, 176; Murphy, *Wild Bill*, 101.

104. Philip Hoffman, "Does the U.S. Supreme Court Need a Woman Justice?," *Parade Magazine* (*Oakland Tribune*), Dec. 11, 1966; Mary McLeod, NAWL President's Letter, Jan. 1, 1967.

105. Abraham, *Justices and Presidents*, 243.

106. Abraham, *Justices and Presidents*, 238–45; Eisler, *Justice for All*, 76; Gronlund, *Controversial Appointment*, 137–46.

107. Abraham, *Justices and Presidents*, 244.

108. Abraham, *Justices and Presidents*, 246.

109. Newsclip, *Fort Wayne News Sentinel*, Sept. 16, 1949.

110. Abraham, *Justices and Presidents*, 245–47.

111. "Young Proposes Enlargement of U.S. High Court," *Plain Dealer*, Sept. 24, 1949.

112. Linda Greenhouse, "Burnita S. Matthews Dies at 93; First Woman on US Trial Courts," *New York Times*, Apr. 28, 1988, D27.

113. Brinson, *Personal and Public Interests*, 150–59.

114. "India Edwards, 82, Still 'Pulling No Punches,'" *Washington Post*, June 15, 1977; Drew Pearson and Robert S. Allen, "Washington Merry-Go-Round," Bell Syndicate, Nov. 30, 1950.

115. A. H. Belmont to D. M. Ladd, "FBI Office Memo Re: Judge Florence Ellinwood Allen," Apr. 14, 1952; FBI Summary, "Judge Florence Ellinwood Allen," Apr. 16, 1952.

116. Organ, "Sexuality as a Category," 231–29; Tuve, *First Lady*, 166–68; Rosalind Bates to Dwight Eisenhower, Feb. 10, 1957; Lula Bachman to Eisenhower, Feb. 5, 1957; Viola Smith to Allen, Feb. 11, 1957; Dolly Butler to Eisenhower, Feb. 12, 1957; Elizabeth Salisbury to Eisenhower, Feb. 14, 1957; Viola Smith to Eisenhower, Feb. 11, 1957.

117. Abraham, *Justices and Presidents*, 251, 262; Boyd, Collins, and Highland, *Supreme Bias*, 25.

118. Tuve, *First Lady*, 168; Ernestine B. Powell to Grace Doering, Jan. 14, 1958.

119. Jefferson and Johnson, *Shortlisted*, 34–35; Neva Talley to Marion Harron and Viola Smith, Mar. 22, 1957.

120. Diary, June 18, 1956.

121. Abraham, *Justices and Presidents*, 250–70; Jefferson and Johnson, *Shortlisted*, 34.

122. Diary, Jan. 10–Mar. 2, 1957; Robert Grey, Special Assistant to Eisenhower to Judge Lorna Lockwood, Feb. 27, 1957, Dwight D. Eisenhower Papers, Eisenhower Presidential Library.

123. Neva Talley to FEA, Mar. 13, 1957; Neva Talley to Marion Harron and Viola Smith, Mar. 22, 1957; Diary, Jan 1–Mar. 2, 1957; "Ohio Businesswomen Keeping Eye on Automation," *Plain Dealer*, Apr. 16, 1957.

124. Frances Bolton to Sherman Adams, Assistant to the President, Feb. 20, 1957, Dwight D. Eisenhower Papers, Eisenhower Presidential Library.

125. Tuve, *First Lady*, 167–68, 174 n.65, 181.

126. Abraham, *Justices and Presidents*, 250–70; Jefferson and Johnson, *Shortlisted*, 34.

127. Abraham, *Justices and Presidents*, 267–72.

128. Justice Stanley Reed to FEA, Mar. 26, 1959.

129. Jacobellis v. Ohio, 378 U.S. 184 (1964).

130. Stevens, "Fond Memory, Cordelia Kennedy," 1008–9.

131. Rosalind Bates to Senator Knowland, Sept. 9, 1953; Dorothea Blender to Hon. Henry Cabot Lodge Jr., Sept. 21, 1953.

132. Abraham, *Justices and Presidents*, 250–70; Jefferson and Johnson, *Shortlisted*, 36, 72: "Miss Donlon Wins Gallant Backing," *New York Times*, July 29, 1955, 10.

133. Cook, "First Woman Candidate," 19, 25; Jefferson and Johnson, *Shortlisted*, 27, 33; "The Court Needs Judges," newsclip, 1946.

134. Cook, "First Woman Candidate," 19, 24 (citing FEA to H. C. Herring, Mar. 17, 1934).

135. Tuve, *First Lady*, 100.

136. Newsclip, *Time*, Mar. 19, 1934; "Woman Judge," *News-Week*, Mar. 17, 1934.

137. Railway Labor Executives Association to President Franklin D. Roosevelt, Dec. 20, 1939.

138. "Still in Race"; Abraham, *Justices and Presidents*, 210.

139. FEA, speech, "I Shall Vote for FDR," Oct. 31, 1932; Cook, "First Woman Candidate," 20–21.

140. Abraham, *Justices and Presidents*, 42–43.

141. Joe Alex Morris, "Judge Allen Studied for Supreme Court," *Cincinnati Post*, Jan. 10, 1938.

142. Legal Defense Committee, Cleveland NAACP, to Senator Robert Bulkley, Feb. 12, 1934; memo, "Record of Judge Florence E. Allen in labor cases and in the Weaver case," n.d., in Franklin D. Roosevelt Presidential Library.

143. "Criminal Syndicalism Law of Ohio Is Upheld," *Cincinnati Times Star*, Dec. 21, 1932, 28.

144. Kusmer, *Black Cleveland*; Greg Hand, "Ohio Tried to Ban D. W. Griffith's Epic 'Birth of a Nation,'" *Cincinnati Enquirer*, Feb. 18, 2020.

145. "Asks Free Speech, Condemns Rioting: Law and Order," newsclip [ca. 1919].

146. SAC, Cincinnati to Director FBI, "Office Memo: Judicial Conference," Apr. 30, 1959.

147. Morris, "Judge Allen Studied."

148. Lemons, *Woman Citizen*, 139–41; "Women Denounce Economy Pay Act," *New York Times*, Feb. 6, 1933; McGuire, "'Most Unjust Piece,'" 516; Scharf, *To Work and to Wed*, 46.

149. Newsclip, *Chicago Daily Tribune*, July 13, 1933; Tuve, *First Lady*, 136–37; "Spinster Breadwinner Hailed as Heroine by Woman Judge," *Washington Post*, Mar. 10, 1934.

150. FEA to Marion Harron, May 1957; Organ, "Sexuality as a Category," 242.

151. Organ, "Sexuality as a Category," 241 (citing Olga Jones to FEA, Mar. 6, 1957).

152. Murdoch and Price, *Courting Justice*, 18–20.
153. Sloan, *Court at War*, 226; Feldman, *Scorpions*, 183.
154. Sloan, *Court at War*, 9; 323 U.S. 214, 233–40 (Murphy, J., dissenting).

EPILOGUE

1. Statement for Judge Burnita S. Matthews, Judge Allen Portrait Presentation, Oct. 14, 1959, prepared by Marion Harron.
2. "Judge Allen Honored by Lawyers," *Plain Dealer*, Oct. 11, 1959, 33.
3. Allen, *Justly*, 148; FEA to Potter Stewart, Oct. 14, 1959.
4. Allen, *Justly*, 145; "Proceedings of Portrait Presentation," Oct. 15, 1959; "Judge Allen Hailed as Magnificent American," *Plain Dealer*, Oct. 16, 1959.
5. "Law as a Career for Women Urged," *New York Times*, Nov. 10, 1935.
6. Ginsburg and Brill, "Three Way Pavers," 281.
7. Elliott Field, "Interesting People: The First Woman Judge of a Common Pleas Court Believes in 'Speeding Up Justice,'" *American Magazine*, Oct. 1921.
8. Cook, "Supreme Court Candidates," 326; Allen, *Justly*, 48.
9. "Assails Delays of U.S. Courts," newsclip, Mar. 21, 1926.
10. FEA to Chief Justice Earl Warren, Oct. 28, 1959.
11. Jordan, "'We Must Forget,'" 101.
12. Jordan, "'We Must Forget,'" 102.
13. Allen, *Justly*, 128; "Women Lawyers Rally," *New York Times*, July 9, 1950, 12.
14. Allen, *Justly*, 121–29; Tuve, *First Lady*, 130.
15. "Women's Influence Wanes," *Christian Science Monitor*, Nov. 14, 1960.
16. Allen, *Justly*, 150–52.
17. Ware, *Partner*, xvii, 146–48; Freedman, "Separatism," 512–29, 514; Lemons, *Woman Citizen*, 111.
18. Boyd, Collins, and Highland, *Supreme Bias*, 40; Gomez, "Female-Neutrality," 674; Kenney, *Gender and Justice*, 3; Dixon, "Female Justices," 21; Kenney, "Critical Perspectives on Gender and Judging," 436.
19. Gomez, "Female-Neutrality," 674; Kenney, *Gender and Justice*, 3.
20. Gomez, "Female-Neutrality," 674.
21. Allen, *Justly*, 150–51; Bible, Micah 6:8 (KJV).
22. FEA, speech, "The Effect of Women on the Administration of Justice" [ca. 1932], 7, LOC Papers; FEA, speech in Detroit, 1946; Allen, *Justly*, 48.
23. Boyd, Collins, and Highland, *Supreme Bias*, 40; Kenney, *Gender and Justice*, 19, 36–37; Palmer, "'To Do Justly,'" 237; Boyd, Epstein, and Martin, "Untangling the Causal Effects," 406.
24. Moyer and Haire, "Trailblazers," 665.

25. Brown-Nagin, *Civil Rights Queen*, 309; Thomas, "Struggle for Gender Equality," 182.

26. For example, State v. Lowenstein, 109 Ohio St. 393 (1924); Norton v. Norton, 111 Ohio St. 262 (1924); Foltz v. Boone, 107 Ohio St. 562 (1923); Cook v. Mozer (Allen, J., concurring); Lewis v. Reed, 117 Ohio St. 152 (1927); The Cleveland Railway Co. v. Merk, 124 Ohio St. 596 (1932); Cleveland Trust Co. & Annie Richardson v. Scobie, 114 Ohio St. 241 (1926); Industrial Commission of Ohio v. Rotar, 124 Ohio St. 418 (1931); Scott v. City of Columbus, 142 N.E. 25 (Ohio 1923); City of Fostoria v Binley, 125 Ohio St. 1 (1932); Burton v. Powers, 124 Ohio St. 564 (1932); Dean v. McMullen, 109 Ohio St 309 (1924).

27. Boyd, Collins, and Highland, *Supreme Bias*, 40, 95.

28. Breedlove v. Suttles, 302 U.S. 277 (1937).

29. Glasser v. United States, 315 U.S. 60 (1942); Ballard v. United States, 329 U.S. 187 (1946); Fay v. New York, 332 U.S. 261 (1947).

30. J.E.B. v. Alabama, 511 U.S. 127 (1994).

31. 335 U.S. 464 (1948); French, "Mixing It Up," 27.

32. Resnick, "Representing What?," 12.

33. Boyd, Collins, and Highland, *Supreme Bias*, 14.

34. Allen, "Participation of Women in Government."

35. FEA, "Effect of Women"; Diary, May 14, 1915; Cook, *Women as Judges*, 21.

36. Resnick, "Representing What?," 12–14; Boyd, Collins, and Highland, *Supreme Bias*, 38; Kenney, *Gender and Justice*, 161, 175–78; Martin, "Representative Role," 166.

37. Varsava et al., "Judicial Dark Matter," 1956; Kenney, *Gender and Justice*, 176; Purvis, "Legal Profession," 295.

38. Resnick, "Representing What?," 14–16.

39. Symposium, "Honorable Paul C. Weick," 617, 620; Bradley v. Milliken, 484 F.2d 215, 259 (6th Cir. 1973) (en banc) (Weick, J., dissenting), *rev'd*, 418 U.S. 717 (1974); Krause v. Rhodes, 570 F.2d 563, 580 (1977) (Weick, J., dissenting), *cert. denied*, 435 U.S. 924 (1978).

40. Douglas Martin, "Cornelia G. Kennedy, a Pioneering Federal Judge, Dies at 90," *New York Times*, May 23, 2014; Jefferson and Johnson, *Shortlisted*, 68–72, 148.

41. Jefferson and Johnson, *Shortlisted*, 3; Thomas, *Sandra Day O'Connor*.

42. "Alice Robie Resnick," biography, The Supreme Court of Ohio, https://www.supremecourt.ohio.gov/courts/judicial-system/supreme-court-of-ohio/justices-1803-to-present/alice-resnick/.

43. David, *Lady Law*, 4

44. "Shirley Hufstedler, Judge and Cabinet's First Education Secretary, Dies at 90," *New York Times*, Mar. 31, 2016; Alexander, "Shirley Mount Hufstedler," 623 n.4.

45. "Women in the Legal Profession," in *Profile of the Legal Profession 2023*, American Bar Association, https://qa.americanbar.org/content/dam/aba/administrative/news/2023/potlp-2023.pdf; Cook, "Women Judges: Preface," 573–75.

46. Boyd, Collins, and Highland, *Supreme Bias*, 33–37; Kenney, *Gender and Justice*, 70–71, 77; Clark, "Carter's Groundbreaking Appointment," 1139.

47. Kenney, *Gender and Justice*, 77.

48. "2024 U.S. State Court Women Judges," National Association of Women Judges, https://www.nawj.org/www.nawj.org/statistics/2024-us-state-court-women-judges; "Judges," in *Profile of the Legal Profession 2024*, American Bar Association, https://qa.americanbar.org/news/profile-legal-profession/judges/; National Women's Law Center, "Women in the Federal Judiciary: Still a Long Way to Go" (Oct. 2016); Purvis, "Legal Profession," 283–94.

49. "2024 U.S. State Court Women Judges."

50. Stephanie Warsmith, "Say, 'Girls Rule!' Summit County's All-Female Bench Marks Milestone with Portrait," *Akron Beacon Journal*, June 30, 2019.

51. "Florence Allen, 82, First Woman on U.S. Appellate Bench, Dead," *New York Times*, Sept. 14, 1966, 47.

52. "Florence E. Allen Dies," *Washington Post*, Sept. 14, 1966, B6.

53. Harron, "In Memoriam," 145, 175–76.

Bibliography

PRIMARY SOURCES

Archival Collections

The majority of archival papers cited are found in the following:

Florence Ellinwood Allen Papers, Western Reserve Historical Society, Cleveland, Ohio
Florence Ellinwood Allen Papers, Library of Congress

Other sources:

Florence Allen Papers, New York University Library
Dwight D. Eisenhower Papers, Eisenhower Presidential Library, Abilene, Kansas
Salmon Levinson Papers, Hanna Holborn Gray Special Collections, University of Chicago
Vadae Meekison Papers, Bowling Green State University
Franklin D. Roosevelt Presidential Library, New York

Works by Florence Allen

Allen, Florence E. "The First Ten Years." *Woman's Journal* (Aug. 1930): 5.

Allen, Florence E. "The Governmental Task." *Annals of the American Academy of Political and Social Science,* 7, no. 10 (July 1932): 161–69.
Allen, Florence E. "Invention American Style." *Journal of Patent Office Society* 40 (1948): 312–21.
Allen, Florence Ellinwood. "The Nuremberg Trial Implements World Law." *Educational Forum* 11, no. 4 (May 1947): 389.
Allen, Florence Ellinwood. "Nuremberg Trial Implements World Law." *Women Lawyers' Journal* 34 (1948): 6.
Allen, Florence E. "Participation of Women in Government." *Annals of the American Academy of Political and Social Science* 25 (1947): 24.
Allen, Florence Ellinwood. *Patris.* Horace Carr, 1908.
Allen, Florence Ellinwood. *This Constitution of Ours.* G. P. Putnam's Sons, 1940.
Allen, Florence Ellinwood. *To Do Justly.* Western Reserve University Press, 1965.
Allen, Florence. *The Treaty as an Instrument of Legislation.* Macmillan, 1952.
Allen, Florence E. "Women in Public Office." *Women Lawyers Journal* 44, no. 2 (1958): 4–25.
Allen, Florence E., and Mary Welles. *The Ohio Woman Suffrage Movement: "A Certain Unalienable Right."* Suffrage Committee, 1952.

SECONDARY SOURCES

Abbott, Karen. *The Ghosts of Eden Park: The Bootleg King, the Women Who Pursued Him, and the Murder that Shocked Jazz-Age America.* Crown, 2019.
Abbott, Virgina Clark. *The History of Woman Suffrage and the League of Women Voters in Cuyahoga County, 1911–1945.* William Feather, 1949.
Abraham, Henry J. *Justices and Presidents: A Political History of Appointments to the Supreme Court.* Oxford University Press, 1985.
Abrams, Jamie R. "Feminism's Transformation of Legal Education and Unfinished Agenda." In *The Oxford Handbook of Feminism and Law in the United States*, edited by Deborah Brake, Martha Chamallas, and Verna L. Williams. Oxford University Press, 2023.
Addams, Jane. *Twenty Years at Hull-House.* SMK Books, 2015 [1910].
Adkins, Judith. "'These People Are Frightened to Death': Congressional Investigations and the Lavender Scare." *National Archives Prologue Magazine* 48, no. 2 (Summer 2016).
Alexander, Janet Cooper. "Shirley Mount Hufstedler, Pioneer." *Stanford Law Review* 69 (2017): 623–27.

Allen, Frederick Lewis. *Only Yesterday: An Informal History of the 1920s.* Harper & Row, 1931.
Alonso, Harriet Hyman. *The Women's Peace Union and the Outlawry of War, 1921–1942.* Syracuse University Press, 1997.
Ambrose, Hugh, with John Schuttler. *Liberated Spirits: Two Women Who Battled over Prohibition.* Berkley, 2018.
Andersen, Kristi. *After Suffrage: Women in Partisan and Electoral Politics Before the New Deal.* University of Chicago Press, 1996.
Anderson, Greta. "Florence Ellinwood Allen, 1884–1966." In *More Than Petticoats: Remarkable Ohio Women.* Globe Pequot Press, 2005.
Aronson, Amy. *Crystal Eastman: A Revolutionary Life.* Oxford University Press, 2020.
Babcock, Barbara. *Woman Lawyer: The Trials of Clara Foltz.* Stanford University Press, 2011.
Banner, Stuart. *The Most Powerful Court in the World: A History of the Supreme Court of the United States.* Oxford University Press, 2024.
Barber, Kathleen L. *Proportional Representation and Election Reform in Ohio.* The Ohio State University Press, 1995.
Barber, Kathleen L. *A Right to Representation: Proportional Election Systems for the Twenty First Century.* The Ohio State University Press, 2000.
Batchelder, Alice. "In Memoriam of Judge Kennedy." *Ohio State Law Journal* 75 (2014): 1008–17.
Batlan, Felice. *Women and Justice for the Poor: A History of Legal Aid, 1863–1945.* Oxford University Press, 2015.
Beachy, Robert. *Gay Berlin: Birthplace of a Modern Identity.* Vintage, 2014.
Becker, Susan D. *The Origins of the Equal Rights Amendment: American Feminism Between the Wars.* Bloomsbury, 1981.
Beeton, Beverly. "How the West Was Won for Woman Suffrage." In *One Woman, One Vote: Rediscovering the Woman Suffrage Movement*, edited by Marjorie Spruill Wheeler. NewSage Press, 1995.
Bennett, James D. "Roosevelt, Willkie, and the TVA." *Tennessee Historical Quarterly* 28, no. 4 (1969): 388–96.
Bennett, Walter. *The Lawyer's Myth: Reviving Ideals in the Legal Profession.* University of Chicago Press, 2001.
Berkson, Larry. "Women on the Bench: A Brief History." *Judicature* 65 (1982): 286–93.
Bernstein, David E. "The Feminist 'Horseman.'" *Green Bag 2d* 10 (2007): 379–86.
Billig, Thomas Clifford. "Book Review." *University of Chicago Law Review* 7 (1940): 753–55.
Biskupic, Joan. *Sandra Day O'Connor: How the First Woman on the Supreme Court Became Its Most Influential Justice.* Harper Perennial, 2006.

Boisseau, Tracey Jean, and Tracy Thomas. "After Suffrage Comes Equal Rights? ERA as the Next Logical Step." In *100 Years of the Nineteenth Amendment: An Appraisal of Women's Political Activism*, edited by Holly J. McCammon and Lee Ann Banaszak. Oxford University Press, 2018.

Bordin, Ruth. *Woman and Temperance: The Quest for Power and Liberty, 1873–1900*. Rutgers University Press, 1990.

Boyd, Christina L., Paul M. Collins Jr., and Lori A. Highland. *Supreme Bias: Gender and Race in U.S. Supreme Court Confirmation Hearings*. Stanford University Press, 2023.

Boyd, Christina L., Lee Epstein, and Andrew D. Martin. "Untangling the Causal Effects of Sex on Judging." *American Journal of Political Science* 54 (2010): 389–411.

Bragg, L. E. "Judge Reah Mary Whitehead, 1883–1972: Lady Justice." In *More Than Petticoats: Remarkable Washington Women*. Falcon, 1998.

Breckinridge, Sophonisba P. *Women in the Twentieth Century: A Study of Their Political, Social and Economic Activities*. McGraw-Hill, 1933.

Bredbenner, Candice Lewis. *A Nationality of Her Own: Women, Marriage, and the Law of Citizenship*. University of California Press, 1998.

Brinkley, Jennifer L. *Justice Was Her Calling: The Fierce and Fascinating Life of Dorothy Kenyon*. University of California Press, forthcoming.

Brinson, Susan L. *Personal and Public Interests: Frieda B. Hennock and the Federal Communications Commission*. Praeger, 2001.

Brown, Dorothy M. *Mabel Walker Willebrandt: A Study of Power, Loyalty, and Law*. University of Tennessee Press, 1984.

Brown, Dorothy M. *Setting the Course: American Women in the 1920s*. Twayne, 1987.

Brown, Victoria Bissell. "Jane Addams, Progressivism, and Woman Suffrage." In *One Woman, One Vote: Rediscovering the Woman Suffrage Movement*, edited by Marjorie Spruill Wheeler. NewSage Press 1995.

Brown-Nagin, Tomiko. *Civil Rights Queen: Constance Baker Motley and the Struggle for Equality*. Pantheon Books, 2022.

Burns, Erik. *1920: The Year That Made the Decade Roar*. Pegasus, 2015.

Cahill, Bernadette. *Alice Paul, the National Woman's Party and the Vote*. McFarland, 2015.

Cahill, Cathleen D. *Recasting the Vote: How Women of Color Transformed the Suffrage Movement*. University of North Carolina Press, 2020.

Canaday, Margot. *Queer Career: Sexuality and Work in Modern America*. Penguin, 2023.

Capuzza, Jamie C. *The Fifth Star: Ohio's Fight for Women's Right to Vote*. Kent State University Press, 2023.

Catt, Carrie Chapman, and Nettie Rogers Shuler. *Woman Suffrage & Politics: The Inner Story of the Suffrage Movement*. Dover, 2020 [1923].

Chandra, Jennie Berry. "Lucile Lomen: The First Female United States Supreme Court Clerk." In *In Chambers*, edited by Todd Peppers and Artemus Ward. University of Virginia Press, 2012.

Chen, Jim. "*Filburn*'s Legacy." *Emory Law Journal* 52 (2003): 1719–70.

Chen, Jim. "The Story of *Wickard v. Filburn*: Agriculture, Aggregative and Commerce." In *Constitutional Law Stories*, 2nd ed., edited by Michael C. Dorf. Foundation Press, 2009.

Chused, Richard, and Wendy Williams. *Gendered Law in American History*. Carolina Academic Press, 2016.

Clapp, Elizabeth. *Mothers of All Children: Women Reformers and the Rise of Juvenile Courts in Progressive Era America*. Pennsylvania State University Press, 1998.

Clark, Mary L. "Carter's Groundbreaking Appointment of Women to the Federal Bench: His Other 'Human Rights' Record." *American University Journal of Gender, Social Policy and Law* 11 (2003): 1131–64.

Clark, Mary L. "The Founding of the Washington College of Law: The First Law School Established by Women for Women." *American Law Review* 47 (1998): 613–76.

Clark, Mary L. "One Man's Token Is Another Woman's Breakthrough? The Appointment of the First Women Federal Judges." *Villanova Law Review* 49 (2004): 487–550.

Cobble, Dorothy. *For the Many: American Feminists and the Global Fight for Democratic Equality*. Princeton University Press, 2021.

Conner, Valerie Jean. *The National War Labor Board: Stability, Social Justice, and the Voluntary State in World War I*. University of North Carolina Press, 1983.

Cook, Beverly B. "The First Woman Candidate for the Supreme Court—Florence E. Allen." In *Yearbook 1981: Supreme Court Historical Society* (1981): 19–35.

Cook, Beverly B. "Florence Ellinwood Allen." In *Notable American Women: The Modern Period: A Biographical Dictionary*, edited by Barbara Sicherman and Carol Hurd Green. Belknap Press, 1980.

Cook, Beverly B. "Moral Authority and Gender Difference: Georgia Bullock and the Los Angeles Women's Court." *Judicature* 88, no. 3 (1993): 144–55.

Cook, Beverly B. "Women as Judges." In *Women in Judicial Process*. American Political Science Association, 1988.

Cook, Beverly B. "Women as Supreme Court Candidates: From Florence Allen to Sandra O'Connor." *Judicature* 65 (1982): 314–26.

Cook, Beverly B. "Women Judges: A Preface to Their History." *Golden Gate Law Review* 14 (1994): 573–610.

Cook, Beverly B. "Women Judges: The End of Tokenism." In *Women in the Courts*, edited by Winifred Hepperle and Laura Crites. National Center for State Courts, 1978.

Corder, J. Kevin, and Christina Wolbrecht. *Counting Women's Ballots: Female Voters from Suffrage Through the New Deal*. Cambridge University Press, 2016.

Cott, Nancy F. *The Grounding of Modern Feminism*. Yale University Press, 1974.

Cushman, Barry. *Rethinking the New Deal Court: The Structure of a Constitutional Revolution*. Oxford University Press, 1998.

David, Sonja White. *Lady Law: The Story of Arizona Supreme Court Justice Lorna Lockwood*. Brighton, 2012.

DeWolf, Rebecca. *Gendered Citizenship: The Original Conflict over the Equal Rights Amendment, 1920–1963*. University of Nebraska, 2021.

Diner, Steven J. *A Very Different Age: Americans of the Progressive Era*. Hill and Wang, 1997.

Dixon, Rosalind. "Female Justices, Feminism, and the Politics of Judicial Appointment: A Re-Examination." *Yale Journal of Law and Feminism* 21 (2010): 297–338.

Doerschuk, Beatrice. *Women in the Law: An Analysis of Training, Practice, and Salaried Position*. Bureau of Vocational Information, 1920.

Downey, Kirstin. *The Woman Behind the New Deal: The Life of Frances Perkins, FDR's Secretary of Labor, and His Moral Conscious*. Doubleday, 2009.

Drachman, Virginia. *Sisters in Law: Women Lawyers in Modern America*. Harvard University Press, 2001.

Drew, E. Harris. "Women and the Law." *Women's Law Journal* 47 (1961): 20–23.

DuBois, Ellen Carol. *Feminism and Suffrage: The Emergence of an Independent Women's Movement in America*. Cornell University Press, 1978.

DuBois, Ellen Carol. *Harriot Stanton Blatch and the Winning of Woman Suffrage*. Yale University Press, 1997.

DuBois, Ellen Carol. *Suffrage: Women's Long Battle for the Vote*. Simon & Schuster, 2020.

Dudden, Faye E. *Fighting Chance: The Struggle over Woman Suffrage and Black Suffrage in Reconstruction America*. Oxford University Press, 2011.

Dudney, Mark. *Sons of the Cumberland: The Early Years of Cordell Hull and John Jordan Gore*. Authorhouse, 2012.

Eckhaus, Phyllis. "Restless Women: The Pioneering Alumnae of New York University School of Law." *New York University Law Review* 66 (1991): 1996–2013.

Edwards, India. "Oral History Interview." Interview by Jerry N. Hess, Jan. 16, 1969. Truman Presidential Library.

Edwards, India. *Pulling No Punches: Memoirs of a Woman in Politics*. G. P. Putnam's Sons, 1977.

Egerton, John. "Walking into History." *Southern Spaces*, May 4, 2009.

Eisler, Kim Isaac. *A Justice for All: William J. Brennan, Jr., and the Decisions That Transformed America*. Simon & Schuster, 1993.
Epstein, Cynthia Fuchs. *Women in Law*. Basic Books, 2001.
Eskridge, William N., Jr., and Philip S. Frickey. "The Making of the Legal Process School." *Harvard Law Review* 107 (1994): 2031–55.
Faderman, Lillian. *Odd Girls and Twilight Lovers*. Columbia University Press, 1991.
Faderman, Lillian. *To Believe in Women: What Lesbians Have Done for America—A History*. Houghton Mifflin, 1999.
Farhang, Sean, Jonathan P. Kastellec, and Gregory J. Wawro. "The Politics of Opinion Assignment and Authorship on the U.S. Court of Appeals." *Journal of Legal Studies* 44 (Jan. 2015): S59-S85.
Feinman, Clarice. "An Historical Overview of the Treatment of Incarcerated Women: Myths and Realities of Rehabilitation." *Prison Journal* 63, no. 2 (1983): 12–26.
Feldman, Noah. *Scorpions: The Battles and Triumphs of FDR's Great Supreme Court Justices*. Twelve Books, 2010.
Flanagan, Maureen A. *America Reformed: Progressives and Progressivisms, 1890s-1920s*. Oxford University Press, 2007.
Frankfurter, Felix, and Roscoe Pound, eds. *Criminal Justice in Cleveland: Reports of the Cleveland Foundation Survey of the Administration of Criminal Justice in Cleveland*. Cleveland Foundation, 1922.
Franzen, Trisha. *Spinsters and Lesbians: Independent Womanhood in the United States*. New York University Press, 1996.
Free, Lauren E. *Suffrage Reconstructed: Gender, Race, and Voting Rights in the Civil War Era*. Cornell University Press, 2015.
Freedman, Estelle B. *Maternal Justice: Miriam Van Waters and the Female Reform Tradition*. University of Chicago Press, 1996.
Freedman, Estelle B. "Separatism as Strategy: Female Institution Building and American Feminism, 1870–1930." *Feminist Studies* 5, no. 3 (1979): 512–29.
Freedman, Estelle B. *Their Sisters' Keepers: Women Prison Reform in America, 1830-1930*. University of Michigan Press, 1981.
French, Amy Holtman. "Mixing It Up: Michigan Barmaids Fight for Civil Rights." *Michigan Historical Review* 40 (Spring 2014): 27–48.
Friedman, Jane M. *America's First Woman Lawyer: The Biography of Myra Bradwell*. Prometheus Books, 1993.
Garner, David D. "Socratic Misogyny? Analyzing Feminist Criticism of Socratic Teaching in Legal Education." *Brigham Young University Law Review* (2000): 1597–1649.
Ginsburg, Justice Ruth Bader, and Laura Brill. "Women in the Federal Judiciary: Three Way Pavers and the Exhilarating Change President Carter Wrought." *Fordham Law Review* 64 (1995): 28–90.

Glasbeek, Amanda. *Feminized Justice: The Toronto Women's Court, 1913–1934*. University of British Columbia, 2009.
Gomez, Alissa Rubin. "The Female-Neutrality Paradox." *Dickinson Law Review* 126 (2023): 673–91.
Gordon, Sarah Barringer. *The Mormon Question: Polygamy and Constitutional Conflict in Nineteenth-Century America*. University of North Carolina Press, 2001.
Greene, Sara Sternberg, and Kristen M. Renberg. "Judging Without a J.D." *Columbia Law Review* 122 (2022): 1287–1388.
Gronlund, Mimi Clark. *A Controversial Appointment: Supreme Court Justice Tom C. Clark*. University of Texas Press, 2021.
Grossberg, Michael. "Institutionalizing Masculinity: The Law as a Masculine Profession." In *Meanings for Manhood*, edited by Mark C. Carnes and Clyde Griffen. University of Chicago Press, 1990.
Gustafson, Melanie, Kristie Miller, and Elisabeth Israels Perry. *We Have Come to Stay: American Women and Political Parties, 1880–1960*. University of New Mexico Press, 1998.
Haire, Susan B. "Rating the Ratings of the American Bar Association Standing Committee on Federal Judiciary." *Justices System Journal* 22, no. 1 (2001): 1–17.
Hamlin, Kimberly A. *Free Thinker: Sex, Suffrage, and the Extraordinary Life of Helen Hamilton Gardener*. W. W. Norton, 2020.
Harron, Marion J. "In Memoriam: Honorable Florence Ellinwood Allen." *Women Lawyers Journal* 52, no. 4 (Fall 1996): 145, 175–76.
Hathaway, Oona A., and Scott J. Shapiro. *The Internationalists: How a Radical Plan to Outlaw War Remade the World*. Simon & Schuster, 2017.
Hays, Anna. *Without Precedent: The Life of Susie Marshall Sharp*. University of North Carolina Press, 2008.
Hessick, Carissa Byrne Hessick. "Race and Gender as Explicit Sentencing Factors." *Journal of Gender, Race, and Justice* 14 (2010): 127–42.
Hirshman, Linda. *Sisters in Law: How Sandra Day O'Connor and Ruth Bader Ginsburg Went to the Supreme Court and Changed the World*. Harper, 2015.
Hubbard, Preston J. *Origins of the TVA: The Muscle Shoals Controversy, 1920–1932*. Vanderbilt Press, 1961.
Hunter, Nan D. "A Century Since Suffrage: How Did We Get Here? Where Will We Go? How Will We Get There?" *Duquesne Law Review* 59 (2021): 125–66.
Isenberg, Nancy. *Sex and Citizenship in Antebellum America*. University of North Carolina Press, 1998.
Iversen, Joan Smyth. *The Antipolygamy Controversy in U.S. Women's Movements, 1880–1925: A Debate on the American Home*. Routledge, 1997.
Iversen, Joan Smyth. "Corinne Allen and Post-Manifesto Antipolygamy." *Journal of Mormon History* 26, no. 2 (Fall 2000): 110–39.

Jabour, Anya. *Sophonisba Breckinridge: Championing Women's Activism in Modern America*. University of Illinois Press, 2019.

Jack, Zachary Michael. *Rosalie Gardiner Jones and the Long March for Women's Rights*. McFarland, 2020.

Jefferson, Renee Knake, and Hannah Brenner Johnson. *Shortlisted: Women in the Shadows of the Supreme Court*. New York University Press, 2020.

Jensen, Joan M. "Annette Abbott Adams, Politician." *Pacific Historical Review* 35 (May 1966): 185–201.

Johnson, David K. *The Lavender Scare: The Cold War Persecution of Gays and Lesbians in the Federal Government*. University of Chicago Press, 2004.

Jones, Martha S. *Vanguard: How Black Women Broke Barriers, Won the Vote, and Insisted on Equality for All*. Basic Books, 2020.

Jordan, Gwen. "'We Must Forget Every Difference and Unite in a Common Cause—Votes for Women': Lessons from the Woman Suffrage Movement." *ConLawNOW* 11 (2020): 91–103.

Kalman, Laura. *FDR's Gambit: The Court Packing Fight and the Rise of Legal Liberalism*. Oxford University Press, 2022.

Kalsam, Kristin. "Feminist Judging: Theories and Practices." In *The Oxford Handbook of Feminist and Law in the United States*, edited by Deborah Brake, Martha Chamallas, and Verna L. Williams. Oxford University Press, 2023.

Karin, Marcy Lynn. "Esther Morris and Her Equality State: From Council Bill 70 to Life on the Bench." *American Journal of Legal History* 46 (2004): 300–33.

Katcher, Susan. "Legal Training in the United States: A Brief History." *Wisconsin International Law Journal* 24 (2006): 335–75.

Katz, Elizabeth D. "'May It Please Her Honor': The United States' First Women Judges, 1870–1930." *Washington University Law Review* 102 (2025): 1729–99.

Katz, Elizabeth D. "Sex, Suffrage, and State Constitutional Law: Women's Legal Right to Hold Public Office." *Yale Journal of Law and Feminism* 33 (2022): 110–93.

Katz, Elizabeth D. "'A Woman Stumps Her State': Nellie G. Robinson and Women's Right to Hold Public Office in Ohio." *Akron Law Review* 53 (2019): 313–57.

Kennedy, James Harrison, and Wilson M. Day, eds. *The Bench and Bar of Cleveland*. Cleveland Printing and Publishing Co., 1889.

Kenney, Sally J. "Choosing Judges: A Bumpy Road to Women's Equality and a Long Way to Go." *Michigan State Law Review* 2012 (2012): 1499–1528.

Kenney, Sally J. "Critical Perspectives on Gender and Judging." *Politics & Gender* 6, no. 3 (2010): 433–41.

Kenney, Sally J. *Gender and Justice: Why Women in the Judiciary Really Matter*. Routledge, 2012.

Kenney, Sally J. "'It Would Be Stupendous for Us Girls': Campaigning for Women Judges Without Waving." In *Breaking the Wave: Women, Their Organizations, and Feminism, 1945–1985*, edited by Kathleen A. Laughlin and Jacqueline Castledine. Routledge, 2011.

Kerber, Linda. *No Constitutional Right to Be Ladies: Women and the Obligations of Citizenship.* Hill and Wang, 1998.

Kerber, Linda. *Women of the Republic: Intellect and Ideology in Revolutionary America.* University of North Carolina Press, 1980.

Keyssar, Alexander. *The Right to Vote: The Contested History of Democracy in the United States.* Basic Books, 2000.

Kohn, Nina A. "Cambridge Law School for Women: The Evolution and Legacy of the Nation's First Graduate School Exclusively for Women." *Michigan Journal of Gender and Law* 12 (2005): 119–61.

Kraditor, Aileen S. *The Ideas of the Woman Suffrage Movement, 1890–1920.* Columbia University Press, 1965.

Kusmer, Kenneth L. *A Ghetto Takes Shape: Black Cleveland, 1870–1930.* University of Illinois Press, 1976.

Ladd-Taylor, Molly. *Mother-Work: Women, Child Welfare and the State, 1890–1930.* University of Illinois Press, 1993.

Ladd-Taylor, Molly. "'My Work Came out of Agony and Grief': Mothers and the Making of the Sheppard-Towner Act." In *Mothers of a New World: Maternalist Politics and the Origins of Welfare States*, edited by Seth Koven and Sonya Michel. Routledge, 1993.

Landever, Arthur R. "Four Remarkable Ohio Women Lawyers—the Cronise Sisters of Tiffin, Florence Allen, and Cleveland Law School's 'Hard-Boiled Mary.'" Manuscript, Oct. 10, 1994. Cleveland State University Digital Commons.

Lemons, J. Stanley. *The Woman Citizen: Social Feminism in the 1920s.* University of Illinois, 1973.

Leng, Kirsten. *Sexual Politics and Feminist Science: Women Sexologists in Germany, 1900–1933.* Cornell University Press, 2018.

Lissak, Rivka Shpak. *Pluralism and Progressives: Hull House and the New Immigrants, 1890–1919.* University of Chicago Press, 1989.

Livermore, Michael, Nina Varsava, Keith Carlson, and Daniel N. Rockmore. "Gendered Judicial Opinions." *Journal of Law and Empirical Analysis* 1, no. 1 (2024): 134–48.

Lopach, James, and Jean Lukowski. *Jeannette Rankin: A Political Woman.* University Press of Colorado, 2005.

Marilley, Suzanne M. *Woman Suffrage and the Origins of Liberal Feminism in the United States, 1820–1920.* Harvard University Press, 1996.

Marino, Kelly L. *Votes for College Women: Alumni, Students, and the Woman Suffrage Campaign.* New York University Press, 2024.

Marshall, Carrington T. *A History of the Courts and Lawyers of Ohio*. American Historical Society, 1934.

Marshall, Leon C., and Geoffrey May. *The Divorce Court, Vol. 2: Ohio*. Johns Hopkins Press, 1933.

Martin, Elaine. "The Representative Role of Women Judges." *Judicature* 77 (1993): 166–73.

Martins, Rachel Louise. *A Most Tolerant Little Town*. Simon & Schuster, 2023.

Masarik, Elizabeth Garner. *The Sentimental State: How Women-Led Reform Built the American Welfare State*. University of Georgia Press, 2024.

May, Allan R. *The Sly-Fanner Murders: The Birth of the Mayfield Road Mob, Cleveland's Most Notorious Mafia Gang*. ConAllen Press, 2014.

McCammon, Holly J. *The U.S. Women's Jury Movements and Strategic Adaptation: A More Just Verdict*. Cambridge University Press, 2012.

McCammon, Holly J., and Karen E. Campbell. "Winning the Vote in the West: The Political Successes of the Women's Suffrage Movements, 1866–1919." *Gender and Society* 15 (2001): 55–66.

McClain, Linda C. "What Becomes a Legendary Constitutional Campaign Most? Marking the Nineteenth Amendment at One Hundred." *Boston University Law Review* 100 (2020): 1753–70.

McDonaugh, Eileen L., and H. Douglas Price. "Woman Suffrage in the Progressive Era: Patterns of Opposition and Support in Referendum Voting, 1910–1918." *American Political Science Review* 79 (1985): 415–28.

McGuire, John Thomas. "'The Most Unjust Piece of Legislation': Section 213 of the Economy Act of 1932 and Feminism During the New Deal." *Journal of Political History* 20, no. 4 (2008): 516–41.

McLeod, Jacqueline A. *The Life of Judge Jane Bolin: Daughter of the Empire State*. University of Illinois Press, 2011.

Mead, Rebecca J. *How the Vote Was Won: Woman Suffrage in the Western States, 1868–1914*. New York University Press, 2004.

Menkel-Meadow, Carrie. "Exploring a Research Agenda of the Feminization of the Legal Profession: Theories of Gender and Social Inquiry." *Law and Social Inquiry* 14 (1989): 289–98.

Moley, Raymond. "Proportional Representation in Cleveland." *Political Science Quarterly* 38 (1923): 652–69.

Monopoli, Paula. *Constitutional Orphan: Gender Equality and the Nineteenth Amendment*. Oxford University Press, 2020.

Monopoli, Paula. "Situating *Dobbs*." *ConLawNOW* 14 (2023): 45–63.

Morello, Karen Berger. *The Invisible Bar: The Woman Lawyer in America 1638 to the Present*. Random House, 1986.

Moyer, Laura P., and Susan B. Haire. "Trailblazers and Those That Followed: Personal Experiences, Gender, and Judicial Empathy." *Law & Society Review* 49, no. 3 (2015): 665–89.

Moyer, Laura P., John Szmer, Susan Haire, and Robert K. Christensen. "'All Eyes Are on You': Gender, Race and Opinion Writing in the U.S. Courts of Appeals." *Law and Society Review* 55, no. 3 (2021): 452–72.

Muncy, Robyn. *Creating a Female Dominion in American Reform, 1890–1935.* Oxford University Press, 1991.

Murdoch, Joyce, and Deb Price. *Courting Justice: Gay Men and Lesbians v. the Supreme Court.* Basic Books, 2001.

Murphy, Bruce. *Wild Bill: The Legend and Life of William O. Douglas.* Random House, 2003.

Nielsen, Kim E. *Un-American Womanhood: Antiradicalism, Antifeminism, and the First Red Scare.* The Ohio State University Press, 2001.

Norgren, Jill. *Belva Lockwood: The Woman Who Would Be President.* New York University Press, 2007.

Norgren, Jill. *Rebels at the Bar: The Fascinating, Forgotten Stories of America's First Women Lawyers.* New York University Press, 2013.

O'Connor, Karen, and Alixandra B. Yanus. "Women as Leaders in Lesbian Organizations." In *Gender and Women's Leadership*, edited by Karen O'Connor. Sage, 2010.

Okrent, Daniel. *Last Call: The Rise and Fall of Prohibition.* Scribner, 2010.

Oldfather, Chad M. *Judges, Judging, and Judgment: Character, Wisdom, and Humility in a Polarized World.* Cambridge University Press, 2024.

Organ, Joan E. "Florence E. Allen and 'Great Changes in the Status of Women.'" In *Builders of Ohio: A Biographical History*, edited by Warren Van Tine and Michael Pierce. The Ohio State University Press, 2003.

Organ, Joan E. "Sexuality as a Category of Historical Analysis: A Study of Judge Florence E. Allen, 1884–1966." PhD diss., Case Western Reserve University, 1997.

Orleck, Annelise. *Common Sense and a Little Fire: Women and Working-Class Politics in the United States, 1900–1965.* University of North Carolina Press, 1995.

Painter, Nell Irvin. *Sojourner Truth: A Life, a Symbol.* W. W. Norton, 1997.

Painter, Nell Irvin. *Standing at Armageddon: A Grassroots History of the Progressive Era.* W. W. Norton, 2008.

Palmer, Barbara. "'To Do Justly': The Integration of Women into the American Judiciary." *Political Science and Politics* 34, no. 2 (2001): 235–39.

Park, Maud Wood. *Front Door Lobby.* Beacon Press, 1960.

Pearson, Drew, and Robert S. Allen. *The Nine Old Men.* Doubleday, 1937.

Peppers, Todd C. "Thoughts on Law Clerk Diversity and Influence." *Harvard Law Review Forum* 137 (Dec. 2023): 109–32.

Peresie, Jennifer. "Female Judges Matter: Gender and Collegial Decisionmaking in the Federal Appellate Courts." *Yale Law Journal* 114, no. 7 (2005): 1759–90.

Perry, Elizabeth Israels. *After the Vote: Feminist Politics in La Guardia's New York*. Oxford University Press, 2019.

Pietrusza, David. *1920: The Year of Six Presidents*. Carroll & Graf, 2006.

Porrello, Rick. *The Rise and Fall of the Cleveland Mafia*. Barricade Books, 1995.

Porter, Philip W. *Cleveland: Confused City on a Seesaw*. The Ohio State University Press, 1976.

Press, John Kenneth. *Founding Mother: Frances Kellor and the Creation of Modern America*. Social Books, 2012.

Price, Mark J. *Mafia Cop Killers in Akron*. History Press, 2017.

Pritchard, Pamela. "The Negro Experience at the Ohio State University in the First Sixty-Five Years, 1873–1938." PhD diss., The Ohio State University, 1982.

Purvis, Alaina. "Women in the Legal Profession: How Gender Barriers and Attrition Are Keeping Women out of the Judiciary." *Journal of Legal Profession* 43 (2019): 283–96.

Quinn, Mae C. "Fallen Woman (Re)framed: Judge Jean Hortense Norris, NYC, 1912–1955." *Kansas Law Review* 67 (2019): 451–512.

Quinn, Mae C. "Feminist Legal Realism." *Harvard Journal of Law and Gender* 35 (2012): 1–56.

Quinn, Mae C. "The Home Term Part: A Second Look at the Nation's First Criminal Domestic Violence Court." *Akron Law Review* 41 (2009): 733–62.

Quinn, Susan. *Eleanor and Hick: The Love Affair That Shaped a First Lady*. Penguin, 2016.

Randolph, Percilla Lawyer. "Judge Florence Allen." *Women Lawyers Journal* 19 (Winter 1932): 15–17.

Resnick, Judith. "Representing What? Gender, Race, Class and the Struggle for the Identity and the Legitimacy of Courts." *Law and Ethics of Human Rights* 15, no. 1 (2021): 1–91.

Ritter, Gretchen. *The Constitution as Social Design: Gender and Civic Membership in the American Constitutional Order*. Stanford University Press, 2006.

Roosevelt, Eleanor, and Lorena A. Hickok. *Ladies of Courage*. G. P. Putnam's Sons, 1954.

Rose, Kenneth D. *American Women and the Repeal of Prohibition*. New York University Press, 1996.

Rosenberg, Rosalind. *Beyond Separate Spheres: Intellectual Roots of Modern Feminism*. Yale University Press, 1982.

Rouse, Wendy L. *Public Faces, Secret Lives: A Queer History of the Women's Suffrage Movement*. New York University Press, 2024.

Ryder, Sandra L. "Clearing the Bar: Catharine Waugh McCulloch and Illinois Legal Reform." *DePaul Journal of Social Justice* 17 (2024): 1–49.

Scharf, Lois. *To Work and to Wed: Female Employment, Feminism, and the Great Depression*. Greenwood Press, 1980.

Scharf, Lois. “The Women’s Movement in Cleveland from 1850.” In *Cleveland: A Tradition of Reform*, edited by David D. Van Tassel and John J. Grabowski. Kent State University Press, 1986.

Schmidhauser, John R. *Judges and Justices: The Federal Appellate Judiciary.* Little, Brown, 1979.

Schreiner, Olive. *Dreams*. Roberts Brothers, 1891.

Schwarz, Judith. *Radical Feminists of Heterodoxy: Greenwich Village 1912–1940*. New Victoria, 1986.

Scutts, Joanna. *Hotbed: Bohemian Greenwich Village and the Secret Club That Sparked Modern Feminism*. Seal Press, 2022.

Siegel, Reva B. “She the People: The Nineteenth Amendment, Sex Equality, Federalism, and the Family.” *Harvard Law Review* 115 (2002): 947–72.

Sklar, Kathryn Kish. “The Historical Foundations of Women’s Power in the Creation of the American Welfare State, 1830–1930.” In *Mothers of a New World: Maternalist Politics and the Origins of Welfare States*, edited by Seth Koven and Sonya Michel. Routledge, 1993.

Sloan, Cliff. *The Court at War: FDR, His Justices, and the World They Made.* Public Affairs, 2023.

Snyder, Brad. *Democratic Justice: Felix Frankfurter, the Supreme Court, and the Making of the Liberal Establishment.* W. W. Norton, 2022.

Sochen, June. *The New Woman: Feminism in Greenwich Village, 1910*–1920. Quadrangle Books, 1972.

Solimine, Michael E., and James L. Walker. “The Strange Career of the Three-Judge District Court: Federalism and Civil Rights, 1954–76.” *Case Western Reserve Law Review* 72 (2022): 909–76.

St. Clair, James E., and Linda C. Gugin. *Chief Justice Fred M. Vinson of Kentucky: A Political Biography.* University Press of Kentucky, 2002.

Stansell, Christine. *American Moderns: Bohemian New York and the Creation of a New Century.* Henry Holt, 2000.

Stanton, Elizabeth Cady, Susan B. Anthony, and Matilda Joslyn Gage, eds. *History of Woman Suffrage, Vols. 1–3 (1848–85).* Privately published, 1881–86.

Stein, Gary. *Justice for Sale: Graft, Greed, and a Crooked Federal Judge in 1930s Gotham.* Lyons Press, 2023.

Steinglass, Steven H., and Gino J. Scarselli. *The Ohio State Constitution.* 2nd ed. Oxford University Press, 2022.

Stevens, Justice John Paul. “Fond Memory, Cordelia Kennedy.” *Ohio State Law Journal* 75 (2014): 1008–9.

Steward, Tyran Kai. “Time Not Ripe: Black Women’s Quest for Citizenship and the Battle to End Jim Crow at The Ohio State University.” *Ohio History Review* 121 (2014): 4–34.

Suk, Julie C. *After Misogyny: How the Law Fails Women and What to Do About It.* University of California Press, 2023.

Symposium. "The Honorable Paul C. Weick: A Lengthy and Distinguished Tenure on the Court." *Akron Law Review* 15 (1982): 617–33.

Tani, Karen M. "Portia's Deal." *Chicago-Kent Law Review* 87 (2012): 549–70.

Terborg-Penn, Rosalyn. *African American Women in the Struggle for the Vote, 1850–1920.* Indiana University Press, 1998.

Thomas, Evan. *First: Sandra Day O'Connor.* Random House, 2019.

Thomas, Tracy A. *Elizabeth Cady Stanton and the Feminist Foundations of Family Law.* New York University Press, 2016.

Thomas, Tracy A. "The Jurisprudence of the First Woman Judge, Florence Allen: Challenging the Myth of Women Judging Differently." *William & Mary Journal of Race, Gender, and Social Justice* 27 (2021): 293–349.

Thomas, Tracy A. "The Long History of Feminist Legal Theory." In *The Oxford Handbook of Feminism and Law in the United States*, edited by Deborah L. Brake, Martha Chamallas, and Verna L. Williams. Oxford University Press, 2023.

Thomas, Tracy A. "More Than the Vote: The Nineteenth Amendment as Proxy for Gender Equality." *Stanford Journal of Civil Rights and Civil Liberties* 15 (2020): 349–78.

Thomas, Tracy A. "Reclaiming the Long History of the 'Irrelevant' Nineteenth Amendment for Gender Equality." *Minnesota Law Review* 105 (2022): 2623–58.

Thomas, Tracy A. "The Struggle for Gender Equality in the Northern District of Ohio." In *Justice on the Shores of Lake Erie: A History of the Northern District of Ohio*, edited by Roberta Alexander and Paul Finkelman. Ohio University Press, 2012.

Thomas, Tracy A., and Tracey Jean Boisseau. *Feminist Legal History.* New York University Press, 2011.

Thurner, Manuela. "'Better Citizens Without the Ballot': American Anti-Suffrage Women and Their Rationale During the Progressive Era." In *One Woman, One Vote*, edited by Marjorie Spruill Wheeler. NewSage Press, 1995.

Trestman, Marlene. *Fair Labor Lawyer: The Remarkable Life of New Deal Attorney and Supreme Court Advocate, Bessie Margolin.* Louisiana State University Press, 2016.

Tushnet, Mark. *History of the Supreme Court of the United States, Vol. 9: The Hughes Court: From Progressivism to Pluralism, 1930 to 1941.* Cambridge University Press, 2021.

Tuttle, William M., Jr. *Race Riot: Chicago in the Red Summer of 1919.* University of Illinois Press, 1996.

Tuve, Jeanette E. *First Lady of the Law: Florence Ellinwood Allen.* University Press of America, 1984.

Tuve, Jeanette E. "First Woman State Supreme Court Judge." *Gamut*, no. 11 (Winter 1984): 51–60.

Upton, Harriet Taylor. "The Woman Suffrage Movement in Ohio." In *History of Ohio, Vol. 2*, edited by Charles B. Galbreath, 333–34. American Historical Society, 1925.

Van Tassel, David D., and John J. Grabowski, eds. *Cleveland: A Tradition of Reform*. Kent State University Press, 1986.

Varsava, Nina. "Opinion Authorship and Precedential Status." *Washington University Law Review* 101 (2024): 1593–1677.

Varsava, Nina, Keith Carlson, Michael A. Livermore, and Daniel N. Rockmore. "Judicial Dark Matter." *University of Chicago Law Review* 91 (2024): 1949–2011.

Von Drehle, David. *Triangle: The Fire That Changed America*. Grove Press, 2003.

Ware, Susan. *Partner and I: Molly Dewson, Feminism, and New Deal Politics*. Yale University Press, 1987.

Warner, Hoyt Landon. *Progressivism in Ohio: 1897–1917*. The Ohio State University Press, 1964.

Weisbrod, Carol. "Images of the Woman Juror." *Harvard Women's Law Journal* 9 (1986): 59–82.

Weiss, Elaine. *The Woman's Hour: The Great Fight to Win the Vote*. Penguin, 2018.

Wheeler, Marjorie Spruill. "A Short History of the Woman Suffrage Movement in America." In *One Woman, One Vote: Rediscovering the Woman Suffrage Movement*, edited by Marjorie Spruill Wheeler. NewSage Press, 1995.

Williams, Joan C., Marina Multhaup, Su Li, and Rachel Korn. "You Can't Change What You Can't See: Interrupting Racial and Gender Bias in the Legal Profession." American Bar Association, 2018.

Willrich, Michael. *City of Courts: Socializing Justice in Progressive Era Chicago*. Cambridge University Press, 2003.

Wilson, Jan Doolittle. *The Women's Joint Congressional Committee and the Politics of Maternalism, 1920–30*. University of Illinois Press, 2007.

Woloch, Nancy. *A Class by Herself: Protective Laws for Women Workers, 1890s–1990s*. Princeton University Press, 2013.

"Xen Hicks: Senior Circuit Judge: Sixth Circuit." *American Bar Association Journal* 33, no. 2 (1947): 127–32.

Zahniser, J. D., and Amelia R. Fry. *Alice Paul: Claiming Power*. Oxford University Press, 2014.

Zimmerman, Joan G. "The Jurisprudence of Equality: The Women's Minimum Wage, the First Equal Rights Amendment, and *Adkins v. Children's Hospital*, 1905–1923." *Journal of American History* 78 (1991): 188–225.

Index

Founded in 1893,
UNIVERSITY OF CALIFORNIA PRESS
publishes bold, progressive books and journals on topics in the arts, humanities, social sciences, and natural sciences—with a focus on social justice issues—that inspire thought and action among readers worldwide.

The UC PRESS FOUNDATION
raises funds to uphold the press's vital role as an independent, nonprofit publisher, and receives philanthropic support from a wide range of individuals and institutions—and from committed readers like you. To learn more, visit ucpress.edu/supportus.

www.ingramcontent.com/pod-product-compliance
Ingram Content Group UK Ltd.
Pitfield, Milton Keynes, MK11 3LW, UK
UKHW042306250926
475588UK00001B/1/J

9 780520 399600